Macro-Policies for Appropriate Technology in Developing Countries

About the Book and Editor

Over the past two decades the concept of appropriate technology has gained increasing acceptance as an essential part of any development strategy that aims to combine economic growth with equity. Yet, appropriate technology has not been widely adopted in the developing world. A major reason for this failure, according to the authors of this book, has been a focus on micro-interventions to the neglect of macro-policies, which determine the context in which all technology choices are made.

Frances Stewart's introduction provides a classification of macro-policies within four broad categories—those affecting the objectives of decision-makers, those determining the availability and price of resources, those influencing markets, and those disseminating knowledge about technological alternatives. The proportion of resources controlled by different types of organization is also critically important. In seven case studies of government policies in developing countries, the authors explore the effects of macro-policies and determine which policies have best promoted appropriate technology. The studies explore the political economy of appropriate macro-policies, examining which groups in society are likely to benefit from alternative policies and technologies.

Frances Stewart is a Fellow of Somerville College and senior research officer at Queen Elizabeth House, Oxford University.

Published in cooperation with
Appropriate Technology International, Washington, D.C.

Macro-Policies for Appropriate Technology in Developing Countries

edited by Frances Stewart

Routledge
Taylor & Francis Group
LONDON AND NEW YORK

To my mother,
Clarissa Kaldor

First published 1987 by Westview Press, Inc.

Published 2018 by Routledge
52 Vanderbilt Avenue, New York, NY 10017
2 Park Square, Milton Park, Abingdon, Oxon OX14 4RN

Routledge is an imprint of the Taylor & Francis Group, an informa business

Library of Congress Cataloging-in-Publication Data
Macro-policies for appropriate technology in developing countries.
(Westview special studies in social, political, and economic development)
1. Developing countries—Economic policy.
2. Rural development—Developing countries.
3. Technological innovations—Economic aspects—Developing countries. I. Stewart, Frances.
II. Series.
HC59.7.M238 1987 338.9'27'091724 86-22433

ISBN 13: 978-0-367-01166-6 (hbk)
ISBN 13: 978-0-367-16153-8 (pbk)

Contents

Preface

Most support for appropriate technology (AT) takes the form of micro-interventions—support for oil processing, for example, in a village in Tanzania, or wool spinning in Nepal.* Yet, despite a multiplicity of such interventions and widespread agreement on the need for AT, progress in achieving appropriate technology on a significant scale is generally acknowledged to have been disappointing. The hypothesis on which this book is based is that this comparative failure, despite successes at the micro-level, has been due to obstacles resulting from macro-policies. The prime aim of this book is to explore how macro-policies affect technology choices in order to identify policies which would promote AT. The second aim is to understand the political economy associated with the policies, so as to explore how and why political economy may influence the chosen set of policies and therefore the possibility of achieving AT.

Chapter One presents an introductory classification of macro-policies, dividing policies into four categories—those affecting objectives, resources, markets and technology—and tentatively identifying policies which would support AT. Chapters Two to Eight are empirical case studies, which were undertaken using the framework presented in Chapter One in order to assess and illuminate the categorisation used there and the policies identified. Six of the studies cover technology choice in the rural areas, while two relate more to the modern urban industrial sector. Chapter Nine summarises and analyses the major findings of the case studies.

The idea for this study originated at a workshop sponsored by Appropriate Technology International (ATI) and organised by Ted Owens, held at Easton, Maryland, in September 1980. The work on macro-policies and appropriate technology, included in this volume, was the focal point of a subsequent workshop held in Washington, DC, in January 1986 and sponsored by ATI and the Overseas Development Council. The project has been financed by ATI. I am very grateful for their continued support. I would especially like to thank Ted Owens, Ton de Wilde and Judith Polsky at ATI. Ted Owens in particular was responsible for initiating the work and has been enormously

*Examples taken from *Appropriate Technology as a Strategy for Development*, Annual Report of Appropriate Technology International, 1984.

helpful throughout. My experience with ATI has shown that large(ish) organisations *can* support small projects, with a minimum of bureaucratic requirements, and in friendship. I would also like to thank Mrs. Abha Ghani for editorial assistance.

Frances Stewart

One

Macro-Policies for Appropriate Technology: An Introductory Classification

Frances Stewart

I. INTRODUCTION

In every case, actual decisions about technology take place at the micro-level. That is, an investment decision embodying a particular technology is made by decision-makers within a productive unit. The productive unit may be a large organization with world-wide activities, such as a multinational corporation, or it may be a very small unit, such as a family firm or farm. Whatever the size of the unit, the level of decision-making is defined here as "micro" since the decisions are taken by the units in question in the light of their own objectives and resources.[1] But while each decision takes place at the micro-level, each is strongly influenced by the external environment in which it takes place. Apart from intervening directly by making particular investment/technology decisions, governments can influence technology decisions only by influencing the external environment. Direct interventions account for only a small proportion of all technology decisions, especially in a mixed economy. Hence a government's greatest potential influence on technology decisions takes the form of influencing a decision-making unit's external environment. Despite this, appropriate technology institutions have tended to confine their activities to direct intervention. This can be seen from the annual reports of almost any appropriate technology institution, which generally consist of a list of particular interventions in technology promotion or dissemination.

This is a revised version of a paper prepared for an Appropriate Technology International Workshop on macro-policies for appropriate technology, which took place at the Institute of Social Studies, The Hague, in March 1982. In preparing this version, I benefited greatly from the discussions at the workshop. The paper appeared as an A.T. International working paper, 1983; a shortened version was published in the *International Labour Review*, No. 122, June 1983.

The full version appears in J. James and S. Watanabe (eds), *Technology, Institutions and Government Policies*, London: Macmillan, 1985.

This paper looks at the government policies that affect the environment in which micro-decision-making takes place, with a view to classifying and identifying the set of policies likely to promote appropriate technology. These policies are described as "macro"-policies to emphasize their general nature, as distinct from direct and particular interventions at the micro-level.

II. DEFINITIONS

It is easy to spend too much time on definitions. Nonetheless, it is necessary to be as clear as possible about the two main concepts under discussion—macro-policies and appropriate technology.

• *Macro-policies:* As used here, macro-policies cover general government policies which influence the environment where micro-decision-making units operate. Micro-decision-making units are normally described as firms in micro-economic textbooks. In this chapter the clumsy term micro-decision-making units is preferred because the units do not consist solely of conventional private sector firms, with owners, employers, and employees, but also include public sector firms, cooperatives and family and household organizations. For brevity the words "units" and "firms" will also be used to encompass this spectrum of micro-decision-making units. The macro-policies go beyond the normal macro-policies of economic textbooks, which are largely confined to policies towards major economic aggregates, such as the money supply, interest rates, public expenditure levels, budget deficits, and so on. While these policies are one subset of the macro-policies considered here, we also include many others—such as policies towards technology supply, market access and so on. Macro-policies are used to describe this great variety of policies to indicate that they apply to the whole spectrum of micro-decision-making, in contrast to particular interventions. The policies may equally be described as general policies towards appropriate technology. In what follows, macro-policies and general policies, will be used interchangeably.

• *Appropriate technology*: A great deal has been written on the definition of appropriate technology.[2] We may contrast two views on its definition. On the one hand there are those who define appropriate technology with reference to welfare economics. According to this view, appropriate technology is that technology which maximizes social welfare: "Appropriate technology may be defined as the set of techniques which make optimum use of available resources in a given environment. For each process or project, it is the technology which maximizes social welfare if factor prices are shadow priced."[3]

In contrast, most groups working in appropriate technology associate it with a specific set of characteristics, rather than with social maximization in abstract. This is also the approach adopted by some social scientists.[4] The list of characteristics varies among authors. Among economic characteristics, a more appropriate technology is normally defined as: more labor-using in comparison with a less appropriate technology (higher L/O); less capital-using (lower K/L); less skill-using; making more use of local materials and resources; smaller scale; and producing a more appropriate product (that is, a simpler product designed for lower income consumers or a product suitable as an input into other appropriate technologies).

Other characteristics sometimes emphasized are that appropriate technologies should not be environmentally damaging and that they should fit in with socio-economic structures of rural life.[5] According to the multidimensional specific-characteristics definition, technologies may be appropriate in some respects, inappropriate in others. Moreover, since societies differ in material resources, culture, and socio-economic structures, technologies may be appropriate for some societies while inappropriate for others. The specific-characteristics approach thus does not uniquely, and for all countries and for all time, identify particular technologies as appropriate or inappropriate. Instead, it points to a multidimensional set of characteristics which tend to be associated with more appropriate technologies.

Both definitions of appropriate technology—the social welfare definition and the specific-characteristics definition—have their disadvantages. The specific-characteristics definition can lead to a situation where an appropriate technology (that is, the one with a more appropriate set of characteristics) is an inferior technology or one which does not best enable a country to meet its objectives. This might arise because the technology with appropriate characteristics is inefficient in a technical sense (of low productivity) compared with a technology with inappropriate characteristics. In some cases, the technology with appropriate characteristics might still be the best choice (despite its technical inferiority), if its effects on some objectives (for example, enabling the poor to participate in economic activity) outweigh its low productivity. The specific-characteristics approach also concentrates on the immediate consequences of a technology, while neglecting the wider, long term effects which might make a technology with appropriate characteristics preferable. For example, a capital-intensive technology might generate exports and thus relax a foreign exchange bottleneck, permitting more employment in the long run than a more labor-intensive technology.

In such situations, the specific-characteristics definition leads to one of two outcomes: either it encourages the adoption of the "wrong" technology, taking all aspects into account; or, it means that technologies with appropriate characteristics should not always be selected (that is, the appropriate technology is not always the best choice). Apart from the fact that this involves a type of linguistic contradiction, it also means that additional criteria (of an efficiency, social cost-benefit type) are necessary in order to decide what the best technology is.

The social welfare definition avoids these problems. The appropriate technology is always (by definition) the right technology to choose. But there are other difficulties with the social welfare/cost-benefit analysis to determining appropriate technology. First, this apparatus has many conceptual and practical problems, especially for determining social values and shadow prices.[6] Second, the social welfare definition can conceal, or even eliminate, the insights offered by the appropriate technology movement, in that the all-embracing terms used by economists, such as social welfare and objective functions, tend to lack descriptive content. Third, there are no signposts for action in the social welfare definition as there are in the specific-characteristics definition. According to the social welfare definition, only one technology out of a set will maximize social welfare and can therefore be called appropriate. Such a technology could be large-scale, capital-intensive, and ecologically damaging. None of these characteristics are indicated by the definition. But indicating that all the technologies in the set are inappropriate in some respects is extremely important in demonstrating the need for search and research in specific directions and areas. This signposting is one of the major contributions of the appropriate technology movement, and one that is lost by adopting the social welfare definition.

The discussion of the relative merits of the two approaches has implications for methodology, whichever definition is finally adopted. On the one hand, if a specific-characteristics approach were adopted, then other criteria (encompassing something of the social welfare approach, albeit rather simply) would be necessary to make sure that social and economic considerations of efficiency, dynamic as well as static implications, and general as well as partial effects were included in determining technology choice. On the other hand, if a social welfare definition were adopted, then a checklist of specific characteristics would be essential to assess each technology to provide signposts for choice, search and research.

Both approaches have to be applied in a dynamic context. Over time the resources available to any country, as well as the technological possibilities open to it, are changing. Consequently, the appropriate technology (according to either definition) will generally change over time. Moreover, technology choice affects a country's development path—most obviously in relation to employment creation. A technology that maximizes short-run employment can be different from one that maximizes long-run growth in productive employment opportunities. Selecting the appropriate technology then depends on the trade-offs and on country preferences in relation to time.

The question of a country's preferences or objectives is at the heart of a social welfare approach to appropriate technology since social welfare can be measured only if social objectives have been determined. Country objectives do not enter explicitly into the specific-characteristics approach. However, in selecting characteristics some objectives are implicit. The characteristics have been selected as those that, broadly speaking, would spread employment opportunities and provide income-earning opportunities for the poor, thus reducing poverty and inequality. The preselection of objectives can be regarded as a strength of the specific-characteristics approach, because it correctly reflects a major element in the appropriate technology movement, which is concerned with objectives as much as the means of achieving them. At the same time, it preempts what should be the choice of the people concerned, rather than that of an outside movement.

Moreover, while the broad elements of the objectives embodied in appropriate technology are generally agreed upon, their precise details are not—especially the importance attributed to different objectives. This lack of clarity is reflected in the uncertainty about precisely which objectives to include and what weight to give them when conflicts occur. With a specific-characteristics approach, a government may reject the appropriate technology because it does not share appropriate technology objectives—for example, because it wishes to modernize and maximize growth and places little weight on reducing poverty. In contrast, with a social welfare approach, government objectives are automatically incorporated in the measure of social welfare. This means a government would never reject the appropriate technology identified by the social welfare approach, but that every technology might not be recognizably appropriate in terms of the normal objectives of appropriate technology. For example, it might involve heavy expenditure on prestige and capital-intensive modernization projects, if that is what the government wants.

The rest of this book adopts a specific-characteristics approach, recognizing its limitations: the selection of precise characteristics and their weighting is often arbitrary and should always incorporate local preferences; the characteristics need to be supplemented by some assessment of social efficiency before the technology is chosen; and it is possible that an appropriate technology, defined by this approach, could be rejected because the objectives implicit in the characteristics do not reflect the objectives of a particular government.[7]

III. THE MACRO-ENVIRONMENT AND THE MICRO-DECISION

We define the micro-unit as the organization (generally a firm) which makes a technology decision: that is, chooses, acquires, installs and operates a particular technology. This unit may be in the public or private sector, may be a capitalist or family unit, in industry, services or agriculture. The unit makes its decision in light of the following factors:

1. Its own objectives (which may be to maximize pre- or post-tax profits, family income, employment, and so forth).
2. The resources available to it and the prices it has to pay for these resources. The resources include material inputs, labour of various skills, and capital equipment. The prices an organization has to pay consist of the actual prices it faces (for example, wage rates for labour) and taxes of various kinds (for example, social security payments).
3. The nature—size, industry and type—of the market it faces. ("Type" refers to the market that makes up the major consuming element—for example, high-income or low-income, local or international). In part, the nature of the market is dependent on the history of the

organization. Thus, a firm that has always manufactured soap tends to stay in that market. A large-scale firm that exports most of its products will be concerned with the international market and so on. But the market is also a variable that can be changed by activities of the firm.

4. The organization's knowledge of available technological alternatives. This is a function of three variables: (i) the actual technology shelf in the industry, which depends on the historical development of technology in that industry; (ii) existing information channels about technology in that industry (for example, consultants, machinery salesmen, information services, and so on); and (iii) the efforts the firm puts into collecting information and the nature of those efforts. For example, one firm may do nothing about acquiring information and simply depend on local machinery salesmen for knowledge; others may actively search, sending engineers abroad to look for suitable second-hand machinery or to come up with innovations through their own research and development.

In sum, technology choice depends on firm objectives, resource availability and cost, markets, and technology, or O, R, M, T. It follows that macro-policies may affect micro-choice of any given unit by affecting any of these four variables. In addition, the government can affect the balance of choice in the economy as a whole by altering the proportion of resources controlled by various units, or what we shall call the *composition of units* in the economy. For example, small-scale units generally use more labor-intensive technologies than large-scale units; whether they are public or private. By shifting the control of total resources the government may bring about more appropriate technology in the economy as a whole, even though it has not altered the decisions of any particular unit.

Macro-policies, considered briefly below, consist of the policies which affect the four variables and those affecting the composition of units in the economy.

The socio-economic framework of an economy is highly relevant in two respects. First, the framework influences many variables affecting technology choice. For example, the organization of productive units, their access to resources and the nature of the markets they serve are heavily influenced by the system of political economy. In most contexts, the broad dimensions of this framework have to be taken as a given, not as a variable. Consequently, conclusions as to appropriate macro-policies may vary according to the socio-economic framework. Secondly, political economy variables influence which policies are feasible in a particular context, and which are not. Thus a strategy that might at first appear best, from the point of view of promoting appropriate technology, may have to be ruled out in a particular context because it appears infeasible, and some apparently second best set of policies may have to be recommended. This is a problem-ridden area because it is very difficult to judge what is and what is not feasible. Yet to ignore it can lead to useless recommendations.

Two extreme views on political economy can be contrasted. On the one hand, economists' first-best recommendations normally completely ignore the limitations or constraints imposed by political economy or assume that they do not exist. In many situations, recommendations made without recognizing the constraints are ignored. Rudra indicates the failures of appropriate technology in India since independence—despite government rhetoric in its favor—and attributes such failures mainly to conflicts with important power groups. A similar dichotomy between rhetoric and action can be seen in Tanzania, and the explanation is also largely a matter of political economy.[8]

In contrast to the no-constraints view, the view is sometimes taken that the forces of political economy are so great that there is little room left to maneuver. Galtung's view of structures comes close to this position. Every technology, according to Galtung, is associated with a certain economic, social and cognitive structure that "produces, filters out and accepts only the techniques that will be accompanied by such structures, thereby reinforcing the structure themselves."[9] The structures associated with Western advanced technology consist of the capitalists, scientists and bureaucrats who benefit from the technology. Their positions would be threatened if an alternative technology were adopted. But these are the people who make most of the technology choices. Consequently, there is little possibility of introducing an alternative technology on any scale in any society where such advanced technology is well established.[10]

Historic experience—and common sense—suggest that there is much truth in a structures or political economy view that leaves little room for choosing alternative technologies. But there is some possibility of choice, as indicated by the wide variety of technologies in use, both in a single country and across countries.[11] More effort needs to be devoted to exploring the forces of political economy and the factors that determine technology choice. One fruitful approach is a game theory, as suggested by Enos.

It is first necessary to identify and delineate the groups affected by alternative technology choices and also to determine what power the various groups have over the technology choices. No group is completely homogeneous. For example, workers are differently affected according to their skills, their experience and versatility, and their family circumstances. Nonetheless, it is usually possible to pick out the main groups which are likely to be affected by technology choices, even though there may be differences among them. We may distinguish between decisions involving the government and those that do not. Decisions that involve the government are those where the government itself plays an active direct role (for example, in choice of technology with respect to public sector investment) and those where the government plays an indirect role by forming, or at least influencing, the rules (prices, tariffs, etc.) which determine the framework in which all micro-units make decisions. This last category is relevant in formulating macro-policies for appropriate technology (although the considerations are similar where the government is acting directly). In all micro-unit decisions, obviously one of the relevant groups is the government. The question is the nature of the government: what interests it represents and hence how it is affected by different decisions, what objectives it holds and what game it is playing—together these will determine the actions it takes.

Implicitly, these two extreme views make different assumptions about the nature of government. The first-best type of view of many economists, implicit in much social-cost-benefit analysis, is that a government is a single entity whose interests are those of the nation and whose objectives are to maximise social welfare. This leaves (an impossible)[12] task of identifying the interests of the nation, especially where (to use Disraeli's term) there are "two nations," in order to make maximization of social welfare meaningful. If this can be achieved, then one does not need to trace the particular interests that are embodied in a government and the effects these have on technology choice and associated policy variables. At the other extreme is the view that a government uniquely and consistently represents one set of interests—in Galtung's example, those of the researchers, bureaucrats, and capitalists. But this view also oversimplifies a complex world. In reality governments are not homogeneous but have ties with numerous groups. The groups vary from society to society, and the ties are sometimes strong and sometimes weak, particularly where conflicting interests occur among the various elements which influence government. Careful empirical work is needed in each situation to delineate the various groups which make up or influence government decision-making. Such research is required before either of the two extreme views just described can be accepted or rejected, although exponents of both views do not seem to view such research as necessary.

If governments are linked to many different groups, then there is potential for conflict of interests among them. Potential rule changes (or macro-policies) are of three types, in terms of the gains or losses for various interest groups:

1. Those where all groups constituting government interests gain;
2. Those where all groups lose;
3. Those where some gain and some lose.

In exploring feasible strategies, it is helpful to classify desired changes into these three categories. Changes that positively affect all major parties (category one) are obviously politically realistic. It might be thought that very few changes would fall into this category, since such changes would presumably already have been put into effect. But in a dynamic world, where new possibilities are continuously arising (which is especially true of technology), new information can lead to the emergence and identification of such changes. Changes in the second category, where all groups lose, are not politically feasible.

Most potentially feasible changes are likely to fall into the third category—some gainers, some losers. The number of possible changes within this category will determine the extent of politically feasible macro-policies for appropriate technology in any particular context.

Two facts prejudice the likelihood of change within category three. First, the very fact that there are losers indicates that the changes will not be politically straightforward. Second, since the changes have not been carried out, we may assume that the losing interests dominate the gaining. However, it is also possible to identify ways to make it more likely that a change in this category will be made. These include altering the proposed change so that the distribution and size of gains and losses are also altered, to make the changes more acceptable; devising new political coalitions to strengthen the gainers vis-à-vis the losers; or providing information which may alter the various parties' assessment of the changes.

A simple example may clarify the discussion. Assume that tractors are being introduced in large farms in a particular area, and that these tractors are being bought with subsidized credit available to the large farmers from government credit institutions. In terms of the specific-characteristics definition of appropriate technology, it appears that the tractors are inappropriate compared with the use of labour plus bullocks, since the tractors are more capital-intensive, large-scale, use imported inputs, etc. Are the tractors also inappropriate according to the social welfare definition? The answer depends on the values (shadow prices) of a social welfare exercise; however, many case studies have shown that tractors do not maximize social welfare.[13] Let us assume that this is the case here. Hence, to ensure that the appropriate technology is selected, the government needs to alter various rules, so that tractors are no longer introduced. The government could make the following changes:

(a) redistribute the land by taking it away from the large-scale farmers (who consequently are no longer relevant to technology choice) and giving it to small-scale farmers who continue to make appropriate decisions;
(b) reduce the availability of credit for the purchase of tractors to large- and small-scale farmers;
(c) increase the price of credit so that the farmers find it more profitable not to buy tractors; or
(d) ban the import of tractors.

All of these changes have been suggested at one time or another in order to promote appropriate technology. The alternatives can be approached at various levels and from various points of view. The economists' approach is to maximize efficiency. In general, this tends to favor change (c), insofar as it could be shown that previously the prices of credit or labor were distorted. Alternatively, those concerned with distributional considerations would favor (a) the redistribution of land followed by (b) the redistribution of credit. While not totally disregarding considerations of economic efficiency or distribution, a political economy approach would look at all alternatives from the perspective of feasibility. Using the classification system suggested above, the first requirement would be to draw up a matrix showing the gains and losses to different groups from the various changes. This has been done (for illustrative purposes only) in table 1.1. In the matrix, option (d) has been divided into two: $(d)^1$ would ban all tractors, including local production and $(d)^2$ would ban imports only. While banning all tractors obviously is more effective from an appropriate point of view, banning imports is the more common policy.

The matrix illustrates a category three conflict situation with some groups gaining and some losing from each change. The size and distribution of gains and losses among different groups differ significantly according to the strategy selected. The redistributive strategies (a) and (b) hurt the large landowners most and help the small landowners most. The landless laborers gain most from the land redistribution strategy because it is assumed that some of the land is redistributed to them. They benefit equally from each of the other strategies except $(d)^2$. Banning tractor imports is less beneficial to them, since it is assumed that some tractorization continues with locally produced tractors. There is nothing in the matrix about the social benefits of the various alternatives because any adding-up exercise depends critically on the weight attributed to various groups.

In order to say something about the political feasibility of the possible rule changes, we need to know the weight the government gives to each interest group. This requires an analysis of the political composition of the government, the sources of its support, and the power of pressure groups. A government whose major concern and support is from landless laborers would choose option (a). In contrast a government that is dominated by large-scale farmers would do nothing. Most governments are subject to a variety of interests of varying strengths. They are concerned about employment and therefore give some importance to landless labourers. But they are also subject to pressure from landowners large or small and therefore would tend to choose options (c) or (d) which benefit the landless while minimizing the cost of landowners. In addition, many governments are subject to pressure from local producers. Consequently $(d)^2$ might be the most attractive option. It benefits a major local interest group (tractor producers), gives the appearance (and perhaps a little of the reality) of helping the employment situation, while only slightly harming large farmers.

In many situations, there can be conflicts between first-best options from the point of view of economic efficiency and/or social justice (options (c) and (a) in our analysis) and those which are politically feasibile (option $(d)^2$) according to at least one plausible political scenario. Where such conflicts emerge (which can inhibit appropriate technology), it is worth investigating possible ways to alter the outcome, as mentioned above. The matrix of benefits and costs of the way the political system processes this matrix could be altered. For example, a new technology might be produced which would benefit all categories, such as a manually propelled tractor. It could be made locally (thus benefiting local tractor producers) and, if associated with some change in taxes or subsidies, it would not be detrimental to large landowners. Alternatively, political action by the landless laborers, joined perhaps by small landowners, might alter the importance the government gives to various groups and therefore the outcome with the given benefit matrix. Possible and effective changes will vary according to the particular case.

It must be emphasized that the example given above has been illustrative. It is close enough to actual cases, however, to help explain why tractorization and other types of inappropriate technology persist despite clear evidence of their negative social benefits. The example is intended to emphasize the conclusion already reached: that designing policies without considering political realities often leads to ineffective recommendations.

Political economy impinges on the timing and sequencing of particular strategies. Certain developments (for example, technology choices) establish a nexus of interests which then become powerful in influencing future decisions—both technically and politically. For example, the establishment of an assembly plant may establish employer and employee interests in continued protection of that industry and its market and create technical needs and political support for ancillary services (for example, transport, local maintenance services, etc.). In the above example, the initial decision to establish a local tractor industry generates political forces which influence the likely choice of strategy. The initial decision should then take into account likely later developments. A different initial strategy might be optimal if later developments are allowed for. This is especially true for technology, where there are strong links (political, technical, and economic) between choice of technique at different stages of production. Decisions about choice of technique at one stage justify choosing compatible techniques at earlier or later stages.

IV. CUMULATIVE FORCES

Political and technical forces tend to lead to cumulative decisions with respect to each of the four variables delineated above, O, R, T, M. To summarize briefly, objectives (O) are mainly a function of the nature of the micro-unit and of the competitive structure of the economy. Particular organizations (for example, foreign owned firms, family firms) establish political pressures for their continued existence; similarly, a highly protected non-competitive structure of the economy generates interest groups whose survival depends on the continuation of this policy. Conversely, a strongly competitive structure forces firms increasingly to become profit maximizers, rather than satisfiers.

R represents access to price of resources. A policy that gives some sectors favourable access—for example, subsidized capital—is difficult to reverse. Similarly, a high wage policy is difficult to reverse.

Market access (M) tends to be cumulative in that it is much easier to maintain than create a particular market; often there is no way of reversing consumer tastes created for a particular set of products.[14] Also, firms acquire experience in serving a particular market.

T, knowledge about technologies, is strongly cumulative. Research, development, and knowledge concentrate on technologies in use (or already known about) so that the direction of technical change is heavily influenced by technologies in use. These cumulative forces mean that changes in strategy should preferably be made early in the development process before too many cumulative forces have been established; marginal changes might be difficult to achieve. A radical break has to occur to generate cumulative forces operating in a different direction.

V. CLASSIFICATION OF MACRO-POLICIES

The description of variables influencing technology choice at the micro-level serves as a way of identifying and classifying macro-policies. In general, such policies have the twin objectives of altering the decisions of particular units and the *composition of units* in the economy in favour of those units likely to choose more appropriate technologies.

Objectives

The objectives of any micro-unit depend on three things. The first is the mode of production the unit represents. Objectives differ, for example, between foreign-owned firms (aiming to maximize world-wide profits) and local firms (concerned with local profits); between family firms (aiming to maximize family income) and capitalist firms (aiming to maximize profits); between publicly-owned and privately-owned firms, and so on. The second is the organization within the firm. In some firms "engineering man" may predominate, in others "economic man" (to use Wells' terms). In some firms, managerial objectives of maximizing output, for example, have come to dominate capitalist objectives of maximizing profits. The third is the economic environment in which the firm operates. In some environments some objectives may not permit the firm to survive. For example, in a protected and oligopolistic environment, firms may be able to pursue "satisficing" objectives, while in a more competitive environment they may be forced to be profit maximizers to survive.

Government policy can influence objectives in a number of ways: directly, through government directives to publicly-owned enterprises; indirectly, by changing the economic environment; and, for the economy as a whole, by changing the composition of units.

It is not immediately obvious which objectives best serve appropriate technology. It is apparent that the effect of the objectives pursued depends on the interaction with the other variables, so that in some contexts, for example, profit maximizing could lead to appropriate choices, while in other contexts it may result in inappropriate choices. In addition, short-run and long-run consequences might differ. For example, if firms in the public sector aim to maximize employment in the short run, they will select appropriate technologies, but, if these technologies are highly inefficient, the long-run possibilities for appropriate technology could be damaged. It is nonetheless possible to draw a few conclusions on objectives.

1. Satisficing type objectives—especially in large firms reliant on foreign technology—lead to inappropriate choices. According to some research (for example, Wells) engineering man is empowered to make the effective decisions, which tend to be for over-sophisticated technologies. According to others (Morley and Smith), foreign-owned firms tend to select technologies similar to those adopted in the home (developed) country. The choices of firms which are profit maximizers will depend on the external environment (prices, markets, etc.) they face. In some environments (oligopolistic competition with product differentiation, high wages, subsidized capital) they will tend to make inappropriate choices; in others they may make more appropriate choices. Hence policies designed to change objectives need to be accompanied by those that will change the economic environment.

2. Foreign-owned firms (or ones with close foreign associations) are generally concerned with maximizing world-wide (after tax) profits. This frequently involves adoption of the technology developed by the firm in its home company. Where the country in question is developed, this often means inappropriate technology and products. Where the country is another developing country, the technology may be more appropriate. Government policies here then may consist of countering such effects by creating incentives or disincentives to encourage the use of local technology, encouraging less developed country multinationals, and shifting away from foreign ownership.

3. In principle, governments may direct publicly-owned firms to take particular decisions, but doing so is too cumbersome if it involves daily interventions. Alternatively, and more efficiently, governments can lay down the criteria public firms should adopt. While this does occur in principle, in practice it is often ineffective because of day-to-day pressures which prevent the firms from carrying out government policy.

Thus, even in countries whose governments explicitly favour appropriate technology, public firms often make inappropriate decisions. Public sector firms seem to be more subject to internal and external pressures that preclude either appropriate or profit-maximizing decisions than private firms.[15] Additional work is needed to determine what the appropriate criteria of choice should be, and given the political economy of the public sector, how the government can assure that the criteria are used.

4. Generally, the small-scale and family sectors appear to make more appropriate choices both in the short- and long-term, partly because of their objectives and partly because of other factors (markets, access to resources). Macro-policies need to be designed to promote this sector and to increase its efficiency. Thus, for governments it is not a question of changing the objectives of this sector, but of formulating other policies.

The effect of cooperative arrangements on technical choice and income distribution depends critically on the form of the cooperative—its objectives and resources. Empirically a range may be observed from associations of members that have virtually no effect on resource allocation (for example, marketing co-ops in parts of Africa) to the more ambitious units which affect objectives and resource allocations radically (e.g., kibbutzim, communes).[16] Government policy needs to promote a structure of cooperative arrangements that will lead to appropriate choices.

Resources

The price package associated with appropriate technology is well-known.[17] It consists of eliminating the subsidies on capital (tax allowances and artificially low interest rates to the modern sector) and trying to eliminate those factors which lead to high wage costs in the modern sector, including social security costs as well as the wages themselves. Exchange rate policies are also relevant; overvalued exchange rates accompanied by high protection tends to reduce the price of imported capital goods.

It should be noted that these policies—basically raising capital costs and reducing wage costs—are all directed at the modern sector. For the rest of the economy, policies with the opposite effects are required. The informal sector and the traditional sector in general require lower interest rates and more access to capital. Distribution of credit is a major element in policies intended to change the composition of units in favor of decision-makers that make more appropriate technology choices. Through credit distribution, investable resources can be directed towards the small-scale sector and away from the large-scale sector.

Other aspects of resource policy are those related to the supply of resources used in appropriate technologies. The human capital element is important here, including policies towards training to generate appropriate skills. In some industries, supply problems with the skilled labour requirements of more appropriate technology are a significant reason why more capital-intensive technologies are introduced.[18] For capital, the promotion of a capital goods industry producing appropriate technologies can be important especially in areas where the international supply of appropriate capital goods is deficient.

Markets

Markets are important with respect to scale and to type. As far as scale is concerned, larger-scale production is almost invariably associated with more capital-intensive techniques.[19] Decisions on scale depend on resource access and markets. But markets play an independent role. Where markets are localized (because, for example, transport costs are high) then small-scale and labor-intensive techniques are often selected. Rural industry should be encouraged rather than leaving rural consumers dependent on urban centres for supplies.

The viability and dynamism of (dispersed) rural industry depends in part on the dynamism of agriculture. Where agricultural incomes are rising fast, then local markets will also be increasing, but these markets will not necessarily be supplied by local small-scale sources. To ensure that they will, local infrastructure (financial, technical, and marketing services) must be developed. The success of rural industry in Taiwan has been attributed in large part to infrastructural and organizational investments in the rural areas. In 1971 non-agricultural income accounted for over half of rural income in Taiwan, compared with between 15 and 20 percent in the Philippines, where the bias against agriculture had been greater and investment in rural infrastructure substantially less.[20]

Transport policy is also relevant—the structure of roads (trunk roads or localized feeder roads) and the way transport charges are calculated, which often encourage long haulage even where it is uneconomical. In India, for example, the system of pricing on the railways has given substantial advantage to large-scale cement production by eliminating the real advantage—in terms of transport costs—that small-scale plants should have in their locality.[21]

As for type of market, here it is a question of the nature of the products in demand. The nature of the products is an important direct aspect of appropriate technology. Appropriate products are products characterized by their compatibility with the income levels and needs of the majority of the population. Products that only a small high-income minority in a society can afford are defined as inappropriate. This is not a watertight definition, but it provides a broad criterion for assessing the appropriateness of products.

Economies produce products to be consumed directly, intermediate products (inputs into further production) and products for export. The criterion of appropriateness just described does not apply to the last two categories. For intermediate products, appropriateness depends on whether the product is an input into appropriate or inappropriate techniques. For export products, the relevant questions relate to the production techniques, rather than to the characteristics of the products. All products are associated with a certain (normally limited) range of production techniques; in general, once the characteristics of a product have been specified in detail there is not much choice of production techniques. Therefore—apart from the appropriateness or inappropriateness of the products—markets are important in determining production techniques.

Nationally, upper-income markets are associated with products with international brand names. Within any product class, these products are often more capital-intensive. In addition, high-income markets tend to consume products from more capital-intensive product groups. Redistributive policies, raising the purchasing power of low-income groups and reducing that of high-income groups, tend to increase the demand for appropriate products and also to tilt production techniques towards more labor-intensive methods. In some cases, however, high-income groups consume more labor-intensive products (for example, craft products such as hand-made carpets and hand-loom textiles). There are also direct policies towards markets and products, such as banning certain inappropriate products (for example, powdered baby milk), limiting advertising, or promoting products with more appropriate characteristics.[22]

The international market usually requires a higher standard and more capital-intensive product within any product market. But this can be offset by selecting more labour-intensive products (for example, textiles) as a consequence of international trade. Trade among developing countries might consist of more appropriate products (and production techniques) than trade between North and South. However, while this is probable within any product group, it might not apply to trade in manufactures as a whole. While international trade policies affect markets, in both quantity and type, their effects are complex and depend on specific policies and circumstances.[23]

Different organizations tend to serve—and even create—different markets. Although each type of organization sometimes does serve each type of market, there is a tendency for the following links between organization and market:

Organization	*Type of Market*
Foreign-owned firms and joint ventures	International markets Middle- and upper-income markets locally
Public sector Large-scale private sector	Middle- and upper-income markets locally Some international markets
Informal and traditional sectors	Low-income markets locally

Technology and Knowledge about the Available Technological Choice

A major area for policy consists in promoting appropriate information channels. The present system of information tends to be systematically biased towards recently developed, advanced country technologies (through salesmen, journals, etc.). Old appropriate technologies are rarely promoted. Information channels are often weak and need improvement nationally and internationally. Methods for so doing are fairly well known but there is a bias against improved information in this area.[24] As Pack pointed out, there can be large private (as well as social) gains for firms that invest in acquiring improved information.

The second major area is research and development (R & D) into appropriate technologies. In general, technical change originating in developing countries will tend to be more appropriate than technical change originating in developed countries, since the local environment influences the area of search as well as the results which will prove economically efficient, as illustrated in figure 1.1.

Suppose R & D tends to be randomly dispersed in all directions around the technology in use (roughly a Nelson and Winter type strategy), then for any initial technology (T) in diagram A, new research results will occur within the circle shown. But the only ones that are taken up will be those which reduce costs compared with the existing technology—that is, those below the budget line given by labour and capital costs. With developing country (DC) costs (KK^1), the area shaded with horizontal lines will represent economically efficient new techniques. With less developed country (LDC) costs (LL^1), the vertically shaded area will represent the techniques that will be developed. Hence techniques developed in DCs will tend to be more capital-intensive than LDC-developed techniques. The difference is much greater if each starts with a different technology, as in diagram B. Here there is no overlapping in the new results. This suggests that the direction of technical change will tend to become cumulative, according to the location of research, since the initial differences in new technologies—even after starting with the same technology as in diagram A—will tend to lead to a different choice of technology and consequently to a different starting point for technological developments in the next period.

In figure 1.1, only the usual capital/labour characteristics have been illustrated. But the environment is much more complex than this and includes the availability of different types of materials, labour of various skills, products required and organizational units.

A major effort needs to be made to promote technical change in developing countries, starting with a careful look at the analysis (see Lall, Katz, and others) of what promotes and inhibits such change. Policies regarding the import of technology, local R & D institutions, the promotion of relevant skills, and local capital goods industries are relevant.

Sources of technology—both as to information and the development of new technology—have been heavily biased towards the modern sector, and within the modern sector towards the relatively large scale. These biases arise because in the main, R & D is carried out in developed countries by larger-scale firms. The informal and traditional sector in developing countries suffers from heavy technical neglect. The diagrams used in figure 1.1 to illustrate how developed-country R & D tends to generate inappropriate techniques for developing countries could also be used to show how technology change initiated by large-scale enterprises in developing countries would tend to generate results inappropriate for the small-scale and traditional sector, as well as those for the modern sector in less developed countries.

VI. CONCLUSION

This brief discussion has attempted to identify and classify the main areas in which we should look for macro-policies for appropriate technology. It has not discussed the policies in any detail, nor has it considered whether such policies would be realistic or effective in particular contexts. Detailed research into comparative country experience with particular policies is necessary to support detailed policy conclusions in each of the areas identified. It is likely that this would lead to a typology of countries, with different policies relevant for countries at differing stages of development and with differing resources.

The general discussion has underlined three conclusions. First, political economy factors are significant and must be built into the analysis from the start and not added as an aside at the end. Second, cumulative forces—political, economic and technical—need to be taken into account because current options may be severely limited by past decisions. Third, changing what we have called "the composition of units" (the proportion of investment decisions in the control of different types of units) can be significant for every variable (objectives, resources, markets and technology) and might be one of the most effective ways of promoting appropriate technology. The dynamics of technology choice need underlining. Since countries are changing, creating resources (for investment in physical capital and human skills), the choice of technique must fit in with this dynamism of the economies, and not simply consist of a static resource allocation exercise. Moreover, technology too is changing at a rapid rate, especially in some industries, rendering many technologies obsolete. The implication of rapid technology change emanating from developed countries also needs to be taken into account in determining policies for appropriate technology.

NOTES

1. Leibenstein, while accepting this definition of "micro-level" has recently identified a need for a "micro-micro" economics, exploring how decision-making takes place *within* the decision-making unit. This too is an important area for those interested in appropriate technology, and one that has already been approached in discussions of "engineering" and "economic" man's relative influence within the firm. See Pickett, et al., and Wells. This is not further explored here.

2. See, for example, Morawetz, Stewart, 1977, chapter three, and Cooper.

3. Morawetz, p. 517. An almost identical definition is adopted by Westphal.

4. See, e.g., Schumacher, Stewart, 1977, and the many references in Singh.

5. In Robinson; see also Singh, who provides a much fuller discussion of the various characteristics that have been associated with appropriate technology.

6. This is not the place to summarize the substantial discussion on the issues of social cost-benefit analysis. See Stewart, 1975, and the special issue of *World Development*, edited by G.A. Amin and J.D. MacArthur, February, 1978.

7. Strictly, the introduction of "social efficiency" considerations would rule this out, where "social" values were elucidated with respect to actual government objectives. However, to avoid ambiguity it is preferable not to eliminate conflicts in this way. Instead, it is assumed that social efficiency is measured with reference to appropriate technology objectives. The use of the term "government objectives" is ambiguous. In fact there are no "government objectives" per se but rather various objectives belonging to various elements in the governments. Moreover, there is no good way of ascertaining precisely (and sometimes at all) what these objectives are.

8. See Perkins.

9. Galtung, p. 133.

10. I have taken a similar view, although I expressed it somewhat differently (see Stewart, 1977, chapter twelve).

11. See, e.g., Ranis, 1973.

12. Formally impossible; see Arrow.

13. See Binswanger's survey.
14. This happened with respect to refined maize milling in Kenya, for which there was no market until one was "created," but where strong demand subsequently developed. See Stewart, 1977, chapter nine.
15. See, e.g., Sobhan, Kumar, Perkins.
16. See Stewart, ed., 1983.
17. See, e.g., Acharya and Eckaus.
18. This applies to many craft industries, for example.
19. See, e.g., evidence contained in Forsyth, McBain and Solomon.
20. See Ranis, 1983.
21. Sigurdson.
22. See James and Stewart.
23. There is some evidence that trade in technology between developing countries is more appropriate than North-South trade (see, e.g., Lecraw), but the limited evidence is ambiguous on trade in general (see Amsden).
24. See Bhalla, ed.

REFERENCES

Acharya, S.N. 1974. *Fiscal/Financial Intervention, Factor Prices and Factor Proportions: A Review of Issues*, World Bank Staff Working Paper, No. 183.

Amsden, A.H. 1980. "The Industry Characteristics of Intra-Third World Trade in Manufactures," *Economic Development and Cultural Change*.

Arrow, K.J. 1970. *Social Choice and Individual Values*. Cowles Foundation Monograph: No. 12, second edition. New Haven, Conn.: Yale University Press.

Bhalla, A., ed. 1979. *Towards Global Action for Appropriate Technology*. Elmsford, N.Y.: Pergamon Press.

Binswanger, H.P., V. Ruttan and others. 1978. *Induced Innovation, Technology, Institutions and Development*. Baltimore: Johns Hopkins University Press.

Cooper, C. 1979. A Summing up of the Conference. In *Appropriate Technologies for Third World Development*, ed. A. Robinson. New York: St. Martin's Press.

Eckaus, R.E. 1977. *Appropriate Technologies for Developing Countries*. Washington, D.C.: National Academy of Sciences.

Enos, J. 1982. *Market Structure, Industrial Organization and Technology: Concepts and Methodology and Evidence*, World Employment Programme Research Working Papers, (WEP 2-22/WP 93). Geneva: International Labour Organization.

Forsyth, D., N. McBain, and R. Solomon. 1980. "Technical Rigidity and Appropriate Technology in Less Developed Countries," *World Development*, 8.

Galtung, J. 1980. *The North/South Debate: Technology, Basic Human Needs and the New International Economic Order*, World Order Models Project, Working Paper No. 12.

James, J. and F. Stewart. 1981. *New Products: A Discussion of the Welfare Effects of the Introduction of New Products in Developing Countries*, Oxford Economic Papers, 31.

Katz, J. 1978. *Technological Change, Economic Development and Intra and Extra Regional Relations in Latin America*, IDB/ECLA/UNDP/IDRC Regional Program of Studies on Scientific and Technical Development in Latin America, Working Paper No. 30. Buenos Aires: Economic Commission for Latin America.

Kumar, R. 1982. The Indian Coal Industry after Nationalization, Ph.D. diss., Oxford University.

Lall, S. 1982. *Developing Countries as Exporters of Technology*. London: Macmillan.

Lecraw, D. 1977. *Direct Investment by Firms from Less Developed Countries*, Oxford Economic Papers, 29.

Leibenstein, H. 1979. "'The Missing Link'—Micro-Micro Theory?" *Journal of Economic Literature*, XVII.

Morawetz, D. 1974. "Employment Implications of Industrialization in Developing Countries: A Survey," *Economic Journal*, 84.

Morley, S.A., and G.W. Smith. 1974. *Managerial Discretion and the Choice of Technology by Multinational Firms in Brazil*, Paper no. 56. Houston, Texas: Rice University.

Nelson, R. and S. Winter. 1974. "Neo-Classical Versus Evolutionary Theories of Economic Growth: Critiques and Prospects," *Economic Journal*, 84.

Pack, H. 1981. "Appropriate Industrial Technology: Benefits and Obstacles," *The Annals*, November.

Perkins, F.C. (1983). "Technology Choice, Industrialization and Development Experiences in Tanzania," *Journal of Development Studies*, 19.

Pickett, J. et al. 1974. "The Choice of Technology, Economic Efficiency and Employment in Developing Countries," *World Development and Cultural Change*, 21.

Ranis, G. 1973. "Industrial Sector Labour Absorption," *Economic Development and Cultural Change*, 21.

Ranis, G. 1983. Alternative Patterns of Distribution and Growth in the Mixed Economy: The Philippines and Taiwan. In *Work, Income and Inequality: Payments Systems in the Third World*, ed. F. Stewart. London: Macmillan.

Robinson, A., ed. 1979. *Appropriate Technologies for Third World Development*. New York: St. Martin's Press.

Rudra, A. 1982. Government Policies for Promoting Appropriate Technology in India. Paper prepared for A.T. International-sponsored workshop, Macro-Policies for Appropriate Technology. The Hague, March 1982.

Schumacher, E.F. 1976. *Small is Beautiful: A Study of Economics as if People Mattered*. New York: Harper & Row Press.

Sigurdson, Jon. 1982. A Comment on Appropriate Technology in Light of Rapid Technological Change for Major Technologies in the Industrialized Countries. Paper prepared for A.T. International-sponsored workshop, Macro-Policies for Appropriate Technology. The Hague, March 1982.

Singh, H. 1981. Appropriate Technology, M.Phil. diss., Oxford University.

Sobhan, R. and M. Ahmed. 1980. *Public Enterprise in an Intermediate Regime: A Study in the Political Economy of Bangladesh*. Bangladesh Institute of Development Studies.

Stewart, F. 1975. "A Note on Social Cost Benefit Analysis and Class Conflict in LDCs," *World Development*, 3.

Stewart, F., ed. 1983. *Work, Income and Inequality: Payments Systems in the Third World*. London: Macmillan.

Wells, L.T. 1973. "Economic Man and Engineering Man: a Choice of Technology in a Low Wage Country," *Public Policy*, 21.

Westphal, L.E. 1982. Macro Policies for Appropriate Technology. Paper prepared for A.T. International sponsored workshop, Macro-Policies for Appropriate Technology. The Hague, March 1982.

World Development, 6 (Special issue edited by G.A. Amin and J.D. MacArthur), February, 1978.

Table 1.1

Costs and Benefits Matrix

Group Affected	(a) land redistribution	(b) credit redistribution	(c) price changes	(d)[1] banning tractors	(d)[2] banning tractor imports
Large landowners	-100	-20	-10	-5	-2
Small landowners	+ 50	+20	+ 5	0	0
Landless labourers	+ 70	+20	+20	+20	+5
Local tractor producers	- 30	-30	-30	-50	+40
Foreign tractor producers	- 30	-30	-30	-50	-50

Figure 1.1 R & D and technical change

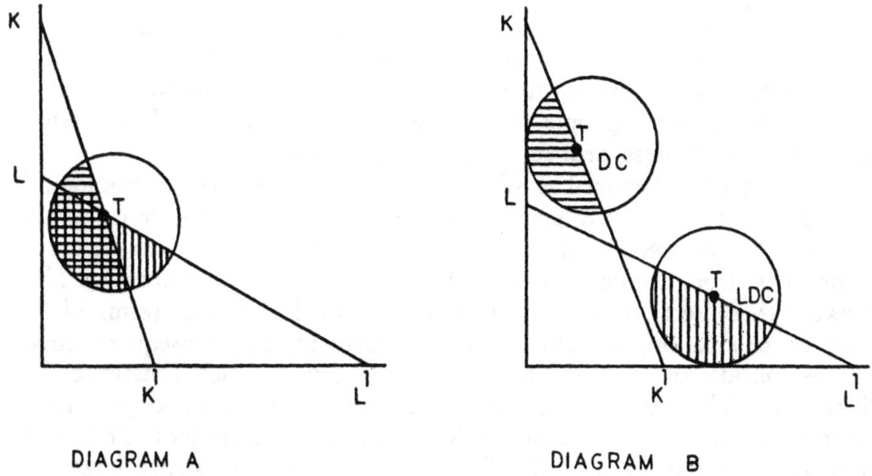

Two

Technology Choice in Agriculture in India over the Past Three Decades

Ashok Rudra

I. INTRODUCTION

Our argument in this chapter will be that India started its development efforts in the post-independence period with a more or less correct approach towards the problem of technological choice in agriculture, based on a balanced assessment of the requirements of growth and equity; however, in the following decades, the technology policy changed to incorporate more and more inappropriate techniques of production. It will be seen that even though Indian agriculture is pre-eminently private, consisting of hundreds of millions of individual cultivators, government policy has had a decisive role in shaping the technological basis of Indian agriculture. This policy has been, to a very large extent, a direct result of Western influence, especially that of the United States.

This chapter will not be concerned with conceptual finesses of what constitutes appropriateness of technology. When we say that the technological choice has become increasingly inappropriate, we mean that other choices could have been made that would have resulted in greater distributional justice, more labour employment, greater use of local resources, more participation by local people, less dependence on imports, less foreign influence, and all these probably with more output.

The chapter is structured as follows: section II presents the technological scenario as it has gradually emerged and promises to become more firmly set in the future. Section III traces the evolution of state policy towards the problem, from the immediate pre-independence period until today. The following three sections evaluate this technological choice in terms of its effects on production, distribution and employment. The subsequent three sections consider in detail the major industrial inputs which constitute the pillars of the New Agriculture—namely, chemical fertilizers and pesticides, irrigation and agricultural machinery. We will not only consider their impact on the agricultural sector but will also look at the industrial interests, domestic and foreign, that have influenced policies with regard to them.

II. THE EMERGING TECHNOLOGICAL SCENE

For about the first two decades after India's independence one could hardly discern a clear pattern in the technological horizon of the country's agriculture. The traditional pattern was no doubt giving way, but what was taking its place remained blurred. However, in the mid-1960s the mist started to clear.

From that time, Indian agriculture has been marked by a strong duality technologically, and this duality will continue. The bulk of agriculture will retain its base in the traditional technology represented by a combination of human labour, bullock labour and cow-dung manure; but there will be within it increasing islands of modern agriculture based on chemical fertilizers, pesticides, powered irrigation and indiscriminate use of farm machinery. The alternative strategy—which is not being followed—would consist of a judicious retention of some of the traditional means of production and farm practices with a discriminating application of science and technology to improve them alongside the new means of production.

Thus, efforts at mobilising various kinds of organic manures have been all but given up. Canal water continues to be wasted because of the inadequacy of feeder channels and the absence of suitable institutional arrangements for the efficient and equitable distribution of water. The shift towards minor irrigation has been largely a shift to privately owned and energised tubewell irrigation without any research being made for tapping non-conventional groundwater and surface water. While farm mechanisation has gone ahead in an indiscriminate manner with imported models of tractors, power tillers and other accessories, there have been few improvements made to the traditional implements.

In quantitative and comparative terms the use of modern inputs is still quite insignificant, as may be seen from tables 2.1 and 2.2. But what is important is the rate at which the increase is taking place in this enclave. As can be seen in table 2.3, there has not been any marked increase in the quantities of traditional inputs.

Two points relating to modern agriculture in India need emphasis. First, the technology that constitutes its basis, which has come to be called *new technology*, is not restricted to chemical and biological innovations, as has often been claimed by its protagonists, but incorporates mechanisation as an integral part. It is erroneous to describe the "New Strategy" as a seed-fertilizer-water intensive strategy as is often done because there cannot be any strategy for the growth of agriculture which does not incorporate greater and more efficient uses of improved seeds, plant nutrients and controlled water supply. It is a particular way of combining these basic inputs and machinery that constitutes the newness of this so-called New Strategy.

Second, it is utter nonsense to say that this technology is scale neutral. The technology is patently biased in favour of larger holdings in two senses: the agricultural machinery that has been introduced requires larger areas for its efficient utilisation, and all the inputs, whether mechanical, chemical, or biological, are extremely costly so that only the richer farmers can afford to make adequate use of them.[1]

III. EVOLUTION OF TECHNOLOGY POLICY: AN HISTORICAL SKETCH

It is convenient to divide the period under consideration into three phases. The first phase begins in 1949 with the publication of the report of the Congress Agrarian Reforms Committee (CARC, 1949) and continues until 1959. The second phase begins with the publication in 1959 of a famous report by a team of experts from the Ford Foundation and continues until 1966-67, which is usually recognised as the beginning of the so-called Green Revolution. The third phase continues until today. The second phase marked a drastic reversal of the policy priorities pursued in the first phase. There was no such reversal with the Green Revolution. The strategy associated with this hackneyed expression is nothing but the consummation of the approach adopted in the second phase.

The balanced approach to the problem of technology in agriculture that prevailed among the leaders of pre-independence India is best reflected in the report of the Congress Party, referred to above. It took a categorical stand on mechanisation—"We do not favour in general mechanisation of agricultural operations"—and qualified its stand only with the following proviso: "Large-scale mechanisation [is] to be restricted to collectivised agriculture on culturable wastes." It supported "every effort to improve the implements used in agriculture" and gave concrete suggestions, for instance, for "inverting ploughs for green manuring, which can be easily drawn by bullocks of an average size, [and for] seed drills and hand-operated fans for winnowing."

As to high-yielding seeds, the report did not wait for Dr. Borlaug, the so-called father of the miracle wheat, to recommend that "large-scale efforts should be made to produce pedigree seeds." However, the Congress Party report differed drastically from Dr. Borlaug's philosophy insofar as plant nutrients are concerned. It recommended the use of green manure, farmyard manure, oil cakes, bone-meal, and even night soil; chemical fertilizers were only mentioned. In relation to irrigation, the report anticipated the later strategists by calling for efforts for minor irrigation works to supplement the major ones.

These emphases remained unchanged in the first two five-year plans, which spanned the remaining period of the first phase. The second plan has been rightly criticised for not saying much about agriculture. This only meant that it endorsed the approach articulated by the first plan. The most important statements in the plan relate to the institutional counterpart to the technological approach of the first phase.

This counterpart consisted of the Community Development Programme, whose underlying philosophy briefly stated: "All aspects of rural life are interrelated and . . . no lasting results can be achieved if individual aspects of it are dealt with in isolation" (Planning Commission, 1952). Blocks, each a cluster of about one hundred villages, were treated as the basic units for development efforts comprehending different economic and social activities from agriculture to industry, from health to education, from housing to transport and communications. The efforts were to be based as much as possible on local resources under local management, in the form of "direct contributions of labour by farmers themselves" (Planning Commission, 1952).

On plant nutrients, the first plan took a more balanced and positive view in words such as, "We do not consider that it is necessary to wait for such full mobilisation before introducing chemical fertilizers. The two processes should and can go on simultaneously. Both these types of manure are necessary for maintaining and increasing soil fertility."

On the irrigation front, the second plan marked the beginning of the shift of emphasis from canals to tubewells. On mechanisation, the stand until the end of this first phase was, "In agriculture, except under certain conditions, in the present stage of development the possible advantages of mechanisation may be more than offset by the social cost of unemployment that such mechanisation will involve" (Planning Commission, 1956).

The drastic change in approach that marks the second phase is not reflected in the third plan. It was not until the fourth plan that the adoption of the New Strategy was announced—already a *fait accompli* in a weak form since 1959 and consummated in 1966-67, a few years prior to the launching of the fourth plan in 1969-70.

The new actor on the scene was the new type of high-yielding wheat and rice seeds; drastic breakthroughs in the development of these seeds were recorded in the mid-1960s. The role of chemical fertilizers was emphasized as if it were a new discovery, significantly underplaying the role of organic manures. Other integral parts of the policy package were the emphasis on water management with "integrated use of ground and surface water," which meant a shift of emphasis from public canal irrigation to private tubewell irrigation; emphasis on multiple cropping involving short-duration crops; proposals for setting up supportive institutions for the distribution of fertilizers and credit; and abandonment of reliance on indigenous materials and local initiative. But the policy still remained shy of mechanisation.

This inhibition was overcome in the fifth plan, which urged selective farm mechanisation, recognizing that an absolute shortage of farm power would inevitably develop if animal power alone were relied upon. Since then there have been no further policy shifts in the successive plans. Selective opening to mechanisation has meant indiscriminate proliferation of all kinds of farm machinery, with the sole exception of harvest combines, which have been frowned upon. Thus, in every aspect—nutrients, water, seed or power—there has been an increasing reliance on industries.

The story above, based on the plan documents, misses some essential facts. These documents constitute the most important source for development policies adopted and pursued by the Indian government. But technology policy in agriculture has hardly been a matter for the government of India to decide on alone. Incredible as it may sound, these decisions have throughout been taken by certain external agencies, and it was left to the government of India to acquiesce to them, with different degrees of reluctance and delay. As such, the account reads a bit like *Hamlet* without the Prince of Denmark. We shall briefly correct the record by bringing in that chief actor to clarify the policy shifts.

The philosophy of overall general development underlying the Community Development Programme (CDP) was also inspired by the United States—the model for the programme was the latter's extension services. From the very beginning the CDP was financed largely by the U.S. government and such agencies as the Ford Foundation and the Rockefeller Foundation. U.S. experts participated in various activities, including the training courses for the staff of the programme. The programme was divided into eight parts dealing with areas from agriculture to social welfare, and for each part there was a U.S.-sponsored supporting project. For instance, there was an operations agreement for the acquisition and distribution of fertilizers, another operational agreement for the acquisition and distribution of iron and steel for agricultural purposes and yet another operational agreement for groundwater irrigation. The minister for community development wrote in 1957 about a U.S. expert: "There has hardly been a basic decision taken on the implementation of this programme in which Dr. Ensminger's observations as an advisor and his views as one identified with this programme have not made some significant contribution." This occurs in the foreword written by the minister for a basic manual for a training course called "A Guide to Community Development," which was written by Dr. Ensminger. This is an indication of the degree to which U.S. experts acted not only as advisors but as leaders of the programme.

It is therefore not surprising that subsequent policy shifts were triggered by reports made by one team after another of U.S. experts. Within a year of launching the programme, a report by the United States Technical Committee (1953) questioned the adequacy of the approach of thinly distributing available resources and knowledge of the existing technology among all villages and villagers and recommended that a part of the CDP funds be reallocated to research and training in the agricultural sciences. This shift from a general welfare oriented approach to a technocratic one, aimed narrowly at crop production, was reiterated in 1955 by a joint Indo-American team on agricultural research and education. The team recommended that agricultural programmes be run by career professionals of agronomy and that these professionals be graduates of agricultural universities similar to the U.S. federal-state land grant universities. While the government of India began to set up such agricultural universities and to bring together under a single administrative control all programmes relating to agriculture, as suggested by the Nalagarh report (Ministry of Food and Agriculture, 1958), the Ford Foundation set up an expert team which made history by its "Report on India's Food Crisis and Steps to Meet It" (Ministry of Food and Agriculture, 1959). It is this report that led to the formation of the New Strategy, adopted initially in the form of the Intensive Agriculture Districts Programme (IADP), later giving place to the so-called Green Revolution Strategy in the mid-1960s. The Ford Foundation not only provided the general idea but also presented a concrete programme in the form of yet another expert team report that followed shortly: "Suggestions for 10-point Program to Increase Food Production." In 1960 the 10-point programme was formally adopted in a memorandum of agreement between the government of India and the Ford Foundation.

While the parentage of the IADP and the Green Revolution is clear, the central thrust of these reports is not easily seen in the summary statements of the recommendations made in them. This thrust expresses itself best in the phrase, "the package principle"—a phrase that was much in use in offical writings of that time and one that encapsulates the entire philosophy behind the strategy. The philosophy is not that seed, fertilizer, water, pesticide, and so on are to be combined in a package in their application, but that anything else, for example, fertilizer without water or pesticide without seed, would hardly make sense. The idea was to apply the inputs in a combination of their maximising doses, which meant allocating the development resources, material and financial, in a highly concentrated and selective manner. Selectivity was to be applied at all levels—regions, crops, farmers, etc. This meant that resources were to be allocated in a selective and concentrated fashion to such regions, and within them to such crops, and with respect to them, to such farmers, which promised to make maximum use of resources. This amounted to pouring funds on regions that were already well-endowed, on crops already profitable and on farmers already rich.

The inequality aggravating implications of the strategy were so glaring, but the policy reversal did not take place as a simple walk-over; there was a great deal of struggle between different personalities and factions within the government that supported and opposed the approach. A good account is found in a book by C. Subramaniam (1979), a cabinet minister in the 1960s. He played a crucial role in making the government adopt the New Strategy policy behind the back of the planning commission, which for him was "a bottleneck that had to be by-passed."

We have stressed that there was nothing new in the search for new seeds. That is not to deny the importance of the break-through in seed innovation that took place in the mid-1960s as a world phenomenon. Developments in India would have been different if the government had not imported in 1965 two hundred tonnes of a Mexican wheat variety that had been newly innovated by a Rockefeller Foundation research team and then imported another eighteen thousand tonnes the next year, made possible by foreign exchange also provided by the Rockefeller Foundation.

Thus a policy that started its career right after independence with the philosophy of all-around and self-reliant development of the rural community was transformed into one narrowly focussing on production alone, concentrated in regions, crops and among rich farmers and depending exclusively on purchased inputs from distant and sophisticated large-scale industries.

IV. GROWTH OF CROP PRODUCTION

Maximum growth of production was the sole objective of the new strategy; neither employment nor equality were considered as objectives. Thus, Ladejinski (1973) wrote, "the aim of the Green Revolution as envisioned by policy makers is productivity; social imperatives were not part of it." Although we shall argue that from the point of view of employment and distributional effects, the technological choice has been far from socially beneficial, in this section we shall assess the performance by the criterion of maximising production.

As far as agricultural production for the country as a whole is concerned, it is by now widely accepted that during the entire period since independence, growth has followed a smooth trend despite all the ups and downs caused by hazards of the monsoon or other cyclical factors. This is an extremely remarkable fact. First, there is no reason why any natural growth of agricultural production should follow a smooth trend represented by a simple mathematical function: in statistical time-series analysis, one often applies such methods as that of the moving averages and obtains so-called trend lines which reveal no regular pattern whatsoever. It is all the more remarkable that the trend that one obtains now with data available for more than thirty years is not different from the fit with data for only the first fifteen or twenty years. That is, whether one considers a period preceding the so-called Green Revolution or one following it or one spanning both, one seems to end up with the same fitted trend curve.

This has important implications for the question of whether there has been a "Green Revolution" in the country. The answer to the question is no, if one thinks of the country as a whole and agriculture as whole and if by revolution one means "a sharp break from the situation that existed before the revolution" (Ladejinski, 1973). There is lack of agreement among experts as to whether this trend in agricultural growth is one of a constant rate of growth or of a diminishing rate of growth. None of the trend fitting exercises can be read as implying an increasing rate of growth. However, there have been differences in opinion as represented by the following two positions: (1) "Output (and yield per unit area) of food crops and all crops grew more or less uniformly over the entire period with no evidence of either acceleration or deceleration since 1967-68" (Srinivasan, 1979), and (2) "The average annual growth rate between 1950-51 to 1954-55 and 1960-61 to 1964-65 was over 3 percent in the aggregate. . . . In the subsequent decade, ending 1970-71 to 1974-75, the growth of crop output was around 2.1 percent" (Vaidyanathan, 1977). Given that the population seems to be growing at a rate of 2.4 percent per year, the first view suggests a growth which just manages to maintain per capita consumption production. But the second view suggests an alarming decline. This is a problem on which many others, including the writer, have carried out extensive and careful exercises and concluded that there is no means of discriminating, by purely statistical means, between a constant rate trend and a decelerating trend. (Interested readers may consult Rudra (1970), Dey (1975), Srinivasan (1979) and Chaudhuri (1980).)

We shall, for our present argument, accept the interpretation that the rate of growth has remained constant—our latest figures are 2.58 percent per year for agricultural production and 2.56 percent per year for food grains (figures 2.1 and 2.2). The significance of these rates can be appreciated if one considers that the rate of growth of agriculture in the fifty years preceding the country's independence was a mere half percent per year. Also, when compared internationally, the record is not to be minimised.[2] But given that the trend has been continuous from the beginning of the 1950s, could this performance be credited to the New Strategy, which, as we saw, picked up momentum only by the mid-1960s? To answer this question it may be recalled that until the mid-1960s growth of production had been mainly based on extending the area under cultivation. No further extension was possible after that, and the production increase since then has been due to an increase in hectare yield. The New Strategy can therefore be given credit for increasing the per hectare yield so as to maintain the overall trend in the rate of growth.

It is no small achievement that the country has, from the mid-1970s, become self sufficient in food-grains—a national objective that has always received a high priority.[3] Not only is India no longer dependent on imports for current consumption, but it has built up a considerable buffer stock, and the spectre of famine, it is claimed, has finally been laid to rest.

The phenomenon of production growth has not been uniform for all crops and all regions. It is now accepted that there have been some extensive changes in the production conditions in some regions for certain crops.[4] The most cited example is that of wheat in the regions of Punjab, Haryana and Western U.P. (Uttar Pradesh). Figures 2.3 and 2.4 show that there have been sharp breaks in the trends of production of this crop in these regions: from less than 3 percent up to the end of the 1950s the rate jumped to 7.28 and 9.88 percent in U.P. and Punjab-Haryana, respectively.[5] There was a similar upward shift in rice production in Punjab-Haryana though such a shift did not take place in the principal rice growing areas (figure 2.5). Such sharp breaks may be qualified as revolutionary. If there have been such upward shifts in the growth rates of certain crops in certain regions, but not for all crops in all regions, it follows that there must have been some regions and some crops for which there have been downward shifts. This means that the New Strategy has affected regions and crops selectively and has increased regional disparity. Those crops and regions not affected have recorded stagnation or even decline, while other crops in other regions have been given such a push upwards that they have made up for the shortfalls in other areas and other crops.

This uneven performance suggests caution against a complacent view about the food situation. Reality does not ride on smooth mathematical curves. There are no bases allowing one to take for granted that the country will remain self-reliant in agricultural products, especially food grains. Many hold the pessimistic view that the new technology has already exhausted itself in the few areas where it has taken place. Various factors at different times have provoked these pessimistic prognoses. Dilution of the potency of the new seeds and an alleged slowing down of the rate of growth of demand for fertilizers are two signals which have raised such alarms. Indirect evidence that has been used is the extremely low inter-farm variation in the adoption of the new technology in Punjab.

We shall now consider the argument that production could have grown even more if a different strategy had been followed. This alternative strategy would have distributed the production-augmenting inputs among more farmers with a lower intensity. The New Strategy is based on the idea that each farmer should apply the combination of inputs that maximises his private profit. The alternative strategy would have a larger number of farmers applying the inputs in smaller doses so as to maximise aggregate production, given a limited supply of a particular input. The argument that the social optimum is different from the results obtained by aggregating individual optima has been elaborately demonstrated for fertilizer use, as we shall see in the following section.

V. AGGRAVATION OF INEQUALITY

It is accepted by all concerned that the new technology has aggravated the already acute inequality of distribution of income and wealth among the population dependent on agriculture. This consensus is based largely on *a priori* reasoning. Whatever quantitative work has been done on the problem—mostly with regional or local data—corroborates or at least does not contradict the reasoning. It is easy to understand that measuring inequality for the agricultural population and comparing it over time are extremely difficult tasks. It is even more difficult to decide what part of the increases in inequality can be ascribed to the introduction of the new technology and what part to other factors.

The *a priori* reasoning is so straightforward that even defenders of the New Strategy have never cared to counter it.[6] The reasoning can be divided into several components, each of which has been shown to be valid in light of empirical evidence. These components are as follows:

1. Since the new technology is intensive in capital inputs per hectare, the adoption rate is higher among bigger farmers than among smaller ones and is higher among owner farmers than among tenant farmers.[7]
2. Because of their better resources position, bigger farmers apply modern inputs in greater quantities than smaller farmers and thus approximate more closely to the private profit maximising combination.[8]

3. These two factors are further accentuated by the fact that bigger farmers enjoy greater access to institutional credit and other production-augmenting facilities provided by the government.[9]
4. While seed, water, and fertilizers are indeed divisible and size-neutral, tractors, tubewells and most other machinery require minimum farm sizes to be used with maximum benefit.
5. The new technology yields a higher rate of return to capital investment than the traditional technology.
6. Yield per hectare under the new technology increases with farm size.[10]
7. The above factors working together generate more income among bigger farmers than among smaller ones.
8. More income among big farmers generates more savings among them. This leads to a cycle of larger income–larger savings–larger capital investments and yet larger income among the big farmers.
9. All that has been said above refers only to owners of land. There are, however, the totally landless, and the polarisation between the landless and the big farmers is yet another dimension of the phenomenon.[11]

It follows, therefore, that both income and wealth would become more unequally distributed with time.

Data on the income of farmers are scarce, and data on savings and capital formation are not very reliable. But one can see with one's naked eye the piling up of farm machinery in a concentrated manner in the bigger farms and the much greater use by them of expensive inputs, like fertilizers, pesticides, and so forth. This unequal accumulation of fixed and working capital must indicate a correspondingly larger income generation among the bigger farmers. A recent study (Chopra, 1984) showed that after land, the next most important factor contributing to the unequal distribution of farm assets (including land) is modern machinery and implements, and it is precisely these items that are concentrated in the bigger farms.

The findings of some of the more important empirical investigations support the *a priori* reasoning. According to a Reserve Bank of India survey (RBI, 1965, and RBI, 1975), the Gini coefficient of concentrations of assets among cultivating families in the rural areas increased between 1961 and 1971 from 0.59 to 0.62. According to another survey (NCAER, 1972), the same coefficient for household income in rural areas increased from 0.41 to 0.46 in the brief period from 1962 to 1968. The distribution of land among the rural population (including landless people) has remained more or less unchanged—the NSS 17th Round (for 1961) yields a Gini coefficient of 0.72 and the NSS 26th Round (for 1971) shows it to be 0.71.

Then there are the so-called poverty calculations, which are calculations relating to the proportion of people below a certain poverty line, understood as a level of living below which the basic requirements of subsistence are not met. The results of different poverty calculations carried out by different research workers are not consistent with each other. There are some who find that the proportion below the poverty line is increasing (for example,

Bardhan, 1974). There are others (for example, Ahluwahlia, 1977) for whom the proportion below the poverty line does not show any clear trend, being subject to fluctuations caused by such variables as prices, per capita output, and so on. There are, however, no studies that show a systematic decrease of the proportion below the poverty line. Given that average rural income has risen in real terms, this alone is a quantitative indication of an increase in income inequality.

The changes in the heartland of the Green Revolution have been much more acute. A survey (Rudra, 1969) conducted in 1968 found that from 1955-56 to 1967-68 bigger farmers (those owning more than 20 acres of land) had increased their land ownership through purchases by about 10 percent, and farmers having between 100 and 150 acres of land had done so by nearly 40 percent. According to Kahlon and Singh (1973), large farmers increased their land ownership by 16 percent in the four years from 1967-68 to 1971-72. During the same period, small farmers lost land by 38 percent. Inequality increase is, however, much more important for assets other than land. For assets other than land, the same investigators found that inequality of distribution increased in the manner shown in table 2.4.

The aggravation of inequality discussed above cannot be ascribed entirely to the adoption of the new technology. It is difficult to sort out the effects of the new technology from those of other contributory factors. Frankel (1971) estimated the direct effects of the new technology in Ludhiana, one of the heartlands of the Green Revolution, calculating that about 80 percent of the farmers shared in its benefits, even if unequally; in the country as a whole the proportions were exactly the reverse.

One aspect of inequality aggravation by the new technology was a change in agrarian relations. This relates to tenancy. Since the new technology is highly profitable, there has been a widespread tendency among landowners to evict tenants and resume cultivation under their own supervision and with the help of hired labourers. This has meant increasing misery of poor peasants and aggrandizement of big landowners. According to some authors (for example, Frankel, 1971), these evictions and rising land rents have caused not only a relative worsening of the lot of poor peasants but even an absolute deterioration.

Alongside evictions, two other developments affected poor land-owning peasants. Some of them have found it more profitable to lease out their tiny bits of land to bigger landowners than to cultivate them themselves, giving rise to what has been called the phenomenon of reverse tenancy. The other phenomenon is that of poor peasants selling land to rich farmers. The extent to which the latter has taken place is a matter on which there is little concrete evidence. It is generally held that this has not been an important part of the agrarian transformation that is taking place in the country.

VI. EMPLOYMENT EFFECT

The employment effect of the new technology is a subject on which there has been, on the one hand, many empirical studies, and on the other, an absence of agreed conclusions. The ambiguity relates chiefly to the effect of mechanisation on employment. There are not many differences of opinion about the employment effect of the seed-fertilizer-water part of the technology packet. It is widely agreed that these inputs augment employment. More irrigation obviously calls for more labour for digging, bunding, and so forth. More fertilizer application also means greater labour requirements. The high-yielding variety (HYV) seeds require more labour by calling for more tending, more weeding, and such improved practices as row-sowing, seed treatment, and so on, and by making possible a higher intensity of cropping by shortening the durations of crop seasons.[12] Increased production, whether due to seed, fertilizer, or water, increases employment during the harvest season.

The type of labour used also seems to be affected by the new technology. There is a shift from family labour to hired labour, which is not surprising given that farmers who can afford the new technology belong to the upper brackets and may therefore be expected to have a higher preference for leisure. There seems to be some effect on the employment of farm servants, but its nature is somewhat ambiguous.[13]

But the employment gains due to biochemical inputs are drastically curtailed by the negative effects of mechanisation. Once again, there is no difference of opinion about the labour-displacing effects of farm machinery, when specific operations are considered in isolation. There is also no difference of opinion about threshers and harvest combines being much more labour displacing than tractors.[14] Differences arise when one attempts to evaluate the net effect on farming as a whole. Those who support and advocate mechanisation point at indirect employment generation of the following kinds:

1. Higher employment generated by manual operations made possible by deeper tillage
2. Employment generated by higher intensity of cropping made possible by the speeding-up effect of mechanisation on certain operations for individual crops[15]
3. Higher employment made possible by energised irrigation
4. Higher employment resulting from crop production on land released from fodder cultivation[16]
5. Employment generated through expansion of facilities for storage, transport, and so forth
6. Employment generated outside agriculture by the maintenance and up-keep of farm machinery and in ancillary industries[17]

Even if all these effects do take place, whether the indirect employment generation fully compensates for the direct labour displacement remains an open question. Some of the dissenting views have been referred to in notes 15, 16, and 17. A different argument is that the net loss due to mechanisation is more than compensated for by additional employment generated by the seed-fertilizer-water combination. While this argument is repeated endlessly by advocates of the new technology, there is important evidence against it.[18]

Another effect on employment which is socially positive and not subject to any controversy is an evening-out of labour demand over the seasons. This stands in contrast to the traditional pattern of labour demand, which is concentrated in a number of peak periods.

An important point often lost sight of is that the labour absorption due to the seed-fertilizer-water technology is subject to a certain ceiling that has already been reached in areas where adoption of the new variety and the associated technology has reached near saturation.[19] This ceiling will be raised only if there is another breakthrough in seed technology. On the other hand the decrease in employment due to mechanisation may be expected to continue indefinitely given that mechanisation has only just begun and there is a continuous process of innovations in the sector.

VII. THE FERTILIZER POLICY

The policy of the Indian government towards soil nutrients since the beginning of the 1960s has been one of vast and continuous expansion of the use of chemical fertilizers by all possible means. All the policy instruments in the hands of the government (for example, import control, industrial licensing policy, fiscal policy, price control policy, and so on) have been applied in a concerted manner to achieve this aim. The numbers involved are all impressively large, as is shown in table 2.5 and figure 2.6. Consumption of nitrogen, phosphate and potash has grown at rates between 15 and 20 percent per annum over the last three decades.[20] Domestic production of nitrogen and phosphate has also grown at about 16 percent per year. The capacity for production of nitrogen has grown at an even faster rate, nearly 22 percent per annum. Even though there has been considerable import substitution, imports have grown at an equally high rate.[21] Raw materials for the industry have also grown but at a slightly lower rate, both in the domestic and the import sectors.[22] Investment in the industry by mid-1983-84 amounted to more than Rs. 40,000 millions, which can be compared with the book value of investments of about Rs. 160,000 millions in public sector industries up to 1979.

This phenomenal rise took place when costs of production were also growing at fantastic rates, largely due to the dependence of industry on the oil industry for feedstocks as well as transportation (table 2.7). Prices of capital goods in the industry have increased in the world market at even higher rates. As a result, investment per ton of nitrogen became four times more expensive from 1969 to 1984.

This growth could have been satisfactory if it were part of an overall mobilisation of all kinds of plant nutrients. There has, however, been no noticeable effort for the maximum mobilisation of organic manure resources even though, according to an FAO report, "everywhere in the world the best yields from all the crops are achieved by appropriate combinations of organic and mineral fertilizers" (FAO, 1976). This wisdom has not yet been challenged by anyone. In India and in the world, there was at one time much appreciation of the potential contribution to agricultural growth from large-scale efforts at the efficient utilisation of plant nutrients from animal wastes, human wastes, industrial wastes, crop residues, legumes and other green manures, and augmenting them with the help of bacterial fertilizers, algae fertilizers and different soil amendments.[23] The Food and Agriculture Organisation published two comprehensive reports (FAO, 1962 and FAO, 1976) which gathered much useful information from agronomists on practices in different countries for the benefit of policy makers in developing countries. The Indian government also published several reports (for example, PEO, 1967; National Commission on Agriculture, 1976(b)) which made similar suggestions and recommendations. In addition, in the earlier days of its development efforts, the Indian government took the trouble of sending expert delegations to China and Japan to learn about improved methods of cultivation which relied more on labour intensive production techniques than on heavy inputs of capital (Ministry of Food and Agriculture, 1956(a); 1956(b)).

These reports contained useful information from many countries; for example, about composts, which provided more than 40 percent of nitrogen, phosphate and potash in Japan in 1946; the large-scale use of night-soil in China; the use of sewage irrigation in Germany and Edinburgh, and so on. One also learned about methods of processing and making use of different organic matters with data relating to their nutrient contents, relative importance, and so forth.[24] There is without doubt a large potential of nutrient resources which has been left unutilized.[25] This is true not only in India but in most developing countries.

There was a serious imbalance in emphasising chemical fertilizers to the neglect of organic manures, and also in the recommended pattern of fertilizer use. Thus, as is known, the standard recommendation is to apply fertilizers in extremely high doses to high-yielding varieties grown on irrigated soils. The combination of irrigation, HYV and high doses of fertilizers constitutes the very heart of the new technology. But even on purely productivity considerations the rationale of this combination has been seriously challenged. It has been held that for the best results for the country as a whole, "fertilizers need not necessarily be concentrated either on irrigated land or on HYV's" (Parikh, 1978). The positive recommendation made is to distribute fertilizers thinly over land, irrespective of irrigation and HYV. It has further been held that "a cultivator may be able to get a large yield from high-yielding variety even without applying fertilizer." This is not just an extreme viewpoint. These conclusions have been arrived at from extensive analysis of fertilizer response data by a team of highly competent researchers.[26]

This leads one to wonder if the path adopted could have come about just as a matter of course, without any forces pushing the country away from the path of balanced development of organic and inorganic resources to that of exclusive reliance on inorganic fertilizers. In French there is a saying, "Cherchez la femme." The male chauvinist idea is that if there is an intriguing problem defying immediate explanation, look out for the woman at the root of all the trouble. It does not take much research to discover the powerful interests that stand to lose from the developing countries relying more on organic manures.

To start with, consider the following facts about the fertilizer industry on a global level and the policies pursued by powerful international agencies towards fertilizer:

- More than 80 percent of exports of nitrogen, phosphate, potash and phosphate rock are made by a handful of developed countries, dominated by the United States, Japan, the USSR and Canada. The industries in these countries are highly oligopolistic. Demand and supply of some of the products are price inelastic (Desai, 1982). Export prices have often been found to be lower than domestic prices. Multinationals in the industry are known to insert clauses in collaboration agreements banning direct as well as indirect dissimulation and adaptation of technology (Menon, 1980).
- Much fertilizer imported by India (for instance, about 85 percent in the late 1960s) is financed by tied aid from aid-giving countries of the West, mainly the United States. According to a study by Kahnert (1971) this has sometimes meant that India had to pay twice as much for importing materials from the United States than for importing similar materials from the Gulf countries (if permitted), with transportation other than U.S. flag ships.[27]
- Much of the aid for agriculture finances fertilizer imports and the establishment of fertilizer plants.[28]
- The fertilizer industry is highly capital-intensive with a high import content—about 60 percent in India.
- The fertilizer industry is the most important industry receiving support from the World Bank—its share in the total loans given to the industrial sector all over the world until June 1978 was 27 percent.
- It has been estimated that projects in India financed by the World Bank have at least 25 percent more foreign exchange content than other projects. As a precondition for receiving World Bank support, the projects have to be larger in scale than the national average.

We now turn our attention to the government of India's policies towards this industry.

- Even though the Indian government's Industrial Policy Revolution earmarks the fertilizer industry as one in which the public sector plays the leading role, the private sector has been allowed to increase its share from less than 15 percent in 1960-61 to about one-third in 1979.
- Foreign capital has been allowed to have majority participation, which goes against the established practice of the government.
- The government intervenes in the market for fertilizers to support a combination of a higher cost of production and lower prices for consumers, mostly big farmers. This is done by price controls and subsidies. While the cost of production varies enormously from unit to unit—the highest

being double that of the lowest—a uniform retail price is maintained for the consumer in all parts of the country (that is, irrespective of production and transport costs). Each plant is paid a retention price that covers its cost of production, however high. The trend is for plants to be set up with higher and higher costs of production. This has led to a huge escalation of subsidies.[29] An important point to note is that the minimum prices of crops have also been controlled by the government, making the ratio of crop price to fertilizer price increasingly favourable to farmers.[30]

We may now look at some of the pertinent features of the domestic fertilizer industry.

• The growing importance of the private sector has gone along with a growing influence of Indian big business and its multinational collaborators. The foreign countries figuring prominently in the industry are the United States, United Kingdom, Japan and West Germany. The multinationals figuring prominently include Halcon International, Inc., International Minerals and Chemicals Corporation, Texaco, United States Steel Corporation, Imperial Chemical Industries, National Iranian Oil Company, BASF, Toyo Engineering Corporation and Hitachi. Indian big business houses figuring importantly include such names as K.K. Birla, Dalmia, Bharat Ram, Kasturbhai Lalbhai and Khaitan.

• Capacity expansion in the industry has been sustained, irrespective of domestic demand, with chronic underutilisation of capacity.[31] Production has always been in excess of demand, leaving a huge carryover stock (Desai, 1979). Growth of production and consumption has not been closely related to movements either of fertilizer prices or of the ratio of fertilizer price to crop price.

These features point to a highly oligopolistic and protected industry.

A Note on Pesticides

The story of pesticides on the supply side is similar to that of fertilizers but on a much reduced scale, although there is a paucity of data on this. Input per hectare in 1981-82 was a mere 377.1 grams, which may be compared with more than 10,000 grams in Japan, nearly 2,000 grams in Europe, and about 1,500 grams in the United States in 1971. Once again, the small absolute figure conceals an extremely high rate of growth—17 percent per year between 1955-56 and 1971-72. At a world level the pesticide industry is also highly oligopolistic, dominated by about 20 multinationals. These multinationals are extremely powerful, evading laws and even exporting items that are banned, and yet receive subsidies from the national governments. Profit to turnover ratio in the industry is as high as 40 percent, about four times higher than in comparable industries.

There is, however, one important difference between pesticides and fertilizers from the point of view of our present study. While there are known non-industrial substitutes or supplements in fertilizers, this is not the case for pesticides. Protection from insects and diseases is essential for the growth of crop production. But traditional agriculture does not provide any solution which could have been retained.

VIII. MECHANISATION POLICY

We have seen that before independence, as well as in the early post-independence period, the country had a well-defined policy of discouraging such mechanisation of agriculture that might adversely affect employment. With the adoption of the new technology this gave way to a laissez-faire policy—letting farmers use whatever machines they could purchase and letting industries produce whatever farm machinery they could sell. As the farmers' and the industrialists' decisions are based on private profit maximisation and not on social welfare maximisation, it is not surprising that this laissez-faire policy resulted in an indiscriminate proliferation of farm mechanisation, as if the government's policy was to maximise mechanisation.

As in the case of fertilizers, the numbers are impressive. The production of tractors has increased at a rate of more than 26 percent per year. Stocks have piled up at a rate exceeding 15 percent. Oil engines and electrically operated pumpsets and tubewells in use by farmers have increased at the rates of 13.5 percent and 19.2 percent per annum, respectively. Electricity in agriculture has grown at the rate of 14.8 percent per year (figure 2.7 and table 2.10).[32] This phenomenal growth in mechanisation has taken place on a very narrow base, with the result that, on a per hectare basis, the importance of this machinery still remains insignificant, as was seen in tables 2.1 and 2.2.

The most important producing industry is the four-wheeled tractor industry beginning in the early 1960s, with an investment in 1979 of Rs. 15,000 millions and an annual production of 60,000 units in 1980. This compares with the annual production of 197,000 in the United States in 1978. Important newcomers are harvest combines and power tillers.[33] The manufacture of a whole range of accessories used with tractors for various operations has also begun.[34] Among them, disc harrows, trailers and seed-cum-fertilizer drills have acquired popularity.

We have discussed (section VI) the labour displacing effects of farm machinery, in particular those of tractors and harvest combines. We have also seen that no one contests that direct employment is adversely affected by most farm machinery. But there are differences of opinion on the net effect after taking into account increased employment following from better cultivation, supposedly made possible by mechanisation. On this matter we can do no better than to cite the conclusions on tractorisation arrived at by Binswanger (1978), who painstakingly reviewed numerous studies on the effects of tractorisation—from large-scale surveys conducted by important research organisations to unpublished Ph.D. and M.A. theses. His views, uncontested so far, are worth quoting:

> The tractor surveys fail to provide evidence that tractors are responsible for substantial increases in intensity, yields, timeliness and gross returns on farms in India, Pakistan and Nepal. At best, such benefits may exist but are so small that they cannot be detected and statistically supported, even with very massive survey research efforts.

The fairly consistent picture emerging from the survey largely supports the view that tractors are substitutes for labour and bullock power, and thus implies that, at existing wages and bullock costs, tractors fail to be a strong engine of growth. It is to be underscored that according to Binswanger not only are the social benefits outweighed by social costs, but even "private returns [from use of] tractors [in] agricultural operations must be close to zero or negative."

Binswanger concedes that "there are probably a few areas remaining where tractors are a pre-condition for area expansion by reclamation." He also recognises various non-agricultural uses of the tractor which are beneficial, like transport. As to the reduction of drudgery which is undeniable, he insists that: "They [agricultural laborers] have accepted to perform the arduous tasks only because they were forced into them by a lack of better alternatives." As such, introduction of the machinery "clearly increases rather than reduces the suffering." He concludes that "it nevertheless is clear that tractors shift the cost advantage in farming towards the larger farms and that they therefore induce pressures towards increased concentration of landholdings in fewer hands. This is inconsistent with the stated goal of policymakers in all these countries to achieve a more equal distribution of landholdings."

Let us now consider the alternatives foregone. There is a vast scope for improving traditional implements and for designing new machinery that would reduce drudgery and improve production and which would be capital saving and labour-intensive. This was recognised officially as early as 1928 in the report of the Royal Commission on Agriculture (RCA, 1928), which recommended the development of such equipment as pneumatic tires for transportation, seed drills for line sowing, and so on. After independence, policy documents, including the five year plans, emphasized the point. A comprehensive countrywide survey of indigenous implements was conducted by the Indian Council for Agricultural Research, and some useful volumes were produced (for example, ICAR, 1960). A machinery division was set up in a number of states. Experiments for the improvisation of a large number of implements have been carried out in these places.[35]

Most of these laboratory experiments have remained in the laboratory, however; they have not been taken up by cultivators.[36] Facile explanations like Indian peasants being conservative cannot be advanced anymore at a time when the fashion is to point to the avidity with which peasants have taken to the HYV-fertilizer technology. More objective factors like lack of service facilities, lack of standardisation, and so forth can be thought of. But the most important factor is that not enough has been done to establish communication between the laboratory and the farmer. Not even a fraction of the energy and organisational effort with which the fertilizer-HYV technology has been sold to the farmers has been expended for taking the improved machinery to the farmers and bringing back their reactions to the laboratories for generating a continuous process of use-feedback-redesigning. This has occurred largely because of the deeply entrenched prejudices of engineers and administrators in favour of big and sophisticated machinery, compared with the small and simple yet efficient.

This also explains why there has been so little research focussed on inventions of the kind made in many other countries for tapping non-conventional sources of energy, such as the sun and the wind, and for increasing the efficiency of energy conversion by imaginative utilisation of the principles of mechanics. It is all the more unfortunate because Indian farmers, far from being averse to the adoption of such inventions, reveal a great deal of untutored and unsupported enterprise in the matter. Throughout the country contraptions are made by the farmers, with the help of locally available materials and artisanal skills and by incorporating various gearing, pedalling and levering devices, for better utilisation of human and animal energy. A piece of bamboo tied to the handles of three hand-operated tubewells in a row and operated by two persons at two ends saves human energy by one-third. This elementary device that we discovered in a village in West Bengal symbolizes the enormous potential that has been allowed to go unutilised. This subjective factor is reinforced by the objective interests of the engineering industries, domestic and foreign, engaged in the manufacture of agricultural machinery. The domestic industry in this field, as in most areas, has shaped itself on models of developed countries. In contrast to the fertilizer industry, trends in the tractor and allied industries have been set not only by the capitalist West but also by the socialist East.

Until 1958 tractors and allied machinery reflected the western technology of the Caterpillars of the United Kingdom, Ford Motor Company of the United States, Massey-Ferguson of the United Kingdom, and the International Harvester of the United Kingdom and the United States, who were the principal exporters in India's market. Since that time, East European countries have entered the Indian market in a big way, so much so that domestic production, started in 1961, has been based largely on collaborative agreements with as many countries in the East as the West.[37] Factor endowments and methods of cultivation in both of these groups of countries call for large and heavy machinery. It is such products that they exported earlier, and it is the technology for such products that they have exported later. That is only to be expected. It is not expected that they would design machines suited to Indian conditions, given the small market that India offers. Nor is it surprising that USAID and the World Bank should give loans for importing machinery.[38]

The story is not very different for power tillers. Even though they have received blessings from many for being small and cheap, a serious economic observer stated, "Judged in terms of the depth of tilling, the two wheeled power tillers (of the Japanese variety) . . . might be an inferior substitute even for ploughs" (Raj, 1973). The foreign exporting interest here is Japan—both for products as well as for technological collaboration.[39]

Domestic industrial interests are not likely to favour a policy reducing the dependence of agriculture on them and promoting a robust growth of small-scale and artisanal industries fabricating tools, implements and light machinery, while saving on purchased energy. Even though the farm machinery industry is much smaller than the fertilizer industry, it involves the interests of such powerful big business houses as the Kirloskars, the Mahindras and the Tatas.[40] They have been able to ban all imports of tractors from 1976-77 as well as to lift industrial licensing from the mid-1970s.

It is ironic that the tractor industry in India is one of the few with a record of independence and self-sufficiency in technology. The Swaraj model of Punjab Tractors, Ltd., is wholly indigenous and better adapted to Indian conditions than all the other models based on borrowed technology. This is ironic because the tractor in itself is inappropriate. Moreover, no originality has been shown in the production of more appropriate varieties of machinery; the industry fabricating various appliances is producing only things which are operated with the help of tractors and which earlier were imported along with tractors.

IX. IRRIGATION POLICY

Irrigation policy also changed around 1959-60, which marked the adoption of the new technology. Until then the emphasis was on major and medium works which used river water and canal systems with the help of barrages and reservoirs. The new technology shifted the emphasis to groundwater irrigation with the help of tubewells, energised by electricity or diesel. The shift was provoked by the greater suitability of the tubewell technology for the new technology because of the control over timing and quantity of water supply that it ensures.

Being the mainstay of agriculture since ancient times, the growth of irrigation in general has not been as spectacular as the other concomitants of the new technology. The annual rate of increase of irrigated acreage has been a mere 2.3 percent. It has been even lower for canal irrigation—2.1 percent. Tubewell irrigation, on the other hand, has grown at a rate of about 26 percent per year, which is comparable to the growth rates for fertilizers and mechanisation.[41]

As in the case of mechanisation and fertilizers, this high rate of growth in tubewell irrigation would have been a matter of satisfaction if it were moving towards a satisfactory solution to the water problem, which is one of the basic problems of cultivation in tropical climates. That, however, is far from the case. For one thing, even if all the potentials of canal and tubewell irrigation are utilised, about half the cultivated area would remain beyond their reach. As such, devices must be found to take care of the water problems of these areas as much as possible. Even within the half irrigated by either canals or wells, the potential for groundwater is limited.[42]

There is no question that irrigation must find a place in whatever technology package is adopted for the development of agriculture. That irrigated areas are more productive than rainfed areas is universally accepted. There are, however, differences of opinion about the relative quantities. While some have advanced crude estimates, there are others who hold that "available data do not permit a meaningful analysis of the effectiveness of irrigation or its influence on productivity" (Manmohan Singh, 1984).[43] There is no difference of opinion that groundwater irrigation has a much greater impact on crop yield than surface water irrigation.[44] But all the same, the way groundwater irrigation has been promoted at the cost of other sources, such as canals, ponds, tanks, and so on, without improving the efficiency of water use by technical, organisational and managerial innovations leaves the state of affairs much worse than it need be.

The advantages and disadvantages of canal irrigation are well known. Yet the advantages seem to have been lost sight of and the disadvantages, from the point of view of the new technology, highlighted so as to prevent necessary steps to extract the full benefits of canals. It is well known that much water flowing down canals is wasted due to conveyance losses and the absence of adequate field distribution systems—seepage loss has been estimated at 40 percent. This sometimes leads to water-logging, which is inimical to the new variety seeds just as irrigation by flooding with canal water is.[45] The soil salinity effect is another drawback of the system. While this is true of all canals, those that dry up during certain seasons or are prone to flooding cause additional difficulties.

Among the advantages of canal irrigation which are easily neglected are (a) in its command area it supplies water more plentifully, and therefore it can benefit many more people than a well can; (b) it does not discriminate between big and small farmers; and (c) it entails certain benefits not reckoned in crop production terms, like non-consumption of any inanimate energy, minimisation of damages due to floods and drought and lessening the fluctuations of crop yields. But the most important point to be noted, when comparing canal irrigation with tubewell irrigation, is that the benefits of the latter are largely enhanced by canal water seepage, which re-charges the groundwater tapped by the wells.

The obvious disadvantages of tubewell irrigation which are lost sight of in the runaway enthusiasm for it by the new technology (because of its qualities of perenniality and controllability) are (a) its dependence on external and scarce sources of energy, such as electricity and diesel; (b) its dependence on repair and maintenance; and (c) its built-in bias in favour of the big farmer, in view of the minimum size of land below which it is uneconomic.[46]

However, the greatest drawback of well irrigation is the deleterious effect it can have on groundwater when not resorted to in a conjunctive and controlled fashion. Thus, the National Commission on Agriculture, despite its support for the new technology, states: "Overpumping results in permanent lowering of the groundwater table. The progressive depression of the water table leads to increasing pumping head, reduced discharge, and high costs making groundwater utilisation ultimately uneconomic. In a scramble for water, people go in for larger and deeper bores or space the tubewells and open wells closer than they should" (NCA, 1976(b)).

If the canals, after the huge investments made on them, can be neglected, it is not suprising that the traditional sources of irrigation like open wells, tanks, ponds, and so forth operated with the help of human and animal energy applied to primitive and inefficient implements should be left in limbo, with total disregard for the vast potential of improving performance which is not only possible but also unavoidable if agriculture in the country as a whole is to develop in a balanced fashion.

It is therefore important to recall some of the advantages of the traditional sources and means of irrigation. The dugwell can be used practically in all types of geological formations except in coastal areas. The tubewell, however, can only exploit water held in sandy aquifers and is not feasible in rocky formations, thus ruling out most of peninsular India. Dugwells and all other small sources, like tanks, ponds, and so on, have the advantage of controllability though obviously not of perenniality. The greatest advantages of dugwells are that (a) they make no demand on any scarce inanimate energy; (b) they make little demand on the services of repair and maintenance and (c) when they do, the services can be provided by locally available materials and skills. Similarly, tanks play an important role in preventing soil erosion. They also recharge soil moisture and sub-soil and groundwater storage.[47]

The technological problem of irrigation does not consist of a choice between canals, tubewells and traditional means. The complementarity of these three irrigation sources is well recognised. The technological problem consists of a systems approach towards an optimal combination of all the different sources that could be tapped in a given area. "It was for this purpose that Command Area Development authorities were established in important project areas. . . . We have from the horse's own mouth, however, the results have not been impressive. . . . In practice, such conjunctive use is not reflected in planning irrigation works, and in particular, groundwater development is taken up in an *ad hoc* manner" (Manohan Singh, 1984).

This is recognised as having been caused by a strong bias among irrigation administrators and engineers in favour of the engineering aspects of the water works, compared with their management aspects. It is the same overriding interest in sophisticated technology at the cost of connected social and human problems which accounts for the inefficiencies of canal irrigation and the total neglect of non-energised surface irrigation. This, along with the overriding climate of private profit maximisation pervading the economy, has resulted in the technological choice to maximise output per unit of area rather than to maximise output per unit of water or to maximise the total area benefitting.

Such has been the weight of conventional engineering thinking that even within the canal and tubewell systems all the different technological options that exist have not been taken into account and decisions have been taken as if blindfolded. Thus, canal irrigation offers choices in technology as well as in related management on the following issues:

1. Choice of material for diversion structures, for example, earth, rocks, concrete, and so forth, with obvious differences in matters of labour absorption, capital requirement, and dependence on local material and skill.
2. Choice between use of heavy earth moving machinery and massive application of human labour.
3. Choice of density and other characteristics of field channels—the greater the density, the more the replenishment of groundwater.
4. Choice of method of controlling sedimentation, vegetation, and so on, in channels with machines or with human labour.
5. Choice between barrages and reservoirs with regard to problems of seasonal scarcities of water, flooding, and so on.
6. Choice between lining of canals and allowing seepage for the benefit of groundwater replenishment.[48]
7. Choice from among different distribution systems, e.g., rotational versus non-rotational delivery.[49]

Similarly, tubewell irrigation offers technological choices in the following areas, among others:

1. Choice of material for the tube from among steel, brass, PVC, bamboo, etc.[50]
2. Choice of size with the choice of the depth of underground water layer, involving considerations of landholding structure in the command area.
3. Choice from among drilling methods—manual, manual percussion, jetting and rotary drilling.
4. Choice from among different kinds of pumps, for example, centrifugal, vertical turbine, and so on.[51]
5. Choice from among different means of delivery, for example, field channels, undergound pipes, and so forth.
6. Choice between sources of energy—human, animal, electric and diesel. Human and animal energy have been more or less excluded from consideration. Diesel and electricity are both inappropriate, being highly expensive and depending on remote sources.[52] Non-conventional sources of energy, such as the sun and the wind, offer potential alternatives.[53]

As has been pointed out, canal and well irrigation can serve at most half the cultivable area in the country. For the remaining half, means have to be found for the more efficient use of tanks, ponds, and other surface water sources. The implements presently used with respect to these sources are so primitive and so wasteful of human energy that one can be sure that potential improvement in this area is vast.

In fertilizers and farm machinery we located domestic and foreign industrial interests that have put all their weight behind the inappropriate technological choice represented by those industries. This factor would seem to play a much less important part in irrigation. Tubewell technology hardly requires any sophisticated products manufactured by multinationals or the big business houses of India. Both electricity and diesel belong mostly to the public sector. The decisive influence here seems to be the profit motive of the big farmer backed by foreign advisors. The interests of the big farmers have also received full support from the bias of engineers and administrators.

X. RESEARCH AND DEVELOPMENT POLICY

Research for the improvement of agriculture in India is conducted in different institutions which may be grouped into three categories—research institutions under the Indian Council of Agricultural Research (ICAR); state departments of agriculture; and agricultural universities. Of these three, the ICAR has the longest history. It was set up in 1929 on the recommendation of the Royal Commission on Agriculture, then named the Imperial Council of Agricultural Research. In 1976 the Commission on Agriculture mentioned nineteen research institutes under the ICAR, many of them specializing in particular crops and covering all aspects of agriculture, including not only crop production but also animal husbandry, fisheries, horticulture, forestry, and so on. The most important among them is the Indian Agricultural Research Institute (IARI), set up in 1905; after independence, it played a notable part in the development of the new variety seeds.

Next in importance are the agricultural universities. Before independence there were no such universities. Some research was carried out in a few of the general universities, including Calcutta, Banaras and Visva-Bharati. Agricultural universities were set up at the insistence of U.S. advisors, and "inspiration was drawn from the United States' Land Grant Colleges" (NCA, 1976(c)).[54] The first was in Pantnagar in Uttar Pradesh. Another is the Punjab Agricultural University in Ludhiana, which was set up soon after the above and has won international fame for its role in the propagation of the New Strategy. Another twenty universities were established by 1976. Many more agricultural colleges have been set up all over the country.

Research and development is known to be weak in India as far as industrial technology is concerned. The story, however, is different with agriculture. The far-reaching transformation the country's agriculture is undergoing results largely from the research institutes and universities mentioned above. The improved variety seeds were not simply imported from Mexico and the Philippines. Much adaptive research was done before they were made suitable for Indian fields. Behind that lay a large accumulation of original research in cross-breeding seeds. Agronomy is a field where India's record of research and development is far from negligible.

It is therefore unfortunate that all this effort should contribute to the proliferation of a technology which is as inappropriate as we have seen the new technology to be. Part of the explanation lies with the extraordinarily large influence wielded by foreign experts and advisors on Indian agricultural policy[55]—but only a part. One may hazard the guess that even if there were no such foreign influence, research and education in agriculture would have been just as much or even more ill-suited to the requirements of the country. The entire higher education system of the country bears testimony to the Indian genius for learning from the West and retaining from India's own heritage precisely such elements that are least suited for the country's welfare—whether values or institutions or technologies.

XI. CONCLUSION

This chapter has established that technological choice made for Indian agriculture has been such that the production of commodities has grown at the cost of distributional justice as well as employment and such social objectives as local resource mobilization, local initiative and national self-reliance. It should be possible to have more growth if better use is made of organic manures, if a more coordinated and efficient exploitation of surface and ground water is achieved, and if greater emphasis is put on the improvement of traditional implements and less on farm machinery of Western models. Of the four components of the new technology, namely, improved seeds, water, chemical fertilizers and farm machinery, only the first may be regarded as an unmixed blessing. While inappropriateness attaches to the roles allotted to the remaining three components there is nothing inappropriate about the seeds. There is no doubt that growth would have been less if certain breakthroughs had not taken place in the form of new variety seeds. We, however, do not equate these breakthroughs with the new technology, which is defined by a certain combination of these four components. The country would certainly have been better off if the new seeds were integrated into an alternative, more appropriate package of water, nutrients and non-conventional farm machinery and implements.

Why did things go this way? A believer in the virtues of the competitive price mechanism may tend to think: the prices have been wrong! With all those controls and subsidies, what else can one expect? The prices of inputs and outputs we are dealing with are subject to serious distortions. However, we would not be so naive as to suggest that things would have been better if only the prices were not thus distorted. Policy economists are given to double-talk about certain supreme virtues allegedly attached to perfect competition. Yet the theorems that they rely on relate only to Pareto optimality. It should be clear from elementary textbooks and not really require a major economist to argue (as, for instance, Amartya Sen, 1975) that Pareto optimality is an extremely unsatisfactory indicator of social welfare. This optimality is well known to be compatible with the most monstrous inequality. Further, the static concept has no relevance for growth: there is no theorem that shows that Pareto optimality ensures a maximal or an optimal rate of growth. Yet another point that is often forgotten is that even for this limited optimality to hold, there has to be perfect competition not only in any one sector like agriculture but in every nook and cranny of the economy. As such, correct input and output prices in agriculture alone would not ensure even Pareto optimality.

Who then killed Cock Robin? The answer has been given in the course of this paper. It is the unique convergence of the interests of rich farmers, Indian big business houses, powerful multinationals, and the aid-giving powers of both East and West, all supported by the deeply entrenched bias in favour of the big and the sophisticated shared by the Indian engineers, mostly trained in the West, and the country's administrators. Given this solid alliance of forces, there is very little chance that the country will see a return to a more balanced development of agriculture, with not only growth but also distributional justice, with more reliance on improved indigenous methods and involving a maximum use of locally available resources.

NOTES

This chapter was completed in a brief period. I could not have possibly carried out the work but for the extremely capable support I received from my research assistants. The person who helped me throughout was Sutapa Bose. Neepa Bisi helped in the first part of the project, and Mithu Ghosh took over when she left. Thanks are due to all of them.

1. This is not a point that is disputed even by the most ardent advocates of the New Strategy. Thus, Ladejinski (1969), citing certain cost figures for a seven-acre farm to adopt the new technology, wrote, "This is where neutrality to scale begins to break down." Also see note 6.

2. The average annual growth rate of agricultural production between 1880 and 1960 has been estimated at no more than 1.5 percent in the United States and 1.9 percent in Japan; the average annual rate in the United Kingdom was barely 1 percent (Johnston and Kilby, 1975).

3. Some of the crops, however, are still in short supply and have to be imported—for instance, oil seeds.

4. An idea of the high regional concentration is obtained from the following figure quoted in Bhalla (1979): 69 high-productivity districts, representing only 20.5 percent of total area, account for 45 percent of fertilizer consumption in the country, 50 percent of the tractors and 38 percent of gross irrigated area. Among crops, rice has benefitted much less than wheat, though it is the most important among the food-grains, and a great deal of effort and attention has been directed at it. The only other crop to benefit to some extent is Bajra (see Srinivasan, 1971).

5. It is usual to locate the so-called Green Revolution in the years 1965-66 and 1966-67. However, as may be seen from Figures 2.3 and 2.4, the upward shift in growth took place much earlier. In the case of wheat in Punjab and Haryana, the

point of departure is visible in 1960-61, the beginning of the IADP period. In the case of wheat in U.P., it is between 1962-63 and 1963-64.

6. Thus, Subramaniam (1979), who was Minister for Agriculture in the mid-1960s and who claims credit for making the government promote the adoption of the New Strategy, writes, "There has also been a cry that it is only the better-off farmers who have been using the fertilizers so that we have been only subsidizing them. But you have to strike a balance because if they do not use the fertilizer they will not produce and the whole nation will have to starve."

7. There has been much evidence supporting this proposition. Reports of the Agro-Economic Research Centres, the Programme Evaluation Organisation of the Planning Commission and individual researchers have presented such data (see, for instance, Griffin, 1974).

8. This again is a proposition that has been supported even by enthusiastic supporters of the New Strategy (for example, Bhalla and Chadha, 1982).

9. This again is not a matter on which there is any dispute. Even such strong advocates of the New Strategy as Kahlon and Singh (1973) present figures that show that in 1971-72 large farmers obtained eight times more institutional loans than small farmers. Similarly, another high priest of the Green Revolution, Ladejinski (1973), had this to say: "Throughout the long history of institutional rural credit the differentiation has always been along the lines of much for the few and little for the many. And there is no mystery about it, for the distribution of such vital resources as credit and inputs reflects a power structure very much biased in favour of the affluent."

10. This proposition is disputed by some, though much less than the proposition about the inverse relation in traditional agriculture. Among those emphasizing this reversal of the relation are Dasgupta (1980), who is a critic, and Bhalla and Chadha (1982), who are supporters of the new technology.

11. See Lockwood (1972) for detailed discussion. There are some who counter the argument by saying that labourers have also gained through more employment and higher wages. However, most researchers agree that this has not prevented the widening gap between the two poles.

12. There are, however, some crops (like cotton) for which HYV seeds absorb less labour than ordinary seeds (see Lakdawala, 1978).

13. In India, one distinguishes between two kinds of farm labourers by their duration of employment: daily labourers and farm servants, who are also often referred to in English as "permanent labourers," "attached labourers," etc. This author (Rudra, 1971) found that employment of farm servants increases with the use of tractors. The same result was found by NCAER (1973). However, some other research workers, e.g., Kusum Chopra (1974), Kanchan Chopra (1984) and Agarwal (1983), found the opposite to take place.

14. Some of the more important references on the subject are Raj Krishna (1975), NCAER (1973, 1980), Manmohan Singh (1979), Singh and Singh (1980), C.B. Singh (1981), Oberai and Ahmed (1981), Joshi (1981), Agarwal (1983), and Laxminarayan and others (1981). Various authors have also presented numerical estimates of the displacement effect. According to the National Commission on Agriculture (NCA, 1976), tractors displace human labour by only 15 percent. This is consistent with C.H.H. Rao's (1979) estimate that tractorisation resulted in reduced labour days by 12 percent to 27 percent in different parts of the Punjab. This, however, is lower than the estimates by Kumar and others (1981) which put the reduction at 41 percent and that of Laxminarayan (1982) who places it at 58 percent for ploughing. Laxminarayan and others (1981) calculated that harvest combines reduce employment

by 95 percent. NCAER (1976) presents a much more benevolent picture for power tillers—labour displacement being only between 10 to 20 percent.

15. This point is affirmed by Kahlon (1976), Ray and Blase (1978) and C.H.H. Rao (1979).

16. This point has been emphasised by NCAER (1980), conceded by C.H.H. Rao (1979) and disputed by Agarwal (1983) and Binswanger (1978).

17. This point is greatly emphasised by the National Commission on Agriculture (NCA, 1976) and among research workers by S. Bhalla (1981). Binswanger (1978), opposing the point, wrote, "A 10 percent reduction is all that is required to offset this off-farm employment and in most cases less than 5 percent reduction in farm labour requirement will do it."

18. For instance, Raj Krishna (1975) carried out a decomposition exercise which showed that the negative effect of the tractor was much more than the positive effect of other factors. Joshi and others (1981) found a similar result. The same conclusion has been drawn from a comparison of the farm management data for Muzaffarnagar district for 1954-55 and 1966-67. Not only per hectare labour input for individual crops decreased but so did the total labour input per hectare, and that by as much as 15 percent. This is in contrast to the picture for the Ferozepur district where labour input into individual crops decreased but where labour input into all crops taken together increased (by 29 percent according to the calculations of Sharma (1974) and by 40 percent according to those of Mehra (1976)).

19. In the country, three-fourths of the area under wheat and half of the area under rice have already been brought under high-yielding varieties. The ratios are much higher in the Green Revolution areas—96 percent and 83 percent for wheat in Punjab and Haryana, respectively, and 87 percent for rice in Punjab.

20. Recently there has been talk about deceleration in fertilizer demand (for example, Nagaraj, 1982). In our judgment, this is a serious mistake made through mechanical interpretation of statistical data. It is true that the geometric rate of growth in consumption of chemical fertilizers, as may be obtained by a comparison of end-points, would be less than what is shown in table 2.5 if one would consider a period like 1967 to 1983. However, there is no reason to attach a greater significance to the geometric rate than to the arithmetic rate. As may be seen from table 2.6, the yearly increment of demand was much higher in 1959-60 to 1975-6 than preceding 1959-60 and much lower after 1975-6.

21. Thus, imports of fertilizers have grown between 1962-63 and 1980-81 at the annual rates of 10.7 for N, 23.6 for P_2O_5 and 17.9 for K_2O.

22. Thus, naphtha production doubled between 1973 and 1983. Natural gas production increased by 4.5 fold between 1970-71 and 1982-83, reflecting its growing universal popularity. Import of ammonia increased at the compounded rate of more than 60 percent per year between 1974 and 1981. Production of rock phosphate grew fourfold and import of sulphur threefold between 1969-70 and 1982-83 (table 2.5).

23. Extensive research has been done to establish the residual effects and the buildup of nutrients in the soil with continuous application of farmyard manure. It has been seen that while farmyard manure is less effective than chemical nitrogen when applied alone, the combination of farmyard manure and chemical fertilizers yields better results than chemical fertilizers alone. (See Kulkarni and Kulkarni, 1982.)

24. Thus, the FAO report of 1976 provides estimates in million tonnes of nitrogen, phosphate, potash, and so on, available from organic matters like animal dung, animal urine, human excreta, effluent and sludge.

25. According to official statistics of the Indian government, rural and urban composts used in 1981-82 amounted to 231 million tonnes and 6.5 million tonnes, respectively. Even if these figures are taken at their face value, they represent less than 1.5 million tonnes of NPK, compared to chemical fertilizers providing 6 million tonnes of the same. In 1981-82 only 3.1 percent of gross cropped area was green manured. This may be compared with more than 33 percent of the same area receiving chemical fertilizers. One of the rare appropriate technology innovations accepted in much of the world for simultaneously improving the heat efficiency of cattle dung as fuel and its nutrient efficiency as manure is the bio-gas plant. But while in China they have put up more than eight million such plants, in India the latest figure available does not reach even ten thousand (see Ramaswamy, 1984).

26. The Fertilizer Association of India commissioned the Indian Statistical Institute to undertake a research project aimed at making future projections of fertilizer requirements. A team headed by K.S. Parikh and T.N. Srinivasan analysed data from 31,000 fertilizer trials in farmers' fields, and the conclusions quoted in the test are from rigorous statistical analysis of the same. Detailed results have been presented in Parikh and Srinvasan (1974).

27. In an OECD sponsored study Kahnert (1971) shows (1) how the f.o.b. prices from the United States are higher than the f.o.b. prices from the Gulf countries; (2) how the free market transport cost from the United States is about four times higher than from the Gulf countries; and (3) how the transport in United States flag ships costs several times more than in other ships. Despite all this, importers from the United States are obliged to carry half the supplies on United States flag ships.

28. According to an OECD estimate, foreign exchange fertilizer imports accounted for about 14 percent of the net official and private financial flows from the aid giving countries to the developing countries and the proportion of capital aid for the fertilizer industry represented about 14 percent of the total aid given to the developing countries for agriculture (OECD, 1968).

29. The total subsidy on fertilizers in 1982-83 was estimated at Rs. 65,000 millions. And the accumulated subsidy between 1976-77 and 1983-84 was estimated at about Rs. 38,000 millions. This may be compared with the accumulated investment in the industry as Rs. 25,000 millions until 1979-80. The rates of subsidies vary from product to product and state to state. A rate of 50 percent is very common.

30. The ratio of the index number of fertilizer prices to the index number of agricultural commodities decreased between 1961-62 and 1973-74 by as much as 40 percent. Even during the sharp rise of fertilizer prices due to the oil crisis the ratio remained 13 percent below that in 1961-62. During the next ten years crop prices were at first systematically decreased and then again increased so as to be a mere 10% higher in 1983-84 than in 1974-75.

31. Capacity utilization has been less than 60 percent in most of the 1970s in both nitrogenous and phosphatic branches of the industry.

32. These growth rates have been calculated from figures presented in different non-official publications like NCAER (1980) and CMIE (1982). We must resort to these sources as authoritative statistics (for which the source is *Livestock Census of India*) though they are extremely backdated.

33. Power tillers entered the scene only in 1965-66 with a supply of less than 700 units from domestic production and imports. Production grew at a fast rate after that and so did imports for some years. By 1974-75 the cumulative total of machines available was about 16,000 (compared to nearly 450 thousand tractors in stock in 1979).

34. The National Commission on Agriculture gives a long list of farm machinery manufactured and used: for example, trailers, cultivators, disc-harrow, mouldboard plough, disc-plough, seed-cum-fertilizer drill, levelling blade, dozer front, scraper, leveller, tractor-mounted sprayers and dusters, tractor-mounted liquid fertilizer applicator, fertilizer speeder, rotavator, spike tooth harrow, chisel plough, mower, clod crusher, wind rower, maize sheller, forage harvester baler, chaff cutter, fodder mill feed grinder, groundnut digger, groundnut decorticator, potato harvester, potato planter, dryer, seed cleaner, thresher, mounted pumping set, loader and lifter, sugarcane planter, sugarcane harvester, blade harrow, farmer stroke picker, cotton picker, soyabean harvester, and so on.

35. A long list of different improved implements that have been developed and are in limited use or for which potential exists has been presented and discussed in NCA (1976(b)).

36. According to the National Commission on Agriculture, some of the improved implements are five to ten times more efficient. The superiority of the iron plough over the wooden plough has been demonstrated for a long time; yet its generalised use has not taken place in the last 75 years. Improved weeders eliminating the backbreaking drudgery of the traditional hand tool have also not gained currency. On the other hand there are examples of improvements that have been widely accepted, for example, the iron sugarcane crusher. There is, similarly, much scope for increasing the efficiency of animal drawn implements and vehicles which have not been exploited despite laboratory successes. (See Kahlon, 1981, and Ramaswamy, 1979.)

37. Out of a total capacity of about 80,000 tractors in 1979-80, as much as 31,000 was the share of the East-European collaboraters and 40,000 that of Western countries; the remaining were indigenous.

38. Such loans for India have been much less than those for Pakistan.

39. In 1974-75 there were only six firms manufacturing power tillers with a total installed capacity of 10,000, each with Japanese collaboration.

40. Voltas is a firm that involves the partnership of the Tatas.

41. As in the case of fertilizers, growth of area under tubewell irrigation would also show deceleration if one were to judge by the compounded rate of growth, calculated separately for two halves of the period. But here again the linear rate of growth shows an increase.

42. The net cultivable area is 140 million hectares and area potentially irrigable is 100 million—70 million by surface water and 40 million by groundwater. Of these potentials the rates of utilisation have been 21 percent for canals and 20 percent for tubewells.

43. According to Dhawan (1983(a)), foodgrain production increases 175 percent with irrigation. This all-India average hides regional variations like 250 percent for peninsular India and 80 percent for central India. These figures are several times less than irrigated yield as observed in demonstration farms. Abbie and others (1982) calculated that value added per hectare of net irrigated land was more than five times that on rainfed land. The difference is largely accounted for by higher cropping intensity on irrigated land.

44. Estimates of differential contributions to production increase by different sources of irrigation are presented in Dhawan (1983(b)).

45. It has been estimated that as of 1975 field channels were yet to be constructed in 2 million hectares in the command areas of the major irrigation projects. Also about 6 million hectares of land were affected by water-logging caused by seepage from canals (Michael, 1976).

46. Superiority of groundwater over surface water is probably not a universal fact. It has been found to be so for Punjab and Tamil Nadu but some researchers have failed to establish it for U.P., Bihar, Karnataka, and Maharashtra.

47. Detailed descriptions of various traditional sources and means of irrigation with their advantages and disadvantages are to be found in NCA (1976(b)) and in Michael (1976) and Dhawan (1982).

48. It has been estimated that of the 40 percent of canal water that gets into seepage only one-third to one-half can possibly be retrieved by pumping. As such, lining is suggested as a better alternative that would prevent about 80 percent of the loss.

49. Rotational irrigation in Japan and Taiwan has been found to save water to the tune of 20 percent to 30 percent. However, this system requires much more supervision.

50. Bamboo tubewells have crossed the stage of experimentation. They are already being used in conjunction with diesel pumps to serve small command areas of two to four hectares.

51. A vertical turbine pump was eight times more costly than a centrifugal pump in 1975.

52. Electricity is cheaper than diesel on both capital and current accounts and this is so even when one takes into account that a diesel pump can be made mobile so as to singly serve several tubewells at the same time. However, dependence of electric pumps on the erratic supply of power has made the more costly alternative more popular.

53. Research is being carried out for the manufacture of solar energy charged cells for irrigation pumps. India is ahead of other Third World countries in this field, though, ironically, it is much behind countries of the West which have much less sun to utilise. Windmills for irrigation are also being tried out in some parts. But these beginnings are mere drops in the ocean of conventional practice.

54. The recommendation in this regard featured most importantly in the reports is referred to in Section 2 of the Joint Indo-American teams of 1955 and 1960 as well as in the one of 1959 that launched IADP.

55. It would be pardonable for a reader not closely familiar with the problem at hand to treat our version of foreign influence as exaggerated. It is no doubt true that Indian intellectuals, no less than Indian politicians, suffer from a deplorable, though understandable, tendency of blaming the country's ills on imperialism. It is precisely the truth of such cases as that of agricultural policy that lends credence to the caricatural presentations of Imperialist conspiracies in every nook and corner. The National Commission on Agriculture writes, "The agricultural research situation as a whole was far from satisfactory. In recognition of this overall view and of the need to reorganise agricultural research the following expert teams were constituted . . ." and then cites five committees of which three are called the First Joint Indo-American Team on Agricultural Research and Education (1955), the Second Joint Indo-American Team on Agricultural Research and Extension (1960), and the Committee for Agricultural Universities' Legislation—Cummings Committee (1962).

REFERENCES

Abbie, Leslie, James Q. Harrison, and John W. Well. 1982. *Economic Return to Investmnet in Irrigation in India*, World Bank Staff Working Papers, No. 536, The World Bank.

Agarwal, Bina. 1983. *Mechanization in Indian Agriculture—An Analytical Study Based on the Punjab*. Allied Publishers Private, Limited.
Ahluwahlia, M.S. 1978. "Rural Poverty and Agricultural Performance in India," *Journal of Development Studies*, Vol. 14, No. 3.
Bardhan, Pranab. 1974. "Inequality of Farm Incomes: A Study of Four Districts," *Economic and Political Weekly*, Vol. IX, Annual Number.
Bhalla, G.S. 1979. "Transfer of Technology and Agricultural Development in India," *Economic and Political Weekly*, Vol. XIV, Nos. 51 and 52.
Bhalla, G.S., and G.K. Chadha. 1982. "Green Revolution and the Small Peasants—A Study of Income Distribution in Punjab Agriculture," *Economic and Political Weekly*, Vol. XVII, No. 20.
Bhalla, S. 1981. "The New Structure of Field Crop Labour in Haryana and Its Impact on Poverty of Landless Agricultural Labour Households," *Anvesak*, Vol. XI, Nos. 1-2.
BICP. 1979. *Industry Profile—2, Nitrogenous and Phosphatic Fertilizers Industry*. Bureau of Industrial Costs and Prices, Ministry of Industry, Government of India.
Binswanger, Hans P. 1978. *The Economics of Tractors in South Asia: An Analytical Review*. Agricultural Development Council, New York, and International Crops Research Institute for the Semi-Arid Tropics, Hyderabad.
CARC. 1949. *Report of the Congress Agrarian Reforms Committee*. The All-India Congress Committee.
Chaudhuri, Maitreyi. 1981. "Is the Rate of Growth of Indian Agriculture Diminishing?" *Economic and Political Weekly*, Vol. XVI, No. 5.
Chopra, Kanchan. 1984. "Distribution of Agricultural Assets in Punjab—Some Aspects of Inequality," *Economic and Political Weekly*, Vol. XIX, No. 13.
Chopra, Kusum. 1974. "Tractorisation and Changes in Factor Inputs in Punjab," *Economic and Political Weekly*, Vol. IX, No. 52.
CMIE. 1982. *Basic Statistics Relating to the Indian Economy*, Vol. I. All India Centre for Monitoring Indian Economy.
Dasgupta, Biplab. 1980. *The New Agrarian Technology and India*. The Macmillan Company of India, Ltd.
Desai, Ashok V. 1982. "World Nitrogen Fertilizer Economy: Developing Countries' Place in Production and Trade," *Economic and Political Weekly*, Vol. XVIII, Nos. 14, 15, and 16.
Desai, Gunvant M. 1979. "Agricultural Development of India—Policy and Problems." In *Agricultural Development in India*. See Shah, C.H.
Dey, Amal Krishna. 1975. "Rates of Growth of Agriculture and Industry," *Economic and Political Weekly*, Vol. X, Nos. 25-26.
Dhawan, B.D. 1982. *Development of Tubewell Irrigation in India*. Agricole Publishing Academy.
Dhawan, B.D. 1983(a). Productivity Impact of Irrigation in India. Delhi: Institute of Economic Growth. Mimeo.
Dhawan, B.D. 1983(b). Source-wise Productivity Impact of Irrigation—a State-wide Analysis. Delhi: Institute of Economic Growth. Mimeo.
FAO. 1962. *Efficient Use of Fertilizers*. Rome: Food and Agriculture Organisation of the United Nations.
FAO. 1976. *Development of a Programme Promoting the Use of Organic Materials as Fertilizers*. Rome: Food and Agriculture Organisation of the United Nations.
Frankel, Francine R. 1971. *India's Green Revolution—Economic Gains and Political Costs*. Princeton University Press.
Government of India. *Fertiliser Statistics*, different volumes.

Griffin, Keith. 1974. *The Political Economy of Agrarian Change*. London: Macmillan.

Johnston, Bruce F., and Peter Kilby. 1975. *Agriculture and Structural Transformation*. Oxford University Press.

Joshi, P.D., et al. 1981. "Direct Employment Effect of Technical Change in Uttar Pradesh Agriculture," *Indian Journal of Agricultural Economics*, Vol. XXXVI, No. 4, Conference Number.

ICAR. 1960. *Indigenous Agricultural Implements of India*. Indian Council of Agricultural Research.

Kahlon, A.S. 1976. "Impact of Mechanisation on Punjab Agriculture with Special Reference to Tractorisation," *Indian Journal of Agricultural Economics*, Vol. XXI, No. 4.

Kahlon, A.S. 1981. "Factors Affecting Adoption of Improved Animal Drawn Implements in India," *Agricultural Situation in India*, Vol. 36, No. 7.

Kahlon, A.S., and Gurbachan Singh. 1973(a). *Social and Economic Implications of Large Scale Introduction of High Yielding Varieties of Wheat in the Punjab with Special Reference to the Ferozepur District*. Department of Economics and Sociology, Punjab Agricultural University, Ludhiana.

Kahlon, A.S., and Gurbachan Singh. 1973(b). *Social and Economic Implications of Large Scale Introduction of High Yielding Varieties of Wheat in the Punjab with Special Reference to the Gurdaspur District*. Department of Economics and Sociology, Punjab Agricultural University, Ludhiana.

Kahnert, F. 1971. *Aid Tying and Export of Nitrogenous Fertilizers from the Persian Gulf*. Development Centre of the Organisation for Economic Co-operation and Development.

Krishna, Raj. 1975. "Measurement of the Direct and Indirect Employment Effects of Agricultural Growth with Technical Change." *Externalities in Transformation of Agriculture*, E.O. Heady and L.R. Whiting, eds. Iowa State University Press.

Kulkarni, K.S., and M.V. Kulkarni. 1982. "Complementary Use of Farmyard Manure and Chemical Fertilisers in Intensive Crop Production," *Fertilizer News*, October.

Kumar, P., et al. 1981. "Estimating Labour Demand Functions and Labour Absorption in Agriculture: A Case Study of Delhi Wheat Farms," *Indian Journal of Agricultural Economics*, Vol. XXXVI, No. 4, Conference Number.

Ladejinski, Wolfe. 1969. "Green Revolution in Bihar," *Economic and Political Weekly*, Vol. IV, No. 27.

Ladejinski, Wolfe. 1973. "How Green is the Green Revolution?" *Economic and Political Weekly*, Vol. VIII, No. 52.

Lakdawala, D.T. 1978. "Growth, Employment and Poverty," *The Indian Journal of Labour Economics*, Vol. XXI, Nos. 1 and 2.

Laxminarayan, H., D.P. Gupta, R. Rangaswamy, and R.P.S. Malik. 1981. *Impact of Harvest Combines on Labour Use, Crop Pattern and Productivity*. Agricole Publishing Academy.

Laxminarayan, H. 1982. "The Impact of Agricultural Development on Employment: A Case Study of Punjab," *The Developing Economies*, Vol. XX, No. 1.

Lockwood, Brian. 1972. "Patterns of Investment in Farm Machinery Equipment," *Economic and Political Weekly*, Vol. VII, No. 40.

Mehra, S. 1976. "World Bank and Transfer of Technology: A Case of Indian Fertilizer Industry," *Economic and Political Weekly*, Vol. XV, No. 34.

Michael, P.R. 1976. "A Dynamic Approach to Irrigation Development and Irrigation Utilization." In *Role of Irrigation in the Development of India's Agriculture*, The Indian Society of Agricultural Economics.

Ministry of Food and Agriculture. 1956(a). *Report of the Indian Delegation to China on Agricultural Planning and Techniques*, Government of India.

Ministry of Food and Agriculture. 1956(b). *India's Rice Revolution: Japanese Method of Paddy Cultivation*, Government of India.

Ministry of Food and Agriculture. 1958. *Report of the Agricultural Administration Committee*, Government of India.

Ministry of Food and Agriculture. 1959. *India's Food Crisis and Steps to Meet It*, Government of India.

NCA. 1976(a). *Report of the National Commission on Agriculture, Part V*, Ministry of Agriculture and Irrigation, Government of India.

NCA. 1976(b). *Report of the National Commission on Agriculture, Part X*, Ministry of Agriculture and Irrigation, Government of India.

NCA. 1976(c). *Report of the National Commission on Agriculture, Part XI*, Ministry of Agriculture and Irrigation, Government of India.

NCAER. 1972. *All India Household Survey of Income, Saving and Consumption Expenditure*. National Council of Applied Economic Research.

NCAER. 1973. *Impact of Mechanisation in Agriculture on Employment*. National Council of Applied Economic Research.

NCAER. 1976. *Fertilizer Demand Study*, Final Report, Vol. I. National Council of Applied Economic Research.

NCAER. 1980. *Implications of Tractorisation for Farm Employment, Productivity and Income*, Vol. I. National Council of Applied Economic Research.

Nagaraj, R. 1982. "Trend Deceleration in Fertilizer Consumption: A Preliminary Exploration," *Economic and Political Weekly*, Vol. XVII, No. 39.

Oberai, A.S., and I. Ahmed. 1981. "Labour Use in Dynamic Agriculture: Evidence from Punjab," *Economic and Political Weekly*, Vol. XXVII, No. 4.

OECD. 1958. *Supply and Demand Prospects for Fertilizers in Developing Countries*. Development Centre of the Organisation for Economic Cooperation and Development.

Parikh, Kirit S. 1978. "HYV Fertilizers: Synergy or Substitution—Implications for Policy and Prospects for Agricultural Development," *Economic and Political Weekly*, Vol. XIII, No. 12.

Parikh, Kirit S., T.N. Srinivasan, et al. 1974. *Optimum Requirements of Fertilizers for the Fifth Plan Period*. Indian Statistical Institute and Fertiliser Association of India.

PEO. 1967. *Study on the Use of Fertilizers and Manures in Agricultural Production*. Programme Evaluation Organisation of the Planning Commission, Government of India.

Planning Commission. 1952. *The First Five Year Plan*. Government of India.

Planning Commission. 1956. *The Second Five Year Plan*. Government of India.

Ramaswamy, N.S. 1979. *The Management of Animal Energy Resources and the Modernization of the Bullock-Cart System*. Bangalore: Indian Institute of Management.

Ramaswamy, N.S. 1984. "Management for Rural Development," *Journal of Rural Development*, Vol. 3, No. 2.

Rao, C.H. Hanumantha. 1979. "Farm Mechanisation." In *Agricultural Development of India*. See Shah, C.H.

Raj, K.N. 1973. "Mechanisation of Agriculture in India and Sri Lanka." In *Mechanisation and Employment in Agriculture*, International Labour Organisation.

RBI. 1965. "All-India Rural Debt and Investment Survey, 1961–62," *Reserve Bank of India Bulletin*.

RBI. 1975. *All-India Debt and Investment Survey, 1971–72*. Reserve Bank of India.

RCA. 1928. *Report by Royal Commisssion on Agriculture in India*. Government of India.

Roy, S., and M.G. Blase. 1978. "Farm Tractorisation, Productivity and Labour Employment: A Case Study of Indian Punjab," *The Journal of Development Studies*, Vol. 14, No. 2.

Rudra, Ashok. 1969. "Big Farmers of Punjab—Second Installment of Results," *Economic and Political Weekly*, Vol. IV, No. 52.

Rudra, Ashok. 1970. "The Rate of Growth of the Indian Economy." In *Economic Development in South Asia*, E.A.G. Robinson and M. Kidron, eds. London: Macmillan.

Rudra, Ashok. 1971. "Employment Patterns in Large Farms of Punjab," *Economic and Political Weekly*, Vol. VI, No. 26.

Sen, Amartya. 1975. "The Concept of Efficiency." In *Contemporary Issues in Economics*, Parkin and Noblay, eds. Manchester University Press.

Shah, C.H. 1979. *Agricultural Development of India—Policy and Problems*. Orient Longman.

Sharma, R.K. 1974. "Green Revolution and Farm Employment: Analysis of Experience in Punjab," *Indian Journal of Industrial Relations*, Vol. 10, No. 2.

Singh, C.B., et al. 1981. "Labour Absorption and Factors Influencing Levels of Employment in Crop, Dairy and Poultry Enterprises," *Indian Journal of Agricultural Economics*, Vol. XXXVI, No. 4, Conference Number.

Singh, H.K. Manmohan. 1979. "Population Pressure and Labour Absorbability in Agriculture and Related Activities: Analysis and Suggestions Based on Field Studies Conducted in Punjab," *Economic and Political Weekly*, Vol. XIV, No. 11.

Singh, I.J., and R.P. Singh. 1980. "Farm Mechanisation Revisited in North India," *Eastern Economist*, Vol. 75, No. 11.

Singh, Manmohan. 1984. The Agrarian Prospects in India. Dr. V.G. Panse Memorial Lecture, Indian Society of Agricultural Statistics.

Srinivasan, T.N. 1971. *The Green Revolution or the Wheat Revolution*, Discussion Paper No. 66, Indian Statistical Institute, New Delhi.

Srinivasan, T.N. 1979. "Trends in Agriculture in India, 1949-50 to 1977-78," *Economic and Political Weekly*, Vol. XIV, Nos. 30, 31 and 32.

Subramaniam, C. 1979. *The New Strategy in Indian Agriculture*. New Delhi: Vikas Publishing House.

Vaidyanathan, A. 1977. "Performance and Prospects of Crop Production in India," *Economic and Political Weekly*, Vol. XII, Nos. 33 and 34.

United States Technical Committee. 1953. *Observations on Indian Agriculture*. United States Technical Cooperation Mission.

Table 2.1

Modern Inputs into Agriculture - Country Comparison

Continent/ Country	Fertilisers: Nitrogenous	Phosphatic	Potassic	Pesticides gm per hectare	Tractors, per 1,000 hectares
	1981-1982			1971-1972	1976
Asia	19.5	6.4	2.3		
India	21.4	6.5	3.7	180.1	1.5
China	29.1	7.6	1.8		
Japan	118.2	128.8	98.3	10,790.0	181.8
South Korea	244.7	56.4	39.9		
Africa	1.9	1.3	0.5		2.1
Egypt	204.5	38.5	4.5		
South America	1.9	2.7	1.6		
Europe	63.8	37.0	38.8	1,870.0	58.3
Netherlands	236.9	40.0	52.6		
Spain	26.2	10.9	7.0		
U.K.	75.7	24.3	25.7		
U.S.A.	23.5	10.2	11.9	1,480.0	23.5
U.S.S.R.	13.8	9.7	8.1		10.6
World	13.0	6.7	5.2		13.1

Units: For fertilisers kg/hectare
For pesticides gm/hectare
For tractors per 1000 hectares

Time reference: for fertilisers 1981-82
for pesticides 1971-72
for tractors 1976

Source: Fertiliser Statistics (1982-83), National Commission on Agriculture (1976), NCAER (1980).

Table 2.2

Intensity of Use of Modern Inputs

Item	Unit		Reference Period
1	2	3	4
Area under HYV			
Paddy		41.7	
Wheat		70.2	
Jowar	percent of	19.0	1978-79
Bajra	gross cropped	25.8	
Maize	area	23.4	
Total		38.1	
Area Irrigated			
By Canals		10.6	
By Tube-wells	percent of net	5.7	1978-79
By all sources	sown area	26.6	
Tube-wells	number per lakh hectare*	2775	1982
Tractors	number per 1000 hectare	2.5	1979
Electricity	kwh per 1000 hectare	100.8	1982
Pesticides	gm per hectare	377.1	1981-82
Fertilizers			
N+P+K	kg per hectare	31.6	1981-82
Area fertilized	percent of gross cropped area	33.8	1976-77
Farmers using fertilizers	percent of all farmers	45.2	1976-77

Note: In some cases the figures are somewhat backdated because later estimates that are available are marked as provisional. For instance, the percentages of Area under HYV will be more by about 5% for most of the crops if one takes the provisional estimates for 1980-81.

* "hectare" here and below refers to gross cropped area.

Source: Fertiliser Statistics (1982-83), CMIE (1982), Indian Agricultural Statistics (different volumes), NCAER (1979) and NCAER (1980).

Table 2.3

Growth of Modern Inputs

(percent per annum)

Item	Growth Rate	Reference Period
1	2	3
Machinery in use:		
Tractors	15.1	1951-79
Tube-wells	23.9	1951-78
Oil Engines	13.5	1951-82
Electrically operated irrigation pumpsets/ tube-wells	19.2	1951-82
Consumption of Fertilizer and Pesticides:		
N	14.8	1952-83
P	18.7	1952-83
K	19.8	1953-83
N+P+K	15.9	1952-83
Pesticides	13.7	1956-82
Net Irrigated Area:		
All Sources	2.3	1951-79
By Tube-well	25.6	1961-79
By Canal	2.1	1951-79
Improved Seeds:		
Area under HYV	23.4	1967-82

Source: For tube-wells, Dhawan (1982). For the rest of the items, see Table 2.2.

Figure 2.1 Index level of agricultural production

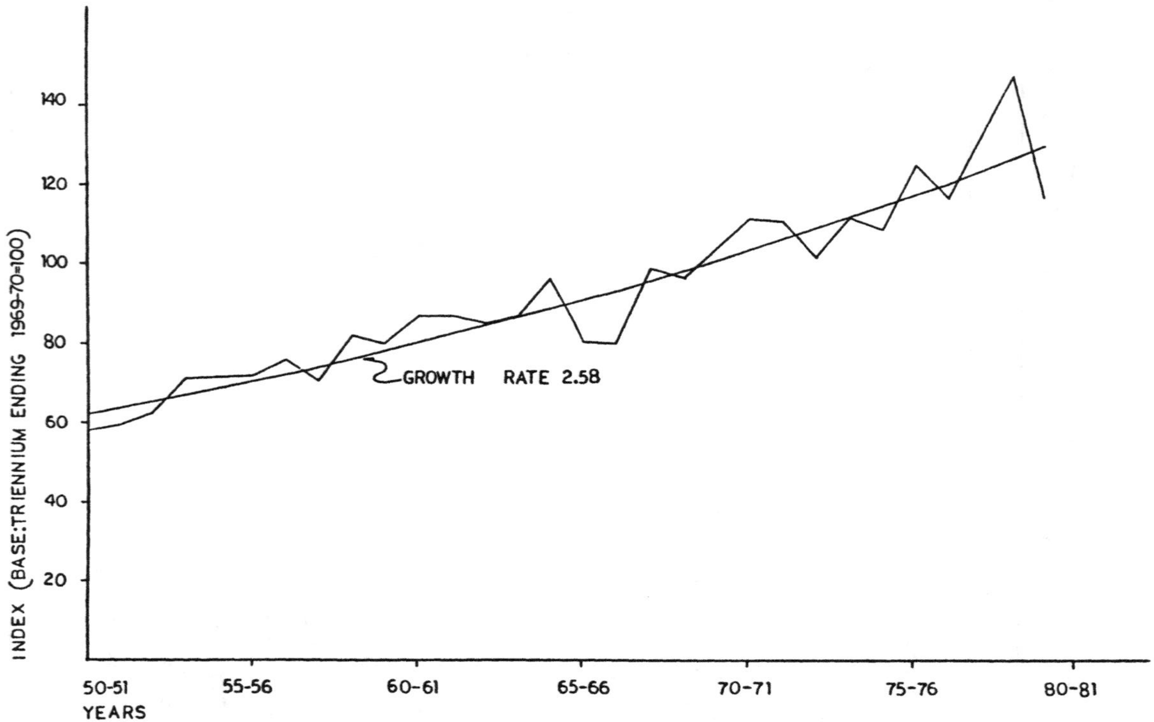

Figure 2.2 Index level of food grain production

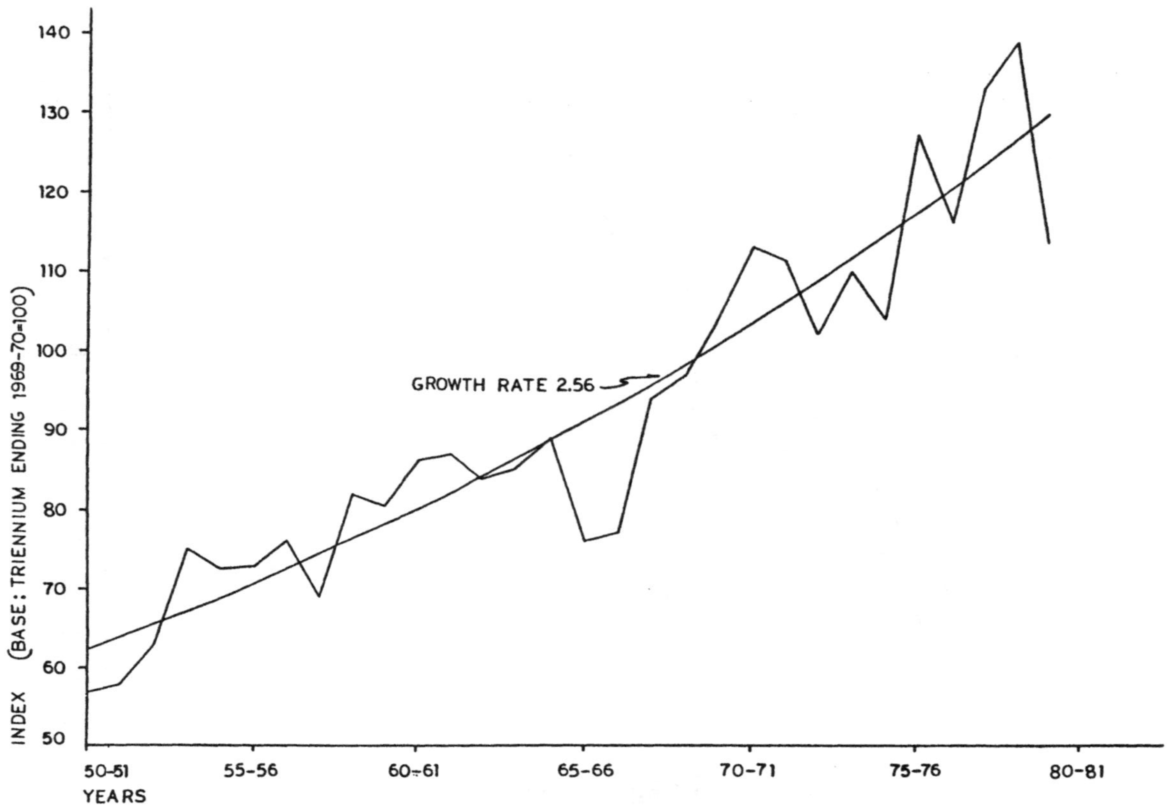

Figure 2.3 Production of wheat: Punjab and Haryana

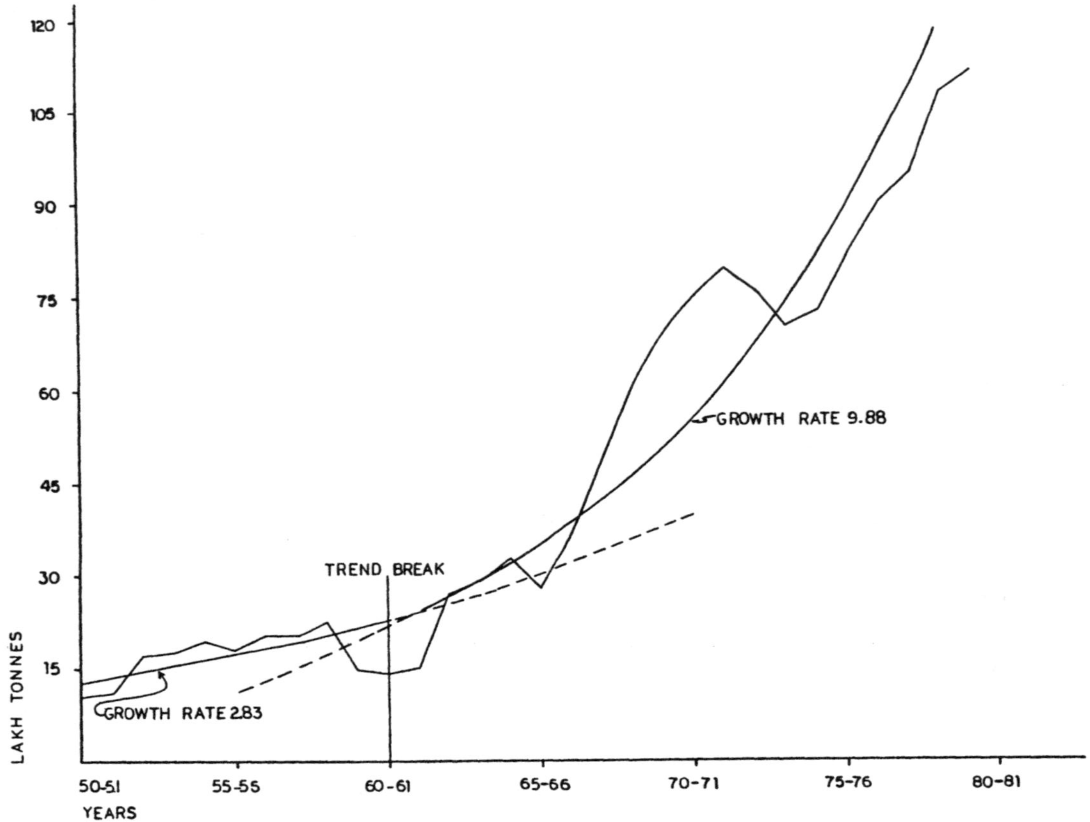

Figure 2.4 Production of Wheat: U.P.

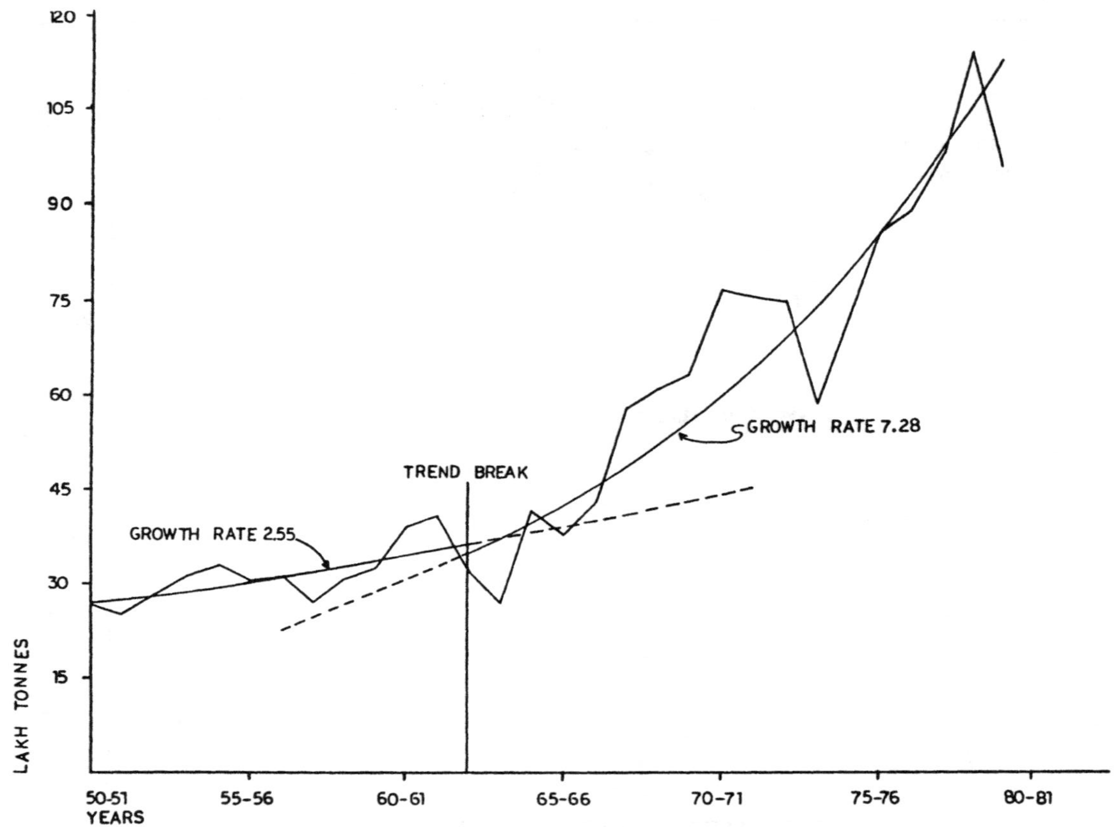

Figure 2.5 Production of rice: Punjab and Haryana

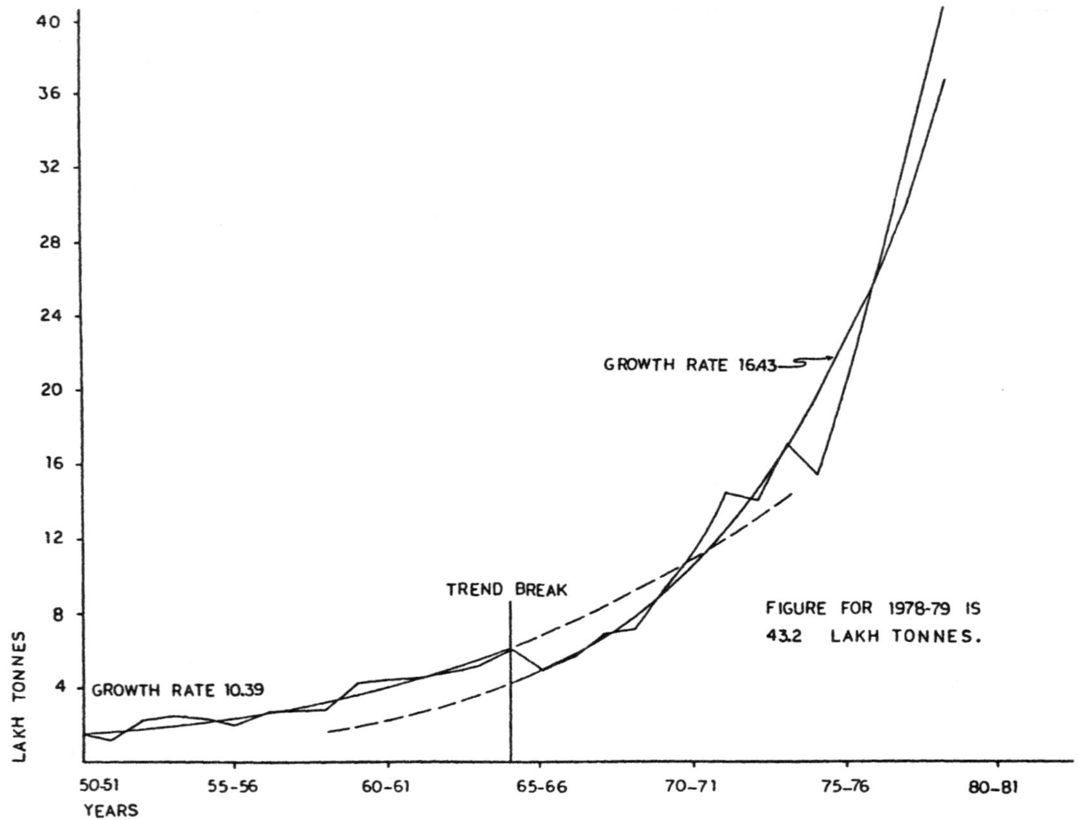

Table 2.4

Ratio of Values of Assets Held by Different Size Categories of Holders in Ferozepur

	Large/small	Large/medium	Medium/small
	1	2	3
1967-68	3.25	1.56	2.08
1971-72	4.21	2.38	1.77

Note: Large farmers are defined as those owning more than 14 hectares; small farmers are defined as those owning less than six hectares. The rest are medium farmers.

Source: Kahlon and Singh (1973a).

Table 2.5

Growth of the Fertiliser Industry

(annual compound rates)

Item	Percent per Year	Period
1	2	3
N		
Capacity	21.7	1951-83
Production	16.7	1952-83
Consumption	14.8	1952-83
P_2O_5		
Capacity	10.7	1951-83
Production	16.0	1952-83
Consumption	18.7	1952-83
K_2O*		
Consumption	19.8	1953-83
Naptha		
Production	6.8	1974-83
Import	-6.9	1976-83
Rock-Phosphate		
Production	12.6	1970-83
Import	6.2	1970-83
Phosphoric Acid**		
Production	9.4	1974-83
Import	30.0	1974-82
Sulphur		
Production	4.6	1970-78
Import	6.9	1969-83

Note: * There is no domestic production of potash at all.
** For the fertiliser industry alone.

Source: Fertiliser Statistics (1982-83).

Figure 2.6 Fertiliser: Consumption and imports

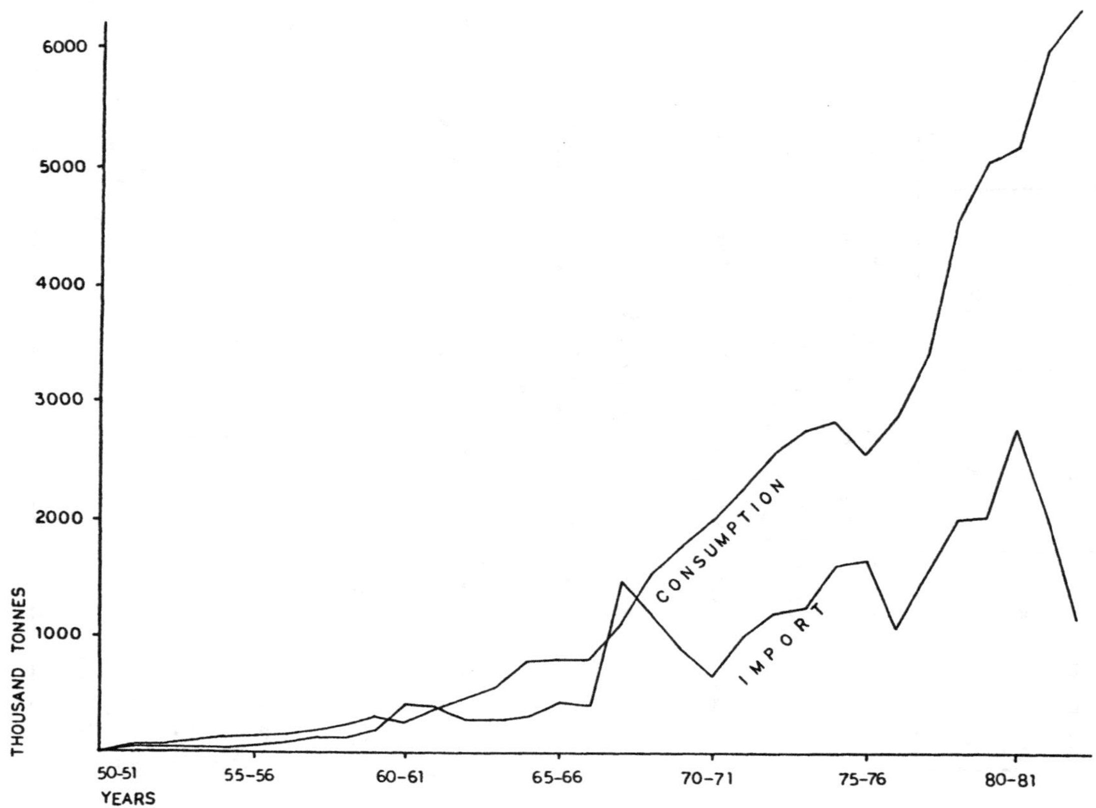

Table 2.6

Linear Rates of Growth of Fertilizer Consumption

(thousand tonnes per year)

	N	P_2O_5	K_2O
First Period	29	32	2.4
Second Period	116	200	36.0
Third Period	300	550	56.0

Note: 1st Period 1950-51 to 1959-60 for N and P_2O_5
1950-51 to 1963-64 for K_2O

2nd Period 1960-61 to 1975-76 for N and P_2O_5
1964-65 to 1974-75 for K_2O

Source: Fertiliser Statistics (Different Volumes).

Table 2.7

Annual Rates of Fertilizer Price Increase

(percent)

Item	1967/1969-73*	1973-74	1974-83
Fertilizer Product			
Urea	3.8	90.5	0.8
Ammonium Sulphate	1.8	68.5	8.2
Di-ammonium phosphate	2.4	25.1	2.3
Muriate of Potash	6.4	82.1	-
Fertilizer Raw Material			
Naptha		88.0	14.8
Sulphur +		71.0	7.2
Rock-phosphate		39.0	2.3

* The period is 1967-73 for urea and Ammonium-sulphate. The period is 1969-73 for the other two products.

\+ The price of sulphur refers to only the part that is imported for the fertilizer industry.

Source: BICP (1979); Fertiliser Statistics (1982-83).

Table 2.8

Product and Feedstock Composition of the Fertilizer Industry

Item	Percentage of Capacity		
	1963	1973	1983
1	2	3	4
Nitrogenous Products			
Ammonium Sulphate	33.8	10.1	4.1
Urea	3.4	65.6	82.0
Phosphate Products			
Simple Super Phosphate	88.4	41.9	20.4
Triple Super Phosphate	NA	2.3	16.3
Feedstocks			
Naptha	NA	75.3	46.4
Fuel Oil	NA	4.4	24.9
Natural Gas	NA	2.3	13.9

Source: Fertiliser Statistics (1982-83).

NA: Not available.

Table 2.9

Role of Imports in the Fertilizer Industry
(percent)

Item	Share of Domestic Production in Total Supply	Year
1	2	3
N	50.1	1951-52
	73.4	1981-82
P_2O_5	38.7	1951-52
	73.5	1981-82
Naptha	92.6	1975-76
	96.7	1982-83
Rock Phosphate	13.0	1969-70
	24.1	1982-83
Phosphoric Acid	67.5	1973-74
	38.0	1981-82
Sulphur	26.8	1969-70
	16.3	1977-78

Source: Fertiliser Statistics (Different Volumes).

Figure 2.7 Availability and production of tractors

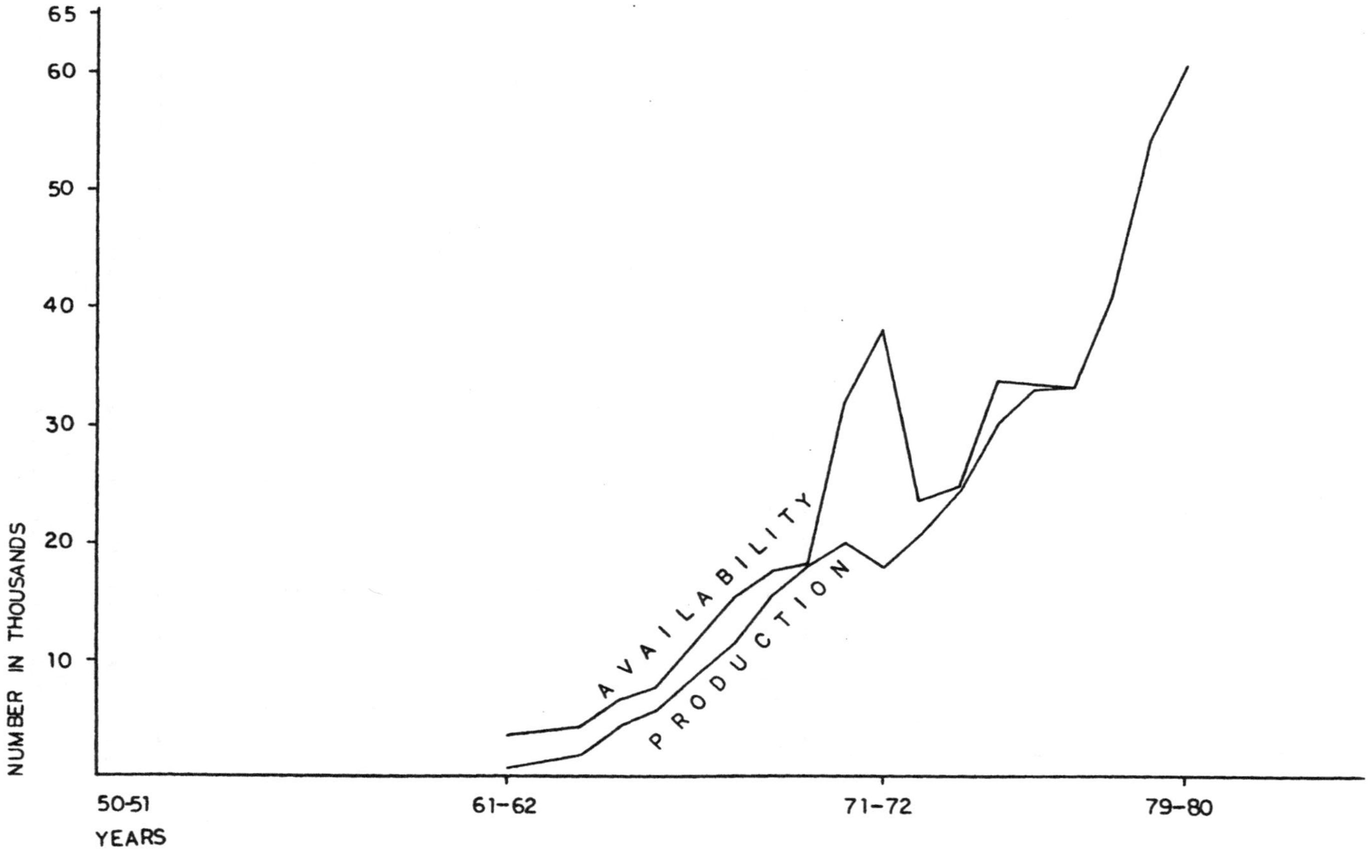

Table 2.10

Share of the Private Sector in the Fertilizer Industry

(percent)

Year	In Cumulative Investment	In Cumulative Capacity	
		N	P_2O_5
1	2	3	4
1956	6.9		
1961	13.1		
1974	39.7		
1977		41.9	44.9
1979	31.5		
1983	26.6	30.0	41.4

Source: Fertiliser Statistics (1982-83).

Table 2.11

Stock of Tractors and Tubewells

(number in thousands)

Year	Tractor	Tube-wells
1	2	3
1951	8.6	3
1961	31	22
1965/66	54	100
1971/72	148	540
1978/79	444	1744

Note: The years 1965, 1971 and 1978 are the reference period for tube-wells; the years 1966, 1972 and 1979 are the reference years for tractors.

Source: NCAER (1980); Dhawan (1982).

Figure 2.8 Net area irrigated by source

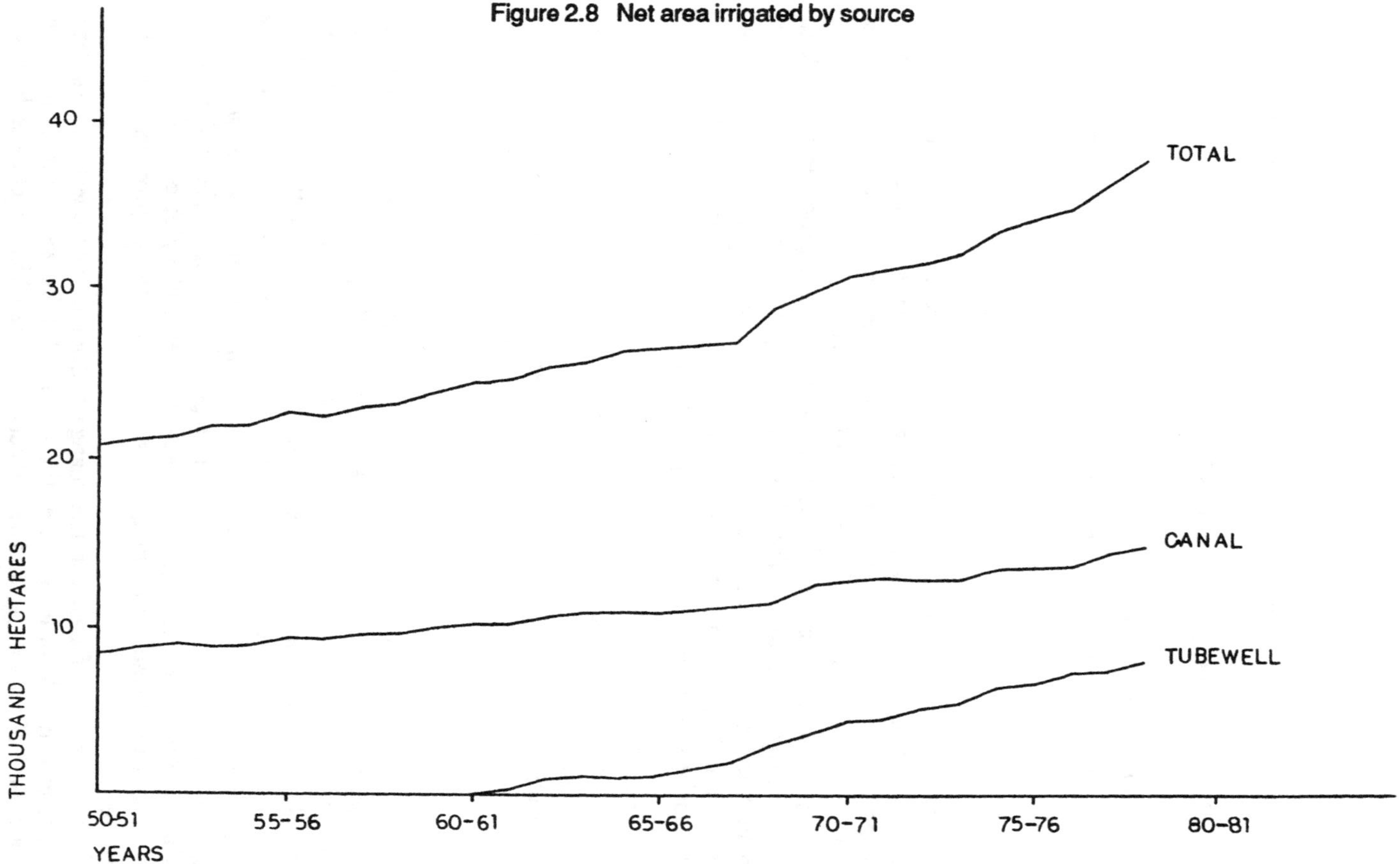

Three

Irrigation in Bangladesh

Stephen Biggs and Jon Griffith

I. INTRODUCTION

In recent years there has been an increasing interest in the development and promotion of appropriate technologies. This has led to the establishment of appropriate technology institutions in developed and developing countries and to a growing body of literature in this area.[1]

There has been considerable debate over what is appropriate technology. In this chapter, we follow the view that multiple and specific criteria need to be used to define what is appropriate technology for any particular physical and socio-economic situation (Stewart, 1983). More specifically, for our analysis this involves that equipment which:

i) is technically viable. For example, it works and does what it is supposed to do;
ii) uses resources efficiently from a national point of view;
iii) is relevant to the priority problems of a specified group of poor people in a rural area.

Sometimes the proponents of appropriate technology claim that suitable techniques exist but that their spread is hampered by the lack of supportive government policies to change institutions, relative prices, credit, and so on. On other occasions it is said that appropriate techniques do not exist and that new research and development is needed. In many situations a whole range of reasons is involved. Generally, however, some factors are far more important than others. In this paper we identify the major factors which led to the diffusion of an appropriate technology in Bangladesh, and the room for manoeuvres in government policy for its promotion in the future.

Our case study focuses on the changing character and effects of irrigation policy in Bangladesh. It examines the relationship between irrigation policy, the choice of technique, and the effects that the different choices have on the distribution of benefits in the society. Within this context, particular attention is paid to an innovative hand-powered irrigation technique.

One of the central themes of our analysis is a recognition that there are special interest groups in aid agencies, in different departments of government, in universities and research institutions, and in rural areas, which stand to gain or lose from changes in government policy. For example, we do not see government or the state as a single institution making uniform policies and programmes.[2] Rather, we see government as being made up of separate, and often competing, ministries and departments. It is because different departments in aid agencies and in government have vested interests in different types of technology that the relative strengths of these departments influence what types of technique are selected and promoted.[3]

The case study shows the way different factions in aid agencies have promoted or obstructed the promotion of irrigation technologies in Bangladesh in recent years. The study concludes by identifying where there is room for manoeuvre for changing irrigation policy in the future.

II. CONTEXT

Agriculture dominates the Bangladesh economy, accounting for 70 percent of total employment and 55 percent of the gross domestic product. Due to rapid population growth, however, there is only about 0.3 acres of arable land (0.12 hectares) per person. Foodgrain imports have increased to over 1.5 million tons per year in the mid 1980s. Moreover, the available resources are unevenly distributed, so that many people have inadequate food intake. While less than 10 percent of households own more than half the cultivable land, 21 percent own none and a further 27 percent own half an acre or less (Januzzi & Peach, 1977). These landless people depend on wage labour for their survival. But, due to an increasing rate of rural under-employment, the value of the daily wage has been declining. Between 1969/70 to 1975, real agricultural wages fell by 30 percent (Clay, 1976).

Increases in agricultural production and employment must be generated by more intensive cultivation. The expansion of irrigation is the most important single contributor to this end. The total irrigated area increased from one million acres in 1960/61 (5 percent of arable land) to 3.6 million acres in 1980/81 (16 percent), and it is planned to double this area by 1985.

In many ways, Bangladesh presents a classic case where labour is relatively abundant, while land and capital are scarce. One would expect, therefore, that irrigation policy would follow a route promoting labour-intensive technology whenever possible.

Government irrigation activities began in the 1950s, but the growth of irrigation started long before this. Indigenous manual systems were used where surface water was available adjacent to low-lying land. These methods included tidal irrigation *polders* and manually operated water-lifting devices such as the *dhone*, the *swing-basket*, and the *dug-well*. Manual systems had expanded to irrigate 1.18 million acres (0.49 million hectares) by 1974 (Ahmed, 1976).

Before independence in 1971, government policy favoured large-scale canal schemes, such as the Ganges-Kobadak and the Demra projects, which increased wet season production by flood protection and supplementary irrigation. Minor irrigation received little attention, and traditional methods were ignored although they contributed most of the irrigated area.[4] After independence, higher priority was given to minor irrigation, with diesel-powered units such as the Low-Lift Pump (LLP), the Deep Tubewell (DTW) and the Shallow Tubewell (STW), with command areas ranging from 10 to 100 acres. These offered the alternative of a new crop in the dry winter season, rather than solely augmenting summer monsoon crops. Moreover, this new season could be made highly productive through precise water control and the "Green Revolution" package of inputs. The minor irrigation approach attracted donors because of the expected rapid impact, in contrast to the slow and disappointing results of the large-scale schemes (Hanratty, 1983).

Minor irrigation has therefore expanded rapidly since 1971 with strong government and donor support for mechanized units. The initial policy favoured Low Lift Pumps and Deep Tubewells, each with a water discharge of two cusecs (60 litres/second) having a theoretical command area of up to 80 acres of paddy (32 hectares). These units were highly subsidized and were provided to farmers' irrigation groups or cooperatives for a nominal rental charge.

Until 1981, almost all mechanized irrigation equipment was owned by the government and rented to irrigation cooperatives for a nominal charge. There was, therefore, virtually no private market in this equipment. Decisions on the choice of technology, and on the quantity to be made available, rested with the government and foreign donors. On the other hand, there has been no government intervention and support to encourage the traditional irrigation methods. The area covered by these labour-intensive methods has declined because they have been replaced by power pumps, or because neighbouring power pumps have drawn down their water resources.

Since 1981 the subsidies on mechanized irrigation equipment have been greatly reduced. The Bangladesh Agricultural Development Corporation (BADC), which formerly hired out pumps and tubewells, now sells them to farmers. The irrigation cooperatives, which had frequently been formed to obtain a pump, are disbanding. Instead, rich farmers are taking bank loans in order to buy a pump and then sell water to their neighbours. This policy of privatisation has promoted demand for similar sizes of power pumps, and the Shallow Tubewell has been particularly successful.

It is evident from table 3.1 that the policy commitment favouring mechanized minor irrigation has been successful in achieving a significant increase in irrigated area. However, once again, the traditional labour-intensive irrigation methods have been ignored. For example, while there have been many studies of the management, performance and coverage of power pumps, there is little such information on manual methods (Biggs and others, 1978). National data, collected by the Ministry of Agriculture and published by the Bangladesh Bureau of Statistics, aggregates all manual methods under the heading of "other irrigation". Thus, for example, there is no data on the increasing coverage of the manual dug well. Moreover, the coverage of the mechanized methods is reported as new irrigation, without accounting for the traditional irrigation systems which may have been displaced.

This bias against labour-intensive irrigation provides concern for two reasons. Firstly, it raises questions about the efficiency of government investment policies. Could the area of irrigation have been increased by using the abundant labour resources rather than by using capital-intensive methods? Secondly, and perhaps more seriously, are the issues of distribution of the benefits of irrigation within the rural society. The mechanized units, being large compared to the average farm size and income, are inaccessible to small farmers and to those who lack access to institutional credit. The richer and more powerful farmers, who are able to control these methods, have benefited disproportionately from their use. The traditional methods, on the other hand, are accessible to many more of the small farmers, are more appropriate for small, fragmented land-holdings, and generate greater productive employment.

There is one irrigation device which is a notable exception to the exclusion of labour-intensive methods from state and donor support. This is the Manually Operated Shallow Tubewell for Irrigation, or MOSTI. This is not a traditional method, but an indigenous innovation first reported in 1975. Since 1976, there have been three donor-funded projects to market and promote a total of 430,000 MOSTI's, to achieve a planned irrigation coverage of 150,000 acres (60,000 hectares).

The MOSTI is worthy of further study therefore, not only as a successful and appropriate innovation, but also as an exceptional case of institutional support in Bangladesh for labour-intensive irrigation. It illustrates, therefore, that there is room for manoeuvre for donor organisations and for different government agencies. It demonstrates that the promotion of appropriate technology is not an impossible objective conceived of by idealistic and unrealistic planners.

III. THE MANUALLY OPERATED SHALLOW TUBEWELL FOR IRRIGATION

The name MOSTI (Manually Operated Shallow Tubewell for Irrigation) describes the traditional hand-pump tubewell when it is used for irrigation. This device was introduced to Bengal, as a domestic water source, in the nineteenth century. Before its recent adoption for irrigation, it was already widely used. By 1971, the Department of Public Health and Engineering (DPHE) had installed 125,000 public drinking water wells, and an even larger number were privately installed and owned. More than fifty local foundries manufactured the cast iron hand-pump, and the well-pipe and strainer were both fabricated within the country.[5]

A private drinking water well at the homestead is a convenience and a status symbol. A national network of distributors and retailers supports this market, and there is also an informal market for second-hand pumps and wells. The well sinking is performed in a day or less by tubewell mechanics, using the manual sludger method which requires only hand-tools and three workers. These tubewell mechanics are found throughout the country, and they are employed as contractors in the government's rural water supply programme, which has installed 50,000 new public drinking water wells per year for the last decade. The number of hand-pump tubewells in Bangladesh is estimated to exceed one million as shown in table 3.2.

The public drinking water wells, installed by the DPHE with assistance from UNICEF, have an average depth of 35 metres. They now use imported plastic well-pipe and strainer, which are cheaper than the traditional galvanized iron components. The irrigation MOSTI wells, however, cannot use plastic pipe because the well is extracted from the ground each season to protect it from theft and because re-sinking improves the water yield. The high cost of galvanized iron pipe means that only very shallow irrigation wells are economically feasible. Their average depth is 12 metres. Intensive MOSTI use is thus restricted to those areas of the country where the geology offers a good aquifer at a very shallow depth.

Private drinking water wells may use either galvanized or plastic well-pipe, and most use the same cast iron hand-pump. A MOSTI can be re-sunk at the homestead for drinking water in the off season. Similarly, public wells have been illicitly diverted to irrigation, and private drinking water wells may be re-sunk for irrigation by their owners, or re-sold for that purpose.

This dual usage of privately owned wells has reduced the impact of institutional MOSTI sales programmes and subsidies (see section IV). The dual usage also makes hazardous any estimation of the total number of MOSTIs in use.

There has been only one national census of MOSTI usage, conducted by UNICEF in 1976 shortly after MOSTIs were first reported.[6] From this survey it was estimated that there were 40,000 MOSTIs in use, of which slightly more than half were irrigating an average of 0.45 acres of rice, and the remainder were irrigating an average of 0.64 acres of dry-land crops. Ninety-seven percent of them used 12 metres or less of well-pipe.

The initial crop selection by most operators was HYV winter rice, and the most common assessment of labour requirement was that one man could pump enough water for one-third of an acre of this crop. Winter rice requires irrigation for about three months. Commonly, two men shared the work of irrigating a larger area, and the highest rate witnessed was three men working shifts for one acre of rice. A man's usual working regimen was pumping for 20 to 25 minutes, followed by 5 to 10 minutes rest, repeated for a total of eight hours, representing about six hours net pumping at a slower rate; women were hardly ever seen. Recent reports suggest that women are now pumping more.

Operators are sensitive to any decline in the water discharge, and they frequently carry spare parts for the pump in case of a break-down. These items are available at local weekly markets in intensive MOSTI areas, and the operators do all the pump repairs themselves. If the problem is a clogged strainer, the owner will have the well re-sunk. In some areas re-sinking once or twice during the irrigation season is a standard procedure, and occasionally farmers do this themselves.

The cost of a MOSTI is equivalent to US$60 to $80, depending on the depth required. This low cost makes it accessible to small farming families, while the small irrigation command area is compatible with the fragmented pattern of small holdings. The MOSTI may be considered appropriate because of its small-scale, because it is indigenously produced, and because local skills and services exist for its installation and maintenance. The very high labour requirement for operation is also important given the high rate of rural unemployment and the government's commitment to increasing employment.

By comparison, the alternative mechanized irrigation methods are larger units, with a higher unit cost and a greater dependence on imported parts and fuel. For comparison with the MOSTI, the Shallow Tubewell (STW) may be considered because it is often in direct competition with the MOSTI, and because it is strongly encouraged by present policy. Both methods are presently on sale in Bangladesh in large numbers, under projects sponsored by the government and aided by foreign donors.

Some of the significant characteristics of the two techniques are listed in table 3.4. The STW uses a diesel powered centrifugal pump-set, whereas the MOSTI uses a hand operated pump. The average command area irrigated by the STW is 10 acres of rice, as compared to half an acre by the MOSTI. However, in terms of investment cost per acre, the two methods are similar (see table 3.4, line 10). The installation cost of the MOSTI is negligible, and the unit can be easily relocated, whereas the STW cannot be easily moved or re-sold. Because the STW is new and depends on skilled maintenance services, its operating life has been less than that of the MOSTI; however, as these services develop in rural areas, this differential can be expected to decline.

These figures show that, per acre of irrigation, the installation costs of the two methods are similar.[7] It is the composition and level of running costs that make the two techniques differ so significantly. Unskilled labour inputs (line 12) for the STW are estimated at 8 days per acre for channel maintenance; whereas with MOSTIs an estimated 160 days of pumping labour are required to irrigate an acre of winter rice. The major running cost for the STW is fuel; for the MOSTI it is labour. When labour is costed at the market rate of Tk. 10 per day the total running cost of the MOSTI is over two and one-half times the running cost of the STW.

However, although the MOSTI appears to be inferior, both they and the STWs are spreading rapidly in Bangladesh. The reasons for the adoption of MOSTIs deserve emphasis:

1. *The dual labour market.* A farmer who has the choice either of leaving his land idle, or of hiring labour to operate a MOSTI, would have to pay the market wage to the labourers. On this basis, cultivation with MOSTI irrigation is not financially attractive to a poorer family who must choose either to seek wage labour, or to work their land with manual irrigation. This is because wage employment is infrequently available to job seekers, particularly during the dry season. Although the imputed daily return to manual pumping is far lower than the daily market wage, the gross return to manual irrigation still exceeds the available wage earnings as labourers are frequently unemployed.

2. *The imperfect capital market.* If credit is required to finance irrigation, the small farmer generally faces higher interest rates than the larger landowner. Where institutional credit is supposed to be available, the small farmer might be debarred by lack of the required collateral, or the limited funds available might be pre-empted by his more influential neighbours.

3. *The effects of scale.* The STW is attractive, on a per acre basis, if its full irrigation command of about 10 acres can be achieved. However, it is rare in Bangladesh for any farmer to own a block of land of this size, so profitable operation depends on collaboration between neighbours. Whether the owner sells water to his neighbours, or whether the well is communally operated, there are hidden management and transaction costs which can be considerable. The MOSTI operator does not face these costs because the scale of the technology is smaller and is compatible with the existing fragmented pattern of land ownership.

4. *The effects of complementary inputs.* The operation of the STW depends on the provision of fuel, lubricant, spare parts and maintenance services. Although the distribution of these inputs is improving, there is a risk that any one might become unavailable, or that a monopoly supplier might demand extortionate prices. The MOSTI, being older and simpler, requires fewer complementary inputs, which are more widely available to the user.

5. *The liquidity of the investment.* Because the MOSTI may be cheaply and simply extracted and re-installed, it can be re-sold if the owner faces any unforseen crises. Once the STW is sunk in the ground, its withdrawal is technically complex and risky. The diesel engine and pump from a STW may be re-sold separately, but depreciation on these complex components is faster than for the more robust hand-pump.

The analysis illustrates that these technologies possess intrinsic economic and organizational characteristics which make them more or less attractive to different economic strata of the rural population. The Shallow Tubewell is more accessible and profitable to large farmers. The MOSTI is more profitable for the small farmer, and its labour requirement indirectly benefits the landless (Howes, 1984).

The capital/output ratio of the two methods is similar, and, on this basis, one would expect national planning to be indifferent between them.

In addition, if we look at the economic costs of running the two machines, we would expect government policy to be directed towards the MOSTIs as the shadow price of labour is relatively low in this labour abundant economy, and the shadow price of imported fuel is relatively high. Finally as regards a social cost benefit analysis of the two techniques, the significant contrast between the methods lies in the distribution of benefits (that is, the value added through irrigation). With the MOSTI, labour derives a greater share of the product, whereas with the STW, its owner gains more. For these reasons, a national policy which prefers the Shallow Tubewell to the MOSTI: (i) is inefficient as regards the best use of scarce natural resources and (ii) supports the interests of larger farmers rather than the welfare of the poor.[8]

IV. THE MOSTI PROGRAMMES

Although farmers have recalled using MOSTIs as early as 1966, it was almost 10 years before the innovation attracted any official attention. In 1974 a flood caused famine in the north of the country, and in the subsequent dry season there was a significant increase in MOSTIs, concentrated in areas where the MOSTI was previously known. In 1975, reports reached the capital that public drinking water wells were being stolen, and in Jamalpur, cooperative societies requested the government to provide wells for irrigation.

The Integrated Rural Development Programme (IRDP), a government agency promoting development of farmers' cooperatives, responded to this request, as did UNICEF. By the end of 1975 UNICEF had arranged funding and materials, and 10,000 MOSTI sets were on sale at cooperative associations in 30 thanas.

This programme was able to start rapidly due to the on-going drinking water programme sponsored by UNICEF and the Department of Public Health Engineering (DPHE). The existing procedures for procurement and manufacture were simply expanded to provide additional MOSTI units. All materials were procured by UNICEF, largely from abroad, including pig-iron and coke for casting the pumps, which was done by local foundries. Storage and transportation of materials were handled by the DPHE up to their divisional stores, from where the Thana Central Cooperative Associations (TCCA) nominated by IRDP collected the complete tubewell sets.

The objects of the programme were to expand the use of MOSTI across the country, to increase food production, and to increase the income of families owning three acres or less by the provision of MOSTI on credit sale. The programme was focussed on those thanas where a fresh-water aquifer was available within a depth of 12 metres, and where a TCCA had been established by IRDP. Tubewell sets were sold by the TCCAs on credit to cooperative members, or for cash to non-members. To encourage sales to small farmers, a small premium was added to the price of cash purchases, and it was directed that preference be given to credit purchasers owning less than three acres.

The tubewell sets were priced at cost, plus the handling charges of the TCCAs. This price implied a small subsidy on in-country management and logistic costs, but the absence of taxes and duties meant that the sets were considerably cheaper than the current market rate. This price differential was significant for galvanized iron pipe, which is taxed at almost 100 percent in the market, but was tax-free within the programme.

The programme was funded by foreign grants contributed through UNICEF. The intention was that higher purchase repayments accruing to IRDP should form a revolving fund to continue the programme. However, the revolving fund never materialized, and the programme ended in 1979.

The programme was evaluated by the Institute of Business Administration in 1979 (Miyan, 1980). The evaluation concluded that 71 percent of the sales were on credit, but that only 43 percent of the sets sold were used for irrigation. The average cultivable land-holding of purchasers was 3.89 acres. At the time of the evaluation, 85 percent of the final credit repayments were 10 months or more overdue. However, repayments subsequently improved to over 90 percent at field level (World Bank, 1981).

The second MOSTI programme was sponsored by USAID, who signed a credit agreement with the Planning Commission in 1976 for $14 million to produce 240,000 hand tubewells. Initially the programme was impossible to implement because no local agency could be found to handle the procurement and distribution of the materials. The state agency responsible for minor irrigation, the Bangladesh Agricultural Development Corporation (BADC), was strongly committed to mechanized methods and was reluctant to promote MOSTI. However, in 1978 BADC became the lead agency for the USAID programme, but further delays occurred in procurement.[9] Distribution of the wells was planned through both the TCCAs, and BADC appointed retail dealers who were able to make cash sales, and to deliver sets to purchasers receiving credit from the Bangladesh Krishi Bank.

An evaluation of the programme was conducted by a USAID mission in February 1982 (Friedkin, 1983). At this time 104,000 hand tubewells had been sold, and the programme had been reduced to 160,000 sets because of cost escalation. The evaluation states that credit sales had been very disappointing, explaining that this was due to red tape and to the reluctance of the banks to handle small credit applications. The average land-holding of purchasers was 4.30 acres. Full data is not available on the pricing policy, but the subsidy on a set selling for Tk. 1,300 was about Tk. 280 (Friedkin, 1983).

The third MOSTI programme was assisted by a World Bank/IDA loan of $18 million for 180,000 hand tubewells to be distributed from 1981/82 to 1983/84. This programme was similar to the first programme except that procurement, formerly done by UNICEF, was now the agreed responsibility of DPHE. Sales were handled by the TCCAs, with provision for medium term credit for 90 percent of the units. The sales price included all costs, but taxes and duties were excluded.

This programme also met initial delays due to problems of procurement, and to a government ban on the importation of pipe. The programme was consequently extended until 1985. There has been no published evaluation, but a study is presently being conducted by the Institute of Business Administration. Initial reports suggest that a large proportion of sales have been for cash rather than credit, and that, as with previous programmes, the majority of sales have not gone to small farmers. There are also suggestions that the price differential between the local market and the tax-free programme MOSTIs led to diversions of some programme components into the market.

In the earlier analysis, it was suggested that manual irrigation would be most attractive to very poor families who have surplus family labour and access to some land. The three programmes reviewed here all intended to supply MOSTIs to this group, but evidence suggests that most sales have been going to larger farmers. The conventional explanation of why large farmers buy MOSTIs is that they use them for drinking water, or to irrigate high-value cash crops like tobacco. This may be true, but it is also possible that these purchasers are profiting by re-selling the wells in the market. Because of the tax exemption on programme MOSTIs, there is a dual price structure: the open market price, related to tax paid components, and the price of programme MOSTIs which are untaxed. In the case of steel pipe, which is the largest item in the cost of a MOSTI, taxes represent almost half of the open market price.

It is quite probable that the larger farmers who have access and influence in the institutions are able to pre-empt the supply of subsidized goods, re-sell them to the poorer users, and appropriate the value of the subsidy to themselves. The existence of subsidized marketing programmes may also deter private producers from investing resources in order to enter the market. Thus the effect of subsidies in this context is to make the price higher for the poor, and lower for the rich.

The MOSTI, as pointed out earlier, is simply a new use of the old drinking water well. The desirable characteristics of a drinking water pump—robustness, reliability, and ease of repair—do not necessarily suit it to irrigation, where efficiency and high yield are more important. It is thus reasonable to believe that research and development could produce pumps better suited to irrigation.

Some research and development was conducted in the UNICEF programme, and a low-cost irrigation well strainer was developed. Several foreign voluntary agencies have also been developing new irrigation hand-pumps and wells, which have now achieved some market success, but this type of initiative has received little state support. The IDA programme provided US$200,000 for research and development (R&D) by local agencies, but this activity was removed by the government during a budget crisis, and there has been little productive R&D by local agencies or institutions.

The minimal research and development work on the MOSTI may be compared to the total absence of work on the other manual irrigation methods, such as the dhone, the swing basket, and the dug well. Although these methods, together with tidal irrigation polders, have been irrigating a million acres for 20 years or more, their technical characteristics and performance were not even measured until very recently (Khan, 1980, 1983).

The traditional manual irrigation methods are extremely simple devices, and they are fabricated in the village from wood and bamboo. By comparison the MOSTI is relatively complex; it requires imported raw materials and is manufactured in urban factories. Perhaps the crudeness of the traditional pumps has deferred engineers and policy-makers from considering them worthy of more serious attention (Biggs, 1978). Indeed, it is the relative complexity of the MOSTI which has made it eligible for foreign assistance, because it is possible to monitor and control the manufacturing and distribution processes in the formal and state sectors of the economy.[10]

Since 1980, an innovative research project conducted by foreign engineers of the Rangpur and Dinajpur Rehabilitation Services (RDRS) has developed a very low-cost version of the MOSTI which is largely fabricated from bamboo by trained village artisans. More than 8,000 of these units were sold in 1983, and sales are increasing in the two districts covered by the project.[11] While this is evidently a highly successful and appropriate innovation with a bright future, it is an endeavor which large institutions find difficult to support because it involves only the informal sector of the economy. There is, after all, no need to finance the import of bamboo.[12]

There is also considerable potential for research and development into manual methods for lifting surface water. The traditional methods are constrained by a maximum lifting height of four feet, whereas the MOSTI has shown that lifting water 15 feet is now profitable for small farmers. It is possible that small investments in research might improve technical performance and social benefits. The absence of such research is attributable to the continuing bias towards mechanized irrigation, the benefits of which go mainly to richer farmers.

V. POLICY ISSUES

This chapter has suggested that the rural poor would have benefited more if policies favouring labour-intensive irrigation had been given higher priority. It has been argued that the MOSTI is an example of an appropriate technology, which is appropriate not only from the growth point of view, but also from the standpoint of contributing to equitable income distribution.

We have shown how special interest groups in aid agencies, ministries, R&D institutions, as well as richer farmers and commercial interests have given rise to policies which have prevented the spread of appropriate labour-intensive irrigation technology. An illustration of the main interest groups which have supported or obstructed appropriate technology are given in the Technology Policy Determinants Diagram (figure 3.1).[13] It can be seen that UNICEF played a major positive role, while the Agricultural Development Corporation and the Water Development Board have played negative roles. USAID has played a mixed role, some projects were positive and others negative.

We now turn to some major areas of policy where we find there is room for manoeuvre in the promotion of appropriate irrigation technology. We restrict our suggestions to the promotion of labour intensive techniques, and do not cover other strategies such as the creation of new landless labourer organizations for owning and/or managing capital intensive irrigation machines (Wood, 1984).

National Irrigation Planning

Table 3.6 shows the actual performance of mechanized and manual methods. During the 1970s growth has been due to mechanization; the area under traditional irrigation has decreased, and the contribution of MOSTI was, on a national scale, negligible.

On reviewing this table one might conclude that the capital-intensive strategy was correct. However, what this table does not tell us is: (1) How much of the growth of mechanized irrigation was at the expense of labour-intensive methods; (2) How much labour-intensive irrigation could have been increased if policy had not been biased against it; (3) What combination of mechanized and labour-intensive technology would have been best for achieving both growth and equity.

Given the physical conditions and technology choices available, we are not suggesting that it would have been sensible to discard mechanization, because the labour-intensive methods available have technical limitations. What we do suggest is that explicit attention be paid to investigating the maximum potential for labour-intensive techniques. This might result in a significant re-orientation of Bangladesh's irrigation planning. It would take only one or two major government ministries or aid agencies to seriously consider labour-intensive techniques to change the ground rules of the policy debate in this area.

Subsidization of Mechanized Irrigation

In the past mechanized irrigation has been subsidized in a variety of ways. For example, water has been supplied free of charge; equipment has been rented out at subsidized rates; fuel has been subsidized; machines have been sold through low interest loans; and repayment of these loans has frequently not been enforced. A reduction in these subsidies would certainly lead to the spread of alternative labour-intensive methods.

At the same time that mechanized methods have been subsidized, the MOSTI has been highly taxed. A policy decision to abolish taxes on steel pipe would double the economically feasible well depth, and more than double the area of the country in which the MOSTI is viable. A change in credit policy such as the experiments of the Grameen Bank (Yunus,

1983) for providing loan and saving services to poor people would also enhance demand for low-cost irrigation devices.

Research and Development Policy

The incredibly low level of research and development into labour-intensive irrigation techniques, and the very limited inter-disciplinary research involving engineers and social scientists, means that there is a whole area of activity which could be explored for the improvement and development of appropriate technology.

Although it is difficult to predict the actual growth potential of this type of innovation, improvements to the traditional methods may offer returns by expanding an already large irrigated area. As in the case of MOSTI, a small increase in technical performance may make the technique applicable over a much larger geographical area. For instance, if the lifting height of the dhone could be doubled from four to eight feet, its potential national command area would be more than doubled. While the potential benefits could be large, the major costs involved would be the funding of research projects. If such projects produced viable innovations, then their dissemination and adoption would be largely spontaneous and at little cost to the government.

While research projects may be seen as risky investments, the potential returns should justify such ventures. Because appropriate hand-pumps must be cheap and simple, it is unlikely that private business would be attracted by the potential profits, and so the research must be sponsored by the state. There are now local institutions competent to conduct appropriate technology research, as has been demonstrated by projects at the Mirpur Agricultural Workshop, the Rice Research Institute and the University of Engineering and Technology.

The past failure by government and aid agencies to sponsor such research must be attributed to the strong bias favouring mechanized irrigation. To some extent, this is due to biased attitudes: machines are modern, and hand-pumps old-fashioned; machines will release people from toil. Yet these attitudes are conditioned by one's position in society. The poor, who depend on manual toil for their daily survival, have had little impact on national policy. It is the rich who want labour-saving machines, and who have influenced R&D institutions and policy.

As the influence of the biases is now being recognized, it is possible for engineering R&D priorities to be geared more towards national development criteria.

The Policies of Aid Agencies

Foreign donors, who provide almost the entire development budget, prefer mechanization because such formal sector projects are amenable to their administrative and financial procedures (Thomas, 1975), and because the machines and expertise are exported from the donors' own countries.

The untying of aid, the financing of local costs, and the reform of administrative procedures in aid agencies would help to reduce the aid agency obstacles to the spread of appropriate technology.

We believe that there is room for manoeuvre to change policy in the four areas outlined here. However, we recognize that the implementation of these policy changes would be difficult. For example the western manufacturers, and the local agents and installation contractors, also have a natural vested interest in mechanization. Large agencies, such as the BADC, have been established to implement the mechanization policy in which they have developed a vested interest, and these bodies have also opposed manual irrigation. An indication of groups who would gain and lose from such changes in irrigation policy are given in the following Pay-Off Matrix (table 3.7).

The mechanized irrigation programmes have been successful in realizing a rapid increase in irrigation coverage and production. These programmes were supported by those groups who benefit from them, and who oppose alternative policies. It would be politically naive to imagine that similar conflicts of interest will not exist in the future. What we have tried to do in this paper is to draw attention to the way in which the narrow interests of different groups in aid agencies and local institutions can influence the choice of technology. In the case of irrigation in Bangladesh this has resulted in the promotion of inappropriate technologies.

NOTES

We would like to thank Gerry Foley, Frank Beran and Frances Stewart for comments on an earlier draft of this chapter.

1. For a recent reader on appropriate technology which reviews much of the literature, see Carr, 1985.
2. These issues are taken up in a more general way for a wide range of government and aid agency policies in Clay & Schaffer, 1985.
3. For a review of theories which place emphasis on institutional factors and other theories concerning the generation and diffusion of agricultural technology, see Biggs and Clay, 1983.
4. Minor irrigation projects have command of areas less than one hundred hectares.
5. The raw materials, such as steel and pig-iron, are imported.
6. Subsequent surveys to evaluate MOSTI sales projects have sampled only the population of wells sold by the project; eg. Miyan, 1981, and Friedkin, 1983.
7. The per acre financial cost of the STW is slightly lower than the MOSTI. However, because taxes and duties are higher on MOSTI components than on STW components, the economic cost of the MOSTI is lower than that of the STW. The imported fuel used by STWs is subsidized.

8. Some economists might argue that it is better for richer households to get the surplus as their propensity to save (and then invest) is higher. However, there is increasing evidence (Yunus, 1983) that the poor save as much from current incomes as richer households if they have access to viable and reliable institutional credit services.

9. It is not known why BADC reversed its stand. At this time BADC held a monopoly in the distribution of subsidized agricultural inputs for which there was generally a good demand and, in some cases, a black market. The MOSTI project certainly involved considerable work in a new field, but perhaps BADC officials also felt that it would not be attractive to their existing client group, or there would not be the same opportunities for patronage as in their existing programmes. It may also be significant that the BADC is responsible to the Ministry of Agriculture, whereas the Ministry of Rural Development supervises the IRDP, whose MOSTI programmes were rather more successful.

10. Thomas has made a similar observation concerning the preference of foreign donors for capital-intensive methods of constructing deep tubewells in Bangladesh (Thomas, 1975).

11. The cost of materials for a pump and well is about US$15, and subsidies on this amount have now been eliminated. RDRS still pays part of the artisan's installation fee of about US$3 to ensure quality control. Total sales up to August 1984 are 21,000 units. This device is not spreading to neighboring districts.

12. A USAID official gave this as a reason for not repeating the USAID-funded MOSTI projecct. The government may not have quite the same procedural difficulties in dealing with the informal sector, but the fact that more than three-quarters of the development budget is provided by foreign aid gives the donors great influence in project selection and technology choice (de Vylder, 1982: 39–61).

13. Illustration of the wider applicability of this diagram are given in Biggs, 1982 & 1984.

REFERENCES

Ahmed, Raisuddin. 1976. *Foodgrain production in Bangladesh: An Analysis of Growth, its Sources and Related Policies.* Washington: International Food Policy Research Institute.

Baumann, E., and R.G. Fuller. 1984. *Manual Irrigation in Bangladesh.* Dhaka: Swiss Development Cooperation.

Biggs, Stephen D., Chris Edwards, and Jon Griffith. 1978. *Irrigation in Bangladesh,* Discussion Paper No. 126. Sussex: Institute of Development Studies.

Biggs, S.D. 1982. Institutions and Decision-Making in Agricultural Research. In *The Economics of New Technology in Developing Countries,* eds. F. Stewart and J. James. London: Francis Pinter.

Biggs, Stephen D., and Edward J. Clay. 1983. Generation and Diffusion of Agricultural Policy. In *Room for Manoeuvre: An Exploration of Public Policy Planning in Agricultural and Rural Development,* eds. E.J. Clay and B.B. Schaffer. London: Heinemann.

Carr, Marilyn. 1985. *The A.T. Reader, Theory and Practice in Appropriate Technology.* London: Intermediate Technology Publications.

Clay, Edward J. 1976. "Institutional Change and Agricultural Wages in Bangladesh," *Bangladesh Development Studies,* IV, 4: 423–440.

Clay, E.J., and B. B. Schaffer, eds. 1984. *Room for Manoeuvre: An Exploration of Public Policy Planning in Agricultural and Rural Development*. London: Heinemann.

Friedkin, Tom, Robert Lester, Herbert Blank, and Nizam U. Ahmed. 1983. *Bangladesh Small-Scale Irrigation*, A.I.D. Project Impact Evaluation No. 42. Washington, D.C.: USAID.

Hannah, L. M. 1976. "Hand Pump Irrigation in Bangladesh," *Bangladesh Development Studies*, Vol. IV (4), pp 441–454.

Hanratty, Martin. 1983. Minor Irrigation Development in Bangladesh. USAID/ Bangladesh. Mimeo.

Howes, Michael. 1984. Whose Water? An Investigation of the Consequences of Alternative Approaches to Small Scale Irrigation in Bangladesh. A report submitted to ODA. Brighton: Institute of Development Studies. Mimeo.

Januzzi, F. Tomason, and James T. Peach. 1977. *Report on the Hierarchy of Interests in Land in Bangladesh*. Washington, D.C.: USAID.

Khan, M.H., and S. M. Nazrul Islam. 1983. Irrigation Equipments and their Performance. Keynote paper presented at First National Symposium on Agricultural Research, BARC, Dhaka, Dec. 1983. Bangladesh University of Engineering & Technology. Mimeo.

Miyan, Alimullah, Mahmood Hassan, and Mahbubul Hassan. 1981. *Manually Operated Shallow Tubewell in Bangladesh*. Institute of Business Administration, University of Dacca.

Stewart, F. 1983. *Macro-Policies for Appropriate Technology: An Introductory Classification*, Working Paper, Appropriate Technology International, Washington, D.C.

Thomas, John W. 1975. The Choice of Technology for Irrigation Tubewells in East Pakistan: Analysis of a Development Policy Decision. In *The Choice of Technology in Developing Countries*, eds. Timmer, Thomas, Wells, and Morawetz. Cambridge: Harvard University.

de Vylder, Stephan. 1982. *Agriculture in Chains*. London: Zed Press.

World Bank. 1981. Bangladesh Hand Tubewells Project.

Wood, Geoffrey D. 1984. "Provision of Irrigation Services by the Landless—An Approach to Agrarian Reform in Bangladesh," *Agricultural Administration*, Vol. 17, pp. 55–80.

Yunus, M. 1983. *Group-Based Savings and Credit for the Rural Poor*. Grameen Bank, Dhaka, Bangladesh.

Table 3.1

IRRIGATION IN BANGLADESH

Area Irrigated
(in thousands of acres)

Method	1960/1	1969/70	1975/6	1980/1	1984/5 -plan-
MECHANIZED:					
Large Scale Systems	...	...	110	200	1,000
Low Lift Pumps (LLP)	70	640	1,313	1,400	2,000
Deep Tubewells (DTW)	0	120	152	550	1,500
Shallow Tubewells (STW)	0	90	31	220	1,600
Subtotal	70	850	1,606	2,370	6,100
MANUAL:					
Traditional Methods	940	1,340	1,000	1,200	1,000
Hand Tubewells (MOSTI)	0	0	20	60	150
Subtotal	940	1,340	1,020	1,260	1,150
TOTAL	1,010	2,190	2,626	3,630	7,250
Percentage of total arable land (a):	5%	10%	12%	16%	32%

Notes: ... data not available
(a) 22.5 million acres

Sources: 1960/1 & 1969/70: adapted from Ahmed (1976: 144).
1975/76: adapted from Hanratty (1983: 14, 17).
1980/81 and 1984/5: adapted from Howes (1984: 4) citing GOB: Medium Term Food Production Plan 12.28.

Table 3.2

NUMBER OF HAND-PUMP TUBEWELLS IN BANGLADESH
(1983 estimates)

Public Drinking Wells	600,000
Private Drinking Wells	300,000
Private Irrigation Wells	200,000
Total	1,100,000

Sources: Baumann & Fuller, 1984: 6.

Table 3.3

COVERAGE OF TUBEWELLS

Method	1975/76 (Actual)	1980/81 (Actual)	1984/85 (Target)
SHALLOW TUBEWELL			
Number of units	5,179	23,400	130,000
Acres per unit	6.0	9.4	12.3
Total acres	31,000	220,000	1,600,000
HAND TUBEWELL - MOSTI			
Number of units	40,000	120,000	500,000
Acres per unit	0.50	0.50	0.33
Total acres	20,000	60,000	150,000

Sources: Data for 1975/76 are from Hanratty (1983: 14,7). Other figures are cited by Howes (1984:4) from various government publications.

Table 3.4

CHARACTERISTICS OF TUBEWELLS

		Shallow Tubewell	MOSTI
1.	Pump type	Centrifugal pump	Hand-pump
2.	Power supply	Diesel 5-7 HP	Manual
3.	Well pipe: Diameter:	G.I. pipe 75 - 100 mm	G.I. pipe 40 mm
4.	Well depth	15 - 45 m	8 - 20 m
5.	Discharge	200 - 300 GPM	8 - 10 GPM
6.	Purchase cost*	Tk. 30,000	Tk. 1,750
7.	Installation cost*	Tk. 2,000	Tk. 50
8.	Total investment*	Tk. 32,000	Tk. 1,800
9.	Irrigation area*	10 acres	0.5 acres
10.	Investment cost/acre*	Tk. 3,200	Tk. 3,600
11.	Fuel & maintenance Tk./acre/season*	Tk. 600	Tk. 300
12.	Unskilled labour days/acre/season*	8	160
13.	Labour Costs Tk./acre/season	Tk. 80	Tk. 1,600
14.	Total running costs Tk./acre/season	Tk. 680	Tk. 1,900

* Average estimates; prices are estimated for the 1983 dry season, including taxes and subsidies. (US$1=Tk.25)

Table 3.5

THE UNICEF - IRDP MOSTI PROGRAMME 1975-79

Year		Target	Sales
1975/76		10,000	9,200
1976/77		20,000	22,000
1977/78		30,000	30,100
1978/79		30,000	26,450
	Total	90,000	87,770

Figure 3.1 Technology policy determinants diagram: Manual irrigation in Bangladesh

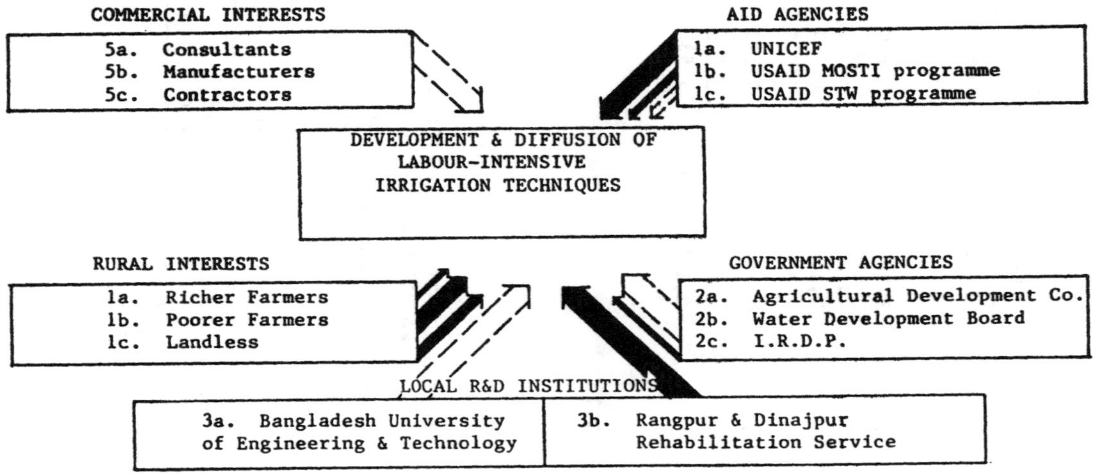

Note: The width of the arrow indicates the relative strength of a specific institution or interest group. A positive influence is shown by a solid arrow and a negative influence is shown by a broken arrow.

Table 3.6

GROWTH OF IRRIGATED AREA

(in thousands of acres)

Method		1969/70 Area	(%)	1980/81 Area	(%)	Increase
MANUAL METHODS						
Traditional	:	1,340		1,200		-(140)
MOSTI	:	0		60		60
Subtotal	:	1,340	(61)	1,260	(35)	-(80)
MECHANIZED METHODS	:	850	(39)	2,370	(65)	1,520
TOTAL	:	2,190	(100)	3,630	(100)	1,440

Sources: See Table 3.1

Table 3.7
IRRIGATION TECHNOLOGY POLICY
PAY-OFF MATRIX

positive benefits: ++
negative benefits: --

Interest Groups		Distribution of Benefits: Mechanized Irrigation	Distribution of Benefits: Manual Irrigation
1.	International Aid Agencies	++	--
2.	Irrigation Departments	+++	-
3a.	Mechanized R&D projects	+++	---
3b.	Appropriate R&D Projects	---	+++
4a.	Large Peasants	+++	-
4b.	Small Peasants	-	+++
4c.	Landless Peasants	+	+++
4d.	Rural Artisans/Workshops	+	+++
5a.	Installation Contractors	+++	---
5b.	Equipment Manufacturers	+++	---

Four

Changes in Small Farm Paddy Threshing Technology in Thailand and the Philippines

Bart Duff

I. INTRODUCTION

Threshing is the final operation in the production sequence. In most small-scale rice production systems, it is also the point where benefits are shared among farmers, labourers, landlords and creditors. Over long periods, sharing arrangements have been developed in most cultural systems which ensure partitioning of the crop among those whose resources (labour, land and capital) have produced it, including those within the community who have no access to land. The introduction of new technology tends to disrupt these arrangements and new systems of sharing emerge to replace older forms. As Hayami (1981) and Kikuchi (1979) have pointed out, innovations may raise production levels, but the gains often create pressures to redivide the crop shares.[1]

Seeking to maximize shares initiates a process of adjustment among those who own productive resources such as labour. The final equilibrium depends on such factors as the relative economic power or position which each group holds in the village or community, alternative employment opportunities, and the strength of established kinship relationships between groups. These factors in turn interact with economic variables in determining the speed and extent to which new threshing technologies are adopted.

In both Thailand and the Philippines there has been a rapid shift from traditional to mechanical threshing techniques over the past ten years. The technical basis for this change was the development and extension of the axial flow thresher by the International Rice Research Institute in the Philippines. The story of the machine's development and promotion through an international network of public institutions and private manufacturing enterprises provides the first major focus of this study. Of particular interest are the factors which persuaded the Institute to invest resources in engineering development activities.

A second theme examines the output and distributive effects of the mechanical thresher on farmers, hired labour and, through backward linkages, on employment and income in the nonagricultural sector. Included is an evaluation of the financial profitability of the thresher and how this has been affected by changing resource and product prices, utilization levels, the stock of machines and the institutional arrangements for contract services.

A third section examines policies and public sector programs which have affected acceptance and diffusion of the axial flow thresher. In addition to government intervention, we also examine the resource commitment by the International Rice Research Institute and attempt to evaluate the benefits from this investment in engineering design and development activities.

II. STUDY DESIGN

To evaluate the adoption patterns and the farm-level impact of the axial flow threshers, field surveys of thresher owners, users and non-users were undertaken at two sites in the Philippines and two sites in Thailand (figure 4.1). A total of 370 farmers were included in these studies. A broad profile of the respondents is given in table 4.1. In addition to farmers, a survey of 64 landless workers involved in threshing operations was conducted in the Philippines (Ebron and others, 1985). These special surveys were supplemented by interviews with thresher manufacturers (Mikkelsen, 1984), reports obtained from engineers (Khan, 1983; 1985), financial institutions (Reyes, 1985) and national and international organizations actively supporting agricultural engineering design and development activities.

III. DEVELOPMENT OF THE AXIAL FLOW THRESHER

IRRI Machinery Program

Beginning with special project funds in 1967, engineers at the International Rice Research Institute (IRRI) focused on the design of equipment specifically tailored for small rice farmers (Duff and others, 1981). The rationale for small, low-cost farm machinery was that private firms in most rice producing countries lacked viable designs and the resources to develop them. In addition, it was felt that the absence of suitable patent protection and incentives to invest in research and development activities made it unlikely the private sector would produce such designs in the short and medium run.

The fabrication of simple farm equipment in Third World countries is carried out by small and medium-scale companies, usually servicing a very localized market and using designs copied from competitors or from imported models. New innovations which demonstrate ready market acceptance and which are easily fabricated are quickly emulated by others. Unless the design is complex, uses unusual materials or methods in its fabrication, or has a tightly circumscribed market, there is little an innovator can do to protect the design from being copied or to capture or restrict the benefits from its use.

Public sector engineering R & D investments by national agencies and academic institutions in the Third World have a poor achievement record (Blackledge, 1974). In almost all cases, such efforts are out of touch with the needs of end users (small farmers). Conversely, reliance on imported equipment from the developed countries is often both expensive and technically inappropriate to the requirements of small two to five hectare rice farmers. Also, before the 1960s, markets for farm equipment were severely limited by the low productivity levels and low investment potential of small farms. Beginning in the late 1960s, biochemical technologies which raised yields substantially improved the productivity of cost-saving, output-increasing devices.

Early proponents of the IRRI engineering program also asserted that the rapid spread of modern varieties, with attendant increases in yields and expanded multiple cropping, stressed available human and animal power resources. Against this background it was argued that the use of mechanical power would complement land and water resources and supplement labour and animal power.

The objective of the IRRI program was to provide local manufacturers with technical support and equipment designs with strong commercial potential. The machines were designed to be fabricated using simple, labour intensive techniques, local materials and labour and to be operated and maintained with a minimum of training and mechanical infrastructure. Because of this commercial orientation, over nearly 10 years IRRI evolved an operational procedure which included assessment of farmer needs and specification of product design parameters followed by design, development, testing and industrial extension (figure 4.2). IRRI's global mandate meant addressing a very wide range of technical and socio-economic conditions, with the inherent danger of diluting the program's focus. At an early stage, therefore, a decision was made to design and develop the machinery for rice farmers with the investment capability to use mechanical innovations profitably. Lowland, irrigated farms were the initial target market.

The program also trained engineers from private firms and national agencies with whom the Institute collaborated in developing local extension programs. The ultimate goal was to institutionalize the design and development process in local agencies.[2] Major collaborative programs involving the placement of personnel and commitments of significant funding resources were established in Bangladesh, Thailand, India, Egypt, Pakistan, Burma, Indonesia and the Philippines.

The Axial Flow Thresher

Work on the design of threshing machines at IRRI began in 1967 (Khan, 1985). At the outset, development focused largely on conventional threshing concepts. In 1970, the investigation shifted to the axial flow principle (figure 4.3) which offered two distinct advantages over conventional concepts: (1) the machine could effectively handle wet materials; and (2) the spiral movement of material along the axis of the threshing drum produced a vigorous threshing action with extended exposure and a high separation efficiency. The concept also resulted in a compact mechanism requiring no complex parts or special materials (Ilyas, 1980). The axial flow concept appears to have originated in Japan (Kishida, 1985), although variations on this principle have been used for rice milling and cleaning equipment for many years and have more recently been extensively adapted for large combine harvesters in the United States, Canada, Australia and Western Europe.

A finished design was released to Filipino manufacturers in 1974. This was quickly modified and multiplied and, after a short period of debugging, rapidly became a major commercial product.The initial model had a capacity of about one ton per hour. It was mounted on rubber tires and was normally pulled to the threshing location by jeep or water buffalo (figure 4.4a). After a series of field studies in Central Luzon, the need for a lighter, more mobile unit for easy access to interior fields was identified and a portable version (figures 4.4b and 4.4c) was developed (Toquero and others, 1985; McMennamy and others, 1978).

Since 1976, the basic design has remained essentially unchanged. Refinements have been incorporated to improve cleaning and separation efficiency, increase capacity (Mongkoltanatas, 1985), extend utility for threshing wheat and corn (Khan, 1985), and tailor manufacturing requirements for local capabilities (Reddy and others, 1985b). By 1985 over 200 manufacturers in 18 countries entered production with the axial flow design.

IV. DISSEMINATION AND ADOPTION

Production of the Axial Flow Thresher

Statistics on the production and sale of the axial flow thresher are incomplete. There are, however, data available from the IRRI extension network which enumerate the production and sale of threshers produced by cooperating manufacturers in several countries. These data underestimate the real volume sold because the design was freely copied by numerous firms having no formal association with the IRRI program. It is estimated that this undercounting might be as high as 50 percent in the Philippines and Thailand. Information presented in figure 4.5 illustrates the rapid take-off of the design in the Philippines and, with a lag of about one year, in Thailand. Sales rose steadily in the Philippines and Thailand until 1982 when world economic conditions dampened economic growth and raised inflation levels. Devaluation in both countries raised the cost of imported parts and the cost of threshing equipment. Despite the unfavorable investment climate, manufacturers in both countries continued to produce and farmers continued to buy the threshers in significant numbers in the mid-1980s. Fewer, but significant, numbers of the machines have also been sold in Egypt, Indonesia, Sri Lanka, Nepal, and India. Prototypes have been shipped and/or produced in Honduras, Pakistan, Ivory Coast, Ghana, Colombia and Mexico. By 1984, nearly 55,000 units had been built by cooperating firms.

Adoption Patterns

Manufacturers were quick to recognize the profit potential of the axial flow thresher. The design spread rapidly from a handful of firms in 1975 to over 70 widely dispersed firms in the Philippines in 1985.[3] The number of firms participating in the IRRI program in Thailand was fewer, but the 20 companies fabricating the thresher in 1985 were larger and had more highly developed marketing channels than their Filipino counterparts.

Philippines

Mechanical threshers have been used in the Central Luzon region since the 1920s (Kikuchi and others, 1979). These machines, locally known as "tilyadoras", were similar to the McCormick stationary thresher used in the United States at the turn of the century. The threshers were owned by large haciendas and used as a mechanism for consolidating the rice crop at harvest time. All tenants were required to thresh their crop with the machine at which time the landlord extracted his share. Technically, the "tilyadora" is a heavy, cumbersome machine, requiring harvesting, consolidation and stacking of the crop several weeks before threshing. Labor requirements were high and the recovery efficiency of the design was low. The machine also performed poorly when threshing wet paddy.

With land reform in 1972, farmers in Central Luzon reverted to hand threshing, largely by hired and exchange labour (Ebron, 1984). In other areas of the Philippines, paddy threshing remained largely a manual operation, although a number of locally fabricated, small threshing machines were used in Bicol and Mindanao as early as the 1960s. During the late 1960s and early 1970s, expansion in irrigation facilities coupled with widespread adoption of short season varieties increased double cropping and raised yields. These changes also increased harvesting and threshing labour requirements, although less than proportionate to the increase in production.

Table 4.2 illustrates adoption patterns of the axial flow thresher in Laguna province. Yields doubled from 1965 to 1978. Per hectare labour for harvesting and threshing increased slightly until 1978 which, with increasing yields and a constant crop share, meant labour productivity also increased. With the introduction of the large axial flow threshers in 1975, labour inputs decreased in 1978 but returned to near pre-thresher levels in 1981.

Demand for axial flow threshers in the Philippines is divided between the portable machine (found principally on Panay Island) and the larger version which is widely used for contract work in Central Luzon and Laguna (figure 4.6). A few portable machines were acquired in Laguna, but principally by individual farmers whose highest priority was threshing their own crop. Contract work was a secondary consideration (Bordado, 1984).

IRRI introduced the portable axial flow thresher to Iloilo province in 1976 (Juarez and others, 1981). In this area all threshing had been done using a traditional foot treading method. Introduction of the improved varieties, followed by the development of irrigation set the stage for the mechanical thresher (figure 4.7). Use of the new varieties in Iloilo increased both yields and incomes, thus raising the investment potential of farmers. Irrigation permitted double cropping which tightened the time constraint between crops and raised incomes further. Similar to the pattern found in Laguna, portable thresher owners in Iloilo were individual farmers whose first concern was using the machines on their own farms.

In villages where machines were purchased, adoption rates were rapid and nearly complete. Since 1978, off-farm use for contract services has also become important in Iloilo. Thresher owners in Iloilo, Laguna and Central Luzon all used their machines in custom threshing operations (figure 4.8). Portable machines were used for contract work less than the larger units.

In the Philippines, almost all threshers were produced by a relatively large number of small firms selling in a localized regional market. By the early 1980s, manufacturing the larger axial flow threshers was in the hands of two or three firms.

Thailand

Introduced into Thailand in 1975, the axial flow design was quickly adapted to local conditions by manufacturers who aggressively promoted the machine in the irrigated rice producing areas (Pathnopas, 1980). Adoption by farmers was also rapid. The Thai market was exclusively for larger units which were used almost entirely for contract work (Krishnasreni, 1981; Mongkoltanatas, 1985). The smaller portable version was tried in 1977 but not accepted. Instead, manufacturers increased the size and capacity of the thresher until output capacity was three to four times that of the original design. Because most threshing is done on a contract basis, improved mobility was also a major aim of the adaptation process. Today the threshing mechanism is often mounted on the chassis of a second-hand truck or car to permit rapid movement over appreciable distances.

By 1975, farmers in Thailand had already widely adopted two and four-wheel tractors for land preparation and low-lift pumps for supplemental irrigation (Sukharomana, 1984). Spread of the high yielding varieties was, however, limited largely because of poor grain quality, a factor of great importance in the Thai export market. Rice farms in the Central Plain of Thailand also were larger than their counterparts in the Philippines, and there was continued growth in the area under cultivation (Binswanger, 1982).

Ownership and Use Patterns

In both Thailand and the Philippines, owning a thresher was not a requirement for using it. Contract rental service has long been a feature of mechanical land preparation in both countries. Hence, many thresher owners purchased the machines not only for their own farm use, but as a source of revenue.

Figure 4.8 presents the breakdown of thresher use between own-farm and contract services. For larger threshers, contract income was clearly important and likely a decisive factor in the machine. In both countries, a majority of the owners were farmers (table 4.1), although 45 percent of the Thai threshers in Chaoengsao province and 40 percent of the machines in the Philippine sample were owned by landless respondents indicating a significant number were owned by non-farmers. Of the 92 thresher owners interviewed in both countries, more than 70 percent indicated they had acquired the machines on a cash basis (table 4.3). In rainfed areas more of the machines were purchased through formal and informal credit arrangements, but both the yields and the size of rainfed farms tended to be lower suggesting a lower investment potential compared to irrigated farms. Credit was also a more important requirement for rainfed compared to irrigated farms in the Philippines.

Utilization of Threshers

While data are not available to examine precise thresher utilization patterns, it has been possible to construct a descriptive profile of both use and contract rates from field studies (Juarez, 1984; Pathnopas, 1980).

Initially, with few threshers available and no demonstrated performance record, annual use levels were low (figure 4.9). Contract terms were on a cash basis of $3.8 to $4.8/ton in Thailand and 5 to 9 percent of the gross output threshed in the Philippines. Annual use levels for the large axial flow thresher increased steadily in the Philippines except in 1978-79 when fuel prices rose significantly. Use levels for portable threshers have remained nearly constant, reinforcing the earlier observation that portable machines are used primarily for threshing the farmer's own crop, with contract work a subsidiary consideration. Using smaller machines is also more localized at the village level, and owners do not solicit threshing contracts over the wide areas covered by the larger threshers.

In Thailand, as machines increased in size, capacity, and mobility, annual utilization increased sharply. Contract rates have not changed appreciably since 1976.[4]

In both countries, the increasing stock of threshers has begun to dampen further increases in annual use. Competition for available threshing contracts has also mitigated further increases in contract rates despite the fact that the investment cost of the machine and fuel prices have more than doubled since 1975.

V. MECHANICAL THRESHERS AND LABOUR

In developing countries, an important policy objective is providing sufficient agricultural employment to absorb the growing number of people living in rural areas. Rapid adoption of threshing machines could critically affect employment opportunities for several reasons. Threshing is one of the most labour intensive operations. Furthermore, it is usually carried out by hired labourers who belong to the poorest segment of rural society—landless and marginal farm households in the Philippines.

Payment for threshing has traditionally been harvest shares. This enabled landless labourers to participate to some extent in the benefits of yield increases accompanying the diffusion of the new rice technology. The adoption of threshing machines could therefore seriously reduce the employment and earnings of landless labourers. On the other hand, theoretically, threshers could have a positive effect on employment by reducing turn-around time and thereby increasing cropping intensity.

Field research in Thailand and the Philippines does not support the claim of higher cropping intensity or reduced turn-around time. Cropping intensity primarily depends on irrigation and water control. Intensive field studies by Toquero and others (1985) support the findings of Juarez (1984) on the lack of intensity effects from mechanized threshing (table 4.4). While farmers using threshers complete their threshing earlier, they do not plant the following crop before others in the same village. Time of planting is closely related to water availability and the need to synchronize crop establishment with others to minimize problems of rodents and pests.

Manual harvesting and threshing require approximately 30 labour days per hectare. The large axial flow thresher performs both threshing and winnowing, and although about four labour days per hectare are required to operate the machine, total labour requirements for post-production operations fall to 20 days per hectare, a decline of about 33 percent (Toquero, 1985).

Results from surveys in Nueva Ecija, Philippines, show post-production labour on mechanized farms is 25 percent lower than on farms in which the paddy was manually threshed (table 4.5). Disaggregated into family and hired labour the data reveal that use of family labour was marginally higher on mechanized farms compared to non-mechanized farms. Hired labour, which comes mainly from landless households, declined by 31 percent. This is consistent with results of a multivariate regression analysis which revealed threshing mechanization as the most important factor accounting for farm differences in post-production labour (Sison and others, 1985). Output had a positive impact on labour use. Its effect, however, was small compared to that of mechanization.

Farmers in both Thailand and the Philippines employed a range of threshing methods. In Iloilo, foot treading from an elevated platform was the most prevalent method. In Laguna, hand beating over a bamboo frame was used. In Thailand, driving water buffalo or a tractor over the crop was used to separate grain from the straw. Winnowing was normally performed with a straw basket or wooden fanning mill.

Labour requirements for traditional methods differed markedly from mechanized threshing. The highest labour requirements and lowest labour productivity were in foot treading (Iloilo) and buffalo treading (Thailand). As shown in table 4.6, the mechanical thresher increased labour productivity by a factor of two to four in Thailand and up to nine times in the Philippines.

On an aggregate basis the mechanical thresher reduced labour requirements by about 25 percent in the threshing operation (Smith and others, 1983). For the Philippines, the impact appears to have been most sharply felt by hired labour. The evidence from Thailand is not clear. Less hired labour is used in the traditional threshing operations than in the Philippines and the overall estimate is that mechanical threshers reduced both family and hired labour by 10 percent (Pongsrikul, 1983).

Economy-wide Employment Impact

For the Philippines, Ahammed and Herdt (1985) used a general equilibrium model with an input/output core to estimate the nationwide employment implications of increasing rice production using alternative production methods. If manual threshing were used to increase rice production by 1 percent, employment in the agricultural sector would increase by 16,000 man-years. The employment effect would be 22 percent lower (12,400) if portable threshers were used.

Ahammed and Herdt estimated the impact of alternative threshing methods on non-agricultural employment by integrating backward and forward linkages. Domestically produced threshers would generate employment in the manufacturing sector. Increased rice output would have a positive effect on employment through consumption linkages. Taking all sectors into consideration, substitution of manual with mechanized threshing would reduce the employment generating potential of increased rice production by about 7 percent (table 4.7).

Although Ahammed and Herdt pointed out that ignoring non-agricultural sectors might result in over estimating the labour displacing effect of machines, it is important to bear in mind that the poorest segment of society lives in the rural areas.

Mode of Payment

Payment for threshing has changed in Thailand and the Philippines since the introduction of the thresher. In Thailand, wage payments to individuals have shifted to cash payments to thresher owners. Rates were $7.0 to $9.6/ton for tractor or animal methods and $3.8 to $4.8/ton when using a threshing machine. As noted earlier the rate for machine threshing has not increased since 1980, largely because more threshers are vying for contract services.

In the Philippines, more complex adjustments took place. Farmers using manual methods previously paid a combined share of the crop for harvesting, threshing and cleaning, usually about 12 to 17 percent. With the introduction of the thresher, the share formerly paid to threshing labour shifted to thresher owners and operators. The arrangements differ slightly between regions, but the normal fee was 3 percent of the crop. Under this rearrangement in sharing rates, labour received a smaller portion of total output. Combined with increases in the agricultural labour force and increasing ownership and operational costs for threshing equipment, there has been a decline in labour's share from one-eighth to one-twentieth of the crop in some areas of Central Luzon.

Since the introduction of the machines, threshing fees have risen in the Philippines and fallen slightly in Thailand.The crucial issue is how the introduction of threshing machines has affected threshing labour, particularly hired labour.

Landless Labor

Most hired labour for post-production operations in the Philippines comes from the landless class, estimated to be as high as 20 percent of rural households in 1984 (Ebron and others, 1985). Workers from the landless class contribute over 50 percent of the labour used for harvesting and threshing. Add small farmers with less than 0.5 hectare of land, and over 80 percent of annual income for landless workers and small farmers is derived from post-production operations.

A study of landless workers in a thresher-using area of Central Luzon revealed several non-income benefits of threshers (Ebron, 1984). Mechanized threshing considerably reduced the arduousness of post production operations. The lighter nature of the work also enabled more women and children to participate in post production activities compared to the pre-thresher period (figure 4.10). Most of the labourers stated, however, that labour was in excess supply at harvest time and that they feared increased mechanization would further reduce earnings.

Wage Rates

In countries with surplus agricultural labour, the introduction and use of machines normally exerts a downward pressure on real wage rates. In the Philippines, the agricultural labour force is projected to grow at 1 percent per annum (David, 1983) while in Thailand it has expanded at about 1.5 percent over the past 15 years (Binswanger, 1982). In the Philippines, real wages in agriculture have been declining and were significantly lower in 1985 than during the mid-1960s. During the same period, the real price of agricultural machines rose with the largest increase during the past five years (figure 4.11).

Evidence describing agricultural wages in Thailand show real wages increased steadily during the late 1960s and through the 1970s (figure 4.12).

There was a decline during the early 1980s when the global economic recession dampened growth.The upward trend appears, however, to have resumed in the mid-1980s.

For the Philippines, it could be argued that seasonality in agricultural wages cannot be ignored. Labour shortages at harvest time might co-exist with a labour surplus during the rest of the year. Data on harvesting and threshing wages in Laguna shows real wages increased prior to the introduction of the thresher (that is, up to 1975), and labour demand at harvest time was increasing more rapidly than supply. The widespread adoption of mechanized threshing since 1978 was accompanied, however, by a steady decline in real wages which in 1981 were below the level prevailing in 1965 (table 4.8).

The decline in real wages for threshing in the Philippines should not, however, be too closely tied to the introduction of threshing machinery. Real wages also fell for other operations in the rice production system and in the industrial sector during this period. The implication drawn from analysis of the wage data is that expansion in employment opportunities has not kept pace with the rapid increase in the agricultural labour force. In addition, while adoption of mechanized threshers may not be directly linked with the decline in real wages, substitution of capital for labour under a falling real wage clearly reduced the income from threshing of workers in rice post-production activities.

Income Shares

Using the concept of factor shares in which the total value of production is partitioned according to the contribution of individual production factors, it is possible to distinguish change in the distribution of income for farms which used the thresher from non-user farms. In Laguna, use of the thresher reduced labour earnings by 6 percent overall (table 4.9). The share of earnings for unskilled (hired/landless) labour, however declined from 33 to 23 percent. The major beneficiaries have been the increased shares to capital and to the farm operator.

In both Thailand and the Philippines, use of mechanical threshers reduced labour requirements significantly from traditional levels. The effect on labour was different in each country. In Thailand, with an expanding land frontier, a small landless worker class, and a rising real wage in agriculture, using threshers was both economically efficient and timely. Rice production increased at an annual rate of 3.8% during the three decades from 1955. Nearly 75 percent of this increase resulted from an expansion in areas under rice cultivation (Barker and others, 1985). During this same period, the available land per agricultural worker increased at nearly 2 percent per year. Under these circumstances, the introduction of threshers along with tractors and water pumps increased labour productivity, sustained increases in rice production and had little or no inimical impact on the level or distribution of rural incomes.

In the Philippines, growth in rice output since 1967 averaged nearly 4 percent, with nearly 80 percent of the increase attributable to higher yields and the remainder to area expansion, primarily increases in paddy land under irrigation (Barker and others, 1985). While nominal wages rose, the real wage rate in agriculture fell continuously since the 1960s. This was paralleled by a fall in the land/labour ratio caused by an increase in the agricultural labour force and little or no growth in cultivated areas. Under these circumstances, using mechanical threshers limited increases in rural employment opportunities and decreased hired labour income. In a succeeding section, we review government policies which made adoption of threshing equipment attractive to owners and farmer-users in spite of falling real wages.

VI. PRIVATE PROFITABILITY

In this section the financial or private profitability of the axial flow thresher is examined from two perspectives. The first is the farmer who does not own but uses the thresher on a contract basis. In this instance, it is the reduction in cost and increased output from using the machine compared to traditional techniques which determines the level of benefits. The second perspective is that of the machine owner. The contract rate, annual use level, investment cost, price of fuel and the price of paddy rice determine the rate of return on investment in the thresher.

Yield Effects

An important benefit of thresher use is that it enables the farmer to recover a higher proportion of the yield from the harvest. Theoretically, manual threshing could be equally thorough. In practice, however, labourers tend to terminate the threshing operation prematurely. Grain remaining with the straw is then appropriated by gleaners, usually elderly relatives or children. Gleaning is highly lucrative and there are claims that diligent gleaners can appropriate up to 10 percent of the harvest (Goodell, 1979). In this situation the thresher is a substitute for additional labour supervisors (Smith, 1983).

In addition to losses caused by labourers working without adequate supervision, the thresher has certain technical advantages over manual threshing methods. It reduces losses caused by repeated handling of both threshed and unthreshed materials. Winnowing and cleaning are an integral part of the axial flow thresher.[5] The effect of these factors has been meticulously measured in on-farm experiments comparing handling, threshing, and winnowing losses from manual and mechanized methods (table 4.10). There is consistent evidence of a reduction in grain losses ranging from 0.5 to 1.6 percent or a net savings over traditional threshing of 0.7 to 6 percent of the total yield. In Thailand, the yield effect of reduced losses was insignificant compared with tractor and buffalo treading. Grain quality under the two techniques was also compared (Toquero, 1985). The only significant differences when using the machine were a 2 percent decline in impurities and a slight increase in the percentage of fermented grain.

Contract Services

Farmers renting threshers are concerned with the comparative costs of traditional and mechanical methods. Other reasons frequently cited for using the machines included lower losses (in the Philippines), less supervision of labour, less handling prior to threshing, and quicker completion of the threshing task. Of these, only the yield effects and contract rates are included in the analysis of financial returns to thresher users.

Table 4.11 lists harvesting and threshing contract rates in the Philippines and Thailand. In the Philippines sharing rates for both traditional methods and machines did not change in Iloilo between 1978 and 1983. In Laguna province, rates for machine threshing increased from 7 to 9 percent and manual threshing was virtually eliminated.

Of particular interest are the *increases* in total shares for all combinations of harvesting *and* mechanical threshing in Laguna, Iloilo and Nueva Ecija. Farmers using threshing machines continued to pay labour at or above the traditional rate for cutting and hauling the crop (harvesting). In Laguna, the harvester's share increased from 6.9 to 10 percent in 1983. Comparing traditional and mechanized threshing, there was an overall increase in the total harvesting/threshing share from 12.5 to 17 percent in 1978 and from 12.5 to 19 percent in 1983. No similar changes in sharing arrangements were observed in Iloilo, and only a 1.4 percent difference existed between traditional and mechanized systems in Nueva Ecija.

Part of the explanation for Laguna farmers' acceptance of higher post-production costs lies in the increased output from using the thresher. A second reason not explicitly obvious in table 4.11 is the rapid urbanization over the past decade of Laguna province, which is close to Metropolitan Manila. By 1985, most traditional threshing had disappeared in Laguna as workers moved to jobs in nonagricultural industries.

Charges for traditional threshing techniques tend to be higher than machine rates in Thailand. The major difference in the financial profitability of the thresher between the two countries is that Thai farmers benefited primarily from the reduced costs of machine threshing compared to traditional methods while Filipino farmers have had the added advantage of reducing grain losses.

The analysis presented in table 4.12 indicates that Thai farmers using the axial flow thresher are able to increase revenues by $2.84/ton compared to traditional methods or $62 per farm, per season.

In the Philippines, the total cost of harvesting and machine threshing is higher in Laguna and lower in Iloilo than traditional methods. The cost of machine threshing increased from 1978 to 1983 in both regions. Despite higher costs, however, farmers renting the machine were able to realize an increase in revenue of $2.23 to $5.79/ton because of increased grain yields and/or reduced costs. The advantage over traditional threshing narrowed slightly in 1983 in Laguna when contract rates for machines increased from 7 percent to 9 percent.

Thresher Owners

For thresher owners, private profitability is determined not only by the contract rate, but also annual amortization charges and operational costs plus the level of use. Table 4.13 summarizes the information on axial flow thresher cost and use patterns for Thailand and the Philippines.

In Thailand, machines thresh nearly three times as much grain per year as similar units in the Philippines. Despite higher initial investment costs and lower contract charges, these machines have very short payback periods and high benefit/cost ratios. The evidence presented earlier in figure 4.9 indicates annual use has begun to level off at about 400 tons/year. In the future, as more threshers enter the contract market, it is likely that the high profitability evident in the present analysis will decline.

Thresher owners in the Philippines have lower use levels resulting in longer payback periods and lower benefit/cost ratios than found in Thailand. Portable threshers in Laguna showed low returns in 1978. This observation was made, however, shortly after introduction when use levels were quite low. Both the portable and large machines operating in Laguna improved financial performance in 1983. The portable thresher operating in irrigated areas in Iloilo gave very high returns in 1978 although machines in rainfed areas were not as attractive, primarily because of low annual use levels.

The comparative performance of threshers in both countries is summarized in figure 4.13. While not shown in the figure for Thailand, breakeven levels have increased since 1978 as machines have become larger and initial investment costs have increased (Mongkoltanatas, 1985). For the Philippines, average annual use levels were sufficient to ensure profitability, although financial performance differed by region and by machine type. With the exception of irrigated farms in Iloilo, threshers in Thailand have been better investments than those in the Philippines.

It is clear from this analysis of empirical use and cost data that the axial flow threshers have been profitable from both a user's and owner's point of view. This profitability has been a major factor in inducing widespread sale of threshers and rapid expansion in the stock of machines in each country. In the next section we examine whether government policies affected the rapid diffusion of threshers.

VII. PUBLIC SECTOR INTERVENTION

As noted, the mechanization of rice threshing is privately profitable in both Thailand and the Philippines. The rapid growth rate in the adoption of the IRRI threshing technology supports this finding. At this juncture, we ask—do government policies and programmes make mechanization artificially profitable? If so, which policies?

Table 4.14 lists the policies associated with farm mechanization currently active in the Philippines and Thailand. In both countries, there is little evidence of direct government intervention affecting decisions to develop, purchase or adopt rice threshers or most other forms of agricultural mechanization. In neither country was there a clearly articulated policy relating to technology design or transfer of farm equipment.

Although there are few specific policies to promote mechanization in general or rice threshing in particular, government was influential indirectly, through policies affecting trade, exchange rates, credit, and interest rates. Price supports for rice in the Philippines and levees in Thailand also indirectly affected the profitability of mechanization. Each of these policies influences the relative costs of capital and labour.

In the Philippines, the World Bank has provided a series of four credit lines since 1965 totaling US$76 million (Reyes and others, 1985). These loans, however, benefited primarily those purchasing four-wheel tractors used in both sugar and rice production. To a lesser degree, imported two-wheel walking tractors for rice cultivation were also financed during the early years of this programme. Beginning in 1975, however, most two-wheel units were made locally and purchased with farmer funds (see table 4.15). Very few paddy threshers were acquired through formal financing arrangements (Juarez, 1984).

In Thailand, the government has taken a generally laissez faire attitude towards small farm mechanization. There have been no formal credit programmes to finance rice threshers, although most dealers provide installment credit to purchasers, although at commercial rates (Chancellor, 1983). Thai farmers also utilize commercial bank credit more often than Filipino farmers purchasing threshers (table 4.16). Farmers in the Philippines use more informal credit facilities or finance the machines from private resources compared with thresher owners in Thailand.

VIII. PUBLIC INVESTMENT IN ENGINEERING RESEARCH AND DEVELOPMENT

The axial flow thresher design was the result of development activities conducted by the International Rice Research Institute (IRRI).The transfer of this technology was also strongly supported by the extension and training activities of the Institute.

Limited social cost analysis by Smith (1984) and Sukharomana (1983) suggests that if the total impact of the costs and benefits from using the thresher were quantified, the design would produce a net social benefit in both Thailand and the Philippines, although in each case, especially the Philippines, this conclusion depends on how the incomes of different groups are weighted.

IRRI's provision of 'free innovation' lowers the price of machinery relative to labour. If private manufacturers had shouldered the development costs, these would undoubtedly have been passed onto the consumer in higher market prices for threshers. This may have reduced or even eliminated its competitive edge over traditional threshing. Given each country's tariff structure, it is highly unlikely private manufacturers would have been willing to invest resources in the development of the thresher. Even after the latest tariff reforms in the Philippines, the effective protection rate (EPR) on agricultural machinery (13.7 percent) is low relative to EPRs on motor vehicles (27 percent) and consumer goods (43 percent). This diverts scarce capital resources away from machinery development towards import substitution in consumer goods and automobiles.

This effect is reinforced by poor enforcement of patents in each country. In addition, the design, though costly to develop, is extremely simple and therefore easy to copy. This makes it difficult for private entrepreneurs to capture the gains from innovation.

At a time when the labour absorptive performance of domestic manufacturing has been disappointing and labour demand from the Middle East is approaching the saturation point, should IRRI be developing machinery which reduces labour demand in the agricultural sector? This question cannot be answered until the efficiency and equity effects of threshers have been more accurately quantified. Futhermore, IRRI's machinery development programme is oriented globally: towards rice growing areas in general and not towards conditions prevailing in particular countries. Even within South East Asia, socio economic conditions vary markedly from country to country. In Thailand where the percentage of landless households is negligible, the efficiency/equity conflict is far less serious than in the Philippines as the labour displaced in Thailand comes from farming households which benefit from the greater efficiency of mechanized threshing.

Under a laissez faire policy, the theory of induced innovation predicts that machinery development will arise, without government intervention, when relative factor price ratios are sufficiently favorable to capital. Under these conditions few equity problems arise. Overall, however, it appears government support of labour-displacing machinery development and purchase is warranted only under rare circumstances. If timely innovation is impeded by distortions in the incentive structure, a gradual dismantling of distortions may be a more effective long run strategy than public support for agricultural machinery. This finding will, however, clearly be dependent on the impact of the machinery on costs and benefits.

A secondary benefit from the IRRI small machinery program has been its impact on research and development of manufacturers participating in the industrial extension program. These companies are given design information, training and technical support in the initial stages of fabricating IRRI designed equipment. A question frequently asked is whether dependency on outside assistance lowers innovation and inventiveness of participants compared with firms that are not in the program.

In a carefully researched study, Mikkelsen (1984) gathered information from a sample of 56 metal fabricating firms throughout the Philippines. Twenty-seven firms were participants in the IRRI Industrial Extension program; the remainder were not. By using the number of patents and the number of modifications made as a measure of innovativeness, Mikkelsen demonstrated that far from becoming dependent on IRRI, these firms exercised considerable initiative and ingenuity to enhance their products.

Because IRRI does not provide exclusive manufacturing rights to a single firm, each cooperator in the IRRI program attempted to improve and differentiate his machine from others fabricating the identical IRRI design. During 1975 to 1983, 18 firms in the IRRI program filed patent applications. Over 50 percent of these were utility patents consisting of modifications to the original IRRI design. Only two were for inventions. In contrast to the nonparticipants in the sample this represented a significantly higher level of innovativeness. In addition, the longer firms were associated with the IRRI program, the more modifications were introduced and the more research and development activities were internalized. According to Mikkelson, " . . . we find that IRRI research has augmented private invention without reducing it, and possibly even increased the level of invention in its cooperating firms."

IX. CONCLUSIONS

The development and extension of the axial flow thresher has clearly been a success in the Philippines and Thailand from the point of view of private profitability to farmers, as judged by its widespread adoption. Its social effects have also been unambiguously positive in Thailand; but in the Philippines its positive effects on output have been accompanied by reduced employment and labour's share of output.

What lessons can be learned from this case study of engineering innovation?

General Findings

1. Proper engineering design and development activities require a sustained commitment of resources with a well focused and identified need.
2. An integrated approach involving market assessment, product planning, design, testing and extension is needed for innovations to be successfully marketed.
3. Rural hardware development requires a clear perception of farm-level production and post-harvest systems.
4. The most viable environment for engineering R & D will be countries in which sustained agricultural development is underway; where lack of patent or legal instruments acts as a disincentive to initiatives by individual firms; where the farm equipment industry is fragmented, composed of small,

undercapitalized firms and where the social opportunity costs of resources are in reasonable balance with private prices.

Specific Findings for Axial Flow Thresher

1. The purchase and use of the thresher has been most successful in Thailand, followed to a lesser degree by its acceptance in the Philippines. Larger farm size, an expanding land frontier and the relatively higher opportunity costs of labour have made the machine an attractive investment and a viable alternative to traditional threshing in Thailand.

2. The major incentive for adopting the thresher is the effect it has on costs. Evidence from the Philippines indicates some increase in yields through lower grain losses. In the Philippines, the major source of savings has been the reduction in harvesting-threshing shares formerly paid to labour. Landless labour has been reduced slightly, although the participation rates for women and children have increased following introduction of the thresher.

3. The private profitability of the thresher is very high in both countries particularly in the early years following release of the design. Over time, the contract rates charged for mechanical threshing have stabilized at an equilibrium level approximating the cost of traditional alternatives available in each country.

4. Adoption of the axial flow design by private manufacturers was rapid in both countries, a result of the IRRI intensive extension effort to demonstrate and promote the design and to provide technical assistance and training to firms cooperating with the program.

5. Individual manufacturers have been quick to innovate and modify the design, principally to differentiate it from similar machines produced by other firms. This process has stimulated a higher level of inventiveness and innovation among cooperating firms compared to noncooperators.

6. There is little evidence of direct government intervention in the farm machinery industry in either Thailand or the Philippines. However, the indirect effect of policies on foreign exchange rates, interest rates, tariffs on fuels and imported parts and the availability of credit have had little effect on the social profitability of the threshers, although there is evidence of a significant divergence between private and social costs of the machines. Policy instruments have subsidized threshers in the Philippines considerably more than in Thailand.

7. It would be conjectural to speculate whether the axial flow or a similar design would have emerged in the absence of formal research and development work conducted at IRRI. It is highly unlikely that a design as efficient or so widely adopted would have resulted from private sector initiatives within the same period. The evident lack of incentives and support for private investment in research and development on small farm machinery would have delayed induced development of such a machine for many years.

The axial flow thresher is a clear case of a viable product resulting from a well focused, integrated engineering design and development program with high accountability. Unfortunately, the result is an exception among publicly supported industrial development institutions operating in the Third World.

The evidence in this chapter is not itself sufficient to conclude that the support of public engineering development programs is warranted. In the case of IRRI, funds allocated to engineering also had a high opportunity cost in terms of other research endeavors such as genetic improvement, disease and insect control, water management and training. Futhermore, the IRRI engineering program has produced other designs which have not had the same commercial success as the axial flow thresher. If the cost of these projects were aggregated into an overall return to the IRRI machinery program, benefit/cost levels would be substantially lower than those of the axial flow thresher examined in isolation.

NOTES

The author gratefully acknowledges the research support and data provided by Dr. Fleurdeliz Juarez of the IRRI Agricultural Economics Department whose own research on rice threshing technology comprises an important share of the contemporary literature on the topic. Ms. Leonarda Ebron and Renu Pathnopas contributed substantially to the data base used in the report and to the impact study on mechanical threshers and employment in the Philippines and Thailand. The present analysis also draws liberally from an earlier report prepared by Smith and Duff (1984) which examines the efficiency of mechanical threshing and its impact on both productivity and equity in the Philippine setting. Ms. Smith's contribution is a substantial one.

1. The details of these investigations are reported in Y. Hayami and others (1981).

2. The process described briefly here closely parallels that enunciated by Hayami and Ruttan (1985) in which they describe technology transfer as a three phase process. The first phase is a simple transfer of materials, for example, tractors, combine harvesters, etc., in which local industry plays little or no role except to assemble and service the machines. In the second phase, designs are transferred from one country to another in the form of blueprints or prototypes. The third and most mature state involves transfer, through development of human capital, the capacity to design and develop technologies tailored specifically to localized needs. The IRRI program targeted the second and third stages of this process. In a 10-year period, the program made available designs aimed at local markets and crafted to local manufacturing capabilities. The program operated through national institutions. Both short and long term training were combined with ongoing technical support at both the institutional and the individual firm level. Over a 10 to 20 year horizon, the objective was to develop indigenous skills and institutionalize the capacity to continue and extend design and development activities.

3. IRRI's policy was not to provide exclusive manufacturing rights to any firm. This arrangement allowed the Institute to minimize the risk that a viable product would not become commercialized because of management or marketing problems within a single firm. It also fostered competition among firms which resulted in better quality and lower pricing to farmers. Lastly, the policy helped to initiate a

process of innovation and a commitment to design and development within individual firms (Mikkelsen, 1984) which improved existing products and produced new ones.

4. The value of the contract has increased in both countries as yields increased. There is not, however, a direct relationship between yield and the time required to thresh a crop. Higher yields require less threshing time per ton of threshed output than low yields.

5. Several versions of the thresher exist. In the larger models, threshing, cleaning, and winnowing are standard features. In the portable models, the cleaning and winnowing mechanisms can be added as options.

REFERENCES

Ahammed, C.S., and R.W. Herdt. 1985. A General Equilibrium Analysis of the Effects of Rice Mechanization in the Philippines. In *Modelling the Impact of Small Farm Mechanization*, Philippine Institute for Development Studies Monograph Series No. 5. Philippine Institute for Development Studies and International Rice Research Institute.

Barker, R., and R.W. Herdt. 1985. *The Rice Economy of Asia*. Resources for the Future, International Rice Research Institute. Baltimore: Johns Hopkins University Press.

Bernas, L. 1985. Power Tiller Manufacturing in the Philippines. In *Small Farm Equipment for Developing Countries.* U.S. Agency for International Development/ IRRI, Los Banos, Laguna, Philippines.

Binswanger, H.P. 1982. Agricultural Mechanization: a Comparative Historical Perspective. Paper presented at Agricultural Development Council Conference on Mechanization of Small-Scale Farms—Economics and Social Implications, Hangzhou, China.

Binswanger, H., and V. Rutton. 1981. *Induced Innovation and Agricultural Development*. Baltimore: Johns Hopkins University Press.

Blackledge, J. 1974. *The Industrial Research Institute in a Developing Country: A Comparative Analysis.* Colorado: Denver Research Institute.

Bordado, G.J. 1984. Factors Affecting the Adoption of Mechanical Threshers in Laguna, Philippines, M. Sc. in Ag. Economics, U.P. at Los Banos. June.

Chancellor, W. J. 1983. *The Sustainability of Mechanization in Thailand*, The Consequences of Small Rice Farm Mechanization Project, Working Paper no. 98. IRRI.

David, C.C. 1983. *Government Policies and Farm Mechanization in the Philippines*, The Consequences of Small Rice Farm Mechanization Project, Working Paper no. 95. IRRI.

David, C.C. 1985. An Analysis of Recent Philippine Rice Trends. Agricultural Economics Department, IRRI. Mimeo.

Duff, B., and A.U. Khan. 1981. Rice Mechanization on Small Farms in Asia. Paper presented at the 1981 Winter Meetings of the American Society of Agricultural Engineers, December 14-18, Palmer House, Chicago.

Ebron, L.Z. 1984. Changes in Harvesting-threshing Labor Arrangements in Nueva Edija, M. Sc. thesis in Rural Sociology, University of the Philippines at Los Banos. May.

Ebron, L.Z., G. Castillo, and P. Kaiser. 1985. "Changes in Harvesting-Threshing Arrangements and Landless Labourers," *Journal of Philippine Development*, Vol. XII, No. 1.

Goodell, G.E. 1979. Ongoing harvest: postproduction labor and income, Agricultural Economics Department, IRRI, Los Banos. Mimeo.

Gonzalo, B.C., and R.E. Stickney. 1985. "MA-IRRI Industrial Extension Program for Small Farm Equipment," *Journal of Philippine Development*, Vol. XII, No. 1, First semester.

Hayami, Y., and M. Kikuchi. 1981. *Asian Village Economy at the Crossroads: An Economic Approach to Institutional Change.* Tokyo University Press.

Hayami, Y., and V. Ruttan. 1985. *Agricultural Development: An International Perspective.* Second edition, revised and updated. Baltimore: Johns Hopkins Press.

Herdt, R.W. 1981. Mechanization of Rice Production in Developing Asian Countries: Perspective, Evidence, and Issues. In *Consequences of Small-Farm Mechanization.* IRRI, Los Banos, Philippines.

Ilyas, M. 1980. An Engineering Analysis of the IRRI Axial Flow Thresher, M. Sc. thesis in Agricultural Engineering, University of the Philippines at Los Banos. Laguna, Philippines, November.

International Rice Research Institute. Agricultural Engineering Department. *Semi-Annual Report Nos. 21–28, 1975–79.* IRRI, Los Banos, Laguna, Philippines.

International Rice Research Institute. Agricultural Engineering Department Trainees. Personal interviews. 1976–85. IRRI, Los Banos, Laguna, Philippines.

Juarez, F., and B. Duff. 1979. *The Economic and Institutional Impact of Mechanical Threshing in Iloilo and Laguna*, The Consequences of Small Farm Mechanization Project, Working Paper No. 1, IRRI, October.

Juarez, F., and R. Pathnopas. 1981. *A Comparative Analysis of Thresher Adoption and Use in Thailand and the Philippines*, The Consequences of Small Farm Mechanization Project, Working Paper No. 28, IRRI, September.

Juarez, F., and R. Pathnopas. 1983. A Comparative Analysis of Thresher Adoption and Use in Thailand and the Philippines. In *Consequences of Small Farm Mechanization.* International Rice Research Institute/Agricultural Development Council. Los Banos, Laguna, Philippines.

Juarez, F. 1984. The Institutional and Economic Impact of Mechanical Rice Threshing in Laguna and Iloilo, Philippines, M. Sc. thesis, University of the Philippines at Los Banos.

Juarez, F. 1985. "The Private and Social Profitability of Mechanical Threshing," *Journal of Philippine Development*, Vol. XII, No. 1, First semester.

Khan, A.U. 1985. The Asian Axial-Flow Threshers. Paper presented at the Agricultural Engineering Workshop on Small Farm Equipment for Developing Countries: Past Experiences and Future Priorities, September, Los Banos, Laguna, Philippines.

Kikuchi, M., V.G. Cordova, E.B. Marciano, and Y. Hayami. 1979. *Changes in Rice Harvesting Systems in Central Luzon and Laguna*, IRRI Research Paper, Series no. 31, July.

Kikuchi, M., F.G. Gascon, L.M. Bambo, and R.W. Herdt. 1982. *Changes in Technology and Institution for Rice Farming in Laguna, Philippines, 1966–1981: A Summary of Five Laguna Surveys.* IRRI Agricultural Economics Department Paper No. 82-22.

Kishida, Y. 1985. Personal Communication.

Krishnasreni, S. n.d. Harvesting and Threshing of Paddy in Thailand. Mimeo.

Loohawenchit, C. 1983. *Indigenous Manufacture of Farm Machinery in Thailand*, Consequences of Small Rice Farm Mechanization Project, Working paper no. 84, November.

Makeham, J. 1979. Thailand's Harvest: Man or Machine. Economic and Social Commission for Asia and the Pacific, Regional Network for Agricultural Machinery. February.

McMennamy, J.A., and J. S. Policarpio. 1978. Development of a Portable Axial-Flow Thresher. In the Proceedings of International Grain and Forage Harvesting Conference by ASAE, Ames, Iowa. Also available as IRRI Agricultural Engineering Paper no. 77-06.

Mikkelsen, K.W., and N. Langam. 1981. Innovation in the Philippine Agricultural Machinery Industry. In Consequences of Small Farm Mechanization, IRRI, Philippines.

Mikkelsen, K.W. 1984. Inventive Activity in Philippine Industry, Ph.D. dissertation, Department of Agricultural Economics, Yale University, New Haven, Conn., May.

Ministry of Agriculture and Food and International Rice Research Institute. October 1984–September 1985. *Industrial Extension Program for Small Farm Equipment*. Annual Report. Bureau of Plant Industry, Ministry of Agriculture and Food, Manila, Philippines.

Mongkoltanatas, J. 1985. Adoption and Diffusion of the Axial Flow Thresher in Thailand. Paper presented at the IRRI Agricultural Engieering Workshop on Small Farm Equipment for Developing Countries: Past Experiences and Future Priorities, September, IRRI, Philippines.

Palacpac, A. 1986. *World Rice Statistics*. Department of Agricultural Economics, The International Rice Research Institute, Los Banos, Laguna, Philippines.

Pathnopas, Renu. 1980. The Economics of Rice Threshing Machines in Thailand: A case study of Chachoengsao and Supanburi Provinces, M. Sc. thesis in Economics, Faculty of Economics, Thammasat University. May.

Pray, C.E. 1985. Private Sector Innovation and Technology Transfer in the Agricultural Sector in Developing Countries. Paper presented at the Regional Conference for Agricultural and Rural Development Officers, May, IRRI, Los Banos, Laguna, Philippines.

Pongsrikul, T. 1983. *A Simulation Model of Agricultural Mechanization in Thailand*, Consequences of Small Farm Mechanization Project. IRRI, Los Banos, Laguna, Philippines.

Reddy, V.R. 1985. Introduction, Local Manufacture and Use of Axial Flow Paddy Threshers in Indonesia. Paper presented at the IRRI Engineering Conference on Small Farm Equipment for Developing Countries: Past Experiences and Future Priorities, IRRI, Los Banos, Laguna, Philippines. September.

Reddy, V.R., F. Kasryno and M. Siregar. 1985. *Diffusion and Commercialization of Technology Prototypes: Rice Post-harvest in Indonesia*, World Employment Programme Research, WEP 2-22/WP, 143. Geneva: International Labour Organization. April.

Regional Network for Agricultural Machinery (RNAM). 1985. *Policies and Strategies for Agricultural Mechanization*. Newsletter no. 23. August.

Reyes, B., and M. Agabin. 1985. "Credit Programs Supporting Agricultural Mechanization," *Journal of Philippine Development*, 12 (1): 211–225.

Ruttan, V.W. 1982. "Changing Role of Public and Private Sectors in Agricultural Research," *Science*, 216: 23–29.

Sison, J., R. W. Herdt and B. Duff. 1985. "The Effects of Small Farm Mechanization on Employment and Output in Selected Rice Growing Areas in Nueva Ecija, Philippines," *Journal of Philippine Development*, 12(1): 29–82.

Smith, J., and B. Duff. 1983. *Efficiency or Equity: The Mechanization of Rice Threshing in the Philippines*, Consequences of Small Farm Mechanization Project, Working Paper no. 99. IRRI, Los Banos, Laguna, Philippines.

Smith, J. 1983. Moral Hazard, Costly Supervision and Agricultural Mechanization. Department of Agricultural Economics, IRRI, Los Banos, Laguna, Philippines. Mimeo.

Sukharomana, S. 1984. The Impact of Farm Power Strategies in Thailand. In *Farm Power and Employment in Asia*. Bangkok: The Agricultural Development Council.

Toquero, Z.F. 1983. A Critical Evaluation of Alternative Rice Post-Production Technologies in Central Luzon and Bicol Regions, Philippines, Ph.D. dissertation, Kansas State University.

Toquero, Z.F., and B. Duff. 1985. *Physical Losses and Quality Deterioration in Rice Postproduction Systems*, IRRI Research Paper Series no. 107, March.

Figure 4.1 Map of study areas, Thailand and Philippines, 1978–1983.
From Juarez and Pathnopas, 1983.

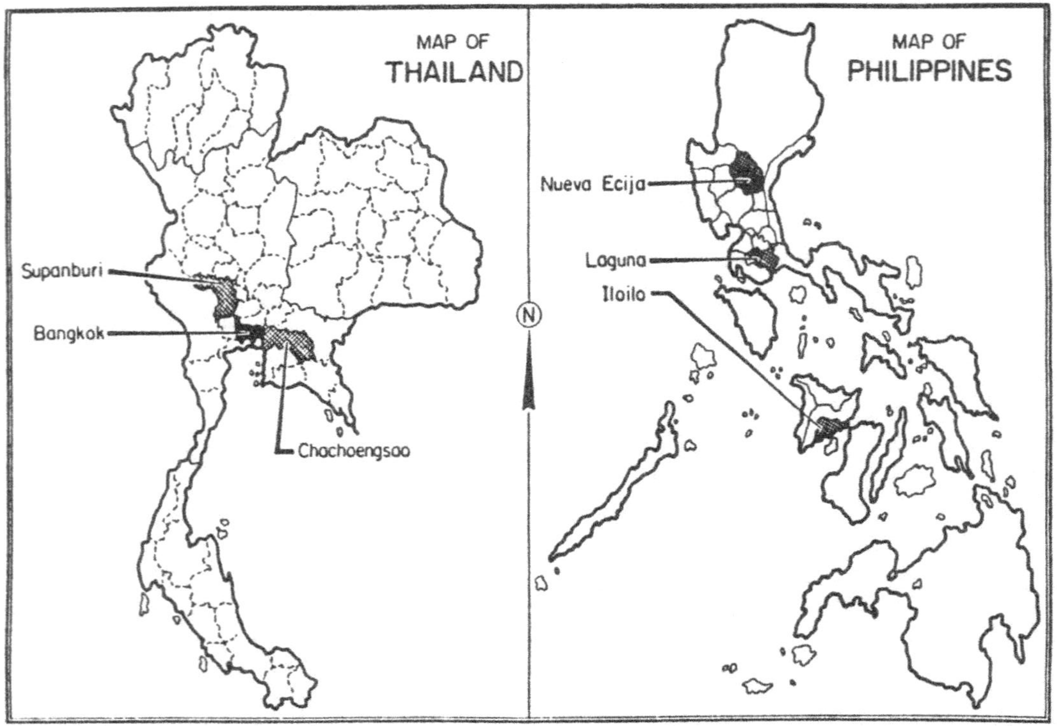

Table 4.1
Profile of Respondents, Thailand and Philippines

Item	Thailand			Philippines					
				Irrigated			Rainfed		
	Thresher Owner Users	Thresher Non-owner Users	Thresher Non-owner Non-users	Thresher Owner Users	Thresher Non-owner Users	Thresher Non-owner Non-users	Thresher Owner Users	Thresher Non-owner Users	Thresher Non-owner Non-users
No. of respondents	63	156	49	18	26	21	5	16	15
Age (yr)	48	48	45	52	50	59	50	49	49
Education (yr)	4	4	4	6.3	4.7	5.0	5.1	6.7	5.4
Tenure (%)									
Landowner, C	55	40	29	56	38	57	60	60	67
S	95	86	98						
Landless, C	45	60	71						
S	5	14	2	44	62	43	40	40	33
Average farm size (ha)	8.9	6.0	7.5	5.1	2.1	1.8	4.4	2.7	2.4
Average yield (t/ha)	2.9	2.7	2.7	3.8	3.9	2.9	2.4	2.8	2.7

C = Chachoengsao Province; S = Supanburi Province.
Source: Juarez and Pathnopas (1983).

Figure 4.2 Design, development, extension system used by IRRI's small farm equipment program

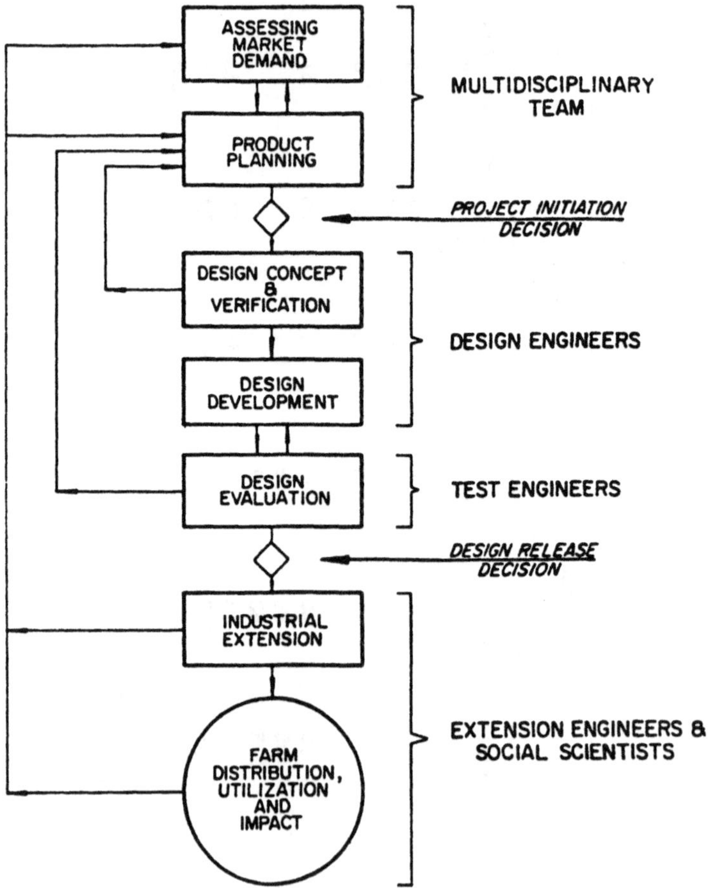

Figure 4.3 Conventional and axial flow threshing concepts.
From Khan, 1985.

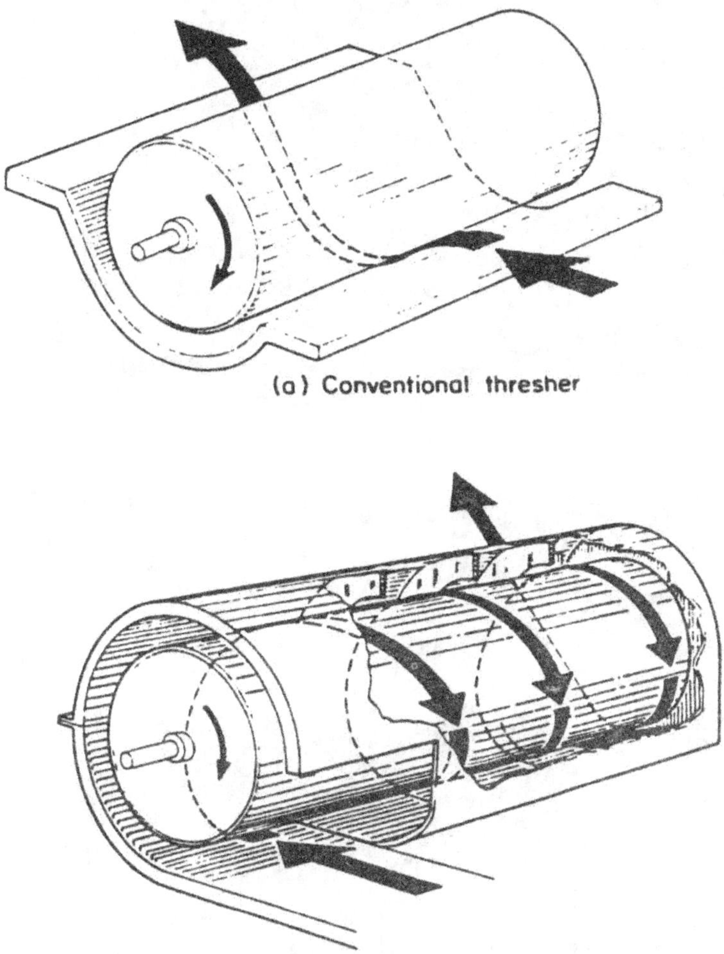

(a) Conventional thresher

(b) Axial flow thresher

Figure 4.4 Axial flow thresher designed and developed at the International Rice Research Institute. Photographs courtesy of Communications and Publications Dept., International Rice Research Institute.

(a) Large axial flow thresher

(b) Portable axial flow thresher

Figure 4.4 (continued)

(c) Moving portable axial flow thresher

(d) Large axial flow converted for shelling corn

Figure 4.5 Production of IRRI-designed axial flow threshers by cooperating manufacturers in selected countries, 1974–1985. From IRRI, Ag. Engineering Dept., 1975–79; Ministry of Agriculture and Food and IRRI, Oct. 1984–Sept. 1985; Khan, 1985; Reddy, 1985.

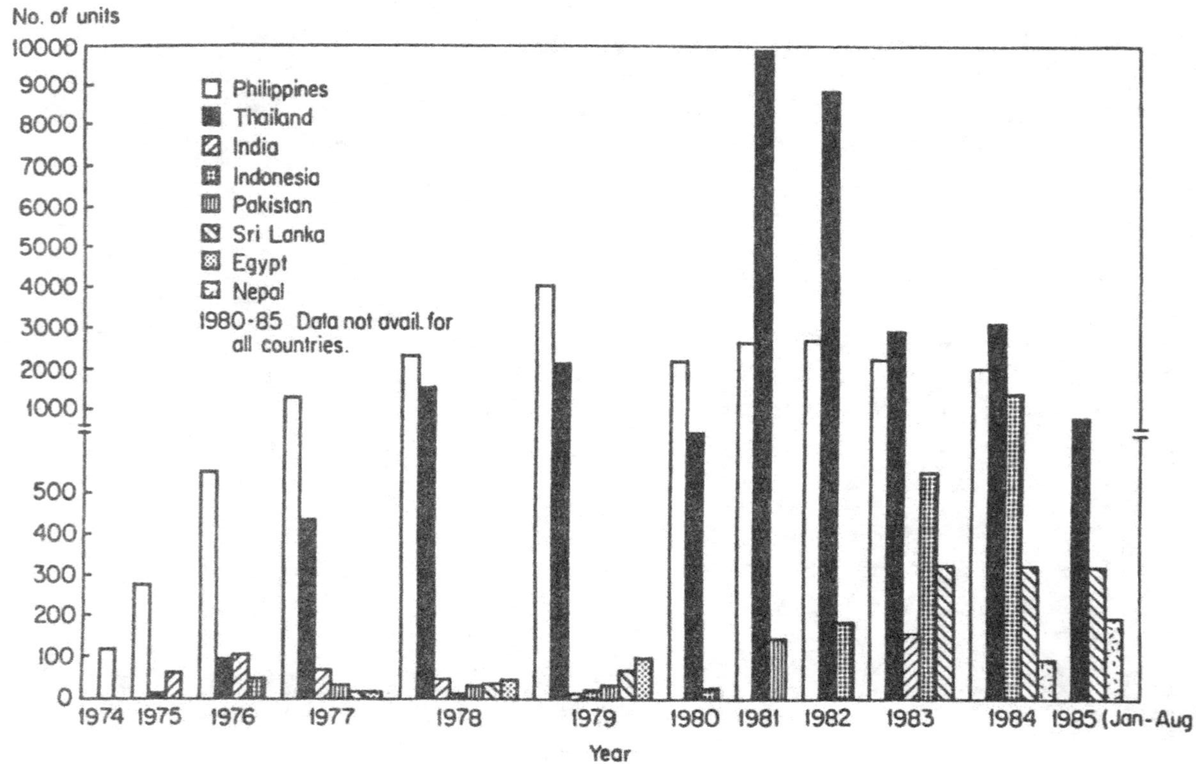

Table 4.2
Thresher Adoption and Labor Use, Laguna Province, Philippines, 1965–1978

Item	1965	1970	1975	1977	1978
Percent of farmers using threshers	0	0	0	67	82
Harvesting and threshing labor (days/ha)	30	32	32	26	31
Yield (t/ha)	2.2	3.1	3.4	3.7	4.6

Source: Kikuchi et al. (1982).

Figure 4.6 Demand for IRRI-designed axial flow threshers, Philippines, 1974–1984. From IRRI, Ag. Engineering Dept., 1975–79; Ministry of Agriculture and Food and IRRI, Oct. 1984–Sept. 1985.

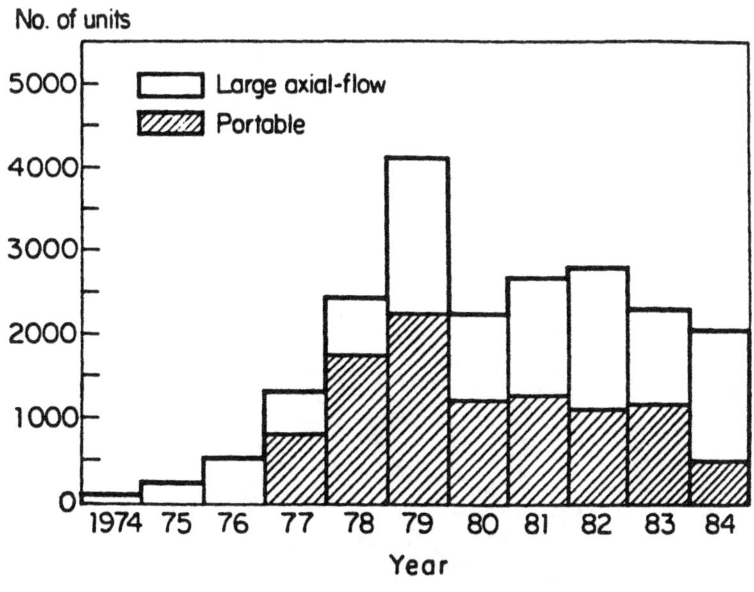

Figure 4.7 Adoption of three rice production technologies in three sample irrigated villages, Iloilo, 1968–1978. From Juarez, 1984; Juarez and Pathnopas, 1981; Juarez and Duff, 1979.

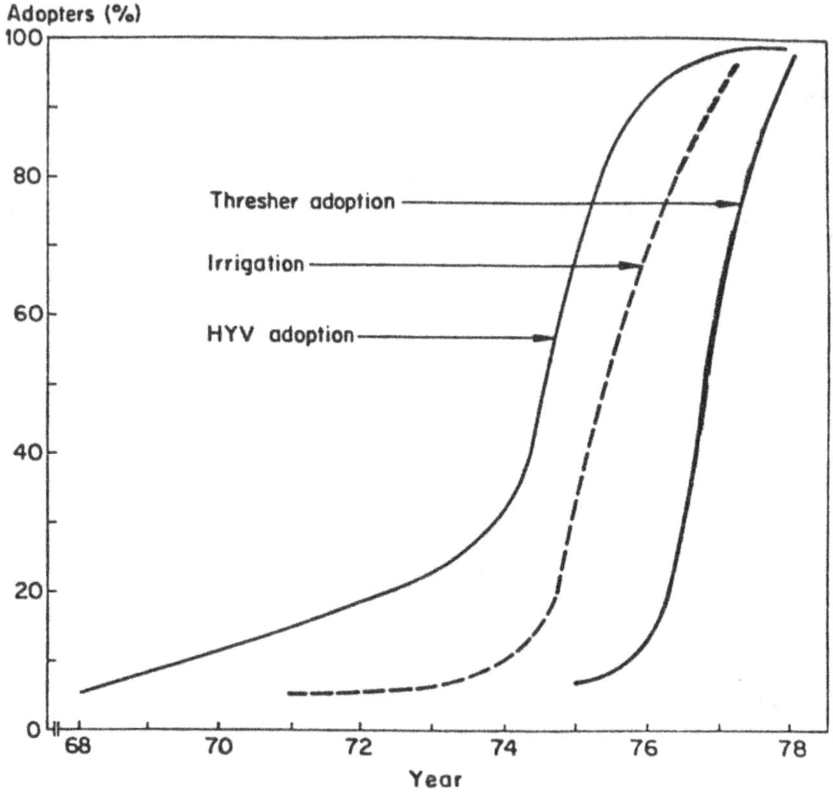

Figure 4.8 Allocation of threshing time, 73 owners, Philippines and Thailand, 1978 and 1983. From Juarez, 1985; Juarez and Pathnopas, 1981.

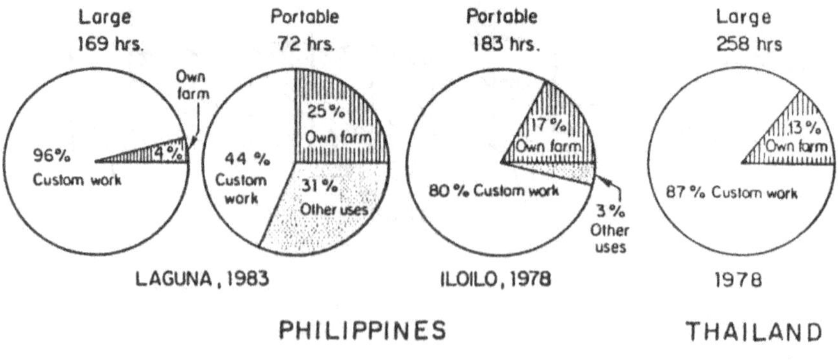

Table 4.3
Sources of Funds for Rice Thresher Investment

Source	Thailand	Philippines Irrigated	Philippines Rainfed
Own cash (%)	69	83	60
Loans (%)	7	--	--
Both cash and loans (%)	24	17	40

Source: Juarez and Pathnopas (1981).

Figure 4.9 Annual utilization and contract costs for mechanical axial flow threshers, Thailand and Philippines, 1974–1983

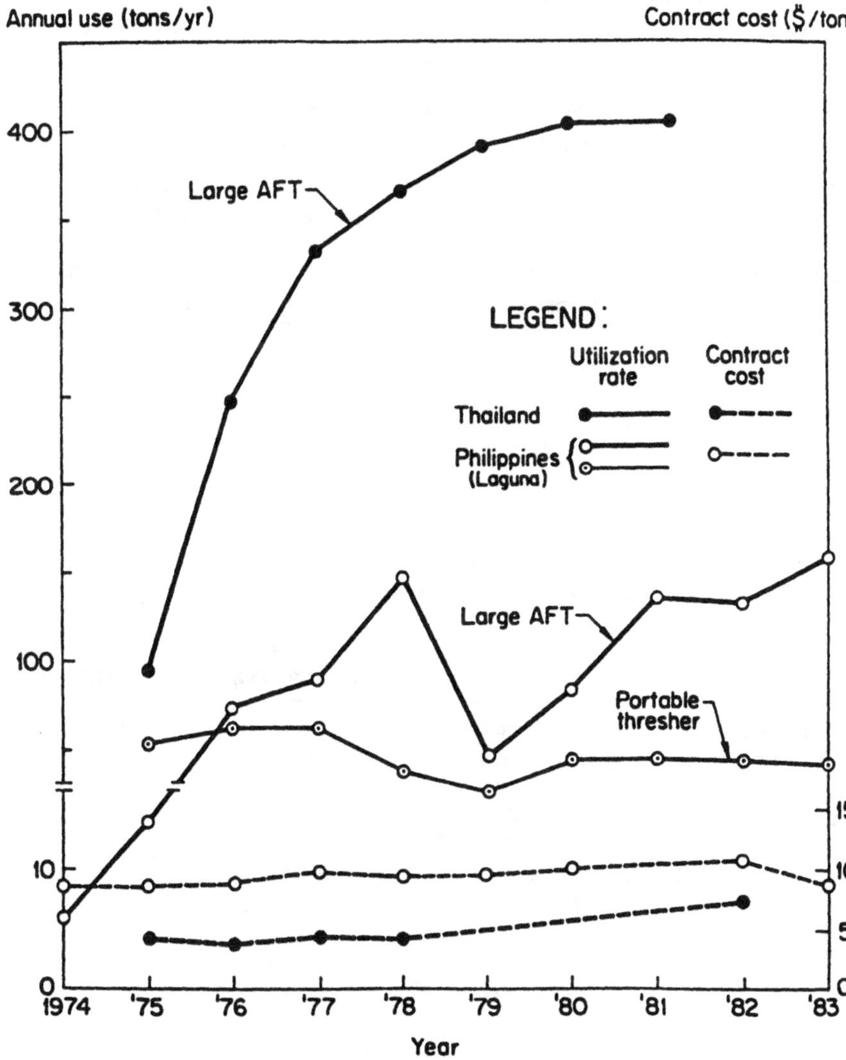

Table 4.4
Summary of Studies on the Impact of Mechanized Threshing on Cropping Intensity in Rice-Based Systems, Asia

Study	Area	Comparison	Cropping Intensity Effect
Juarez, 1984	Iloilo, Philippines	Foot treading vs. power threshing	1.68 (irrigated) + 13%
Juarez, 1984	Iloilo, Philippines	Foot treading vs. power threshing	1.55 (rainfed) +4%
Juarez, 1984	Laguna, Philippines	Hand vs. power threshing	1.43 (irrigated) + 22%
Toquero and Duff, 1985	Central Luzon, Philippines	Hand vs. power threshing	1.78 (irrigated) –23%

Table 4.5
Hired and Family Labor Utilization in Postproduction Activities, Central Luzon, Philippines, 1979–1980

	Hired Labor	Family Labor (labor days/ha)	Total
Manual threshing	29.0	2.3	31.3
Mechanized threshing	20.1	2.9	23.0
Labor displaced	8.9	–0.6	8.3
Percent displaced	31.0	–5.0	26.0

Source: Smith et al. (1983).

Table 4.6
Labor Requirements and Labor Productivity for Rice Threshing Using Alternative Methods in Thailand and the Philippines

Method	Man days/t	Kg/man-day
Thailand		
Buffalo treading	4.85	206
Tractor treading	2.40	415
Large axial flow thresher	1.33	752
Philippines		
Foot treading (Iloilo)	7.69	130
Hand beating (Laguna)	5.49	182
Portable axial flow thresher	0.81	1,230
Large axial flow thresher	0.94	1,070

Source: Juarez and Pathnopas (1983).

Table 4.7
Employment Implications of a One Percent Increase in Rice Production Using Manual or Mechanical Threshing Methods, Philippines

Method	Direct Increase (agri sector)	Indirect Increase (non-agri sectors)	Total Increase
		'thousand man-years	
Manual threshing	15.9	27.1	43
Portable thresher	12.4	27.6	40
Percent difference	22	2	7

Source: Smith et al. (1983). Adapted from Ahammed, C., and R. W. Herdt (1985).

Figure 4.10 Changes in the composition of labor in harvesting and threshing, Philippines.
From Ebron et al., 1985.

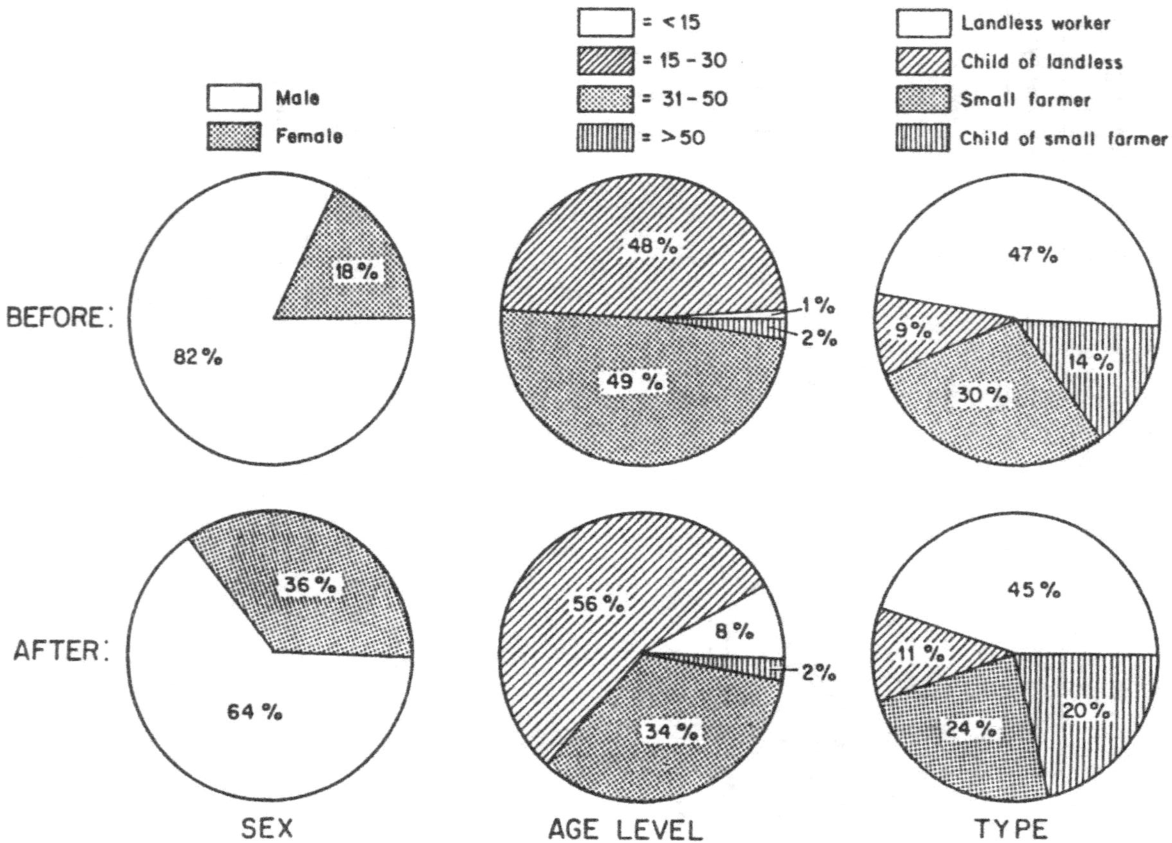

Figure 4.11 Ratio of indices of prices of inputs (labor and machinery) to paddy price in the Philippines. From David, C. C., 1985. "An Analysis of Recent Philippine Rice Trends," IRRI, Ag. Economics Dept.

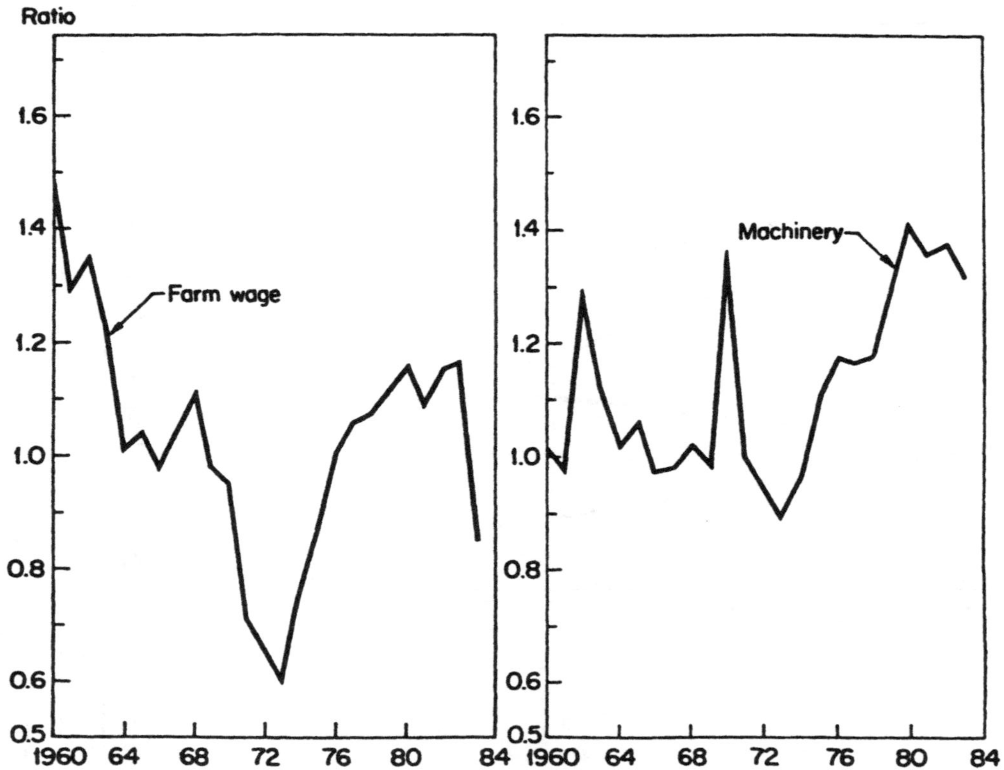

Figure 4.12 Ratio of indices of price of labor to paddy price in Thailand. From Palacpac, 1986; World Rice Statistics, IRRI, 1984; Ag. Eng'g. Trainees, IRRI.

Table 4.8
Agricultural Wage Rates in Rice Production, Laguna, Philippines, 1965–1981[a]

Item	1965	1970	1975	1978	1981
Harvesting and threshing					
Nominal wage[b] ($/day)	1.08	0.91	2.32	2.48	2.38
Real wage ($/day)	1.08	0.70	0.78	0.64	0.40
Index of real wage	100	101	140	113	79
Transplanting					
Index of real wage	100	121	104	83	85

[a]1US$ = P3.88 in 1965, P6.44 in 1970, P7.50 in 1975, P7.38 in 1978, and P8.20 in 1981.
[b]Deflated by Consumer Price Index (CPI) outside Manila.
Source: Smith et al. (1983).

Table 4.9
Division of Factor Shares for Paddy Farmers Using and Not Using Mechanical Threshers, Laguna, 1983[a]

Item	Thresher Renters		Non-thresher Users	
	$/ha	%	$/ha	%
Land owner	87.86	17	87.86	18
Total labor[b]	139.63	27	160.03	33
Unskilled[c]	116.71	23	160.03	33
Skilled[d]	22.92	4	0	0
Capital	80.01	16	45.63	10
Current inputs	80.49	15	80.49	17
Operators residual	127.49	25	104.16	22
Value of production	515.48	100	478.17	100

[a]1US$ = P14.66.
[b]Including gleaners at $16.85/ha.
[c]Excluding thresher operators.
[d]Thresher operators.
Source: Smith et al. (1983).

Table 4.10
Yield Effect of Axial Flow Threshers, Philippines and Thailand

Study	Area	Threshing Method	Physical Grain Loss (% of yield)	Grain Savings (% of yield)
Toquero, 1983	Central Luzon, Philippines	Axial flow thresher	1.10	
		Threshing frame	2.40	+1.30
	Bicol, Philippines	Axial flow thresher	0.48	
		Threshing frame	1.56	+1.08
		Flail or stick	1.20	+0.72
Juarez, 1984	Laguna, Philippines	Axial flow thresher	1.60	
		Hand beating	7.34	+5.74
		Portable axial flow thresher	1.34	
		Hand beating	7.34	+6.00
	Iloilo, Philippines	Portable axial flow thresher	1.34	
		Foot treading	1.65	+0.31
Juarez and Pathnopas, 1981	Supanburi, Thailand	Axial flow thresher	1.66	
		Animal treading	1.12	–0.54
	Chachaoengsao, Thailand	Axial flow thresher	1.66	
		Tractor threshing	0.97	–0.69

Table 4.11
Harvesting and Threshing Contract Rates in the Philippines and Thailand, 1978 and 1983

Location	Traditional Harvesting and Threshing[a]		Traditional Harvesting and Mechanical Threshing		
	Harvester-thresher share	Thresher share	Total shares	Harvester share	Machine share[b]
Philippines			*% gross output*		
Laguna, 1978	12.5	5.6	17.0	10.0	7.0
Laguna, 1983	12.5	5.6	19.0	10.0	9.0
Iloilo, 1978	16.6	5.5	16.6	11.1	5.5
Iloilo, 1983	16.6	5.5	16.6	11.1	5.5
Nueva Ecija, 1983	14.2	--	15.6	9.1	6.5
Thailand			*$/ton*		
Chachoengsao, 1978		6.9 (tractor treading)			3.8
Supanburi, 1978		7.5 (tractor treading)			4.8
		9.6 (buffalo treading)			

[a]Traditional threshing in the Philippines refers to hand beating; in Thailand it refers to tractor and buffalo treading.

[b]Machine share includes charges for fuel, oil, grease, operators, and the machine itself. In both countries about 33–40% of the machine share is paid to operators and helpers and the remainder accrues to the machine owner who pays for fuel, oil, and grease. In most cases, the cost of the machine includes cleaning, particularly when the large axial flow thresher, which has a built-in cleaning mechanism, is used.

Sources: Juarez and Pathnopas, 1981; Juarez, 1984.

Table 4.12
User Benefits from Axial Flow Threshers Compared with Traditional Methods, Thailand and the Philippines, 1978 and 1983

Location	Cost Saving Over Traditional Method ($/ton)	Value of Grain Losses Saved ($/ton)	Total Mean Gain ($/ton)	($/ha)	($/farm)
Thailand, 1978					
Large thresher vs. tractor/buffalo treading	3.55	–0.71	2.84	17.0	62.0
Philippines, 1978					
Large thresher vs. hand beating (Laguna)	–1.84	7.63	5.79	26.0	113.0
Portable thresher vs. foot treading (Iloilo)	2.36	0.38	2.74	9.1	23.0
Philippines, 1983					
Large thresher vs. hand beating (Laguna)	–3.36	5.68	2.32	10.4	45.2
Portable thresher vs. foot treading (Iloilo)	1.92	0.31	2.23	7.6	19.2

[a]Sample includes only farms growing high yielding varieties.
[b]Includes meal expense savings.
Sources: Juarez and Pathnopas, 1983; Juarez, 1985.

Table 4.13
Financial Analysis of Large and Portable Mechanical Thresher Investment in Thailand and the Philippines, 1978 and 1983

Item	Thailand 1978	Philippines					
		Iloilo, 1978		Laguna, 1978		Laguna, 1983	
	Large	Portable (Irrigated)	Portable (Rainfed)	Large	Portable	Large	Portable
Initial cost ($)	1699.00	748.00	789.00	2136.00	837.00	1569.00	546.00
Fixed costs ($/yr)							
Depreciation	250.35	134.64	142.02	320.40	150.66	235.35	98.28
Interest	110.15	49.37	52.07	140.98	55.24	129.44	45.04
Repair and maintenance	166.90	74.80	78.90	213.60	83.70	156.90	54.60
Tax and insurance	33.38	14.96	15.78	42.72	16.74	31.38	10.92
Total fixed costs	560.78	273.77	288.77	717.70	306.34	553.07	208.84
Variable costs ($/t)							
Fuel	0.14	0.63	0.63	0.87	0.50	0.83	0.75
Oil	0.06	0.04	0.04	0.07	0.03	0.03	0.04
Grease	0.01	0.00	0.00	0.01	0.00	0.01	0.00
Labor	1.56	2.20	2.20	3.74	3.74	3.56	3.56
Total variable costs	1.77	2.87	2.87	4.69	4.27	4.43	4.35
Contract rate ($/t)	4.27	6.72	6.72	9.31	9.31	8.90	8.90
Annual use (t)							
Average	366.90	145.00	75.00	149.00	39.00	155.20	37.60
High	377.00	162.60	75.00	175.00	60.00	186.80	62.70
Breakeven point (BEP) (t/yr)	224.31	71.13	75.01	155.35	60.78	123.73	45.90
Payback period (PBP) (yr)							
Average annual use	2.75	1.79	5.56	7.34	20.47	4.17	9.02
High annual use	2.64	1.54	5.56	5.19	5.70	8.03	3.12
Benefit-cost ratio (BCR)							
Average annual use	1.26	1.38	0.95	0.06	0.75	1.08	0.88
High annual use	1.28	1.45	0.95	1.04	0.97	1.18	1.13

Source: Computed from basic data in Juarez (1984) and Juarez and Pathnopas (1981).

Figure 4.13 Breakeven levels for mechanical thresher investments, Thailand and Philippines, 1978 and 1983

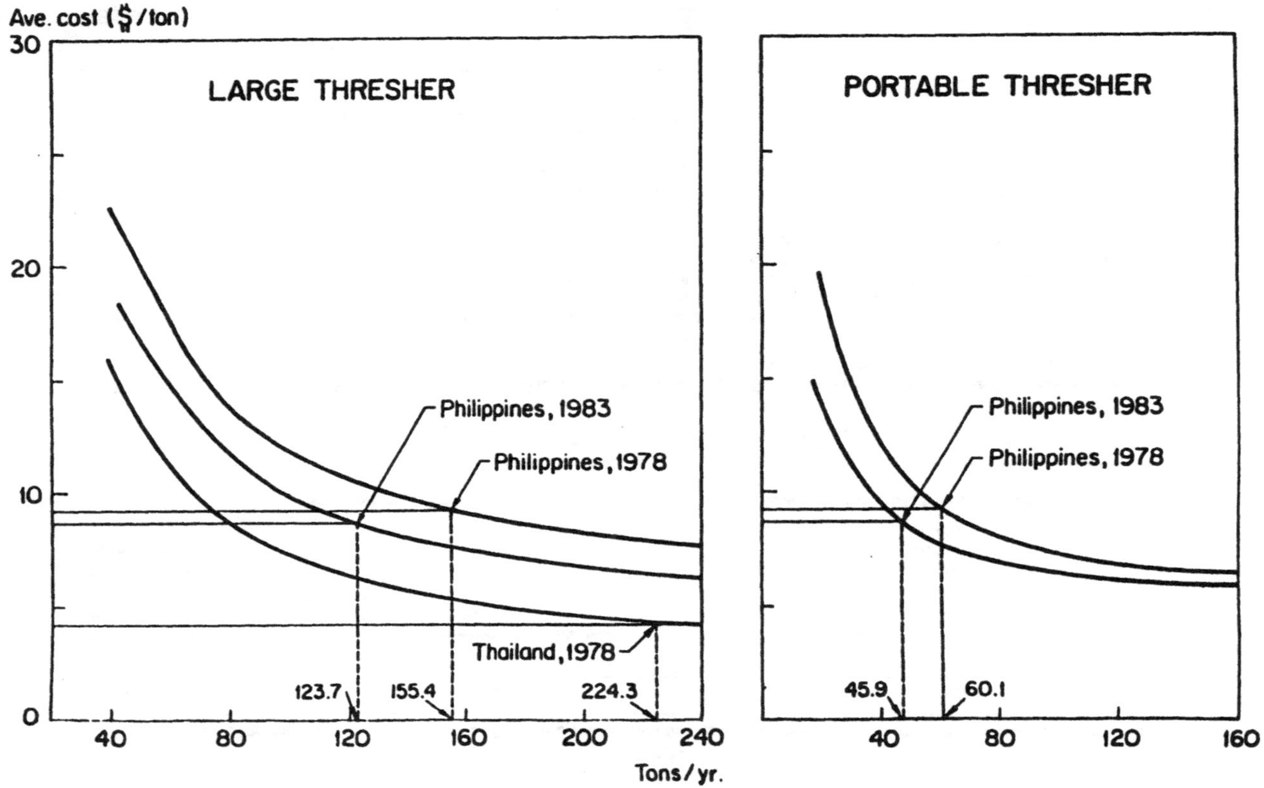

Table 4.14
Summary of Policy and Institutional Programs Affecting Development and Extension of Farm Machinery in the Philippines and Thailand

Policy Instruments	Philippines	Thailand
Tariffs		
Assembled or CKD ag. machines	Engines, sprayers, 4-wheel tractor, harvesting thresh machinery = 10% hand tractor = 30%	imported unit and/or engine = 33%
Components and spare parts	30%	internal parts = 15% roller chain and steel = 25% rubber parts = 50%
Quotas	No import restriction	import restriction at 5337 units for second-hand two-wheel tractors and 705 four-wheel tractors
Taxes	10% advance sales tax	3% business tax 11% profit tax 10% locak tax
Credit programs	Available for each food crop; CB:IBRD provided 4 credit lines amounting $76M from 1965–1984.	Direct installment distributors; Bank for Agriculture and Agricultural Cooperatives gives credit through fabricators and distributors
Manufacturing support programs	Board of investments Ag. Investment Incentive Act; rural artisans training courses; machine drawings and technical assistance provided by Ministry of Agriculture and IRRI Industrial Extension Project; Agricultural Machinery Manufacturers and Distributors Association	Domestic production of small engines of less than 30 hp; technical assistance provided by FAO/UNDP Ag. Mech. Project with Ag. Eng. Div.; technical information through quarterly *News Digest*; Thai-IRRI Industrial Extension Project; Ag. Mech. Manufacturers Association
R&D programs	Ag. Mech. Inter-agency Committee directs mechanization development activities; Ag. Mech. Development Program (AMDP) designs and develops machines and sets quality and safety standards; Ag. Mech. Test and Evaluation Center tests and evaluates locally manufactured machines; IRRI Ag. Mech. Dev. Program; AMDP and IRRI study effects of mechanization.	Ag. Engineering Division Min. of Ag. Cooperatives nationwide surveys of ag. machinery industry; socio-economic studies; provides technical assistance with Reg. Network of Ag. Machinery research coordination with MA, cooperatives and universities
Income tax incentive	Inventors Incentive Act (PD1423) provides a 5-year tax holiday	none
Exchange rate	P18.43/US$ (floating rate since October 1984)	Bhat27.37/US$ (floating rate since 1983)

Compiled from personal communication with Zia Ur Rahman and Chak Chakkapak, Regional Network for Agricultural Machinery, Philippines, and Dept. of Agriculture, Thailand, respectively; Bernas, L. (1985).

Table 4.15
Percent Distribution of CB:IBRD Loan Grants for Farm Machinery as of June 30, 1980

Item	First (1966–1968)		Second (1969–1973)		Third (1974–1977)		Fourth (1977–1980)		Total	
	No.	Value	No.	Value	No.	Value	No.	Value	No.	Value
Four-wheel tractors			56.5	85.2	56.8	86.2	29.6	65.2		
	86.8	93.9							87.4	92.9
Power tillers			31.4	11.4	34.6	11.8	51.8	17.9		
Irrigation systems and wells and distribution works	11.6	4.9	10.6	2.7	6.8	1.3	1.7	0.6	7.8	1.5
Sprayers, grain dryers, threshers and other farm machinery	1.6	1.2	1.5	0.7	1.8	0.7	2.0	1.4	1.7	0.9
Rice mills	--	--	--	--	--	--	14.9	14.9	3.1	4.7
Total	100.0	100.0	100.0	100.0	100.0	100.0	100.0	100.0	100.0	100.0

Source: SGV and Co. and U. P. Business Research Foundation, cited in Reyes et al. (1985).

Table 4.16
Sources of Loans for Rice Thresher Investment

Source	Thailand		Philippines	
	Threshers (%)	Interest rate (%/yr)	Threshers (%)	Interest rate (%/yr)
Bank	74	12	17	12
Agricultural cooperative	16	15	--	--
Private moneylender	5	20–30	33	25–90
Relative	5	0	17	0
Not specified	--	--	33	--

Source: Juarez et al. (1981; 1983).

Five

Rural Linkages in the Philippines and Taiwan

Gustav Ranis and Frances Stewart

I. INTRODUCTION

Expansion in agricultural activity is of fundamental importance to rural prosperity and the growth of industrial and service activities in the rural areas. However, the extent to which non-agricultural activities respond to agricultural expansion varies. In some situations, the sustained growth in agricultural output that has occurred in recent decades, with the introduction of the new seeds, has led to a considerable expansion in non-agricultural output in the surrounding area. Expansion in rural industry has then provided additional impetus for further increases in agricultural productivity, leading to a mutually supportive cycle of agricultural and industrial growth. In other situations, however, increases in agricultural output have had a much smaller effect on local industrial activity.

There is a strong presumption that decentralised rural industrialisation will be associated with appropriate technologies (AT), both in terms of process of production (factor use and scale) and in product characteristics. Consequently, an important element in government policies to promote AT will be those which support high linkages between agriculture and the development of local industrial and service activities.

This chapter explores the conditions that generate local linkages in order to identify policy changes which would increase the magnitude of these linkages. To do so, we compare developments in the Philippines and Taiwan over recent decades, as well as examine linkages in particular areas within each country. In both the Philippines and Taiwan, there has been a sustained expansion in agricultural output. In the Philippines agricultural output grew by 4.3 percent per annum in 1960–1970 and 4.8 percent per annum in 1970–1980. In Taiwan the expansion was somewhat lower in terms of output, 4.0 percent per annum for 1960–1970 and 2.1 percent per annum for 1970–1980, but higher in output per person in agriculture, during the period. However, the expansion of non-agricultural activity was much faster in

Taiwan. From 1961 to 1971, employment in manufacturing in the rural areas grew by 6.1 percent per annum. From 1956 to 1966, non-agricultural employment in rural Taiwan grew by 7.5 percent per annum and manufacturing employment by 7.4 percent per annum (Ho). In the Philippines total rural non-agricultural employment grew by 3.3 percent per annum from 1971 to 1981. Although the dates and classification differ somewhat, all indications support the conclusion that the expansion of non-agricultural activities in the rural areas in Taiwan was substantially greater than the Philippines, despite similar growth in agricultural output in the two countries. A comparison between the two countries therefore provides some important evidence on the factors underlying local linkages. In addition, examination of linkages in particular areas of each country provides an illuminating source of information on linkages.

In both countries, the evidence suggests that the technologies adopted in rural activities have generally been appropriate as compared with urban industrialisation. Rural technologies have tended to be of relatively lower capital-intensity, smaller scale, making more use of local materials and producing more appropriate products.

Evidence for the Philippines shows concentration of large-scale activities in the most urban area (Manila), as compared with other areas (see table 5.1). Capital/labour ratios vary systematically by size of enterprise according to Philippine data, as shown in table 5.2.

Evidence for Taiwan shows a similar preponderance of small establishments in the rural areas. In 1961, 96 percent of rural establishments were classified as small. The evidence "strongly suggests that the rural non-farm sector is comparatively labour-intensive" (Ho). Comparisons of capital intensity by industry between the five major cities and rural Taiwan show that in 1961 rural industry was substantially more labour-intensive than urban industry except food processing and paper and pulp. Data for 1971 show that the average size of establishment was much smaller and that capital-intensity was less in rural than urban industries (Ho). Some details of the differences in capital/labour ratio in 1966 are shown in table 5.3. The data thus strongly confirm the view that rural industry tends to be more appropriate from the point of view of method of production (scale and labour-intensity).

We conducted a small survey of rural non-agricultural activities in the province of Quezon in the Philippines. This gave strong support to the view that rural technologies are generally associated with more appropriate products. In every case, product characteristics were more appropriate than typical urban enterprises. For example, the furniture was simple, low-cost and used local timber. Cakes and sweets used local materials, were non-standardised and had minimal packaging. Rice processed locally was usually unpackaged and had a high proportion of "broken" heads (this was also shown in the IRRI Survey discussed below). Local metal-work shops manufactured and repaired simple agricultural tools. Local transport consisted of jeepneys (adapted from the U.S. jeep to form a basic small bus/lorry), and trimobiles (motorised and non-motorised) with accommodation for passengers and goods. Although the basic components of these (appropriate) products were imported into the area, local workshops adapted and repaired them. In the Bicol area, local firms in small towns manufacture and repair such vehicles, as well as other appropriate transport modes, especially designed for local conditions, including skates (vehicles designed to be pushed along railway tracks) and carabao sleds (see Ocampo).

In some cases, rural industries are "inappropriate." For example, in both countries the paper and pulp mills were large-scale and capital-intensive. Technology in food processing varied; as we shall see below (section III), technologies used in the Philippines in pineapple canning and banana processing have tended to be markedly more capital-intensive and associated with more inappropriate product characteristics than in Taiwan.

On balance, however, rural industries are associated with appropriate technology. It is for this reason that the promotion of such activities—which forms the focus of this chapter—constitutes an important element in the achievement of appropriate technology.

The chapter is organised as follows. The next section (II) gives a brief overview of the general economic performance of the Philippines and Taiwan. Section III considers the factors underlying the linkage relationship, first looking at demand factors and then supply, drawing on evidence from both countries and comparing the two. Section IV summarises the policy conclusions derived from the earlier analysis. Section V considers the political economy of the policy changes required, in order to elucidate the political potential of alternative policy combinations.

II. PHILIPPINES/TAIWAN: SOME BASIC COMPARISONS

The Philippines is much larger than Taiwan, in area (300,000 square kilometers compared with 36,000 for Taiwan), and in population (around 45.6 million people in 1978 compared with 17 million in Taiwan). Taiwan is poor in natural resources and land compared with the Philippines. The colonial experiences of the two countries differed: the Japanese encouraged food production in Taiwan and established a considerable network of rural infrastructure; in the Philippines, both Spanish and U.S. colonial powers promoted cash-crop production, and neglected infrastructural investments.

Conditions in 1960

Apart from these factors, there were many similarities between the two economies in 1960:

- Per capita income was $321 (1978 prices) in the Philippines compared with $443 in Taiwan.
- Structure of production was similar. Agriculture accounted for 26 percent of GDP in the Philippines and 28 percent in Taiwan, while

61 percent of the labour force in the Philippines was in agriculture, compared with 56 percent in Taiwan. The share of industry in GDP was 28 percent in the Philippines compared with 29 percent in Taiwan. Agricultural productivity (both labour and land) was higher in Taiwan. Land productivity was about five times higher. Population was much less dense in the Philippines. Labour productivity in agriculture in Taiwan was about 1.6 times the level in the Philippines.

- Exports were 11 percent of GDP in each country. However, in the Philippines there was a heavier concentration on primary commodities; agricultural products formed 86 percent of exports and manufactured goods only 4 percent. In Taiwan agricultural products accounted for 68 percent of exports and industrial products for 32 percent. About four-fifths of Taiwan agricultural products were processed.
- Gross investment as a share of GDP was higher in Taiwan (at 20 percent, compared with 16 percent in the Philippines).
- Social indicators were mostly better in Taiwan than the Philippines.
- Life expectancy was 64 in Taiwan and 51 in the Philippines in 1960 with corresponding differences in child mortality figures.
- The availability of nurses and doctors was better in Taiwan. For example, there were 1,661 people per doctor in Taiwan compared with 6,940 in the Philippines.
- 24 percent of the population in the Philippines had piped water compared with about 50 percent in Taiwan.
- Public consumption as a share of GDP was higher in Taiwan at 19 percent, as compared with 8 percent in the Philippines.
- There was a remarkable similarity in education; adult literacy was estimated to be 87 percent in 1975 in the Philippines, compared with 82 percent in Taiwan. In both countries, primary enrollment ratios were 100 percent in 1960; secondary enrollment ratios were estimated at 26 percent in the Philippines, 33 percent in Taiwan.
- Income distribution: In the 1950s income distribution was more unequal in Taiwan than the Philippines by every measure (see table 5.4). However, since then income distribution has become much more equal in Taiwan, with the Gini co-efficient falling from 0.56 in 1953 to 0.29 in 1972, while in the Philippines there has been little change in the degree of inequality as measured by the Gini co-efficient, which is around 0.5, indicating substantial inequality. The share of income of the lowest 20 percent of the population has fallen over the period, from 4.9 percent in 1956 to 3.9 percent in 1971. Since the early 1960s, inequality has therefore been substantially greater in the Philippines than in Taiwan.
- Land distribution: In 1960 the estimated Gini co-efficient for land distribution in Taiwan was 0.457 compared with 0.534 in the Philippines. (Fei, Ranis, Kuo, 1979, table 5.17). Land reform in Taiwan had effected a substantial reduction in inequality (of 26 percent in the Gini co-efficient). However, earlier there was a high degree of inequality, so that even after the reform, the Gini co-efficient remained quite high.

Average farm size was substantially smaller in Taiwan at 1.52 ha. compared with 2.7 in the Philippines.

Comparative Performance since 1960

As indicated above, the initial conditions were similar in the two countries. However, since then performance has differed markedly, with Taiwan experiencing a much higher growth rate than the Philippines. On average, from 1960 to 1980, growth in income per head was 6.9 percent per annum in Taiwan compared with 2.8 percent per annum in the Philippines. By 1980 this discrepancy meant that income per head in Taiwan was over 2.5 times that in the Philippines. (For a breakdown of sectoral growth rates see table 5.5.)

A significant factor underlying the more rapid growth in output per head in Taiwan was the faster growth in labour productivity in agriculture which, between 1960 and 1979, increased by 3.6 percent annually in Taiwan compared to 2.1 percent in the Philippines (see table 5.6). The rate of growth of output in the industrial and service sectors was significantly higher in Taiwan throughout the period. The growth of output in agriculture was similar in the two countries from 1960 to 1970 and higher in the Philippines from 1970 to 1982.

The rapid growth of industry in Taiwan absorbed an increasing proportion of the labour force. In 1960, employment in industry accounted for 25.2 percent of the total and agricultural employment for 52.7 percent. By 1979 industrial employment accounted for 47.7 percent and agriculture for 21.5 percent. From 1965 onwards employment in agriculture fell quite substantially. The rate of growth of labour productivity was substantially greater in Taiwan in both agriculture and industry as table 5.6 shows.

The growth of exports in Taiwan was far higher than in the Philippines, especially in the 1960s. The growth in exports in Taiwan consisted chiefly of food processing, textiles and clothing, and electronics, with food processing dominating in the early period (especially from 1954 to 1961), textiles being the major source of expansion from 1961 to 1971 and electrical machinery playing an increasingly important role from 1966.

In both countries, the composition of exports moved away from primary products, but much more dramatically in Taiwan, where industrial products accounted for over 90 percent of exports by 1979, compared with 45 percent in the Philippines. Industrial exports grew by 30 percent per annum in Taiwan, compared with 21 percent in the Philippines (see table 5.7).

Several studies have analysed the causes of these differences in performance (see for example Galenson, ed.; Ranis, 1983; ILO, 1974; Oshima, 1983, 1984). One part of the explanation lies in the major differences in the policy package adopted, with the Philippines pursuing import substitution, with high levels of protection and subsidised interest rates, and Taiwan being much more open and export-oriented, and with more realistic factor prices.

Other explanations include differences in initial conditions, in cultural attitudes and in organisational structure (see Ranis, 1983). We shall not pursue this question further, except insofar as it bears on the issue of rural industrialisation and rural linkages. We shall return to policy issues in section IV, after examining the extent and determinants of rural linkages.

III. FACTORS AFFECTING THE MAGNITUDE OF RURAL LINKAGES IN THE PHILIPPINES AND TAIWAN

Both systems experienced sustained agricultural growth in recent decades. Consequently, their experience provides plentiful evidence of the extent and causes of linkages.

Linkages occur where expansion in agricultural output leads to expansion in other activities, and conversely where additional non-agricultural activity in the rural areas provides opportunities and incentives for raising agricultural productivity. These linkages may take a number of forms: first, *consumption* linkages, where incomes generated in agriculture lead to consumption of output produced locally; second, *production* linkages, which may be backward or forward. *Backward* linkages occur where production in one sector uses inputs produced in other sectors—for example, machinery or fertiliser. *Forward* linkages occur where production in one sector provides inputs for productive activities in other sectors, for example, food supplies for food processing.

The extent of any linkage depends in part on the area in which the linkage is defined as occurring. Any increased demand following extra agricultural output will be met partly by additional local supplies, partly from goods produced in the major urban centres in the country, and partly from imports from outside the country. Our focus here is on local rural linkages: that is, on how far an increase in agricultural production in a particular area leads to greater local activity in the same area. We are focusing on the rural subsector of the economy because, for the most part, local rural activities use appropriate technologies.

The boundary defining what is local and rural is inevitably somewhat arbitrary. In general we would include local market towns. In practice, we have to follow the definitions adopted in the available studies (which are by no means always consistent). However, since the conclusions which emerge are consistent across studies, a change in definition would be likely to alter the precise magnitudes, but would leave the major conclusions unaffected.

We conducted a small survey of rural non-agricultural activities in the province of Quezon. This, together with other studies of rural linkages in the Philippines and Taiwan, provides the basis for a number of conclusions about the nature and causes of rural linkages.

Magnitude of Linkages

1. The linkage effects from additional agricultural output are very substantial, even where policies are not especially conducive to promoting them.
   - In the Gapan area in the Philippines an annual increase in agricultural income of 5.5 percent per annum (from 1961 to 1967) was accompanied by an annual increase in non-agricultural employment of 8.2 percent, while between 1967 and 1971, an annual increase in agricultural income of 8.2 percent was accompanied by an increase in non-agricultural employment of 9.0 percent per annum (Gibbs).
   - An Upper Pampanga River project which roughly doubled net farm income was associated with an annual increase in non-farm employment of 7.0 percent per annum, 1975–79 (Sander).
   - In Oton and Tigbauen between 1974-75 and 1979-80, agricultural production rose by 6.7 percent per annum, while output of non-agricultural activities grew by 8.4 percent per annum (Wangwacharakul).
   - Between 1960 and 1975, there were high rates of growth in small rural establishments in those areas in the Philippines with rapid agricultural growth. In Luzon (excluding Manila and Rizal), small establishments grew by 8.3 percent per annum. There is a strong association between agricultural growth and the growth of manufacturing establishments by regions in the Philippines (Anderson and Khambata).
   - In Taiwan between 1952 and 1965, as a whole agricultural production grew by over 4.8 percent per annum, while between 1955–66, non-agricultural rural employment grew by 7.5 percent per annum (excluding public services) (Ho).
2. Rural non-agricultural employment is dominated by consumption-linkage activities—that is, activities which supply consumption goods and services to people in the area—especially in the Philippines.
   - Our survey found that over 80 percent of establishments were consumption-related (including barbers, furniture makers, general stores, and food processers).
   - In the survey of the Gapan area, consumption-related activities accounted for 58.6 percent of total non-agricultural employment in 1971, with public services accounting for 24.4 percent, and forward and backward linkages for 18.1 percent. Table 5.8 provides a detailed breakdown, which is illuminating for showing the type of rural industries that are of significance.
   - In the Upper Pampanga River area forward and backward linkage industries accounted for only 6.8 percent of employment in the two towns investigated in 1979, with consumption linked activities (including public sector) accounting for the remainder (Saner).

- In Taiwan, about two-thirds of rural non-agricultural employment in 1966 was consumption-related, including public services (see Ho and Sen hsu-Yeng). This is significantly less than the figure of around 80 percent indicated by the Philippine studies. However, consumption-related activities remained the most significant source of non-agricultural employment in rural Taiwan. This was largely because of the significance of service employment, which is mainly consumption-related (see table 5.9). It is impossible to allocate activities precisely between different types of linkage in Taiwan because of the way the data has been collected. But it seems that about 10 to 15 percent of employment was in backward linkage activities in 1966, including machinery and equipment production and servicing, and about 10 percent in forward linkage activities. Activities not directly linked to the agricultural sector were more important in Taiwan than the Philippines. These included some textile and clothing production for urban consumption and for export, which were located in the rural areas to make use of the cheap and abundant labour (see Ho); it also included some mining.

3. Increases in agricultural output are accompanied by high increases in all types of "linked" activities (backward, forward, and consumption). There appears to be some tendency for the greatest proportionate increase to be found in forward linkages.
   - In Gibbs's study, forward linkage industries (chiefly rice trading and milling) increased employment by 9.6 percent per annum, 1961–71; employment in industries supplying agricultural inputs increased by 7.9 percent per annum, and consumption-related industries employment increased by 8.4 percent per annum.
   - In the Upper Pampanga project area from 1975 to 1979, employment in forward linkage activities rose by 17.1 percent per annum, in backward linkage industries by 6.7 percent per annum, and in consumption-related industries by 6.5 percent per annum.
   - In Oton and Tigbauen, output of production linkage industries grew by 10.3 percent per annum from 1974–79, while output in consumption-related industries grew by 4.0 percent per annum.
   - In Taiwan, there was a high and sustained growth in rural non-agricultural employment in every category for the economy as a whole, over the period from 1930–1956, accelerating in 1956–66 (see table 5.10). For 1930–56 the percentage increases were similar for different types of linkage. For 1956–66, the highest proportionate increases were recorded for industries not catering solely to local consumption but also supplying urban and export markets or producer goods (that is, textiles and wood, chemicals and metal products, and transport equipment). The more strictly consumption-related activities (trade, transport and communication, personal services, and construction) showed below average increases.
4. The explanation of employment in absolute terms was invariably significantly the highest in consumption-related activities in the Phil-

ippines. This occurred, despite the proportionately lower increase, because of the large proportion of non-agricultural employment accounted for by consumption-related activity, as described in 2. above.

- In the Gapan area, from 1961–71, consumption linked employment expansion accounted for 62.8 percent of the total expansion.
- In the Upper Pampanga, over 80 percent of additional jobs were in consumption-linked activities.
- In Oton and Tigbauen, expansion in consumption-related activity accounted for over 70 percent of the total expansion in employment.
- In Taiwan, 80 percent of the extra rural jobs created between 1956 and 1966 (outside the public sector, in industries where classification is possible), were in sectors serving local consumption needs. But most of the industries also provided goods or services as inputs for agriculture or as exports outside the area. Probably between 40 and 50 percent of the employment increase was for local consumption. This is less than in the Philippines and is due to the greater significance and more rapid growth, in Taiwan, of other types of output and employment. Employment in consumption related activities increased at a similar rate in the two countries.

5. In general among production-related activities in the Philippines, forward linkages are of much greater significance for absolute employment and employment expansion than backward linkages.
   - In Gapan, in 1971, employment in agricultural input supplies accounted for only 3.1 percent of total non-agricultural employment, while forward linkages accounted for 15 percent. Backward linkages constituted 3.2 percent of the employment expansion from 1961–71, and forward linkages for 16.6 percent.
   - In Upper Pampanga backward linkages in 1979 formed only 1.9 percent of total employment, and forward linkages 4.9 percent. Backward linkages accounted for 1.8 percent of employment expansion from 1975–79, and forward linkages for 9.8 percent.
   - In Taiwan, food processing was an important source of employment, accounting for a fifth of manufacturing rural employment in 1956 and 16.6 percent in 1966. Backward linkage industries were more developed in Taiwan; metal products, transport equipment, machinery, and equipment accounted for nearly as high a proportion of manufacturing employment (16.2 percent) in 1966. The backward linked manufacturing sector showed a higher proportionate increase than the food processing sector from 1956–66.
6. The ranking of linkages in terms of employment derives partly from the labour-intensity of the different types of linkage. The study of Oton and Tigbauen found that production-related activities accounted for substantially the greatest share in output expansion, but the labour-intensity of production-related activities was low relative to consumption-related activities, so that the consumption activities dominated in terms of *employment* expansion.

Conclusion on Magnitudes of Linkages

This survey of the evidence has established that linkages of non-agricultural activity with agricultural production have been a substantial source of employment in both countries. Consumption linkages have dominated in terms of the absolute number of employment opportunities created, despite a tendency for production-related activities to show a greater proportionate growth in output. The next section analyses the major determinants of the magnitude of the various linkages.

Causes of Magnitude of Linkages

The three kinds of linkage involve different types of relationships, so that causes need to be discussed separately.

Consumption Linkages

The nature and extent of consumption linkages depend on how income generated in agriculture is allocated between consumption and savings and among different types of consumption expenditure. Household disposal patterns depend mainly on the level of household income. For the rural economy as a whole, disposal patterns then depend on the average level of household income and the distribution of income among households.

Household income, Yh, may be divided into savings, Sh; imports of goods from outside the area, Ih; expenditure on locally produced food, Fh; and expenditure on local non-agricultural output, Dh. In fact, there is not a sharp distinction between expenditure on food and non-food, because a good deal of expenditure recorded as food includes non-agricultural services, such as processing, packaging, distribution, etc.

If s, i, f, and d represent the marginal propensity to save, import, spend on locally produced food, and local non-food, respectively, then $s + i + f + d = 1$. For any given increase in agricultural income, the consumption linkage is determined by the value of these propensities, which in turn depends on the level and distribution of income among agricultural households and the distribution of the extra income between households of different income-levels.

Agricultural households consist of landlords and tenants, owner-occupiers with different size farms, and agricultural labourers, with some overlap between the categories. In general, the higher the share of high income households (landlords and large farmers) and the lower the share of low-income households (small land-holders, tenants and wage-earners) in additional income, the less local consumption linkages are likely to be. This is because:

- high-income households tend to have a higher propensity to save than wage-earners; $sr > sp$; (r refers to "rich" households; p to "poor" households);

- high-income households tend to consume more imported goods and less local goods: ir > ip;
- however, high-income households tend to consume less food as a proportion of income: fr < fp. Consequently, while total local linkages will tend to be greater where the share of low-income households (small farmers and wage-earners) is greater, expenditure on non-food items will not be so much greater and could even be lower, dr >or < dp.

The evidence on consumer behaviour and linkages from Oton and Tigbauen broadly supports these hypotheses. The study investigated non-agricultural households (which had a much higher income than the farming households) as well as farming households at three levels of income.

As can be seen in table 5.11, the stimulus to local production was greater the lower the income of the household, because of differences in propensity to save. Import behaviour did not differ substantially, according to this study. But the study assumed the same propensity to import for each category of expenditure, irrespective of the income of the household.

A general equilibrium model, estimating variations in consumption and import propensities for the economy as a whole as the distribution of income changes between landlords and wage-earners, shows a lower share of consumption and a higher share of imports as the share of the landlord rises for the Philippines (Ahammed and Herdt). The employment resulting from extra consumption is substantially lower the higher the share of extra income received by the landlord class. Since high-income households tend to have a higher propensity to consume urban-produced goods (for example, consumer durables) than low-income households, the same approach to a rural subsector would show a stronger relationship, with local linkages increasing as the share of low-income classes rises.

Evidence from Taiwan shows the share of food in rural expenditure declining as household income rises, both at a particular point in time and over time. Families with incomes below T$20,000 allocated 64 percent of consumption to food and drink, while those with incomes above T$20,000 allocated 55 percent to food and drink (1966 Survey of Family Income and Expenditure). As average household incomes rise over time, the rising proportion of expenditure on non-food consumption increases opportunities for local non-agricultural employment. Moreover, over time there is a less marked tendency for savings propensities to rise as household incomes rise (as compared with differences between households of different income levels at the same point in time). The Taiwan evidence shows a strong tendency for rising expenditure on urban-produced consumer durables, as incomes rise. For example, the 1960 Census showed that less than 10 percent of farm households had electric fans and 23 percent had radios. By 1970 over half of farm households had some consumer durable.

To summarise the evidence on consumer linkages:

(a) the more unequal the income distribution among agricultural households, the greater the leakages out of the local economy from agricultural income;
(b) similarly, the more unequally distributed any additional agricultural income, the lower extra is demand for locally produced goods (including food and non-food);
(c) local linkages with non-agricultural sectors tend to be greater the more equally distributed income is, since the tendency for low-income households to spend more proportionately on food is offset—in terms of local linkages—by the tendency for higher-income households to save more and spend more on goods produced outside the rural area. Moreover, expenditure on food also involves local non-agricultural services.
(d) as average farm household incomes rise, local linkages rise in absolute amounts, as shown in the Philippines and Taiwan, where a one percent rise in agricultural income led to more than a one percent rise in non-agricultural employment. The relative significance of local linkages (as a proportion of total activity) as average incomes rise is the outcome of conflicting tendencies. On the one hand, there is a rising propensity to spend on non-agricultural items; on the other, some tendency for a rising proportion of expenditures to go to imported items. How strong this latter tendency is depends partly on supply factors—that is, whether local supplies of goods and services change in quality and quantity to keep pace with rising demands.

One major influence on the distribution of agricultural income is the distribution of land; this has a direct influence (determining the distribution of rent) and an indirect influence through the effects on labour-intensity of land use, since small farms generally use relatively more labour. The labour-intensity of land-use (and therefore the share of labour in agricultural income) is also strongly influenced by the extent of mechanisation and by the crop composition of output. Because of the importance of distributional effects in determining consumption linkages, these both become important issues for policies towards linkages.

Crop composition is one determinant of labour absorption in agriculture. The precise labour use for any crop depends on technology and organisation of production and varies between countries and regions, across seasons, and over time. Table 5.12 shows labour-use according to selected crops in Taiwan.

The data from Taiwan show considerable variations in labour-intensity of every crop over time. Labour use per hectare increased quite substantially from the early 1950s until the late-1960s. Since then it has fallen in every crop, reflecting the increasing mechanisation which occurred in response to a growing labour shortage in agriculture in Taiwan, as successful industrialisation led to the end of labour surplus.

Despite the variations for particular crops over time, the data also show broadly consistent variations in labour use between crops. Sugar has tended to be more labour-using than rice, but has shown a sharper fall in the last 15 years, indicating the high potential for mechanisation in sugar (to be discussed more below). While sugar can be a relatively labour-using crop, there are enormous seasonal variations in labour use. Of the new export vegetables, asparagus is highly labour-intensive; mushrooms are less so, but still markedly more labour-using than rice. Fruit export crops (bananas and pineapples) tend to use less labour than rice and sugar. The least labour-using category is "other crops" which includes rootcrops. Data from the Philippines and other Asian countries (see Aguilar, Bartsch, Ishikawa) suggest similar conclusions about the relative labour-intensity of different crops.

A comparison between Taiwan and the Philippines on crop composition and labour-absorption is shown in table 5.13. Around 1960, Taiwan had a higher proportion of the most labour-intensive crops (vegetables) than the Philippines, with over 10 percent of the total produce as compared with 3.0 percent in the Philippines. At that time, Taiwan also had a higher share of the least labour-intensive crops, with over 45 percent of crops being root crops, compared with 18 percent in the Philippines. Between 1960-61 and 1977-78 the crop composition in Taiwan became more labour-using as vegetables increased their share dramatically (to 33 percent of total tonnage), as Taiwan expanded growth of vegetables for export, such as mushrooms and asparagus, while output of root crops fell. In the Philippines, vegetables remained insignificant, but the share of bananas and pineapples increased so that in aggregate, crop composition in the Philippines became less labour-using. However, the actual change in labour-use depends also on the overall increase in output (higher in the Philippines than Taiwan) and changes in technology and organisation.

Technology and Mechanisation. A major influence on consumption linkages is the degree and nature of mechanisation, since this determines the direct employment associated with production and consequently consumption linkages.

There is strong evidence for the Philippines that mechanisation tends to be *labour displacing*, both with respect to family and hired labour. In rice production, labour displacement occurs in land preparation and in threshing (see Ahammed and Herdt, Gonzales, Herdt and Webster, Sison, Herdt and Duff). Labour displacement is significantly greater for large machines than for small (that is, for four-wheel tractors compared with power tillers and for large axial flow threshers than for portable threshers). In contrast, irrigation generally increases labour use. The differences in direct employment effects of differing technologies are large. According to the study by Ahammed and Herdt, one percent extra rice production would create 23,700 extra jobs in agriculture using animal horse-power, a four inch irrigation pump and a hand thresher, compared with only 5,300 using a four-wheel tractor, and a large axial flow thresher in rainfed conditions. The distribution of income tends to favour landlords, the more capital-intensive the methods. (More details of the estimated effects on direct employment land landlord share are shown in table 5.15.)

Direct employment effects—and therefore consumption linkages—are likely to be greatest with pump irrigation. Within each irrigation system, the least mechanised combinations tend to create most direct employment, while substantially less direct employment is associated with the most mechanised combinations (four-wheel tractors and large axial flow threshers).

While tractors and power tillers displace labour, they do not significantly affect yields. (See Duff, and Workshop (1983) passim, especially Gonzales, Herdt and Webster.) However, irrigation does have marked positive effects on yields, and mechanised threshing also has positive effects.

Mechanisation is even more dramatically labour-displacing in sugar cane cultivation where it is estimated that the reductions in labour requirements per hectare are 90 percent or more per task, with the greatest displacement in weeding. In sugar cultivation there are substantial economies of scale, such that full mechanisation is only economic for farms over 25 hectares. Mechanisation is yield increasing and permits Philippine sugar cultivation to remain economic in the face of adverse world prices. Small sugar farms using labour-intensive methods may not survive. Consequently, there is a strong trend towards reduced consumption linkages in sugar cultivation (See Aguilar).

Estimates of consumption linkage effects depend on the level of the real wage associated with employment in agriculture. A lower real wage would have smaller linkage effects for any given increase in agricultural employment. The determinants of the real wage in agriculture are many and complex. They divide into factors affecting *demand* and those affecting *supply* of labour in the agricultural sector. Demand for labour is influenced by mechanisation, other things being equal, higher mechanisation will tend to depress the real wage. Supply of labour depends on population growth and demand for labour elsewhere, especially in the urban centres.

In the Philippines, real wages in agriculture have been stagnant or even declining, despite rising agricultural production per head. One contributory factor has been the labour displacement caused by mechanisation (see David, p. 404). In contrast, in Taiwan mechanisation came later, once the exhaustion of the labour surplus had led to a sustained rise in real wages. In Taiwan, before 1970, there was much greater reliance on low-level mechanisation. In Taiwan in the mid-1960s power tillers accounted for 84.5 percent of total mechanical horsepower, compared with only 4.5 percent in agriculture in the Philippines (Barker and others). Since then the proportion of power tillers in the Philippines has risen substantially, but was nonetheless estimated to be only 20 percent in 1976 (David). Moreover, the supply of labour to agriculture was greater in the Philippines. Taiwan has had a lower population growth (a rate of 2.0 percent per annum from 1970–78 compared with 2.7 percent in the Philippines), and a much more rapid growth in industrial employment, with labour-intensive industry absorbing a steadily increasing proportion of the economy's labour force. In contrast, in the Philippines industrial growth has been comparatively slow and capital-intensive (see table 5.6 above and ILO, 1974).

Consequently, in the context of the overall development strategy, mechanisation in the Philippines has tended to have doubly negative effect on linkages—by reducing direct employment in agriculture and depressing the real wage.

Backward Production Linkages

As noted above, these are relatively small numerically in the Philippines, but are increasing rapidly. In relation to employment, by far the most important are distribution outlets—for fertiliser, seeds, and machinery. For example, these accounted for 196 employees in Cabantuan and Talevera (1979), while only 21 people were employed in actual equipment manufacturing. However, equipment servicing and manufacture generally develop fast as mechanisation proceeds, as is indicated by their greater role in Taiwan. Employment in these areas is likely to depend on the extent of use of modern inputs (fertilisers, seeds, machinery) and the machinery used. Small pumps, hand tillers and threshers, and power tillers can be produced in small workshops in the rural areas, while large tractors and axial flow threshers are almost invariably produced in the urban areas, with much of their parts imported.

The production of tools used in association with carabaos is almost entirely local (that is, ploughs, harrows, and hand implements) (Lantin). Modern mechanical methods involve varying degrees of rural, urban, and imported content. For the Philippines table 5.14 shows how labour content varied as a proportion of the selling price.

For the Philippines as a whole (urban and rural) backward linkages are substantially greater for power-tillers than for tractors, while there is not much difference between portable and large threshers. Rural production occurs only for the smaller machines (power tillers and portable threshers) (See Mikkelson and Langam). Consequently, rural backward linkages tend to go in the same direction as consumption linkages.

Using a general equilibrium approach, Ahammed and Herdt put production and consumption linkages together to estimate the total indirect employment created by different types of water regime and mechanisation. They found that total indirect employment created was very large, outweighing the direct employment (see table 5.15). In general, the direct and indirect employment effects are closely related. Taking production and consumption linkages together, the linkage effects are similar for the most labour-intensive techniques and the intermediate techniques, and smaller for the most mechanised techniques.

In Taiwan, purchased inputs among farm households have risen rapidly. Between 1952 and 1972, purchased inputs (including hired labour) doubled per farm household in real terms. This was due to the widespread adoption of chemical fertilisers (in 1970 93 percent of Taiwan's farm households used chemical fertilisers and 87 percent used pesticides). As the labour market tightened in the late 1960s, there was a dramatic increase in the use of power-tillers, from a few thousand in the early 1960s to 24,000 in 1972

(Ho, p. 28). The ownership of mechanised aids has varied with the size of the farm.

Policies towards Mechanisation. The evidence summarised above shows that large-scale mechanisation has had negative effects on linkages in the Philippines, mainly because of the labour displacing effects of these technologies. Moreover, for tractorisation in rice cultivation, there does not appear to be a consequential rise in yields which could justify the mechanisation from the point of view of maximising output. The situation is different in Taiwan where most mechanisation has consisted of small-scale methods, and where a labour shortage began to emerge from the late-1960s. Despite these conclusions, mechanisation in agriculture in the Philippines has been proceeding quite rapidly over the past few decades, as table 5.16 shows.

Three types of policy have influenced the rate and nature of mechanisation—policies towards land distribution; policies towards prices and credit; and policies towards research and development.

1. *Land distribution:* The size of landholding influences the rate of mechanisation, with larger farms more likely to mechanise, and, when they do so, to adopt tractors rather than power-tillers. This is one reason why Taiwan, with much smaller farms, has a much higher proportion of power-tillers in the total mechanised horsepower in use. Land reform in the Philippines, which occurred from 1972 and involved dividing some large-scale rice farms into smaller units, led to a greater proportion of tillers in the total. Power-tillers accounted for 46 percent of the total number of tractors and power-tillers in the years 1960 to 1971, and 83 percent of the total in 1972–1980. Another reason for this switch towards power-tillers was the growing use of machinery in rice farming. Early mechanisation was almost entirely in large sugar estates, where tractors predominate.

The size of farm is the major determinant of mechanisation in sugar. Large estates (50 hectares and over), which account for the bulk of land devoted to sugar, were the first to introduce tractors in the Philippines, and have recently begun to introduce many other mechanised techniques, including mechanical harvesting. Small sugar farms continue to use labour-intensive techniques (Aguilar).

2. *Prices and credit:* These include policies towards interest rates, tariffs, the exchange rate, and fuel prices. Since 1966 four credit programmes involving subsidized credit have been agreed upon between the Central Bank of the Philippines and the World Bank (the implicit subsidy is estimated to be 12 percent). Studies show that this programme was the major factor affecting sales of tractors and power-tillers (Duff, 1975 and Sanvictores, 1977, Sycip, Gorres and Velayo, 1980). The programmes tended to favour tractors over power-tillers, financing a much higher proportion of total tractor sales (30 percent) than power-tiller sales (7 percent) between 1966–1979.

Tariff policy in the Philippines has been designed to promote domestic production of power-tillers and has thereby increased the price of power-tillers relative to tractors. In the 1970s, the net implicit tariff on power-tillers (including the effect of exchange rate overvaluation) was 19 percent, while there was a zero tariff on tractors.

The overall combined impact of the interest rate subsidy, exchange rate overvaluation, tariffs and fuel tax has been estimated to have resulted in a subsidy on use of power tillers and water pumps in the Philippines in the mid-1970s of 32 percent, and one on tractors of 47 percent (see David). Factor price distortions were the main cause of tractorisation, according to David. The main element in these distortions was the subsidised credit programme.

3. *Research and development:* The main effort in the Philippines has been that of IRRI in developing small-scale methods. They were especially successful in the development of a small-scale portable thresher, which has begun to replace the large-scale axial flow thresher on small farms. In Central Luzon it is estimated that 92 percent of farms are using mechanical threshers.

There has also been some success in the development of hand tractors. Since 1966, increased use of hand tractors for land preparation has been in evidence. This was made possible by the increase in farm incomes and the greater availability of credit.

Domestic production of hand tractors started in the early 1970s with an important stimulus arising from the introduction of a simple prototype designed by IRRI. Table 5.17 demonstrates not only the continued increase in the use of hand tractors but also the increased share taken by the domestic variety. Growth of domestic sales from 1972–1978 was 5.7 percent, with IRRI-designed machines accounting for nearly half of the 1975 domestic production.

In a sample survey of Philippine agricultural machinery manufacturers (Mikkelson), 37 percent of the firms sampled had less than 10 employees, averaging five employees per firm. The survey respondents considered that IRRI machinery designs and technical assistance were significant sources of new technology.

Forward Linkages

It appears that more processing of agricultural commodities takes place in rural Taiwan than in the Philippines. In 1966, two-thirds of those employed in agricultural food-processing in Taiwan were in the rural areas and another 10 percent were in the newly emerging towns. In the 1950s and early 1960s, rapid growth in exports of processed agricultural products (canned vegetables) led export growth. Since then there has been a switch to manufactured exports. Processing of vegetables was largely decentralised. Many features influence the degree of local processing. One factor is the type of commodities grown and the sort of processing required. Another is the location of consumption. In general, processing for local consumption takes place locally; the main choice of location arises for commodities which supply urban or export markets. In this context, the technological facts that are relevant to the location of processing are perishability of the product, economies of scale, and considerations of product quality. For example, the rapid growth of exports of canned mushrooms and asparagus in Taiwan were naturally associated with dispersed processing because of perishability and difficulties in transporting the raw vegetables. The insignificance of these commodities as major exports in the Philippines partly accounts for the smaller degree of rural processing. However, deficient processing facilities might be one cause of the weaker performance in exports of this kind.

There are, however, a number of commodities where there appears to be a genuine choice of processing technology and of location. Below we discuss three examples. In pineapple processing and canning, and in preparation of bananas for export, the choice is illustrated by a comparison between developments in the Philippines and Taiwan, since the two countries have made different choices. In rice processing, the range and determinants of choice are illustrated by developments in the Philippines, where mechanised methods are being actively promoted and are likely to displace more decentralised and labour-intensive methods.

Example: Pineapples. In both the Philippines and Taiwan exports of canned pineapples are substantial. In 1970, the Philippines exported 100,000 metric tons, while Taiwan exported 81,000 metric tons.

There is a sharp contrast between pineapple canneries in the two countries (see Armas, 1975, 1976). Two companies account for pineapple canning in the Philippines, both subsidiaries of multinationals, Dolephil (Dole) and Philpack (Del Monte). In contrast, in Taiwan there are 23 different (national) companies (Armas, 1975, table 3).

The processing and canning technology adopted in the Philippines is more integrated than in Taiwan, while the plants are more capital intensive and of larger scale. The two producers in the Philippines have all their processing facilities on one site, while the Taiwanese operations are dispersed, not only because of the large number of companies, but also because operations are often dispersed within a company. For example, the Taiwan Pineapple Corporation uses five different plants. Differences in technology are illustrated in table 5.18. As this table indicates, there are significant differences between the two plants in the Philippines as well as between each of the Philippine plants and typical Taiwanese plants.

The differences in plant characteristics between the Philippines and Taiwan lead to differences in product quality. Taiwanese canned pineapples supply a lower quality segment of the market, both because of a lack of well recognised brand names and because of less even quality. Nonetheless, there is a large (and sustained) market for this quality, as indicated by Taiwan's sustained share of the market. From 1969–73 both the Philippines and Taiwan accounted for the same share of the market of leading importers (18.3 percent each of the exports of main exporting countries). However, over the 1960s, the growth in Philippine exports, starting from a lower level, was greater than that of Taiwan.

Differences in technology choice and concentration of processing facilities can be accounted for by several factors:

(i) Minimum wage legislation in the Philippines was such that average wages in pineapple canneries in the Philippines were above those in Taiwan, especially in the early 1960s, as shown in table 5.19.

(ii) Infrastructure: Infrastructural deficiences in the Philippines (see below) meant that canneries in the Phillippines had to provide some of their "own" infrastructure, encouraging concentration of facilities (Dolephil supplied some social investments).

(iii) Organisational differences in processing: The many local companies in Taiwan naturally led to a smaller scale and more dispersed processing, in contrast to the situation in the Philippines with only two companies. But as noted there was also more dispersal within companies. This was in part due to differences in wages and infrastructure, etc. It was also due to the differences between multinational subsidiaries and local companies. Multinational companies tend to concentrate facilities, thus economising on local knowledge and contacts and decision-making, and making use of their familiarity with larger scale techniques from other parts of the world. In contrast, local companies have more dispersed local knowledge and contacts.

(iv) Organisational differences in farming: The Philippine plants were largely (not wholly) supplied by plantations, which could provide uniformity of quality and large-scale supplies, suitable for large-scale and automated processing. In Taiwan, each of the plants were supplied by small holder farms, with a number of farms supplying each plant. This reduces the uniformity of product and therefore the relative efficiency of large-scale and automated processing plants. Smaller scale and less automatic plants can cope better with less uniform commodities for processing.

Example: Bananas. In Taiwan, bananas have been grown by small holders in two provinces, Taochung and Kaohsiung, at a low level of capital and technology, but with considerable government assistance with fertilisers, pest control, irrigation, and erosion control. Exports are organised by three groups of exporters—two producer groups and representatives of Japanese importers. Before 1963, the Japanese market was entirely served by Taiwan, with homogeneous fruit "subject to little quality control, no branding and produced as low-scale, low yield, low technological input enterprise" (Read).

In 1963, the Japanese liberalised the market for banana imports. From 1963–1966, Taiwanese production and exports grew very rapidly, from 3.4 million to 20.4 million 40 pound boxes. After 1966, the major multinational companies entered the market, and after a short period in which they procured supplies from Ecuador, they adopted the Philippines as their main source of supplies. Three companies developed facilities in the Philippines: the Standard Philippine Fruit Company (Castle and Cooke), Philpack (Del Monte) and United Brands. The three companies had varied arrangements to secure supplies. Stanfilco and Philpack contracted local businessmen to acquire land and provide supplies. United Brands entered into an agreement with the Tagum Agricultural Development Company, a large Filipino company which operates plantations. Each provided technical assistance, fertilisers, pesticides and financial assistance to local suppliers. Each operated on a large-scale and with expensive and sophisticated equipment for branding, packing, transport, and refrigeration.

The effects of multinational companies' production in the Philippines was to reduce the Taiwanese share of the Japanese market sharply, as shown in table 5.20. Taiwan's share of the market fell because Taiwanese exporters could not compete with high quality, pleasant looking, differentiated (by branding) and advertised bananas. Tie-ups between the MNCs and Japanese retailers were largely responsible.

In some ways, the comparison is similar to the pineapple case, with dispersed smallholder production and decentralised processing facilities with low levels of capital and technology in Taiwan, and multinational dominated organisation in the Philippines, using sophisticated and expensive equipment, and securing supplies mainly from large scale farmers or plantations. In Taiwan, the government provided various facilities—advice, fertiliser, pesticides, etc.—which made smallholder production possible. In the Philippines, there was less government assistance and the MNCs provided these facilities.

The major difference between the two examples is that the MNC product quality in bananas combined with restrictive marketing arrangements (achieved through a combination of high quality control, branding, and advertising) successfully ousted the lower-quality and unadvertised Taiwanese product. The Taiwanese did not find a sufficient market for the lower quality product, as they succeeded in doing with pineapples.

Example: Rice Processing (Pre-milling and Milling). One of the most significant forward linkages in rice-growing areas is rice processing. This includes threshing, drying, handling, and milling. The implications—in terms of income distribution and employment—of this forward linkage depend critically on the choice of technique for these activities. There are a great variety of methods for post-harvest rice processing, ranging from traditional methods which are very labour-intensive, to large-scale mechanised techniques, for both pre-milling (threshing and drying) and milling activities. Most of the technology used in this area in the Philippines is highly labour-intensive, but more capital-using techniques are being introduced, while government policy is accelerating mechanisation.

It is helpful to analyse the implications of technology choice in pre-milling and milling separately.

1. *Pre-milling.* In the Philippines, there are two areas where machinery is being introduced—for threshing and for solar drying. In both, traditional methods use no power, with very simple tools. For example, a stick may be used for threshing and rice may be dried by laying it out in the sun. Labour requirements fall sharply with mechanisation; mechanical threshing reduces labour used by about three-quarters, while drying machines use about half (or less) the labour of solar drying (see IRRI, 1978, and table 5.21). In absolute terms labour requirements per ton are much greater for threshing than for drying and the labour saving from mechanisation is

much greater in threshing (on the order of 32 hours per ton) than drying (with a saving of four to eight hours per ton). Grain losses during processing are somewhat lower with mechanised techniques. On average, it is estimated that the loss is 3.6 percent with mechanical techniques, compared with 4.6 percent with traditional methods (IRRI, 1978). There are also slight quality differences. More mechanised techniques lead to slightly higher quality.

A survey in the Bicol area showed that sun-drying was substantially cheaper than mechanical drying, but mechanical threshing was significantly cheaper than manual methods, when labour costs were calculated at the market wage rate. However, these labour costs for manual methods were all in kind rather than in cash since family labour was employed or other labour paid in kind, whereas over half the costs of mechanical threshers were in cash. For farmers with limited access to cash (that is, subsistence farmers), manual methods would be preferred. Family labour may have a much lower real (opportunity) cost than the market wage rate in those cases where family members would not seek outside work at all, or where they might but only at a much higher wage than they are prepared to work for on the family farm. Thus the cost estimates (shown in table 5.22) suggest that mechanical threshing is likely to be the most profitable choice for commercial farmers who have to hire labour for threshing, but manual methods may be the appropriate choice for family farms. The solar method of drying is unambiguously the best method for all types of farmer, according to this survey. These calculations are at market prices, not social or shadow prices. But there is no reason to believe that, in this context, social prices would differ substantially from market prices, except for family labour which has already been discussed.

The evidence on costs, reported above, concerns axial flow threshers. Portable threshers have substantially lower capital costs (one quarter or less) than axial flow threshers. They are also more suited to areas with poor roads. Their breakeven output levels are substantially less, and they are simpler to produce and maintain. However, they also displace labour and reduce the wage scale, as shown in chapter four.

To summarise: In post-production pre-milling activities, a combination of hand threshing or low cost portable machines and sun-drying methods seems to be the most appropriate choice for small farmers in the Philippines, except where real labour costs are extremely low (substantially below market rates), when traditional manual methods of threshing remain appropriate. A survey of 137 farmers in three villages in the Bicol region in 1976-77 showed 38 percent using mechanised threshers, with the rest adopting a variety of manual methods. Almost all farmers used sun-drying methods (IRRI).

2. *Milling.* There is a distinction between village mills which process locally produced rice for local consumption, and commercial mills which handle supplies for the urban areas. While most rice in the Philippines is milled in decentralised and fairly small-scale mills (compared with modern integrated plants), the commercial mills adopt a different technology from

the village mills and are generally on a somewhat bigger scale (see table 5.23). The most commonly used village mill is a kikisan type which consists of a steel huller, but some mills combine steel hullers with rubber-rolls. Commercial mills chiefly use cono type mills. Village mills are generally small, and need to be able to mill rice in small batches. While commercial mills tend to be larger, there is some overlap, the smaller commercial mills being no larger than medium size village mills.

Technical comparisons between the mills observed in the Bicol survey showed no marked differences in recovery rates. Steel hullers have a significantly higher proportion of broken rice than cono-type mills or mills combining rubber rolls with steel hullers. Total capital costs are lowest for the steel hullers and greatest for the cono mills. Labour costs and other variable costs are rather similar across mills per ton milled.

The relative profitability of different mills depends critically on capacity utilisation. With 100 percent capacity utilisation (defined as 12 hours per day and 24 days per month), the costs per ton of the steel hullers would be the lowest, at $4.09, compared with $6.69 for the largest (and cheapest) of the cono mills. A national survey in the Philippines also showed that with equal capacity utilisation, the village mills were the cheapest (see *A Profile of the Philippines Rice Milling*). But the IRRI survey showed that the actual utilisation rate was very low for the steel hullers (12 percent) and very high for the large cono mill (97 percent), and at these rates costs were lower for the cono mill. One village mill which combined a steel huller and a rubber roll had a fairly high utilisation rate (77 percent) and its costs per ton were below those of the large cono.

In general, it is probable that village mills will have low capacity utilisation because of the small lots involved in milling for local consumption. This is likely irrespective of the technology. The level of utilisation of the commercial mills should be much higher—again irrespective of technology. Consequently, in analysing the net benefits from different technologies, equal capacity utilisation should be assumed, within each category.

The cost analysis (contained in table 5.23) suggests that for rural consumption—where in principle a 50 percent capacity utilisation is achievable—steel hullers are the most appropriate technology, with lower total costs and lower capital costs. But this conclusion only holds if the lower quality of rice is acceptable to rural consumers. As quality requirements rise, the combined steel hullers and rubber roll mills become the appropriate choice.

For *commercial* production (that is, for urban consumption), the rubber-roll/steel huller combination is preferred over the cono mills. The quality of rice produced is very similar, while the costs per ton are lower, given equal capacity utilisation. Capital costs in total and per worker are much lower; the smaller scale and lower capital costs make the technology more accessible to small local entrepreneurs. It is possible that local manufacture of this technology could further reduce capital costs and increase linkage effects.

As rural per capita incomes rise, the marketable surplus consumed outside the area will rise, increasing the extent of commercial milling. With existing milling patterns, this would lead to a switch towards large-scale cono techniques which would both reduce opportunities for small-scale entrepreneurs as compared with smaller scale mills, and be associated with lower local linkages costs since local production of the machinery is possible for the steel huller/rubber roll combination but not for the cono mills.

Therefore, to maintain the high forward linkage effects of rice production, it is important to encourage the use of the steel huller/rubber roll type mills for commercial supplies. Technological improvements in this type of mill (which are being investigated by IRRI) would help. Government and aid donor policy towards the industry is also of major importance.

3. *Government Policy in the Philippines towards Rice-Processing.* Until recently small-scale decentralised techniques have dominated rice-milling in the Philippines. However, government policy in the Philippines is to encourage modernisation and mechanisation of post-production rice processing methods. The major objective seems to be to maximise the supplies of high quality rice to the urban areas and eventually for export. Effects on rural employment and income distribution do not seem to be taken into account in formulating this policy. For example, the government is encouraging farmers' associations to acquire threshers by offering credit facilities on easy terms and by providing threshers (of the large-scale variety) for its grain centers. It is also providing mechanical dryers.

In milling, the National Food Authority has decided to set up four integrated milling complexes in the major rice producing areas to produce a better quality of rice. It has also launched a modernisation programme for private sector (cono-type) mills, making licensing dependent on milling efficiency and providing credit facilities for modernisation.

Government policy is supported by some aid-donors. In the Cagayan Valley, the Asian Development Bank (ADB) is helping to finance a major integrated rice-processing complex, designed to process 100,000 tons of paddy annually. This compares with an annual capacity of 1,630 tons for the largest cono-mill in the Bicol survey, and 619 tons capacity of the steel huller/rubber roll combination, the technology identified above as most appropriate. The ADB project will also provide a number of large threshers and mechanical driers. In addition, the ADB is supporting a modernisation programme for cono-mills, providing relatively low-cost credit for approved modernisation. The scheme covers mills of 1,000KG. to 4,000KG.—which are larger than the cono-mills described above, but much smaller than the new complexes being built. Estimated cost per mill is $38,857 (that is, five times the cost of a single steel huller/rubber roll combination).

Government policies (supported in this case by the ADB) are thus promoting mechanisation of rice processing, with greater concentration of milling in a few large-scale centres. If the policy continues, the decentralised small-scale processes which have been prevalent in the Philippines, and have been reflected in the high forward linkage effects of rice production (illustrated above), will be displaced as rice production grows.

Conclusions from Examples of Forward Linkages. Comparisons between the Philippines and Taiwan with respect to bananas and pineapples show similar differences in location of processing and choice of technique in the two cases. Taiwan has used more decentralised and labour-intensive methods in each case. The major factor accounting for this is the organisational difference, with multinational companies dominating in the Philippines and local companies in Taiwan. The Taiwan government provided more technical support, thus facilitating local companies. For both fruits, the product quality associated with large-scale multinational processing was "higher" than when local companies were responsible. For pineapples, Taiwan's local companies succeeded, nonetheless, in maintaining their share of the international market, aiming at the lower-income segment of the market. However, in bananas, the multinational brand names and marketing arrangements ousted the apparently lower quality Taiwanese bananas in the Japanese market.

The examples of rice processing were taken from the Philippines. In pre-milling activities, sun-drying methods were superior to mechanical driers in the Philippines context. Low-cost portable threshers were more appropriate (and lower cost) than large-scale axial flow threshers and, in most circumstances, more efficient and lower-cost than manual threshing. In milling there are a variety of low-cost small-scale techniques in the rural areas. The most labour-intensive tend to produce a low-quality rice. But quality can be improved by a rubber-roll/steel huller combination which results in lower-cost milling than the cono-mills, for equal capacity utilisation, and produces rice of similar quality. Since the capital cost per mill is substantially lower, this technique permits a much greater spread of opportunities.

In both pre-milling and milling, Philippine government policy—in collaboration with the Asian Development Bank—is promoting substantial increases in mechanisation. The policy has been justified as required to raise the quality of rice-processing and to ensure a steady supply of high-quality rice for the urban areas and eventually for export. However, the quality of rice can be raised by improvements to the village mills. The assessment of the mechanisation programme seems to have neglected the costs involved in the destruction of rural opportunities.

In Taiwan, decentralised methods of canning vegetables (mushrooms and asparagus) also provided substantial rural employment opportunities. These were not present in the Philippines, since these crops were not grown.

In addition to the factors discussed above, differences in infrastructure have influenced choices and opportunities in every case. These are discussed in the next section.

Infrastructure

The discussion above has focussed on the factors leading to high local linkages from the perspective of demand. Favourable demand factors lead to a potential for rural linkages. But the actual development of non-agricultural activities depends on supply factors as well. A major influence here is the state of infrastructure. Most indicators show that provision of rural infrastructure in Taiwan has been substantially greater than in the Philippines (see table 5.24). In 1950, Taiwan had five times the installed electricity capacity of the Philippines. In 1975, only 26.6 percent of households in the Philippines had electricity, compared with 99 percent in Taiwan (1979). Taiwan has 2.5 times the highways per square kilometre, compared with the Philippines. Taiwan's roads are also of a higher standard, with over one-half paved compared with just over one-quarter paved in the Philippines. Taiwan also has extensive railway coverage. In the Philippines, the railways are of minor significance, representing an addition of only 4.0 percent to the highway coverage, compared with 33 percent in Taiwan.

The extensive coverage of rural electrification in Taiwan facilitated the rapid growth of decentralised industry, including those meeting local demands and those supplying urban and export markets. A study of the impact of rural electrification projects in the Philippines—covering 397,000 people—showed that within one year of the provision of energy, over one hundred new enterprises were established, including rice mills, welding shops, meat processing, ice plants, bakeries, and banana cracker plants (see Dumol).

The extensive transport network in Taiwan was especially important for industries supplying urban and export markets. Indeed, the rapid development of this type of industry—notably food processing and textiles—in the rural areas could not have taken place without the extensive and high quality transport network. As noted above, growth in the output of these industries represents the most significant difference between rural industrialisation in Taiwan and that in the Philippines. Differences in infrastructure are responsible for a large part of the differences in rural industrialisation between the two countries.

A notable feature of infrastructure in the Philippines is its uneven distribution as table 5.25 indicates. The rural areas in Taiwan benefit from a more even distribution as well as from higher average levels of infrastructure facilities than the Philippines.

There have also been significant differences in credit distribution in the two countries. In the Philippines, credit has been distributed from the top downwards through a handful of major institutions (for example, the Philippines National Bank). In Taiwan, in contrast, credit institutions have been much more dispersed, with banking and credit facilities attached to farmers' associations.

IV. POLICY IMPLICATIONS

The study has shown that non-agricultural activities in the rural areas can become an important source of work and income. Growth in agricultural output is a vital precondition for expansion of non-agricultural activities in the rural areas. The Philippines experience shows that even where conditions are not especially conducive to high linkages, growth in agricultural output leads to substantial growth in non-agricultural opportunities, especially in the production and distribution of consumer goods and services. The elasticity of non-agricultural employment with respect to growth in agricultural output is greater than one, according to Philippine evidence: that is, for a one percent increase in agricultural production, more than one percent growth in non-agricultural employment is likely. Consequently, all policies aimed at increasing agricultural output are relevant to raising non-agricultural employment opportunities. These include irrigation, research and development and extension, improving the availability of inputs for agriculture, such as new seeds and fertiliser, policies towards agricultural credit, and sustaining the real prices farmers receive for their produce. Where agricultural output has been stagnant (as in much of sub-Saharan Africa) reversing this situation is the single most important aspect of promoting appropriate technology in the rural areas.

The study has shown that the magnitude of linkages, for any given increase in agricultural output, varies according to the pattern of agricultural growth. In particular, the more labour-absorbing the growth, the higher the linkages. In the Philippines, labour absorption would be increased by extending *irrigation*. In 1950 in the Philippines, only 13.9 percent of cultivated land was irrigated, compared with over 50 percent in Taiwan. By 1975, 26 percent of the rice-growing areas, or 37.6 percent of potentially irrigable land (according to World Bank estimates) in the Philippines was irrigated, but there were considerable regional variations, with an average of 47.2 pecent in Luzon (where the land frontier had been reached) and 17.3 percent in Mindanao. Further investment in irrigation is an important policy tool for promoting agricultural growth and associated non-agricultural activities.

Labour absorption tends to be greater in small farms than in large farms, partly because small farms are usually less mechanised, and adopt more labour-using machinery. This was shown in the Philippines after the land reforms of the early 1970s, when the ratio of power tillers to tractors increased substantially. In Taiwan, with typically smaller farms, mechanisation has consisted predominantly of small-scale methods (power tillers and small threshers). Further measures of *land reform* would therefore increase linkages.

Agricultural mechanisation in the Philippines—in which four-wheel tractors have been important—is largely labour-displacing and has little positive effect on yields. Small-scale machines (power tillers and portable threshers) are not only less labour-displacing, but also have greater backward production linkages, because they are often made locally. Mechanisation has been artificially encouraged in the Philippines by programmes of subsidised credit, jointly developed by the World Bank and the Government. The net effect of these and other measures (tariffs, exchange rate, etc.) has been to provide a large subsidy to mechanisation, especially great for the larger machines. The negative effect on local linkages further supports the view that there is no justification for subsidising mechanisation in agriculture in the Philippines.

Crop composition also affects labour-absorption. Other things being equal, high value labour intensive crops generate the greatest consumption linkages, as with asparagus and mushroom production in Taiwan, which had the additional advantage of being associated with high forward linkages.

The study has shown that choice of technology can vary considerably with respect to forward linkage activities. In the Philippines, centralised and capital-intensive methods were adopted in bananas and pineapples, largely because of the dominance of multinational companies; in contrast, in Taiwan, local companies adopted more dispersed, small-scale, and labour-intensive methods. Rice milling created very large numbers of employment opportunities in the rural areas in the Philippines, with the growth of rice output associated with the seed revolution. But government policy, with the participation of the ADB, is promoting large-scale, capital-intensive, integrated rice-processing complexes. The aim, in part, is to secure regular high quality supplies of milled rice for the urban areas, and ultimately for export. The implications for rural job opportunities and income distribution do not seem to have been taken into consideration. The appropriate alternative—which has been established as technically feasible—is to upgrade small-scale rural mills.

The availability and distribution of infrastructure are critical factors in determining the supply response to demands generated by rising agricultural output and incomes. Extensive rural electrification was essential to Taiwan's pattern of rural industrialisation. In the Philippines, rural electrification has been much less extensive, and shows considerable regional imbalance. Taiwan's high quality and extensive road and rail networks have also been important in making rural Taiwan attractive for location of some unlinked activities, for example, textile exports, which located in the rural areas to a much greater extent than normal. A more balanced distribution (and high level) of social infrastructure (doctors, nurses, clinics, schools, and so on) in Taiwan has also provided the conditions for decentralised industrialisation by reducing the power of "urban pull" for successful entrepreneurs.

Taiwan's general development strategy—with more realistic prices and less import protection—undoubtedly favoured rural industrialisation, comparatively, since the policy gave much more importance to genuine (as against artifically created) cost advantages. Consequently, the low cost of labour in the rural areas and the competitive advantages of small-scale and labour-intensive techniques gained more leverage than in the Philippines.

Taiwan has had more favourable conditions with respect to local linkages on every count that we have identified as important—size of farm and land distribution, mechanisation and labour absorption in agriculture, organisation of forward processing activities, and extent and distribution of infrastructure. However, growth in agriculture in the Philippines has been associated with flourishing non-agricultural development in the rural areas, though not at the same rate of expansion as in Taiwan, suggesting a similar potential if the policy environment were as favourable. In the final section, we shall consider the political dimension to securing a more favourable policy environment.

V. THE POLITICAL ECONOMY OF APPROPRIATE POLICY CHOICES

This section discusses the political factors underlying policy choices. The analysis is concerned primarily with the Philippines, since it is there that we have identified the need for some substantial policy changes.

In the last section we identified the following policies as promoting appropriate technology in the rural areas, through enhancing rural linkages:

- Policies to promote agricultural production, including policies towards agricultural prices and credit, and investment in infrastructure;
- Land reform;
- Removal of any artificial encouragement of mechanisation;
- Encouragement of high value labour-intensive crops;
- Development of rural infrastructure, both "productive" (electrification, roads/rail) and social (schools, hospitals, etc.);
- A balanced provision of credit (in quantity and terms) as between urban and rural, large and small-scale activities;
- Support for small-scale local companies for forward processing activities, as against the large-scale integrated plants of the MNCs and government. This involves assistance in technological upgrading and technical information services, as well as policies towards infrastructure and credit.

The main interest groups that would be affected by these policies may be classified as follows:

Domestic: Rural
- Landowners and large-scale farmers
- Small farmers/tenants
- Landless labourers
- Rural entrepreneurs

Domestic: Urban
- Elite/"cronies"—bureaucrats managing parastatals, owners and managers of large-scale private farms, managers in MNCs
- Urban workers employed in formal sector
- Urban employed in informal sector and urban unemployed

Foreign
- Aid donors, bilateral and multilateral
- MNCs

Matrix 5.1 shows gains (G) and losses (L) from the various policy measures identified. N indicates a neutral position, while U indicates uncertainty.

The political economy of decision-making depends not only on potential gains and losses of various groups, but also on their political power. This varies between countries and over time, according to changing circumstances. It is difficult, and inevitably somewhat subjective and arbitrary, to attribute political power to different groups. Table 5.26 provides an illustrative system of weighting for the Philippines, roughly reflecting the situation in 1984 while Marcos was still in power.

Applying this weighting to the various policies provides a way of indicating (very roughly, of course) the net political advantages of the various policies, as shown on matrix 5.2.

Analysis of matrix 5.2 permits identification of (i) political feasibility of various policies in the current context; (ii) location of possible intervention by international donors, and where they might plausibly influence the outcome; and (iii) possible changes in policy mix following political changes. While clearly the outcome shown in the matrix is neither definitive nor fully objective, the approach permits a more analytic discussion of political elements than is normally undertaken. (See Timmer and Falcon for a somewhat similar approach, in the context of international comparisons of policies towards rice.)

1. Political feasibility: In the present political system, where the influence of large landowners, the elite, and foreign interests are paramount and the influence of the small-scale sector, especially in the rural areas, is small, many of the policy changes which would promote rural industrialisation show negative net political advantages. Three policy changes have a positive outcome: policies of agricultural investment; expenditure on rural infrastructure; and policies to change the crop composition towards high-value labour intensive crops. In so far as the first two policies require additional public expenditure, there may be negative effects from reduced expenditure elsewhere and/or increased taxation. In addition, especially in the present climate, international aid donors might oppose increased expenditure. Nonetheless, these policies are less likely to meet decisive political opposition than most others. Moreover, additional revenues are likely to become available at the local government level if the expenditures are for locally planned infrastructural projects. Policy towards crop composition requires further research to identify possibilities, obstacles, and incentives required.

2. By strongly supporting (or opposing) particular policies, aid donors can influence the outcome, especially where they are directly involved. For example, if the World Bank reversed its policy for credit for agricultural mechanisation, and the ADB reversed its policy supporting integrated rice processing complexes, this might be decisive. Where the net gain or loss is relatively small, the aid donors might change the outcome. According to the matrix, this might be the situation in relation to agricultural prices and credit.

3. The matrix makes it clear that the present policy set broadly reflects (as one would expect) current political influence in the Philippines: in particular, the small influence of landless labourers and rural industrialists, and fairly small influence of small farmers, leads to the net disadvantage of measures such as land reform, reform of credit to favour small-scale entrepreneurs and general support for small-scale processing and production. It is possible that the changing situation in the Philippines—after Marcos—will change the perception of political significance of various groups. The matrix of net advantages would then change.

Taiwan adopted most of the policies discussed above during the 1950s and 1960s. This reflected a different conjuncture of political interests. The

Chinese from the mainland, who ruled from 1949, were free from the oppressive influence of local elites (landlords and urban capitalists). They were anxious to achieve self-sufficiency in food, and were therefore pro-agriculture; they wanted to avoid large inequalities emerging, especially in view of the implicit comparison with Mainland China. Rural industrialists had more influence over government policy, and this was cumulative; as their economic power grew, so did their political power. In addition, the United States exerted leverage over the economy at this time, and used it to achieve price and trade policies which proved conducive to the rapid expansion of labour intensive exports of food and textiles. Multinational companies had only a minor role, and a correspondingly small influence.

The political matrix of the Philippines put forward here largely reflects short-term advantages and disadvantages. The Taiwan experience shows that from a longer run perspective, the advantages and disadvantages may change. For example, long run prosperity enhances the long run security of the elite, and may therefore be considered to be worth short run losses.

VI. CONCLUSION

This chapter has shown that agricultural growth can be a very substantial source of rural employment opportunities in industry and services. Significant effects may occur even where the policy environment is not especially favourable. Where government policies towards agriculture, processing, and infrastructure support linkages, the employment effects of increases in agricultural output may be doubled. Even without such favourable policies, agricultural growth using appropriate technology can be more important to the spread of employment in the rural areas than any other single policy to promote AT. A development strategy which strengthens the agricultural sector and supports rural industrialisation leads to stronger growth in both agriculture and rural industry since linkages between the two mean that their growth path is mutually strengthened.

REFERENCES

Aguilar, F. 1984. *The Making of Cane Sugar, Poverty, Crisis and Change in Negros Occidental*, La Salle Social Research Center, Monograph Series, 2.

Ahammed, C., and R. Herdt. 1983. A general equilibrium analysis of the effects of rice mechanisation in the Philippines. In *The Consequences of Small Rice Farm Mechanisation in the Philippines*, Workshop Papers, Development Academy of the Philippines, Dec. 1–3 1983 (referred to as "Workshop Papers" below).

Anderson, D., and F. Khambata. 1981. *Small Enterprises and Development Policy in the Philippines: A Case Study*, World Bank Staff Working Paper No. 468.

Armas, A. 1973. "Implications of legislated minimum wages on the choice of technique in the agro-canned pineapple industries in the Philippines: a micro-approach," *The Philippine Economic Journal*, XII, 23.

Armas, A. 1975. "The constraint of minimum wage legislation on the long-run choice of technology in the canned pineapple industry," *The Philippine Review of Business and Economics*, XII, 2.

Barker, R., W. Meyers, C. Cristostomo, and B. Duff. 1972. "Employment and technological change in Philippine agriculture," *International Labour Review*, 106, 2–3.

Bartsch, W. H. 1977. *Employment and Technical Choice in Asian Agriculture*. Praeger.

David, C. 1983. Government Policies and Farm Mechanisation in the Philippines. In Workshop Papers. (see Ahammed, 1983).

Duff, B. 1976. "Mechanisation and use of the modern rice varieties," *Economic Consequences of the New Rice Technology in Asia*. I.R.R.I., Los Banos, Philippines.

Duff, B. 1978. Output, Employment and Mechanisation in Philippine Agriculture. Report presented at an International Symposium on Farm Mechanisation in Asia, Institute of Developing Economies, Tokyo, Japan.

Dumol, P. 1973. "Rural electrification and employment generation: A case study of two pilot projects," *Philippines Economic Journal*, XII.

Fei, J., G. Ranis, and S. Kuo. 1979. *Growth with Equity: the Taiwan Case*. Oxford University Press.

Galenson, W., ed. 1979. *Economic Growth and Structural Change in Taiwan*. Ithaca: Cornell University Press.

Gibbs, A. 1974. Agricultural Modernisation, Non-Farm Employment and Low Level Urbanisation: A Case Study of a Central Luzon Subregion of the Philippines, Doctoral Thesis, University of Michigan, Ann Arbor.

Gonzales, L.A., P. Herdt, and P. Webster. 1983. An Ex-ante Evaluation of National Mechanisation Policies in the Philippines. In Workshop Papers. (see Ahammed, 1983).

Ho, S.P.S. 1976. *The Rural Non-farm Sector in Taiwan*, World Bank Studies in Employment and Rural Development, 32.

Hou, Chi-ming and Tzong-Shian Yu, eds. 1982. *Agricultural Development in China, Japan and Korea*. Taipei: Academia Sinica.

I.L.O. 1974. *Sharing in Development: A programme of Employment, Equity and Growth for the Philippines*. Geneva: I.L.O.

Industry Development Planning Division, Philippines. 1983. *A Profile of the Philippines Rice Milling Industry*.

I.R.R.I. 1978. *The Technical and Economic Characteristics of Rice Post Production Systems in the Bicol River Basin*. Los Banos, Philippines.

Ishikawa, S., S. Yamada, and S. Hirashima. 1980. *Labour Absorption and Growth in Agricultural China and Japan*, I.L.O., A.R.T.E.P.

Ishikawa, S. 1980. *Essays on Technology, Employment and Institutions in Economic Development*. Tokyo: Kinokumiya Co. Ltd.

Kuo, S., G. Ranis and J. Fei. 1981. *The Taiwan Success Story*. Colorado: Westview Press.

Lantin, R. 1983. A review of Past, Present and Proposed Mechanisation Strategies in the Philippines. In Workshop Papers. (see Ahammed, 1983).

Li, Kwoh-Ting and Tzong-Shian Yu, eds. 1982. *Experiences and Lessons of Economic Development in Taiwan*. Taipei: Academia Sinica.

Mikkelson, K.W., and N.M. Langam. 1981. "Technology change in the Philippines agricultural machinery industry," *The Consequences of Small Farm Mechanisation Project*, Working Paper 20, I.R.R.I.

Mikkelson, K.W. 1984. *Inventive activity in the Philippine Agricultural machinery industry*, Paper 13 of National Science Foundation Final Report, Economic Growth Center, Yale.

Ocampo, R.O. 1982. *Rural transport in the Philippines: Jeepneys, Trimobiles and other simple modes in two Bicol towns*, World Employment Research Working paper, I.L.O., Geneva.

Oshima, H. 1984. *The significance of off-farm employment and incomes in post-war East Asian growth*, Asian Development Bank Economic Paper, 21.

Oshima, H. 1983. "Sector sources of Philippine postwar economic growth: the overall record in comparative perspective," *Journal of Philippine Development*, X, 1.

Philippine Development Planning Studies. 1981. *Regional Development: Issues and Strategies on Agriculture*. Manila, Philippines.

Philippine Development Planning Studies. 1981. *Regional Development: Issues and Strategies on Infrastructure*. Manila, Philippines.

Philippine Development Planning Studies. 1981. *Regional Development: Issues and Strategies on Industry*. Manila, Philippines.

Ranis, G. 1983. Alternative patterns of distribution and growth in the mixed economy: The Philippines and Taiwan. In *Work, Income and Inequality, Payment Systems in the Third World*, ed. F. Stewart. London: Macmillan.

Read, R. 1982. *Corporate foreign direct investment strategies and trade liberalisation in the Japanese market for bananas 1960–1976*, University of Reading Discussion Papers in International Investment and Business Studies, 60.

Reyes, B., and M. Agabin. 1983. A history of credit programs supporting agricultural mechanisation in the Philippines. In Workshop Papers. (See Ahammed, 1983).

Sander, W. 1979. *The Upper Pampanga River Project's Impact on Non-farm Employment and Regional Growth*, Discussion Paper 7918, School of Economics, University of Philippines.

Sanvictores, H. 1977. Studies of Agricultural Mechanisation in the Philippines. Paper presented to International Agricultural Machinery Workshop, I.R.R.I., Los Banos, Philippines.

Sison, J., R. Herdt, and B. Duff. 1983. The effects of small farm mechanisation on employment and output in selected rice-growing areas in Nueva Ecija, Philippines. In Workshop Papers. (see Ahammed, 1983).

Sycip, Gorres and Velayo. 1980. *CB-IBRD Mechanisation, Final Report Draft*, Vol. 1, Manila, Philippines.

Tai, Hung-Chao. 1974. *Land Reform and Politics*. University of Califonia Press.

Timmer, C.P., and W.P. Falcon. 1975. The political economy of rice production in Asia. In *Agriculture in Development Theory*, ed. L.G. Reynolds. New Haven: Yale University Press.

Tzong-Shian, Yu. Industrial policies in Taiwan: an historical review. Institute of Economics. Taipei: Academia Sinica. Mimeo.

Wangwacharakul, V. 1984. Direct and indirect impact of the new cropping systems technology and irrigation in a community economy: the case of Oton and Tigbauen Municipalities Iloilo Province, Philippines, Doctoral Thesis, University of the Philippines.

TABLE 5.1

Size of establishment by region, Philippines, 1975

% of employment in	Manila & Rizal	Luzon	Visayas	Mindanao
Households	29.9	56.8	68.2	51.7
Ests. with < 10	12.6	19.8	12.7	24.9
Ests. with > 10	57.5	23.4	19.1	23.4
Total	100	100	100	100

Source: Anderson and Khambata, Table 6.9.

TABLE 5.2

Capital/labour ratios in manufacturing, Philippines, 1974

Households	1.4
5-19 emp.	4.7
20-49	8.7
50-99	15.2
100-199	19.7
200+	25.8

Source: Anderson and Khambata, Table 8.7.

TABLE 5.3

Ratio of urban to rural capital/labour ratios

	1966		1970
Manufacturing	8.2	Manufacturing	2.0
Food processing	11.7	Mining	1.4
Textiles	20.1	Construction	4.6
Non-electric machinery	29.5	Utilities	5.5
		Trade	1.6
		Services	4.2

Source: Galenson, Table 3.12; Ranis (1983), Table 5.

TABLE 5 .4

Income distribution in the Philippines and Taiwan

	Philippines			Taiwan				
	1956	1961	1971	1953	1959	1964	1972	1981
Share of income of lowest 40% of households:	12.6	12.1	11.9	11.3	15.4	20.3	21.9	22.6
Share of income of lowest 20% of households:	4.9	4.8	3.9	3.0	5.7	7.7	8.8	8.8
Share of top 20% of households:	55.1	56.4	53.9	61.4	51.0	41.1	38.6	37.1
Gini coefficient:	0.48	0.50	0.49	0.56	0.44	0.33	0.29	

Source: Kuo et al. Table 2.15, 3.1, 5.2; ILO (1974), Report on the Survey of Personal Income Distribution in the Taiwan Area, DGBAS.

TABLE 5 .5

Average growth of GDP by industrial origin
% p.a.

		1960-1970	1970-1982
GDP	P.	5.1	6.0
	T.	9.6*	8.7
Agriculture	P.	4.3	4.8
	T.	4.2*	1.4
Industry	P.	6.0	8.0
	T.	15.4*	10.6
Services	P.	5.2	5.2
	T.	9.7*	9.1

*1962-70

Source: World Development Report, 1980 and 1984, World Bank; Statistical Yearbook Republic of China, 1984.

TABLE 5.6

Changes in employment and labour productivity

%p.a.

	Taiwan 1960-79	Philippines 1960-80
Employment:		
Agriculture	- 0.9	2.4
Industry	7.3	3.9
Labour Productivity:		
Agriculture	3.6	2.1*
Industry	5.7	2.7*

*1960-79

Source: Oshima, H. (1983 and 1984); Li, Kwoh-Ting and Tzong-Shian, Yu (eds.).

TABLE 5.7

Export performance

% growth in exports p.a. (real terms)

	1960-70		1970-1978	
Philippines	2.2		5.5	
Taiwan	23.7		9.3	
Composition of exports:	1960		1980	
	T.	P.	T.	P.
% agricultural products	67.7	86	9.2	39[a]
of which processed	55.7	n.a.	5.6	n.a.
Industrial products	32.3	4	90.8	45[a]

[a]1981

Source: World Development Report 1980, 1984, World Bank; Monthly Statistics of Exports and Imports, Taiwan; Tzong-Shian Yu.

TABLE 5.8

Formal Sector Employment, Gapan Area, Philippines, 1961-1971

	Employment 1961	Employment 1971		Employment 1961	Employment 1971
RETAIL TRADE-			CONSTRUCTION-		
C-goods	308	611	Contracting	48	196
Durable goods	14	89	Materials supply	30	61
SERVICES-			Cement prod.	-	84
Restaurants, refresh.	47	177	Gravel/sand	57	70
Barbers	51	120	SPECIALITY INDUSTRIES-		
Billiards	23	60	Sandals	80	346
Amenity shops	32	49	Rattan furniture	38	123
LIGHT TRANSPORT-			Needlework	43	125
Passenger jeepneys	71	164	Other	195	196
Servicing shops	24	79	PUBLIC SERVICES	914	1,560
Calesas/pedicabs	350	10	AGRO-INDUSTRIES PRIMARY-		
Tricycles(motorised)	-	900	Agric. input dealers	16	45
TRADES-			Rice mills, trucking	268	730
Tailoring	55	151	Rice dealers	56	140
Dressmaking	16	57	Other	40	80
Bakeries	37	101	SECONDARY-		
CRAFTS-			Service stations	23	78
Sash works	8	51	Transport shops	35	56
Iron works	6	20	Vehicle body builders	21	33
Furnishing	27	51	Equip. assembly	1	30
			TOTAL	2,934	6,643

Source: Gibb, Chapter VII.

TABLE 5.9

Rural non-agricultural employment in Taiwan

	1930*	1956	1966
TOTAL, '000s	384	573	488
% of total rural employment	24.4	29.3	48.8
% non-agricultural employment			
Mining	4.4	6.4	3.6
Manufacturing	20.4	26.8	22.2
Construction	4.7	4.7	3.0
Utilities	0.4	1.1	0.8
Commerce	27.5	15.9	11.1
Transportation and Communication	9.9	6.8	4.6
Services**	16.7	36.1	41.8
Other	12.3	2.1	12.8

*Includes nine second-rank towns.

**Includes public service, education, personal services and other.

Source: Ho, Table 2.

TABLE 5.10

Annual growth rates in rural employment, Taiwan

	1930-56	1956-1966	
	Rural and Towns*	Rural	Towns
Mining	3.0	3.4	9.2
Manufacturing	3.3	7.1	6.9
Food	4.3	3.2	4.7
Textile	4.1	3.2	4.7
Wood, etc.	0	7.9	6.0
Furniture	7.7	6.9	6.9
Chemical	5.7	6.0	9.2
Non-metals	4.7	6.0	4.1
Metallic Products		12.6	11.7
Machinery	4.7	6.1	-0.5
Transportation equipment		10.7	10.7
Construction	2.5	9.0	9.2
Utilities	6.5	6.6	5.9
Trade	0	5.1	5.3
Banking, etc.	12.2	12.7	9.8
Education	7.3	6.4	7.2
Personal services	6.1	4.0	1.4
Other services	2.5	5.3	6.1

*Includes nine towns second in rank after seven largest cities.

Source: Ho.

TABLE 5.11

HOUSEHOLD TYPE	INCOME PER HOUSEHOLD pesos	SAVINGS PROPENSITY[a]	LOCAL PRODUCTS LINKAGE[b]	FOOD EXPORTS as % of consumption
Non-agricultural	17,930	0.28	0.435	42.5
Irrigated farm	7,876	0.19	0.655	54.6
Rainfed lowland	5,097	-0.01	0.744	58.7
Rainfed upland	3,408	-0.27	0.944	65.5

Source: Wangwacharakul, Table 7, A41, 8.

[a]Expenditure on consumer durables is not included in consumption.

[b]Local production linkage is % increase in local production, including food, in response to 1% increase in household income.

TABLE 5.12

Labour-use per Ha in Taiwan
Days per hectare

BY CROP

	Rice (2 crops)	Other Common Crops	Sugarcane	Mushrooms	Asparagus
1950	191	117	270	n.a.	n.a.
1960	209	123	275	n.a.	n.a.
1964	217	126	255	270	700
1970	206	131	225	270	730
1980	124	107	130	200	530
1982	111	109	110	180	300

BY REGION

	Mainly rice-growing	Rice/sugarcane	Bananas/pineapple	Tea
1952	287	296	314	276
1965	357	355	312	302
1974	321	363	227	227

Source: Taiwan Agricultural Council; Galenson, Table 2.15.

TABLE 5 .13

Crop Composition, Philippines and Taiwan

	Metric tons as % of total of crops shown					Index of Growth	
	Philippines			Taiwan		Philippines	Taiwan
	1960	1978	1983	1961	1978	1977/1960	1978/1961
Rice	48.7	40.5	40.6	26.7	28.7	1.8	1.2
Rootcrops	18.4	16.9	14.0	45.8	17.2	2.0	0.5
Sugar	23.6	18.4	18.0	12.2	8.5	2.0	0.8
Bananas & pineapples	5.7	20.3	24.3	3.7	5.1	6.5	1.6
Citrus	0.6	0.7	0.7	0.7	1.5	2.9	6.8
Vegetables	3.0	3.2	2.5	10.8	33.1	2.2	3.5
TOTAL	100	100	100	100	100	2.2	1.1
Most labor-using[a]	3.0	3.1	2.5	10.8	33.1	2.2	3.5
Least labor-using[b]	24.7	39.5	39.0	50.2	23.8	3.0	0.6
Intermediate[c]	72.3	57.5	58.6	38.9	27.2	1.9	1.9

[a]Vegetables.

[b]Rootcrops, citrus fruits, bananas and pineapples.

[c]Rice and sugar.

Source: Hou and Tzong-shian; Taiwan Agricultural Yearbook; Philippines Statistical Yearbook.

TABLE 5.14

Agricultural machinery

Type	H.P.	Phil. value added as % selling price	Labour cost as % selling price
Power tiller	6-8	43.9	7.3
Tractor	35	41.0	2.2
Irrigation pump, 4"	5	52.6	15.8
Portable Thresher	7	49.8	6.8
Large axial flow thresher	12	45.7	7.8

Source: Ahammed and Herdt, Appendix B.

TABLE 5.15

Direct and indirect employment effects of increasing rice production

Effects of 1% extra rice production

	Power	Irrigation	Thresher	Direct emp. 000s	Indirect	Total	Share of income of landlord
1.	Carabao	gravity	hand	14.5	27.5	42.0	0.44
2.	Power tiller	gravity	hand	15.9	27.1	43.0	0.41
3.	Power tiller	gravity	small portable	12.4	27.6	40.0	0.50
4.	Tractor	gravity	large axial flow	11.2	24.8	36.0	0.49
5.	Carabao	4" pump	hand	23.7	31.3	55.0	0.37
6.	Power tiller	4" pump	hand	21.7	31.3	53.0	0.37
7.	Power tiller	4" pump	small portable	17.4	31.6	49.0	0.46
8.	Tractor	10" pump	large axial flow	9.0	28.0	37.0	0.58
9.	Carabao	rainfed	hand	11.0	20.0	31.0	0.33
10.	Power tiller	rainfed	hand	9.7	18.3	28.0	0.45
11.	Power tiller	rainfed	small portable	7.3	19.7	27.0	0.51
12.	Tractor	rainfed	large axial flow	5.3	17.7	23.0	0.54

Source: Ahammed and Herdt.

TABLE 5.16

Sales of agricultural machinery, Philippines

Year	Four-wheel tractor	Power tiller
1960	588	n.a.
1964	950	1,505[a]
1968	1,630	1,873
1972	1,120	1,408
1976	1,074	8,937
1980[b]	433	2,298

[a]Cumulative total, 1960-65.
[b]Includes sales from January to August only.

TABLE 5.17

Production and sales of hand tractors in the Philippines

Year	Domestic machine	Imported machine	Total	% domestic
1972	336	1,072	1,408	24
1973	2,073	1,047	3,120	66
1974	2,338	4,383	6,721	35(63)*
1975	5,225	5,852	11,077	47(58)*
1976	5,670	3,682	9,352	61
1977	6,206	2,659	8,865	70
1978	6,519	2,794	9,313	70

*Numbers in brackets indicate share of domestic production, when special purchases of imported machines by the Department of Agrarian Reform are excluded.

Source: Mikkelson.

TABLE 5.18

Technology in pineapple canning: Philippines and Taiwan

	PHILIPPINES (i)	PHILIPPINES (ii)	TAIWAN
Capital* cost: 1972 prices, $	141,348	56,555	23,382
Labour requirements	26-33	25-37	25-33
Capacity per minute (cans)	75	60	32
H.P.	24	13	12.5
Capital per worker, $	4,283-5,436	1,529-2,262	709-935

(i) Dolefil
(ii) Philpack
*All operations, including pineapple corers, cutters, and canning.

Source: Armas, 1975, Table 1.

TABLE 5.19

Average wage rates in pineapple canning

(U.S. $ p. hour)

	PHILIPPINES	TAIWAN
1960	0.225	0.070
1965	0.192	0.125
1969	0.190	0.177

Source: Armas, 1975, Table 9.

TABLE 5.20

Banana imports into Japan

(million 40 lb. boxes)

	1960	1967	1970	1976
Ecuador	-	4.4	25.8	1.8
Philippines	-	-	3.0	39.4
Taiwan	2.3	21.8	11.8	4.5
Rest of world	-	0.4	6.0	0.2
TOTAL	2.3	26.5	46.5	45.9

Source: Read.

TABLE 5.21

Labour Requirements: man hours, per ton

All traditional	56
Mechanical threshing, solar drying	23
Mechanical threshing, drying machines	18

Source: IRRI, 1978, Table 10a.

TABLE 5.22

Costs of alternative techniques

	$ per ton Manual	Mechanical
Threshing		
Cash	-	2.08
Non-cash	7.91	2.21
TOTAL	7.91	4.31
Drying		
Cash	-	6.30
Non-cash	1.61	0.65

Source: IRRI, 1978, Tables 19 and 21.

TABLE 5.23

Rice Mills in the Philippines*

	Labour cost per ton	Total cost per ton Utilisation rate- Actual**	50%	100%	Capacity, KG/hour	Quality Recovery %	Head rice %	Capital cost $	K/L (approx.)
"VILLAGE" MILLS:									
Steel Huller	1.70	10.80 (12)	5.00	4.09	105–520	63.1–68.7	32.0–48.1	4,734	3,150
Rubber roll/steel huller	2.20	6.50 (77)	7.91	5.91	245	69.2	71.3	7,633	5,090
"COMMERCIAL" MILLS:									
Large Cone	1.80	6.80 (97)	10.91	6.69	830	70.63	76.75	42,700	17,080
Small Cone	1.80	16.04 (38)	13.50	9.30	240	66.25	75.55	13,301	8,870

*Selection from IRRI Survey.

**Bracketed figures show actual utilisation rate in 1977 survey. Full capacity defined as 12 hours per day, 24 days per month.

Source: IRRI, 1978, Tables 25, 28, 51, 53, 54, 56.

TABLE 5.24
Infrastructure, Philippines and Taiwan

UTILITIES		Philippines		Taiwan	
% households with electricity		1975		1952	1979
		26.5		33.0	99.7
Installed electricity capacity: Kw per 1,000 people	1950		1970	1950	1970
	27.0		95.8	139.1	719.3
% households with telephone		1975		1952	1979
		1.1		2.0	71.3
% households with piped water		1975		1952	1979
	Urban	Rural	Total	Total	
	55.1	10.1	23.8	14.4	63.8
TRANSPORT					
Highways, metres per sq. km.		1983		1974	
		179		458	
Paved roads as %		26.3		51.7	
Railways, metres per sq. km.		7		153	

Sources: Statistical Abstracts of Transport and Communications 1974, Taipei, 1975;
Philippines, Ministry of Public Works and Highways;
Philippine Development Studies, Regional Development: Issues and Strategies on Infrastructure, N.E.D.A., 1981;
Kuo, Ranis and Fei, Table 2.17;
Ranis in Stewart (ed.), Tables 4.1 and 4.2.

TABLE 5.25
Regional distribution in the Philippines

	All Philippines	Luzon	(Metro Manila)	Visayas	Mindanao
% of population	100	54.0	(23.7)	24.1	21.9
% infrastructure expenditure, 71-71	100	73.8	(28.3)	13.5	12.7
% gross value added in utilities, 1974	100	84.3	(71.9)	11.8	3.9
Power capacity per 1,000 people, Kw. 1975	74	98		40	50
% of GVA in agriculture 1974	100	46.9	(17.8)	30.5	22.6
% of GVA in industry 1974	100	74.1	(45.4)	17.2	8.7

Source: Philippine Development Planning Studies, Regional Planning Series, No. Two, Three and Four, National Economic Development Authority, Manila, 1981.

MATRIX 5.1: GAINS AND LOSSES

INTEREST GROUP	POLICY CHANGE Promote agric. Prices/credit	Investment	Policies within agriculture Land reform	Credit/mech.	crop comp.	Rural infra. Elect./trans.	Forward Link Credit	Support Small-scale
Large landowners/ farmers	G	G	LL	L	N	G	N	
Small farmers	G	•GG	G	G	G	G	N	
Landless labourers	G	G	GG	G	G	G	N	
Rural industrialists	G	G	G	G	G	GG	GG	G
Elite/cronies	l	l	L	l	N	N	L	
Urban workers	LL	l	N	N	N	N	N	
Urban u/e, informal	LL	l	N	N	N	N	N	
Aid donors	G	G	N	U	N	U	U	U
Foreign Cos.	N	N	L	L	N	N	L	

g: small gain
G: medium gain
GG: large gain

l: small loss
L: medium loss
LL: large loss

N: neutral

TABLE 5.26

Hypothesised political weight of interest groups

Large Landowners, farmers	15
Small farmers	10
Landless labourers	2
Rural industrialists	1
Elite/"cronies"	25
Urban workers	15
Urban u/e and informal sector	5
Aid donors	17
Foreign Cos.	10
Total	100

MATRIX 5.2: POLITICAL VALUE OF GAINS AND LOSSES*

INTEREST GROUP	POLICY CHANGE Promote agric. Prices/credit	Investment	Policies within agriculture Land reform	Credit/mech.	crop comp.	Rural infra. Elect./trans.	Forward Link Credit	Support Small-scale
Large landowners/ farmers	+1.5	+1.5	-3.0	-1.5	-	+1.5	-	-
Small farmers	+1.0	+2.0	+1.0	+1.0	+1.0	+1.0	-	-
Landless labourers	+0.2	+0.2	+0.4	+0.2	+0.2	+0.2	+0.2	+0.2
Rural industrialists	+0.1	+0.1	+0.1	+0.1	+0.1	+0.2	+0.2	+0.2
Elite/cronies	-1.8	-1.8	-2.5	-1.8	-	-	-2.5	-2.5
Urban workers	-3.0	-0.8	-	-	-	-	-	-
Urban u/e, informal	-1.0	-0.3	-	-	-	-	-	-
Aid donors	+1.7	+1.7	-	?	-	?	?	-?
Foreign Cos.	-	-	-0.5	-1.0	-	-	-	-1.0
NET GAINS/LOSSES	-1.3	+2.8	-4.5	-3.0	+1.3	+2.9	-3.3	-3.1

*Calculated by multiplying gains and losses shown in Matrix 5.1 by % political weight (given in Table 5.26), (where gains/losses count as +1, -1 (for G.L), +1/2, -1/2 for g.1, and +2 for GG; N counts as zero).

Six

Appropriate Technology in Sugar Manufacturing

Raphael Kaplinsky

I. INTRODUCTION

The choice of technology in sugar processing has been debated in the literature for some time.[1] In this chapter, we build on these various analyses in order to subject the specification and choice of appropriate technologies to more scrutiny. In particular, we aim to illustrate how innovation is determined by both micro-technological and intra-enterprise factors and by the macro-political, economic, and social environment. In the following section, we consider the specification of appropriateness in light of the recent debate on appropriate technology (AT) and choice of technology in the sugar processing industry. In section III, we draw upon evidence from project implementation in both India and Kenya to determine the pattern of innovation in this industry. This is followed in section IV by the application of a particular mode of analysing the political economy of technical choice (as developed by Stewart, 1983) and, in section V by a brief assessment of the strengths and weaknesses of this approach.

Before we proceed, it is necessary to point to the single major difference in the technologies available for sugar processing. While there exist many engineering options in a number of separate sub-processes, it is in the evaporation stage that the crucial technological difference arises. Sugar crystals ("non-invert sugar") are produced by evaporating the water in cane juice. To maximise the availability of this crystal sugar, the major trick is to avoid producing "invert-sugars" which are dissolved in the molasses and which cannot be converted into crystals. While many factors affect the extent of invert-sugar production, once the crushed juice has been cleared of impurities the major determining factor is the temperature at which the juice is boiled. The higher the temperature, the greater the proportion of invert sugars produced. Hence, about 150 years ago the first technologies which boiled the juice under vacuum conditions were introduced. This lowered the boiling point of the juice and hence increased the yield of sugar crystals, but at the same time it made the process inherently capital-intensive and subject to economies of scale. By the early 1970s, the optimal size of these vacuum-pan (VP) plants gradually increased to a daily crushing capacity of around 5,000 tons of cane (tcd). Because of the difficulty in ensuring the availability of such large volumes of cane, many vacuum-pan plants were either designed to operate at a lower capacity[2] or, de facto operated at a lower rate[3] whatever their designed crushing capacity.

An alternative process, basically modelled on pre-vacuum pan technology, continued to be used, especially in South Asia. In essence, the major difference was that after clearing the juice of impurities, this process boiled the cane juice off under atmospheric pressure in open-pans, hence its acronym "open-pan" (OP) technology. The cost of this small-scale technology, usually crushing around 100 tons of cane per day, was found in its lower crystal-sugar recovery rate and a slightly discoloured and unevenly granulated product which in India at least (but not in Kenya), sold at a lower price in the final market.[4] Given these disabilities, the profitability of these OP plants was at best marginal (Baron, 1975), although, because of the complexity of market imperfections and government controls, this was not always clear or reflected in the real-world of plant operation (Kaplinsky, 1983). Then between 1978 and 1982, a series of improvements was made in the crushing and boiling sub-processes of the OP technology. These followed a long period of sporadic research and development. Because these improvements significantly increased sugar recovery rates, cut the labour input, saved fuel, and realised other minor productivity gains, they seem to have switched the balance of private profitability in favour of the OP plants (Kaplinsky, 1983).[5]

II. SPECIFYING APPROPRIATE TECHNOLOGY: THE DEBATE ON SUGAR PROCESSING

Stewart (1983) suggests that there are two contrasting views on the definition of appropriate technology (AT). The first is derived from welfare economics and, through the use of shadow prices, allows the determination of the AT. The other involves the detailing of particular characteristics of the choices in question, and is well-represented by the following quotation from USAID.

> In terms of available resources, appropriate technologies are intensive in the use of the abundant factor, labour, economical in the use of scarce factors, capital and highly trained personnel, intensive in the use of domestically-produced inputs.
>
> In terms of small production units, appropriate technologies are small-scale but efficient, replicable in numerous units, readily operated, maintained and repaired, low cost and accessible to low income persons.
>
> In terms of the people who use and benefit from them, appropriate technologies seek to be compatible with local cultural and social environments. (USAID, 1976, p. 191)

Stewart, in discussing the relative value of each of these methodologies, suggests that the specific-characteristic approach has two major benefits. First, it stands back from a universal determination of AT for all environments.[6] And second, it is more likely to signpost particular problems which require action—discounted NPVs have a tendency to "hide" information and disguise the complexity of choice.

Both perspectives are found in the literature on sugar processing. Consider, for example, the following extracts from Forsyth (1977) applying shadow prices in the estimation of "Appropriate Technology in Sugar Manufacturing." He arrives at a specification of AT after calculating net present values based upon plant-life, shadow-prices, and discount rates of 10 and 20 percent. He observes that "despite the plethora of comment on the issue [of AT], there is as yet virtually no hard evidence on what actually constitutes the appropriate technology" (p. 184). This observation is footnoted (after "technology"): "Here defined as that technology which maximises social welfare when products and factors are shadow priced" (p. 201). Then following a detailed working of numbers, Forsyth concluded that "the choice of technology embodied in existing sugar factories in this scale range (for example, in medium to large-scale VP plants) can be justified and the recent literature which emphasises the potential of labour-intensive methods is clearly misleading" (pp. 199–210).

The alternative view of listing and contrasting the particular operating conditions of both VP and OP plants is found in a variety of commentaries, especially that of M. K. Garg, the individual responsible for much of the recent technological improvements made in OP technology. (In his last years Garg worked in The Appropriate Technology Development Association (ATDA), financed by the Uttar Pradesh state government). Garg lists 15 socio-economic benefits obtained from the mini-sugar technology, including the production of 10 percent of India's sugar; a capital investment of Rs 1 billion in rural areas; the employment of 300,000 people in the agricultural off-season; the generation of Rs 40 million in tax revenues; the establishment of a machinery building sector with a turnover of Rs 100m; use of only 60 percent as much iron and steel as VP plants of similar capacity; minimal use of mechanised transport (compared to 60 percent for VP); provision of repair services to surrounding industry; the filtering down of technology to the jaggery industries; and a significantly shorter gestation period than VP mills (Garg, 1979, pp. 13–14). In addition, whereas OP is "producer-owned," VP is "entrepreneur-owned" involving "an element of exploitation" (p. 27). Based on this analysis of the specific operating characteristics, Garg (as well as the ATDA, the Intermediate Technology Development Group and others) concludes that in most LDCs, OP constitutes the appropriate sugar processing technology.

For reasons which are now well articulated in the literature (see Stewart, 1983 and the bibliography therein), we believe that the specific characteristics approach—highlighting choice along a range of dimensions—is far richer than the social-welfare maximisation methodology in which the AT is specified in terms of a single, discounted number. It is as well, however, to remind ourselves that the specification of an AT is not only a complex process, but also one which is inherently variable and relative—it all depends upon whose interests are being considered. As Hagelberg, in his rebuttal of the application of social welfare maximisation methodologies to the specification of AT in sugar processing, points out, "Where a product or process not only admits a choice of technologies, but several are actually practised, the thesis that one is universally appropriate must be sceptically examined. Appropriate technology is inherently relative" (Hagelberg, 1979, p. 894).

III. OPERATING CHARACTERISTICS OF ALTERNATIVE SUGAR PROCESSING TECHNOLOGIES IN INDIA AND KENYA

Insofar as it is possible to specify appropriate technology, we agree with Stewart and others that the specific-characteristic approach offers a richer perspective than that of social-welfare economies. Thus, in illustrating the operating characteristics of these two alternative sugar processing technologies, we abstain from presenting a net present value (NPV) figure incorporating shadow prices which not only adjust for market imperfections (for example the undervaluation of capital) but also consider welfare weightings (for example rural-urban weighting). Rather we illustrate the implications of the two alternative technologies with respect to seven issues: factor utilisation, foreign exchange content, gender division of labour, the decentralisation of economic activity, backward linkages to the local capital goods sector, the farming systems implied, and the quality of product. Other issues could have been picked (for example the role of foreign investment, or the environmental impact), but because we are constrained by space, and because we are primarily concerned with exploring methodological issues, this selectivity is unproblematic.

This discussion of the operating characteristics of the two types of plants is based upon fieldwork in India and Kenya and two different ecological zones.[7] In both cases, the analysis considers the performance of the improved OP plants, operating in two size categories, 100 tcd and 200 tcd. In India these are contrasted with the performance of the median-sized 1250 tcd VP mill; in Kenya with that of the best practice 7,000 tcd Mumias mill. Exchange rates at the time of research (1982) were Rs16.6 = 1 pound sterling and Ksh18.67 = 1 pound sterling. All values are converted into sterling at these rates.

Factor Utilisation

Taking into account the differential sugar recovery rates, it is possible to estimate total factor utilisation (of land and labour) in the two countries if total 1980-81 sugar production had occurred through the sole utilisation of any one of the three types of technologies under consideration. (As we shall see in later discussion, it is only in India that product quality becomes an issue, where it is reflected in lower market prices for OP sugar; this discount has been taken into account in the estimation of private profitability—see Kaplinsky, 1983). The results of this analysis are striking. In India, if 200 tcd OP technology is considered, there is a threefold increase in aggregate employment using only 70 percent of the investment in VP; in Kenya, the employment increase is almost sixfold, and the capital cost only 27 percent.

With regard to land utilisation, the attractiveness of OP to LDC policy is less obvious; because of its lower sugar recovery rate, the land needed for cane is higher by about 15 percent. In both countries land is scarce and ready alternatives exist to cane production. To some extent—that is, insofar as the "social value" (whatever that means) of sugar is reflected in relative agricultural prices—this differential land utilisation has been considered in the analysis since the higher physical input of cane is reflected in the higher cane costs incurred by the OP plants. Nevertheless, precisely because prices hide distributional concerns, the issue of land utilisation remains pertinent to evaluating technical choice in this sector.

Foreign Exchange Utilisation

In India, both VP and OP machinery is produced domestically with local raw materials, although in some specialised parts of VP plants, small quantities of special steels have to be imported. Additionally, key items of VP equipment are produced under license from foreign firms, involving marginal payment of foreign exchange. While around 14 percent of VP sugar is exported, it could be argued that it is the provision of OP sugar for domestic needs which facilitates these exports; if necessary, say the proponents of OP technology, domestic needs could be met with OP sugar and specialised VP production would take place for the export market. Finally, with regard to exports of equipment, both VP and OP technology are sold abroad. Therefore, the foreign exchange implications of choosing amongst these alternative technologies in India are incidental.

The same is not the case for Kenya, where only OP technology is made locally, though with some imported inputs (probably one-third to one-half including indirect imports by final value). This is reflected in the differential in the relative prices of VP and OP equipment in India and Kenya; comparing the installed costs of similar sized plants, the Kenya:India cost rates are 9.45:1 for VP, and only 4.07:1 for OP.[8] A similar situation to that of India exists with regard to potential sugar exports (Kenya has a small quota of 50,000 tpa under the Lome Convention), but as yet the country is not self-sufficient in sugar, and, in 1982, domestic prices were almost double the free-market world prices. Finally, most of the VP mills operate under management contracts with foreign firms—in the case of one mill, the annual cost of this contract is equivalent to the erection of nearly four 200 tcd OP mills. Thus, in Kenya, the choice of VP technology is undoubtedly accompanied by significantly higher foreign exchange costs.

Gender Relations in Production

In Kenya, this is largely a non-issue since, with the exception of office cleaning staff and secretaries, almost no women are employed in sugar production. The situation in India is however more complex because there are significant differences between the North and the South. In the South, women (and children) are employed in OP plants in all processes. In VP mills they are largely confined to marginal tasks in the office; a plus thus for OP, if the objective is to increase the employment of women. In the North, the situation is more complex since historically the only directly productive role played by women was in the drying of bagasse, a task which has been eliminated (displacing around one-fifth of the labor force) by the recent technological improvements mentioned later. Thus, outside of the impact of these recent technological improvements, it is not so much the technologies themselves which affect the gender division of labour, but the pattern of social relations within which these alternative technologies are generally innovated.

The Decentralisation of Economic Activity

Reference to table 6.1 makes it clear that the alternative technologies have very different implications for the location of economic activity. In India, production via 200 tcd plants involves eight times as many plants as via 1250 tcd VP; in Kenya where the comparison is with larger 7000 tcd VP mills, the differential in plant-number is 31 times. This is an important consideration not only because the absolute size of enterprises may have an intrinsic importance,[9] but also because it enables smaller sized agricultural areas to be exploited. In Kenya, for example, to feed a 7,000 tcd sugar mill requires around 42,000 hectares, equivalent to 420 square kilometres, whereas a 200 tcd OP plant requires only 10.4 square kilometres. Moreover this also has implications for transport (and hence imported energy and fixed capital) costs, since the large mills frequently require cane to be hauled over long distances.[10]

Linkages to the Capital Goods Sector

This point is almost self-evident, especially with reference to production in Kenya. There, almost all of the VP equipment is imported as well as some of the commissioning services involved in plant establishment. However, OP mills are largely made locally and plans are afoot to have the pans—one of the more complicated items of equipment—cast locally, perhaps in the well-equipped workshops of the Kenya Railways. The backward linkages here are self-evident, but so too are they in India. There VP machinery manufacture is concentrated in a handful of sites within close proximity to major cities, and manufacture and most maintenance and repair are internalised within the mills. By contrast, OP machinery manufacture is dispersed widely, many near rural towns rather than major cities. Moreover, particularly in repair and maintenance, they are less specialized than the suppliers of VP equipment and hence respond to the needs of other rural industries aside from sugar production. The differential linkages of these two types of plant are clear, in this case affected more by the imperative of the technologies themselves than by the social context in which innovation occurs.

Farming Systems

The question of farming systems is complex for two reasons. First there are important issues arising from the choice of crops. Often (especially in Kenya where sugar production is expanding rapidly and farmers are moving out of other crops and into cane) this has important distributional implications since the substitutes for sugar are maize and beans, crops generally controlled by women. Cane production, however, is generally controlled by men who appropriate the cash proceeds; the choice of crops, therefore, affects not only the gender division of power, but also the nutritional health of the family. This is because directly consumed and nutritious foodstuffs are being displaced by a cash crop where proceeds are often used for schooling and consumer durables, spending decisions generally made by male heads of households. A second factor reflecting the complexity of analysis on farming systems is that we often categorise them into two distinct types, whereas the production function is often much more continuous, merging at the margin. Thus the type of farming systems considered in the analysis may be much clearer in theory than in the real world.

Nevertheless, despite these difficulties there are interesting observations which can be drawn with regard to the farming systems associated with the two sets of technology.[11] This can be seen in India, where OP plants are generally fed by marginal (less than 2.5 acres devoted to cane) and small farmers (2.5–5 acres under cane). While the VP mills are fed by medium (5–10 acres under cane), and larger farmers (over 10 acres), and estates. The implications of these farm systems for factor and input utilisation is shown in table 6.2; most AT practitioners would approve that the balance of favourability lies heavily in favour of the marginal and small farmers. Yet their land productivity—at least traditionally—has generally been much lower, and this is surely an objective favoured by few.[12]

Product Quality

Much has been made in the literature of the "inferior quality" of OP sugar, for which there are three explanations. First, poor supervision leads to the carmelisation of sugar crystals and thus slight discolouring. Second, this discolouring is exacerbated by the cane sugar recovery rate which results in OP sugar having a higher molasses content. It also means that OP sugar takes slightly longer to dissolve and has a stronger taste. And, third, the manual control of processing leads to the production of three to four distinct sizes of crystals in OP.

To some extent the perception of these qualities as being undesirable is a cultural phenomenon, but it also reflects the extent to which sugar is processed.[13] In Kenya, refined white sugar is not produced and the OP product sells interchangeably in the market place with VP raw sugar—in fact the management of some of the VP mills is so bad that the better quality OP sugar actually fares better in relation to the criteria used by the VP mills themselves! By contrast in India, where sugar production has a long history and where refined white sugar is widely processed, the OP product is easily recognized and sells at a discount (around 10 percent) in the final market. Whether the product characteristics are any less acceptable in the social sense is a moot point—if anything the higher molasses content makes it slightly more healthy. However, it is important to recognize the perceived "inferiority" of the OP product. But it is equally important to note that even when this price differential in India is taken into account, production by OP technology remains at least as profitable as that using the VP alternative.

IV. ANALYSIS OF THE POLITICAL ECONOMY OF TECHNICAL CHOICE: AN APPLICATION OF THE STEWART/ENOS APPROACH

The old neo-classical formulation of technical choice—that is, at the point of tangency between the (well behaved) production function and the factor-price line—has long been debunked. It is clear to most AT practitioners and observers that this formulation of technical choice has to be rejected not only because of the non-homogeneity of factors or prices, but also because societies are not composed of the atomistic human units assumed in the neo-classical formulation. Instead, with the gradual evolution of the division of labour, human beings assume social roles. These roles are limited in number, and hold identities of interest, hence giving rise, inter alia, to the concepts of "class" and "interest groups." Moreover, the definition and division of such roles reflects the social relations underlying production—the mode of production.

The recognition that there are coherent identities of interests between different groups of individuals underlines the general recognition in the AT field, even amongst the social-welfare economics school, that appropriateness, if it has any meaning at all, is inherently relative. It depends upon the differential impact of innovation on diverse groups who may not only be poor, but who may also share a common role in the social division of labour (e.g., gender, class). It also, however, has another spin-off in the literature, in that it offers insights into processes whereby particular technologies become the dominant method of production, either in terms of static production-efficiency, or in relation to changes in productive efficiency. This is because the generation of new technology or the improvement of existing technology does not follow an immutable, Darwinist direction. Instead, it reflects the application of resources designed to overcome specific objectives which are defined by the class or interest group directing these technical-change resources.

Yet behind this general recognition of the need to generate a political economy approach, there lies a measure of intellectual disagreement. This has important implications for the room to manoeuvre in promoting socially desirable patterns of innovation as well as for the widespread diffusion of appropriate technologies. Analytical perspectives vary from vulgar Marxist formulations, which suggest that there is no room for manoeuvre at all without fundamental changes in the pattern of social relations, to those explicit in the perspective of many AT practitioners, namely that with sufficient persuasion, almost anything is possible. In this morass of views, Stewart (building upon the earlier formulation of Enos), suggests a way of handling the analysis of technological diffusion. Since we shall attempt to explore this methodology via the case study of sugar processing technology, it is necessary to describe this approach in a little more detail. (Interested readers are referred to Stewart (1983) and Enos (1982) for greater clarity.)

Their game-theoretic approach begins with the conception that given the existence of two particular interest groups, three alternative resolutions are possible. Either the innovation is in the interest of both groups, in which case it will take place easily; or it is against both sets of interests, in which case it will clearly not take place; or, (the most common situation, it is argued), it is in the interests of only one of the two groups, in which case the outcome is uncertain. It is in this last category that they offer political-economic tools to analyze the spread of innovation. The method offered is the construction of a matrix—the row entries comprise the various interest groups, while the columns are made up of the items of choice under consideration. Ideally, argues Stewart, it should be possible to weight each of the entries so that is becomes possible to forecast the pattern of choice. This would allow alternative permutations of choice which are more easily implementable by circumventing the power of particular interest groups or by offering a "sweetener" or a dilution of the costs.

The suggestion that the individual entries might be weighted is more problematic than it might at first seem. The easiest conception of these weights, which inherently relate to private costs and benefits, is one which calculates the discounted benefit/cost of every option, expressed in units of money. However, aside from the problem of estimating these numbers, this implied conception of power relations is inherently economistic (we return to this in section V). Therefore, for these and other reasons, in constructing the matrix we stand back from estimating the value of parameters. Instead, we reflect each entry in terms of "positive" or "negative", that is, is the innovation basically in the favour of a particular group or to its cost? On this basis we turn to matrix 6.1 to examine the balance of interest groups in favour of each of the two major sets of sugar processing technology; this not only assesses the balance of impact for each interest group, but also offers some judgement of the power of these groups in the wider political sphere.

In Direct Production

Here we have four different sets of interest groups: two types of capitalists, management, workers, and the specific interests of women. With the exception of gender relations (where women found work in OP plants in the South), there is little difference in the balance of impact between Kenya and India. Thus large-scale entrepreneurs favour VP while their small-scale counterparts benefit more from OP. Management as a specialized profession, rather than as manager/owners, tends to be more structured and career oriented in VP; whilst workers have ambivalent interests—on the one hand, salaries and working conditions are far superior in VP and skills are more explicitly recognized, but on the other hand, overall employment is much lower.[14] It is probable therefore that there will be conflicting interests between the core payroll workers and the marginal casual workers who would be likely to find more reliable employment if the small-scale labour intensive technology was more widespread. It is striking, however, that insofar as the direct actors are concerned, the relative weight of political power very much favours the VP technology.

Machinery Suppliers

India has a full range of indigenous machinery suppliers, with those producing VP equipment operating under technical service agreements. Clearly there exists an identity of interests between these large-scale capital-goods firms and foreign machinery suppliers in favour of VP technology. Only the small-scale machinery suppliers benefit from the choice of OP technology, although in view of the growing attractiveness of the small-scale alternative, a number of the larger VP supplying firms are actively considering the manufacture of OP technology.

In Kenya, the situation is much clearer—there is no large-scale domestic capital-goods supplier and hence the interests of local machinery supplying firms (which are not powerfully articulated in the political sphere partly because they tend to be immigrant-owned) are squarely lined-up against those of foreign suppliers. Because of their links to individual decision-makers, these foreign machinery suppliers influence government decisions in Kenya.

Interest Groups in Farming

Again we perceive a broadly similar pattern of group interests in India and Kenya. The interests of smaller farmers, who are located far from the VP sugar mills, or whose production is too small to cover the costs of transport, or who are far from the road-network, are generally better served by OP mills.[15] In direct contrast, estate production or large farm production might suffer from the diseconomies imposed by small-scale OP plants, and thus their interests are best served by the large-scale mills. The interests of medium sized farms can be met by either VP or OP mills, depending upon the particular circumstances. It is important that despite regional variations in both countries, it is the medium and large-farmers whose power predominates in the political arena.

The State

The state apparatus comprises heterogeneous interest groups, particularly in India where the class composition of individual state-governments differs sharply from that in the central government. For ease of analysis we distinguish between senior decision-takers, whose personal decisions are often instrumental in final policy, and the bureaucracy, whose task is largely to implement (or undermine) these executive decisions.[16] In India and Kenya both groups have historically favoured VP. This is easy to understand with respect to the senior decision-makers who gain greater credit from a briefly visible single project, or who gain personally from project implementation in both of these rent-seeking economies.[17] At the bureaucratic level of the civil service, the rationale may be more difficult to understand, but the effect is similar.[18] Thus both groups, especially the extremely powerful senior decision-makers, seem to be lined up in favour of VP.

Aid Agencies

Aid agencies have a large profile in Kenya. Individual bilateral loans have been provided for plant acquisition as well as for the provision of infrastructure, especially for roads. Almost without exception these bilateral loans have been linked to the sale of equipment which naturally, given the specialization of developed-country machinery suppliers, involves the choice of developed-country technology. Multilateral-aid has also played an extremely important role in Kenya, particularly through the World Bank which has coordinated much of the aid to the sugar sector.

While there is no inherent reason why this multilateral aid should necessitate VP technology, there has never been any question but that it does. Why this should be the case is partly a reflection of the world view of decision-makers in the state, the implicit and explicit output-maximising criteria they use (see James, 1986) and the widespread use of developed country consultants, often funded by aid-agencies.

Given Kenya's balance of payments problems and the perceived absence of finance for non-aided sugar processing investments, these aid agencies have assumed an extremely important role in directing choice towards VP technology. In India, by contrast, the sugar industry has been a domestic issue for some time and aid agencies have had little role to play.

The "Public Interest"

The "public interest" has a much more important role to play in economic theory than in the real world where it is poorly articulated. It is relevant to the choice of sugar processing technology in three major ways. The first is with respect to price, where OP sugar is more favourable. The second refers to the amorphous concept of welfare which includes such diverse issues as the dangers of monocropping (more prevalent with VP), intra-family welfare, and the nutritional content of sugar. For both of the latter, and in most other respects, OP sugar would be considered preferable by most observers. And, third, the public interest includes consideration of environmental impact where because OP technology is typically associated with smaller farms which use less pesticides and fertilisers, the balance tends to be in its favour. It would appear, therefore, that the balance of public interest favours OP technology. But since these interest groups are so diverse and poorly-articulated, this bears little relation to the actual choice of sugar processing technology.

V. EXPLORING THE POLITICAL ECONOMY OF TECHNICAL CHOICE: THE STEWART/ENOS APPROACH APPRAISED

Before we appraise the Stewart/Enos methodology for explaining the political economy of technical choice, it is helpful to summarize why VP has tended to be the dominant choice of technology in both countries. We begin first by observing the pattern of private profitability in this sector, but since government policy on sugar pricing is crucial, this must be considered in tandem. Next we appraise the effect of other government policies on the choice and generation of technology and conclude by trying to theorise about the political economy of technical choice in this sector in the two countries under consideration and in light of the earlier application of the Stewart/Enos methodology. The analysis is also useful in illustrating the interplay between the micro and the macro in the diffusion of alternative sugar processing technologies.

Private Profitability in Sugar Processing: India and Kenya

The analysis of relative profitability in the two countries' sugar sector is extremely complex. Three factors are particularly problematic. First, there is no single, widely accepted and clear criterion which can be used as a suitable measure; each has its drawbacks.[19] Second, it is necessary wherever possible to obtain operating data, rather than projected performance. This is important not only because actual performance is often different from projected operation, but also because individual enterprises will often pay very different prices for the same material inputs, services, and factors. And, third, in a situation where the sugar price is controlled—the case in both Kenya and India—the valuation of output has a critical bearing on the analysis.

In the face of these and other difficulties, we have made a number of simplifying steps. While these are often inherently crude, they offer a reasonable picture of the basic parameters. First, instead of calculating the rate of profit or a discounted NPV figure, we consider costs of production to determine whether plants can operate at particular sets of prices. This is probably the most relevant measure to use, given the difficulty encountered in the valuation of output, a point considered below. Second, we have attempted to estimate the performance and cost structure of typical OP and VP plants. We believe this is a valid procedure since the inter-technology variations are much more significant than the intra-technology ones. And, third, we have made an important adjustment to the valuation of output. In India and Kenya the controlled price of sugar is estimated on the basis of historic-cost accounting with little recognition of the need to depreciate at replacement values. This is advantageous for the VP plants which are inherently more capital intensive and for whom the effective omission of depreciation costs significantly affects operating costs. We therefore show the effect on the cost structure if capital is depreciated at replacement costs.

Taking these factors into account we can roughly gauge, with a fair measure of confidence, the relative cost-structure of the two types of plants (table 6.3). The results are unambiguous. Given the existing price-structure of sugar, the improved 200 tcd OP plants can just about cover their costs of production; this assumes however, that the OP plants depreciate at replacement costs, while VP mills depreciate at historic costs.[20] However, if sugar prices are set to reflect VP plant acquisition at replacement costs, the capital intensive VP mills are hard-hit and the balance of cost-competitiveness swings heavily in favour of OP. In the light of their lower investment costs, this implies the significantly greater profitability of OP, whatever the measure of profitability chosen.

Given this conclusion it is striking that OP plays such an insignificant role in sugar production, especially in Kenya. There it accounts for only 1.7 percent of output, and in India for around 30 percent. Relative real profitability is given little chance to determine allocation since it is so comprehensively masked by the sugar pricing policies in both countries. But, it addition, there are other government policies, especially in India, which have an important bearing on the allocation of investment between OP and VP technology. It is to these policies which we now turn our attention.

Other Government Policies towards the Sugar Sector

India

In India, there are a maze of policies which affect investment in the sugar industry. These stretch back to the 1932 Sugar Protection Act which initially protected local producers from imports for 14 years. Within four years of the Act being passed, India was virtually self-sufficient in sugar. Production grew at 7.1 percent per annum between 1932-33 and 1977-78, with an especially rapid increase after independence. This reflected the political importance of sugar as a foodstuff, which consequently became one of the priority sectors in agriculture.

The initial protection of producers, by effectively excluding dutied imports, had a major adverse impact on government customs revenue. So in 1934, the first excise duty was imposed on locally produced sugar and latitude was given to state governments to specify minimum prices for cane. With the onset of the five year plans, new and expanded mills required licenses and the government hence controlled not only imports but also production. Finally, control over prices goes back to the war years and subsequently passed through a series of controls, partial decontrols, and full decontrols. By 1982 (when fieldwork was undertaken), in addition to the exclusion of imports and minor controls over wages, molasses prices, etc., the VP mills were subject to three major restraints: on prices (where 65 percent of output had to be sold to the government at prices around 45 percent of the wholesale market price); on cane (minimum prices, varying by state, plus a marginal cess tax); and on capacity (all expansions and new plants were subject to license).

In the light of these controls—especially those on prices—some VP mills ran into difficulties in the early 1970s. A government commission (The Sompath Committee) was set up and made four major recommendations: first, new and expanded mills could sell a greater percentage on the wholesale market rather than at the lower price to government;[21] second, state governments could subsidize cane purchases;[22] third, soft loans were made available for new or expanded plants; and finally, VP mills were given credit to purchase cane.

In contrast to the VP mills, controls over OP plants have been more recent. A small excise duty was imposed in 1939, but withdrawn in 1952. In 1959-60, following protests from the VP mills, excise duty was reimposed on OP sugar but only at 25 percent of that on VP sugar. From 1962, OP plants were offered a choice between this excise duty or paying a fixed weekly tax on the size of the centrifuge, a key piece of equipment.[23] In 1965, following representation, a distinction was made between two different sorts of OP plants and the non-sulphutation mills were freed from compound duties. OP mills pay the same marginal cess tax on cane as VP mills.

The overall picture is thus enormously complex. Government controls exist over inputs, production, and prices, and vary not only by type of technology but by size of investment, ecological zone, and region. The key control is over prices since VP mills were supposed to sell 65 percent of their output at significantly lower (by 55 percent) prices in 1982. However, new and expanded mills were exempt from much of this control for up to eight years. It is clear, therefore, that when comparing the impact of state policies in India on the choice of technology, it is not easy to determine which sector the state favours. If older plants are considered, then OP technology is substantially favoured since the VP mills are required to sell the major proportion of their output at very low levy prices. New or expanded mills, however, particularly the larger ones, are effectively freed from the brunt of these levy controls and are moreover offered additional incentives. In this case new OP plants almost certainly stand at a disadvantage compared to new VP mills.

Kenya

The situation in Kenya is much easier to discern. Shortly after independence in 1963, a decision was made to move towards self-sufficiency in sugar production, despite the growing shortfall in overall food production. By 1982, at replacement capital costs, around Sterling £354 million had been invested in VP sugar mills, with additional infrastructural investment of around Sterling £182 million. This makes the sugar processing industry the largest single recipient of investible funds outside of agricultural production. All but a minute fraction of this has gone into VP mills, initially joint ventures with foreign firms. But as price controls eroded profitability, the state came to own most of the equity in these VP enterprises. Two of the three OP mills (one of which burnt down and will probably be reconstructed) were established with funds from government schemes to promote small-scale industry. But there appears to be little expectation in the state system that this type of investment holds any promise.

It is worth noting two aspects of the Kenyan situation since they have a major impact on the choice of technology in this sector. First, many senior civil servants and politicians own large tracts of land which are under cane; returns to this ownership came about entirely from rent since the farming of the crop, from preparation to final harvest, is contracted out to the VP mills. The straddling nature of their economic activity (that is, in addition to formal government jobs they own many other businesses) makes it impossible to actively manage these farms, a task which would be required if they were to sell cane to the smaller-scale OP mills. And, second, by virtue of the state assuming ownership for the VP mills, setting a sugar price which does not allow the effective recoupment of depreciation costs and therefore allowing the VP mills to run at a loss, VP sugar production is heavily subsidised.[24] By contrast, OP plants (for which, given their labour-intensity, depreciation is a less significant item anyhow) *are* expected to recover their depreciation costs. These two factors give a major incentive to the continued expansion of VP mills, to the virtual exclusion of OP technology, despite the government's stated policies appearing to favour OP rather than VP sugar processing technology.

Policies towards the Generation of Technology

The significance of the sugar processing case study lies not only in the extent to which the choice of technology is explained by the interaction between micro and the macro factors. It also relates centrally to the problem of generating technologies, particularly those which are to be considered in some sense as being appropriate to the needs and operating conditions of developing economies. The policy environment required to produce such appropriate technologies is not always easy to specify, since it will necessarily change over time, between sectors and between countries. It also covers a wide range of potential policies, including those directed towards R&D, higher education, skill-acquisition, foreign-trade and competition.

At this particular juncture, much of the policy debate—especially in aid-agencies—concerns the confluence between trade and infant-industry policies. The question at stake is the extent and duration of the protectionist barriers required to facilitate technological change and innovation, especially in new infant industries. Here there has been an important change in perception over the past five years or so with the hegemonic view increasingly being one which points to the dangers of "excessive protection," particularly insofar as it reduces competitive pressures and hence inhibits technological progress. In the case of one of the most influential proponents of this view (Balassa, 1982) it has been suggested that protection can only really be justified over a period of 5–8 years and that it should be limited to effective rates of 10 percent. In this case, protection of the Indian sugar processing industry from imports—stretching back over fifty years—must be considered difficult to justify. So too, by analogous argument, must it be difficult to justify the internal protection of OP and VP sugar.

In actual fact—as can be seen from figure 6.1—the evidence suggests the contrary. First, there has been technological progress in India in both OP and VP technology, occurring behind market interventions which not only limit imports but also protect the OP sector from competition from the large-scale "inappropriate" sector. Second, it is doubtful whether Balassa's ten-year time horizon is realistic. Insofar as the historical experience of the cane-sugar industry in the industrially advanced countries is concerned, similar time-spans have pertained. Moreover, the experience of the beet-sugar industry (table 6.4) leads to analogous conclusions. All this points to the interaction between the macro-policy environment and technological change—not only in India but also in nineteenth century France, Germany, and the USA. But it does not necessarily suggest that the policy environment which pertained was efficiently geared to minimizing the costs of technological progress, since for almost two decades it was quite clear what steps were required to upgrade OP technology without any effective action being taken. It took enormous resolution and persistence by M.K. Garg and others to force through these technological developments in the face of overwhelming inertia and opposition from parts of the central and regional state systems. The conclusion which emerges from this is that the inducement of technological change required state support, probably greater than the equivalent of ten percent effective protection and certainly for longer than 5–8 years, even if the fifty years which it did take was of unnecessarily long duration.

Appraising the Political Economy of Technical Choice

We return to the Stewart/Enos formulation of the political economy of technical choice by summarising and extending the discussion. The social-welfare economies formulation of appropriateness, based upon the generation of shadow-priced NPVs, is rejected. Instead the analysis discusses the specific characteristics of individual techniques, taking into account the appropriateness of both process and product. However, it is recognised that choice of technique decisions are not made in a vacuum, and a distinction is drawn between the micro-environment and the macro-environment. This distinction is important since it allows the analysis to question the composition of the macro-environment, ultimately leading Stewart/Enos to a game-theoretic approach which weighs up the costs and benefits of each alternative choice for a variety of interest groups.

There is much to command this approach, particularly in comparison with the arid social cost-benefit (SCB) techniques in favour with the economics profession and aid-agencies. Among its many positive features, three stand out. First, unlike the formal SCB analysis, this formulation begins with the recognition that society is not composed of atomistic individuals. Rather it is made up of large groups of individuals who share common roles in the social division of labour (for example, as workers, capitalists, civil servants, women—see table 6.2) and who consequently share common interests. Unless these common interests are clearly recognised, the forces shaping technical choices will be unrecognised and the prediction/explanation of what will occur is likely to be unhelpful. A second virtue of the Stewart/Enos approach, is that it "endogenises" technical change. That is, once interest groups are recognised, it then becomes evident that they might have interests in directing technical progress in particular directions. By contrast in the SCB model, technical progress tends to be exogenous. There is no necessary reason for this perspective in SCB analysis, but unlike the Stewart/Enos formulation the methodology does not force a consideration of the issue. In the case of sugar, for example, technical progress is a relative non-issue for Forsyth (1977 and 1978), while for Garg (1979), Hagelberg (1979) and Kaplinsky (1983) it is much more prominent.

And, a third major strength of the Stewart/Enos game-theoretic formulation is that it tends to force a more systematic consideration of the issues influencing technical choice. In the case of sugar it forces the discussion beyond a history of individual characteristics—capital/labour ratios, foreign exchange content, backward linkages, etc.—to incorporate a perspective on the way in which bureaucrats in the civil service, agricultural workers, or small farmers are likely to be affected by choice. This, as we have seen, is important not only in relation to the impact on welfare, but perhaps more importantly, because it directs attention to the socio-political forces promoting/blocking individual innovations.

There is a danger, however, that this game-theoretic approach to political economy abstracts from a long history of analysis of these types of phenomena. Handled sympathetically there is no reason why the two approaches should be at variance. But in order to remind ourselves of the insights which can be derived—especially with respect to the dynamic components of technological choice—it is instructive to run briefly through some elements, especially in relation to the theorisation of the state and the theorisation of capital. It is also worth pointing to the dangers of incorporating an economistic conception of power relations.

The Theorisation of the State

The game-theoretic conceptualisation of technical choice, and the extension of Stewart to incorporate the importance of government in setting the macro-environment in which choices are made, addresses itself squarely to the role of the State. Indeed the analysis goes on to address the importance of policy-formulation and the way in which this can be used to alter the benefits and costs to particular interest groups, therefore affecting the economics of technical choice.

However, if the analysis ends at this point, there will be a tendency to under-theorise the role of the state in the pattern of technical choice and technical progress. This is not to suggest that there is any such beast as *the* role of *the* state, but there nevertheless exists a number of analyses which provide useful insights into the role which the state plays in relation to the generation and diffusion of AT.[25] Consider for example the discussion by White (1984) who argues that the ability of the state to intervene positively in the process of industrialisation hinges on three basic factors. These are (a) its social nature, considering the relative autonomy of the state apparatus itself, the influence of particular classes (or coalitions of classes) on the state, and the perception of the "national interest"; (b) the state's politico-administrative capacity, involving its political legitimacy, the efficiency of administration and its technical efficiency; and (c) the specific modes of involvement which range from "parametric" measures in which individual enterprises have a high measure of autonomy to pervasive measures in which state involvement is detailed. The advantage of the White-type approach is that it not only makes explicit the pervasive and parametric role of the state (and in this sense it is similar to the Stewart/Enos formulation), but in addition it draws the analysis further to explicitly consider the social roots of the state and its administrative capability.

This broader theorisation helps us understand the pattern of technical choice in sugar processing. Thus, if we widen the theorisation of the social basis of the Indian and Kenyan states and make this a central fact of the analysis, continuity in the pattern of technical choice becomes clearer. For example, at the crudest level the Indian state can be taken to represent the interests of national capital, whereas the Kenyan state more clearly is associated with international capital.[26] Hence we immediately obtain insights into the significant role played by the indigenous small-scale technology in India and not in Kenya. Another example is the establishment of VP technology in Maharashtra State in India. This resulted from a specific attempt to break the class-power of the small-scale rural capitalist in bonded-labour and money-lending, rather than because of the economics of technical choice (Baviskar, 1980). These, of course, are only the briefest outlines of the sort of analysis which might be pursued.

The Theorisation of Capital

In the same way that we suggested that the analysis of the generation and diffusion of AT would be assisted by an explicit theorisation of the state, it is also useful to move to a more explicit theorisation of the trajectory of accumulation adopted by particular fractions of capital. It is not that the class-divisions of the capitalist class are ignored in the game-theoretic approach, but a focus on the (static) balance of forces lining up for and against a particular technology may lead to an ahistorical viewing of evolving structures. Again, relating this analysis briefly to sugar processing, in Kenya two divisions are evident among the capitalist class. In industrial capital, the indigenous bourgeoisie is effectively absent, particularly in the large-scale sector. Frustrated in its attempts during the latter years of the Kenyatta era to exclude foreign capital, it has once again become a rentier-class; the advance of the indigenous industrial class is thus largely confined to the small-scale sector. Given the hegemonic role of this rentier-class ("senior decision makers" in figure 6.2), VP technology triumphs. In agricultural capital it is the same rentier capital (of absent civil servants and politicians) but it is in this case allied to an emergent peasant middle class. This provides a strong impetus to VP mills, which allow for some economies of scale in farming; also, the emergent peasant middle class may undertake much of the farming itself under contract to these rentiers.

It is not that the game-theoretic approach ignores these class divisions, but an insensitive application may place them in a more static framework. Their analysis moves to a conceptualisation of bargains which can be struck between factions of capital, rather than to a recognition of the long-term drive to hegemony by any one of these particular subsets of capital. It thus assumes a mobility of capital between various types of technology and economic activity—which is belied by reality.

An Economistic Conception of Power

A final danger facing the game-theoretic approach is that it might tend towards an economistic conceptualisation of power relations. The situation is most clearly evident in the attempt to place weightings in the individual cells of the matrix drawn-up to display the relationship between particular interest groups and combinations of technical choice. The implicit message carried by the analysis is that investment decisions are made, or not made, after each of the parties sums up the pecuniary costs and benefits of each alternative. As a corollary of this, it is also often implicit in such analyses that capital is mobile, transferring investments to alternative technologies depending upon the rate of return involved.

Yet our analysis of allocative decisons in the sugar processing sector belies this approach. In India many of the OP plants are run by families who have no other businesses; their commitment to small-scale sugar processing is such that they are likely to sustain and even expand their investments whatever the actual rate of return, even if it is negative. In Kenya, foreign capital (often supported by aid agencies) forces choice towards the VP alternative, not so much because it represents an optimal economic decision, but rather because it sustains the sale of VP equipment or management services, areas in which, as MNCs, their global competitive survival is ensured.

Thus the extent to which the power of individual classes or fractions of classes, is buttressed by the choice of particular technologies, is not adequately reflected through an analysis focusing on the economic rationale of technical choice. Within technologies (for example in relation to the choice of a type of machinery or whether to mechanise particular sets of sub-processes), an economistic perception of choice may hold. But, it helps little in explaining why particular groups are wedded to types of technology, almost irrespective of the relative rate of return.

VI. CONCLUSION

In this paper we have attempted to explore the meaning of appropriateness through the choice of technology in the sugar processing sector. In addition the discussion has been extended to evaluate the methodology by which the choice of technology can best be understood.

With regard to the definition of appropriateness we have concluded that the concept has little real relevance. It is not so much that it is inherently relative—a point widely made in the literature—but rather that all technologies are inherently both appropriate and inappropriate at the same time. The significance of this recognition is that it draws analysis of appropriateness directly to the political economy of technical choice, that is to a consideration of the methodology which best illuminates the social processes whereby technologies are generated and chosen. Stewart (1983) and Enos (1982) have made welcome additions to the literature in this regard. They expose the aridity of economic analyses and suggest an alternative based upon a game-theoretic approach.

After considering the relevance of this game-theoretic approach to the choice of technology in sugar processing, there is little doubt that it offers superior insights to those offered by social cost-benefit analysis. However, perhaps because this valuable work is still in its formative stages, we have reservations about the way in which it might be applied. In particular our concern is that while widening economic analysis to political-economy, this broader perspective is still somewhat tangential, almost as if it is a second-stage add-on. Instead, by reference to the sugar processing industries in Kenya and India, we have been concerned to show that the pattern of technical progress and technical choice is best understood if some of the lessons of the political-economic analyses are brought to the central stage. This involves a more concrete theorisation of both the state and the capitalist class, as well as a non-economistic conceptualisation of power relations. Nevertheless, despite these reservations, the game-theoretic formulation of technical choice is a welcome addition to our perception of the generation and choice of technology.

NOTES

1. See Baron, 1975; Forsyth, 1977 and 1978; Garg, 1979; Hagelberg, 1979; Kaplinsky, 1983; Tribe and Alpine, 1982; and Alpine and Pickett, 1980.

2. In India median plant size was about 1400 tcd.

3. In the Sudan, the Kenana sugar factory had a crushing capacity in excess of 20,000 tcd; but in reality it seldom crushed more than 6,000 tcd due to lack of cane.

4. In average Northern Indian conditions VP plants had a crystal sugar recovery rate of around 9.5 percent of cane input, while for OP plants it was around 7.2 percent.

5. Under the same Northern Indian conditions, the sugar recovery rates rose from around 7.2 percent to 8.1 percent.

6. But so does the social-welfare economic analysis which, in theory, inputs different sets of shadow prices.

7. In Northern India, where rainfall is more limited, the cane crushing season is 4 to 5 months; in Western Kenya it is around 10 months. This ecological variation also affects sugar yield, which in VP plants averages around 9.6 percent in Northern India and 10.7 percent in Western Kenya.

8. The reasons for these disparate ratios between the two countries are diverse including the use of different-sized VP plants as points of comparison, different relative machinery prices and different crushing seasons. The significance of differential machinery prices is discussed below.

9. Some observers argue, like Schumacher, that the quality of social life is higher in smaller units.

10. In Kenya, government policy is that smallholders should not devote more than one-third of their land to cane. If therefore the 7000 tcd mill were to be fed entirely by smallholders, the cane catchment area would expand over a 20 kilometre radius encompassing 1260 square kilometres. In India, one of the 1250 mills we visited was hauling cane from as far away as 200 kilometres.

11. It is not always easy to ascribe causality to this pattern of association. In some cases—for example, where the degradation of the sucrose content in cane is caused by the delay in processing and where proximity is thus important—it is clear that farming systems are determined by scale. In other cases—for example in relation to the productivity of different sized farms—the primary causality lies in the realm of social relations and there is no necessary link with the type of sugar-processing technology involved.

12. However, in eastern Uttar Pradesh at least, some observers have noted a major improvement in smallholder yields in recent years (Personal communication from Sanjay Sinha).

13. In India they are disfavoured, in Africa they are not noticed, and in the UK there is a swing back in consumer preference to discoloured raw sugar which is remarkably similar to the OP product.

14. In India, for example, VP workers generally operate on a three-shift, six day a week basis; in OP, they work two twelve-hour shifts throughout the season with no regular rest period.

15. Which ranges from bullock-carts to tractors to pick-ups to large trucks.

16. This group includes elected politicians, their appointees in the civil service and career civil-servants.

17. A 10 percent "commission" on a multi-million dollar VP plant, possibly paid into a Swiss bank account, is a lot more attractive than that on a small OP plant. It is also much easier to obtain and involves less visible negotiation.

18. In Kenya, the Sugar Authority was for a long time reluctant to divulge any information to potential OP manufacturers, but leaned over backwards to satisfy the VP sector.

19. For example, discounted cash flow creates a demand for detailed information over a long time-period, with attendant uncertainties with respect to data; rate of return analysis has ambiguities concerning whether it is net (of what?) or gross as well as with respect to what is included in the denominator (working capital, buildings, what valuation of capital, etc.).

20. A necessary assumption since the improved technology has only recently become available. By contrast many Indian VP mills are over 30 years old, and the Kenyan VP mills have been built (and expanded) over the past 20 years.

21. The percentage varied by size of plant, ecological zone and whether expansions or new investments were involved. The resulting complex formula meant, inter alia, that large new plants in poorer ecological zones could sell all of their output at the higher free market price for seven years.

22. In one VP mill visited, then in Mrs. Ghandi's own constituency, cane prices were subsidised by 40 percent.

23. This tax (compound duty) varied by the size of the centrifuge. The unintended side-effect of this was to bias the development of centrifuges towards a specific size which had no particular technological logic. This not only affected the choice of centrifuge technology in India, but also in foreign markets (where there was no tax on centrifuges) since Indian OP machinery manfacturers only offered centrifuges in the sizes favoured by Indian legislation.

24. Even the best-practice 7,000 tcd Mumias plant, with a sugar recovery rate of over 11 percent and depreciating on historic costs of sterling £32 million (rather than on replacement costs of around sterling £120 million) was running at a loss in 1980-81.

25. White (1984), for example, cautions thus: "This diversity (in the historic role of the State in different LDCs) undermines the validity of general judgements about the role of the state in industrialisation and general policy presumptions which flow from them."

26. See Review of African Political Economy 17 for a discussion of the indigenous capitalist class in Kenya.

REFERENCES

Alpine, R., and J. Pickett. 1980. "More on Appropriate Technology in Sugar Manufacturing," *World Development*, Vol. 8, pp. 167–176.

Balassa, B. 1982. Reforming the System of Incentives in Developing Economies. In *Development Strategies in Semi-Industrialised Economies*, B. Balassa and Associates. Baltimore: Johns Hopkins University Press.

Baron, C.G. 1975. Sugar Processing Techniques in India. In *Technology and Employment in Industry*, ed. A.S. Bhalla. Geneva: ILO.

Baviskar, B.S. 1980. *The Politics of Sugar—Sugar Cooperatives in Rural Maharashtra*. New Delhi: Oxford University Press.

Deer, N. 1949. *The History of Sugar*, Vols. 1 and 2. London: Chapman and Hall.

Enos, J. 1982. *Market Structure, Industrial Organisation and Technology: Concepts and Methodology and Evidence*, World Employment Programme Research Working Paper, WEP 2-22/WP 93. Geneva: ILO.

Forsyth, D. 1977. "Appropriate Technology in Sugar Manufacturing," *World Development*. Vol. 5, No. 3, pp. 189–202.

Garg, M.K. 1979. *Project Report and Feasibility Study of Appropriate Technology and Mini-Sugar (OPS Khandsari)*. Lucknow: Appropriate Technology Development Association.

Hagelberg, G.B. 1979. "Appropriate Technology in Sugar Manufacturing; A Rebuttal," *World Development*, Vol. 7, pp. 893–9.

James, J. 1986. The Choice of Technology in Public Enterprise—A Comparative Study of Manfuacturing Industry in Kenya and Tanzania. Paper presented at A.T. International conference, Macro-Policies and Appropriate Technology, January, Washington, D.C.

Kaplinsky, R. 1983. *Sugar Processing: The Development of a Third World Technology*. London: Intermediate Technology Publications.

Kaplinsky, R. 1984. "Indigenous Technical Change: What can we learn from Sugar Processing?" *World Development*, Vol. 12, No. 4, pp. 419–432.

Stewart, F. 1983. *Macro-Policies for Appropriate Technology: An Introductory Classification*, Appropriate Technology International Working Paper. Washington, D.C.

Tribe, M.A. and Alpine, R.L.W. 1982. *Economies of Scale in Cane Sugar Manufacturing in LDCs*. David Livingstone Institute of Overseas Development.

UNIDO. 1980. *Appropriate Industrial Technology for Sugar*, Monographs on Appropriate Industrial Technology, no. 8, Vienna.

USAID. 1976. *Proposal for a Program on Appropriate Technology*. (Washington: U.S. Government Printing Office, 1976) pp. 11–12, cited by F. Stewart, International Mechanisms for Appropriate Technology. In A.S. Bhalla, op. cit. p. 191.

White, G. 1984. Developmental States and Socialist Industrialisation in the Third World. In R. Kaplinsky (ed.), op. cit.

Table 6.1 Factor utilisation required to meet national annual sugar output (5,150,000 tpa in India, 380,000 tpa in Kenya)

	India			Kenya		
	No. of Plants	Capital cost (£stg)(b)	Employ-ment	No. of Plants	Capital cost (£stg)(b)	Employ-ment
VP mills(a)	327	1,576	284,490	2.6	362	4,420
OP mills						
100 tcd	5,365	1,175	954,970	162	124	29,160
200 tcd	2,682	1,114	836,784	81	98	25,920

(a) Operating at 1250 tcd in India, 7,000 tcd in Kenya (see text)
(b) Replacement costs 'based upon' estimates from machinery suppliers and consultants' reports

Table 6.2 Characteristic cane farming system in N. India

Type of activity	Type of farm: Marginal (<2.5 acres)	Small (2.5-5 acres)	Medium (5-10 acres)	Large (>10 acres)
Land Preparation	bullock	bullock	bullock some tractors	tractors
Planting	bullock & manual	bullock	bullock	tractors
Inter-culture	manual	manual	bullock	tractor
Plant protection	manual	manual	manual	power-operated equipment
Irrigation	canal no pumps	canal & bore holes	canal & bore holes	canals & tubewells
Harvesting	manual	manual	manual	manual
Transporting	bullock cart	bullock cart	some tractors bullock	tractors & lorries
Fertiliser	negligible	30-40 lbs of urea/acre	50-60 lbs of urea/acre	100 lbs of urea/acre
Pesticides	none	none	marginal	non-marginal (no norms)
Approx. output (tons/hectare)	30-40	40	40-45	>50

Source: Conversations with the Indian Sugar Cane Research Institute, Lucknow.

Matrix 6.1 Costs and Benefits

	India VP	India OP	Kenya VP	Kenya OP	Significance of political power
In direct production					
Entrepreneurs - large	+	-	+	-	large
- small	-	+	-	+	small
Management	+	-	+	-	medium
Workers	+;-	+;-	+;-	+;-	small
Women	-	+	-	-	very small
Machinery Supply					
Foreign	+	-	+	-	medium in Kenya
Local - large	+	-	N/A	N/A	large in India
- small	-	+	-	+	small/medium
In farming					
Marginal	-	+	-	+	very small
Small	-	+	-	+	small
Medium	+;-	+;-	+;-	+;-	medium
Large/Estate	+	-	+	-	large
Workers	-	+	-	+	very small
In the state					
Senior decision-takers	+	-	+	-	very high especially in Kenya
Bureaucrats	+	-	+	-	high, especially in India
Aid Agencies					
Multilateral	N/A	N/A	+	-	very high in Kenya, small in India
Bilateral	N/A	N/A	+	-	high in Kenya small in India
'Public interest'					
With respect to price	-	+	-	+	small
With respect to 'welfare'[1]	-	+	-	+	very small
With respect to environmental impact	-	+	-	+	very small

+ positive interest
- negative interest
+; ambivalence

1. For example, production of cane as a monocrop or via mixed farming

N/A Not applicable

Table 6.3 Operating costs of VP and OP in India and Kenya (£Stg. per ton sugar)

	India		Kenya	
	200 tcd improved	1250 tcd	200 tcd improved	7000 tcd
	OP	VP	OP	VP
Official price of sugar ie at historic cost of capital	NA	196	NA	193
With replacement cost of capital	201	238	190	287

Figure 6.1 Developments in VP and OP technology

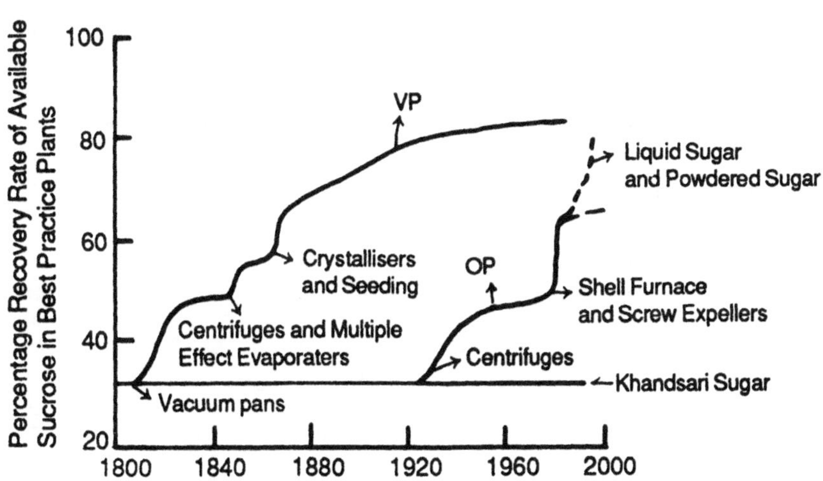

Table 6.4 <u>Sugar beet recovery rate in Germany (% on roots)</u>

1836	5.5
1837-45	5.97
1846-55	7.46
1856-65	8.06
1866-75	8.41
1876-85	9.97
1886	12.31
1896	13.9
1906	15.63
1916-24	16.04
1925	17.15
1926-35	16.19

Source: Deer (1949)

Seven

The Choice of Technology in Public Enterprise: A Comparative Study of Manufacturing Industry in Kenya and Tanzania

Jeffrey James

I. INTRODUCTION

Despite the divergent approaches to development that have been adopted in Kenya and Tanzania—with the explicitly capitalistic orientation of the former usually regarded as standing in sharp contrast to the type of socialism espoused by the latter—public enterprises have come to assume an important position in the manufacturing sectors of both countries. Motivated perhaps primarily to expedite Africanization (that is, to rectify the marked racial imbalance in positions of power and privilege that existed at independence), direct participation in manufacturing activity by the Kenyan Government increased sharply during the 1970s, leading a recent World Bank mission to observe that: "Financial participation by government in industrial ventures has been an important feature in the expansion of Kenya's manufacturing sector" (International Bank for Reconstruction and Development 1983, p. 146). And according to a government report published in 1979, the investments of these and other enterprises in which government has participated in Kenya accounted "for a very sizeable proportion of the total capital formation in the country" (Ndegwa 1979, 22). In Tanzania, the rapid expansion of public enterprises in the manufacturing sector was of course far more ideologically motivated, forming an integral part of the transition to socialist ownership of the means of production after the Arusha Declaration of 1967. By 1974, the public sector accounted for as much as 50 percent of manufacturing value added and employment (Clark 1978).

In view of the rise to prominence of public enterprises in the manufacturing sectors of the two countries, an understanding of the technological choices made by these firms is central to explaining what happened to output, employment, and other major macro-economic variables during the 1970s. An adequate explanation of these choices is also needed because they do not appear to have conformed to what one might have expected. In particular, the highly disparate development strategies that were adopted could reasonably have been expected to produce a correspondingly diverse pattern of technological behaviour by the public enterprises concerned, for these enterprises are often considered an extension, or creature, of the state, so that the divergent goals of Kenya and Tanzania would presumably be reflected to a high degree in their technological choices. But even if this were not the case, and the firms in the two countries had similar goals, their choices might still be expected to differ because of the contrasting macro-environments in which these choices are made; in particular, in Tanzania, market forces are replaced by administrative (or non-market) forms of resource allocation to a greater extent than in Kenya.

Yet, from available evidence one is struck not only by the *similarity* rather than the *differences* in technological behaviour between the two sets of firms, but also by the outcome of this behaviour which diverges from many important national development goals of both countries. The purpose of this chapter is to explain these unexpected findings, using data from a detailed study of how technology decisions were made in a sample of publicly-owned firms in the manufacturing sectors of Kenya and Tanzania. It is contended that, in general, technology decisions are dominated by a single objective which the parastatal holding companies are able to pursue without countervailing pressures from either the macro-environment or from other government agencies. This objective predisposes managers to search for investment projects in which, through various mechanisms and with varying degrees of directness, developed-country patterns of scale, factor-intensity, and product characteristics are invariably closely reproduced.

Section II describes and compares data on the technological characteristics of public enterprise in the two countries. In the following section, a framework is proposed to explain these observations. In section IV, the framework is applied to the case studies. The concluding fifth section considers the main policy implications of the findings.

II. THE TECHNOLOGICAL CHARACTERISTICS OF PUBLIC ENTERPRISES IN MANUFACTURING IN KENYA AND TANZANIA: AN OVERVIEW OF A COMMON PROBLEM

Parastatals in Tanzania have been analysed more than in Kenya. With respect to the technological aspects of the behaviour of these enterprises in particular, the two major studies of the Tanzanian experience are more extensive than the corresponding evidence for Kenya (Clark 1978; Perkins 1980). As a result, the assertions based on these studies juxtaposed in Table 7.1 differ in the degree to which they can be said to accurately characterise the manufacturing sector as a whole. But what comparative data do exist, strongly suggest an interesting paradox common to *both* countries—that the essentially *unplanned* character of the technological behaviour of public enterprises coincides with, and is largely produced by, the *systematic* tendency for large-scale and (often inefficient) capital-intensive technologies to be associated with each other and with excessively sophisticated products. It is this paradoxical combination of features that underlies the striking *similarity* of what has occurred in Kenya and Tanzania. This chapter is designed to contribute to an understanding of this similarity.

III. THE ANALYTICAL FRAMEWORK

According to Gillis, the traditional view in economics is that managers of public enterprises are "cosmic maximisers." That is, they are "motivated solely by a desire to maximise a clearly defined measure of social welfare, as defined by the parent government, under conditions of perfect information on all shadow prices, externalities, and risk" (Gillis 1980, p.3). However, it is apparent even from the brief description of the common problem presented in the previous section that this idealised model (which assumes not only that government is able to provide the firm with a clear set of goals but also that managers actually seek to maximise according to them) will not do. In both Kenya and Tanzania, what has to be explained is why the technological behaviour of public enterprises *diverges* so sharply from many of the most important objectives of their governments. Therefore, an alternative theoretical framework is needed which both posits an alternative behavioural assumption at the level of the enterprise and also contains an alternative and more realistic model of the relationship between the firm and government agencies. Both these modifications are necessary for an alternative framework, for even if public enterprises pursue goals different from those articulated by government, leading to the technological outcomes observed in Kenya and Tanzania, it is necessary to explain the relationship between the firms and the government agencies that enables this to occur.

With respect to the behavioural aspect of an alternative framework, our point of departure is the view that conditions in both Kenya and Tanzania in the 1970s were basically such as to produce what David Williams has termed the bureaucratic-man mechanism, a hypothesis that differs from the neo-classical approach and the engineering-man model (Wells 1975).

Formulated specifically to explain the choice of technology in Tanzanian public enterprises, the bureaucratic-man thesis takes off from the connection between the economic environment and managerial goals (Williams 1975). In the environment in which parastatals for the most part operate in that country, market forces have been substantially replaced by government controls. "The price-control system, for example, is in many cases based on a cost-plus formulation which both shelters the inefficient and gives only a weak incentive to become more efficient. . . . The incentive structure to which the parastatal manager responds offers little in the way of personal financial rewards and, in any case, may focus on surpluses which are more related to windfall gains from the pricing system than to productive efficiency" (Williams 1975, p.7).

Thus deprived of much of an incentive to minimise costs, the manager turns to other goals that appear to offer greater advancement in the eyes of his superiors in the planning hierarchy. In particular, he is said to shift his attention to initiating as many projects as possible. But the manager is constrained in pursuing this goal by financial needs (especially foreign exchange), and he accomplishes this by searching for aid-related projects rather than seeking funds from the planners. "The project which can be secured, presented, moved past the planners, delivered, and staffed fastest and at the least effort to the parastatal is the one that is chosen" (Williams 1975, pp.7–8).

The key element of this hypothesis is that, given the goals of the Tanzanian manager, securing finance becomes critical to achieving his objective. And since the technology for projects is usually closely associated with the financial source (for example, aid donors or export credits), it follows that "the 'choice of technique' in any particular project *is often merely a fallout from the chosen source of finance and related project inputs*" (Williams 1975, p.8). The bureaucratic-man hypothesis may be expressed more strongly as "the bureaucratic decision-maker attempts to achieve objectives which *eliminate* [emphasis added] the choice of technology from the decision process" (Williams 1975, p.8).

What can be said about the characteristics of the technological choices that emerge from this process? According to Williams, it is large-scale, turnkey projects that usually best meet the requirements of rapidly raising finance for projects and ensuring their rapid delivery and construction. Such projects also have the advantage of providing economies of scale in terms of scarce managerial resources at headquarters.

But while the bureaucratic process has, therefore, a systematic bias associated with large-scale production (that is also highly packaged), it does *not*, according to Williams, have a systematic factor-intensity bias. Instead, the factor-intensity of the technology that results from the bureaucratic-man process is thought to be random.

This hypothesis accounts for some of the observed characteristics of the choices made by parastatals in Kenya and Tanzania. But, it fails to explain the tendency towards capital intensity that was noted above in relation to both countries and the sophisticated nature of the products that invariably appear to accompany this tendency. It is possible, however, to modify the implications of the basic model in a direction that is more consistent with these empirical observations by incorporating a more realistic view of the finance bias that is imparted to the technological features of the projects that are selected. And central to this modification are the systematic historical links between the various dimensions of technology that Frances Stewart has described in relation to the experience of the developed countries (Stewart 1977).

The first point that needs to be recognized is that most of the offers of foreign finance to Kenyan and Tanzanian parastatals that seek this means of expanding investment, emanate from the developed market economies.

Thus, despite its socialist orientation, even in Tanzania in the mid-1970s, "Almost 35 percent of Tanzania's assistance is in the form of bilateral aid from Western capitalist countries, while another third comes from the World Bank" (Okumu 1979, pp.244–45). And in Kenya, not surprisingly, aid from these same sources is a much higher percentage of the total (Okumu 1979). Secondly, the "fall-out" (to use Williams' phrase) from this type of finance normally produces a combination of technological characteristics that is not at all random but rather has evolved systematically out of the socio-economic circumstances prevailing in the developed countries with which the finance is associated.

Stewart first elaborated the view that a technology was a "vector" of characteristics (comprising, among other things, the nature of the product and the scale of production) and that changes in these characteristics in the developed countries (where almost all technical change occurs) are mutually interrelated. On the one hand, "As incomes rise, wages rise, making existing technology uneconomic compared with labour-saving innovations. Rising incomes allow greater expenditure on investment per employee" (Stewart 1977, p.7). On the other hand, "Technical change in products in developed countries occurs in line with the rising incomes (and is partly responsible for those rising incomes), so that the balance of characteristics offered by new products corresponds to the changing demands of consumers as their incomes rise. The rising incomes have the effect of shifting demand towards different products with more sophisticated, labour-saving, higher-quality, etc. characteristics" (Stewart 1977, p.17). Moreover, since an increase in the size of the market is another consequence of the rise in average incomes, the scale of output tends to increase with economic growth. "Historically, in the advanced countries the typical size of plant has grown faster than the market as a whole" (Stewart 1977, p.12).

Therefore, insofar as the argument of the two previous paragraphs has validity, the finance bias that defines the bureaucratic-man hypothesis has implications not only for the scale of output, but also for the factor-intensity of technology and the nature of the product. In this way, the behavioural implications of the theory become more consistent with the empirical observations described in Table 7.1. But even this version of the bureaucratic-man mechanism does not adequately describe the relationship between the parastatals and the government agencies that permits the pursuit of a managerial goal, the technological implications of which are, for the most part, inimical to the proclaimed goals of development. The remaining part of the conceptual analysis is devoted to this issue.

Apart from specific problems that vary from one country to another, there are intrinsic difficulties in ensuring that public enterprises are effectively used for implementing government policies. Much of this inherent difficulty can be explained in terms of agent-principal theory.

Raymond Vernon expressed the basic problem in this branch of theory as follows: "How does the principal ensure that the agent acting for him responds to the same information and the same congeries of objectives as the principal would do if acting on his own behalf?" (Vernon 1981, pp.10–11). While by definition this problem pervades all organisations in which agents act on behalf of principals, its severity depends largely on the degree to which the behaviour of the former can be made accountable to the latter. Without an adequate system of accountability, control of the agent by his principal becomes extremely difficult.

Howard Raiffa correctly observed that the problems of accountability and control are usually less acute in private than publicly owned firms. In private firms, "Managers usually have a bottom-line figure that holds them accountable to some extent. In private enterprise, the profit motive is strong and serves as a sieve through which gross incompetents are weeded out and others rewarded" (Raiffa 1981, p.57). In public enterprises, however, as is well-known, the objectives are usually far more diffuse because these firms are formed to fulfill a variety of different functions.

In itself, however, the diversity of objectives of the public enterprise creates no particular problem for the accountability and control system. If, as is assumed in the "cosmic maximisation" model described above, the numerous objectives of the enterprise are combined into an unambiguous objective function, managers could be judged, and held accountable, according to this function, in the way that the private enterprise manager is held accountable in terms of profits. In practice, however, a clear objective function is rarely presented to the managers of the public enterprise and the multiplicity of goals consequently creates severe problems of enterprise accountability and control.

The difficulties in aggregating multiple objectives into an operational composite index have been lucidly described by Raiffa, in relation to the chief executive officer (the principal) of a public enterprise, whose problem it is to communicate the multiple conflicting objectives of the firm to his agents so they can act as the principal would in the same situation. The dilemma facing the chief executive is this: on the one hand, if he is to control his agents he will need to formalise the trade-offs between the conflicting objectives of the firm (for only with such formalisation can an unambiguous objective function be derived). On the other hand, because there is unlikely to be any kind of consensus among the board members about the various trade-offs, whatever formalisation of these that he enunciates will get him into "political trouble" with at least some members of the board. "Thus, the chief executive officer is in an uncomfortable squeeze; he is damned if he formalises his trade-offs and damned if he does not" (Raiffa 1981, p.62).

Raiffa's example can be extended to the case where the government is the principal and the public enterprise its agent; the problem of distilling from the different government agencies a comprehensive set of trade-offs among conflicting goals is likely to be no less serious than it is for the board of directors in the firm. Vernon points to, "The disconcerting fact that, where conflicting and mutually inconsistent goals seem to exist, politicians may find it undesirable, even dangerous, to try to clarify the ambiguity" (Vernon 1981, p.12).

The political difficulties of formalising trade-offs (and consequently of controlling public enterprises effectively) may be severe in open, participatory democracies where there are diffuse and opposing interest groups. Fewer difficulties might be predicted in less participatory regimes where political power is more concentrated among a small group of decision-makers. But even then, considerable disagreement about fundamental trade-offs among development goals can exist.

What we have shown in this section is that there are some inherent (and perhaps intractable) difficulties in making public enterprise conform to national goals. These difficulties often confer substantial autonomy on the enterprises. But there are also measures that can be actively pursued by managers to further their autonomy. The degree to which managers are successful in these endeavours is a further determinant of the likelihood that the outcomes of the behaviour of public enterprises will be at variance with what is intended by government. According to Aharoni, a variety of variables bear on the ability of the manager to increase his autonomy (Aharoni 1981). Among the most important of these are finance, the legal organisation of the firm, and the efficacy of the control functions exercised by government.

IV. APPLICATION TO KENYA AND TANZANIA

It follows from the discussion of the previous section that to apply the analytical framework to Kenya and Tanzania we shall need to concern ourselves with three major issues in these two countries:

1. the conditions that give rise to the operation of the bureaucratic-man mechanism;
2. the technological fall-out from this mechanism, that is, the manner in which the factor-intensity, scale of output, and type of product are derived from financial and other inputs embodied in the sample projects; and
3. the relationships between the parastatals and relevant government agencies that bear (theoretically and in practice) on this fall-out.

The Common Origins of the Bureaucratic Mechanism

It will be recalled that bureaucratic-man tries to start up as many projects as possible. For, it is this focus that is said to be "the way to survive and prosper." But what pressures produce this sort of managerial motiviation is not clear from Williams' statement of the hypothesis. In this part of the chapter it is argued that the source of these pressures in both Kenya and Tanzania can be traced to the extent of, and rapidity with which, output increases were sought (especially in key sectors) and the ease with which this objective of government could be assumed by managers of the parastatals.

It will be argued, furthermore, that the goal of rapid (and sizeable) increments in output was pursued by managers in both countries without much pressure for cost-minimization from the macro-economic environment.

The juxtaposed entries in the first half of Table 7.2 dealing with national goals and goals for the textile and sugar industries support the view that a common desire for rapid growth in domestic output (of wage goods in particular) can be discerned from a study of official and other documents from the 1970s. In both Kenya and Tanzania, this desire was shaped by both political and economic factors: the former because of the significance attributed to meeting the excess demand for many wage goods (see, for example, Barclay's view of this for the Kenyan sugar industry in Table 7.2); and the latter because of the foreign exchange crisis that beset these countries during much of the decade. In the Tanzanian case it should be noted that there was also an ideological basis for the quest for self-reliance in basic goods that formed an essential part of the so-called basic industry strategy (International Bank for Reconstruction and Development 1977(a), App.V).

The admittedly rather sketchy evidence in the second part of Table 7.2 suggests that these political and economic imperatives underlying the national goal for industries such as textiles and sugar translated themselves, at the level of the parastatal holding companies (in which most important decisions regarding manufacturing subsidiaries are made), into a predisposition to initiate a large *number* of projects. The manner of this translation as well as its effects derive from the facts that maximising current output is an objective that is easily measured (and in terms of which, therefore, *kudos* can be *unambiguously* earned). It is also a goal that can be rapidly achieved (as the last quotation for Tanzania in Table 7.2 suggests) on the basis of foreign-financed projects—the more so given that, as Table 7.3 clearly indicates, pressures from the macro-environment to minimize costs were largely absent from both countries. This common absence of pressures on costs stemmed largely from government interventions that broke the link between economic efficiency and profitability at the level of the enterprise.

Of course, maximising output could be achieved by the fuller use of existing projects, and, to some extent, this method was used by parastatal managers (for example, in the attempted reduction of excess capacity). But given the often severe foreign exchange constraints on the efficient operation of these enterprises and the difficulty of raising foreign capital for a fuller utilisation of existing capacity—foreign aid, for example, is usually not available for repairs and spare parts—output maximisation tended to translate in practice into a concern with new projects.

In brief, then, the parastatal holding companies searched for foreign finance (as was explicitly stated by the Kenyan Industrial Development Bank in the final quotation of Table 7.2) and were receptive to offers of such finance. In practice, this usually meant finance from the developed market economies for two main reasons. First, it was this type of finance that, even in Tanzania, tended to be most abundant. Clark observed, "The socialist overtones, far from repelling Western donors, attracted them. . . . What it meant to most donors was that the elite in Tanzania, because of the leadership code, would not enrich themselves on foreign aid, and would in fact strive to enact programmes to better the mass of the population. The Nordic countries, Canada, and the World Bank all found this a striking contrast to the situation in most of the Third World" (Clark 1978, p.182). The second reason is the relative speed (and certainty) of the output increases that are associated with Western finance. "Western firms offer quick, reliable delivery of capital goods. To buy from countries like China takes time and involves uncertainty" (Clark 1978, p.213). (Perhaps a third reason is that developed-country suppliers are more able than their counterparts in the Third World to afford the hard-currency bribes that are not infrequently made to government officials in these countries.)

The Technological Fall-out from the Bureaucratic Mechanism: Case Studies from Kenya and Tanzania

In each country a small sample of publicly-owned firms was selected for analysis. The purpose of these case studies was not to attain statistically significant explanations; rather, it was to study the subtleties of how decisions on technology are made in public enterprises through a detailed study of the decision-making process. The selection of firms was made first for Tanzania from among industries where, for the most part, a considerable data base already existed—sugar, textiles, footwear, detergents, printing ink, grain, and oil milling. The selected cases generally relate to the Third Five Year Plan period from July 1976 to June 1981 (James 1985). In Kenya, an attempt was made to select government majority-owned firms from some of these same industries for a comparable period. These criteria, and formidable problems of data availability and access, produced a sample of enterprises drawn from the following industries: textiles, sugar, salt manufacturing, bottling, cashew processing, ceramics, furfural, and power alcohol. In both countries, data were sought from a variety of documents, such as feasibility studies, board minutes, annual reports, ministerial papers, and tender bids. There was greater access to these documents in Kenya, permitting a more complete reconstruction of the technology decision process in the Kenyan sample than in Tanzanian firms, which should be borne in mind in interpreting the results.

Kenya

The case studies from Kenya provide clear confirmation of the decision-making process for technology envisaged by the notion of bureaucratic-man. They also clearly disprove the implication drawn by Williams that the technological fall-out from this process tends to be random. The confirmatory evidence is contained in Table 7.4 which shows the predicted link between the choice of managing agents (who were generally also minority partners) and the source of technology for the sample enterprises. Table 7.5, however, suggests that when, as is the case for most of the examples studied here, developed-country collaborators are involved, the technological fall-out from this collaboration is more likely to be systematic than random. That is, Table 7.5 points to some tendency for the large-scale of output to go with high capital intensity on the one hand and a sophisticated type of product, often intended for export, on the other.

One could infer from Tables 7.4 and 7.5 an underlying decision-making process in which, because of the lack of concern with the technological aspects of the projects that is assumed to be exhibited by bureaucratic-man (in the form of the parastatal holding companies), the fall-out from the developed-country collaboration proceeded entirely unquestioned, a process in which the appropriateness of the technology to national development goals might, therefore, never be raised. But a close scrutiny of the actual negotiations reveals that this depiction of what occurred is only part of a more complex story.

It is only a partial explanation, not so much because the parastatal holding companies were generally more active technologically than the theory posited, but because other institutions frequently questioned the desirability of the technology proposed. What is interesting, therefore, is the question of how the evident closeness of the fall-out was sustainable in the face of the various challenges to its desirability. Four of the cases are especially revealing in this regard.

Consider first the salt refining and Nzoia sugar projects. In both cases, the World Bank was critical of the lack of attention the Industrial Development Bank (IDB) paid in appraisals of the technological choice aspects of the project. In relation to the salt refining project, the World Bank drew attention specifically to what it regarded as the excessively capital-intensive equipment selected. The Industrial Development Bank's unenthusiastic response to the suggestion that more labour-intensive alternatives be considered is worth quoting in full because it reveals this institution's perception (and arguably, to some degree, rationalization) of the limits of technological choice, given the constraints imposed by the scale of output and the prior selection of developed-country collaborators. "As IDB is involved mainly in fairly large-scale industrial projects, for which technology has to be imported from the developed countries, the possibility of maximising employment (mainly unskilled labour) is severely limited by the inability of the foreign technical collaborator to adapt the technology involved to local needs. We do try to make changes in project design but our experience has so far shown that the scope to make substantial changes is limited, partly because of the technological environment to which the technical participants or sponsors are used. Some of the processes in any case have naturally to be sophisticated, for example a salt refinery or fertilizer plant" (IDB, Project correspondence files). Apparently not satisfied with this response, the officials of the World Bank offered a rejoinder to the effect that a less capital-intensive technology, even if less profitable, ought nevertheless to form part of the holding company's frame of reference. The question, as the World Bank officials saw it, was "by how much [it was less profitable] and whether it would be worthwhile to accept the trade-off." They added, however, that "the project is far too advanced to raise this question at this stage; this question should be raised in the context of the government industrialization and employment policy and should be discussed between the government, the IDB and the promoters in the early stages of project preparation" (IDB, Project correspondence files).

In the Nzoia sugar project, the World Bank's admonition (regarding the inadequate attention that IDB's appraisal had paid to the suitability of the technology selected by the French collaborators) seemed well founded because IDB's management "was not able to assess the technical suitability of the proposed plant or to establish whether the price agreed on was reasonable and competitive" and has therefore "to make do with assurances received regarding Fives-Cail Babcock's many years of experience in supplying similar plants to various countries" (IDB, Project correspondence files). But here, as in the previous case, the late stage in the negotiation at which this issue was raised seemed to make any effective countervailing action very difficult.

It was noted in Table 7.4 that Seditex, the German managing agents of the Rift Valley textiles project, chose German-made equipment for this project. This firm had, however, been asked (apparently by the International Finance Corporation as a minority shareholder and lender) also to consider bids from Japanese and American machinery suppliers. Although these bids were considerably cheaper than the German quotations, they were rejected by Seditex on the following grounds:

> From our viewpoint, two vital aspects have to be considered. The first is operational costs, involving quality and efficiency; the second is the practical and psychological conditions. By opting for the cheapest, we have no doubt that the mill's efficiency and fabric quality will be lower, that supervision, labour, and maintenance costs, as well as consumption of electricity and spares will be higher. On the other hand, as European promoters, with our main office in Hamburg, it would undoubtedly be more difficult and costly to plan and coordinate with Japanese or American suppliers the multitude of details before and during the construction period. Loopholes in tight coordination and planning can have grave financial consequences.
>
> We shall equally have considerable difficulties in coping with urgent problems that would probably require the manufacturer's assistance, once the mill is in operation. Moreover, our natural source of recruiting technicians is Europe. Such European technicians will have to become acquainted with Japanese or American equipment; this would involve more expenses and, in general, contacts would be more difficult and complicated. (ICDC, project correspondence files)

In the case of Kenya Furfural, both the Agricultural Development Corporation and the Industrial and Commercial Development Corporation (ICDC) raised strenuous objections to the technological (and other) aspects of the project. The former noted that, "one or two of the intended equity holders and/or lenders whatever the case may be are also the suppliers of the plant" and sought reassurance that the plant would be purchased "on an international tender basis." Such reassurance did not however materialize as the project leader argued that the plant and equipment, because of its specialized design, "could only be supplied by Escher Wyss," and consequently, an international tender was not possible. The ICDC objection focused on the high capital cost of the project and on an inability to obtain a detailed breakdown of this cost from the sponsor. In spite of these criticisms, other government agencies, (the IDB, the Treasury and the Development Finance Company of Kenya) favoured the project, which was approved in apparently unmodified form.

For a variety of reasons, then—the fragmented government involvement, the attitude of the holding company, the stage at which objections were raised, and the alleged hidden costs of cheaper machinery—the closeness of the technological fall-out was able to be preserved in these cases. But apart perhaps from the hidden costs argument, these reasons offer little basis for supposing that the preservation had anything whatsoever to do with economic efficiency. Rather, it is probable that the outcome was inimical to this objective (the continuous financial losses made by all these enterprises are consistent with, though not proof of, this assertion).

Tanzania

We have seen that the Kenyan case studies generally conformed closely to the bureaucratic-man notion with respect to its prediction of a role for technology that is essentially derivative of the source of foreign (mostly developed-country) finance and related managerial inputs into the project. And in this derivative process there was a tendency for the technological characteristics of the project (scale of output, factor-intensity, and type of product) to take on a systematic form. While some cases in Tanzania (mostly in sugar and textiles) also followed this general pattern, other cases did not.

In these other cases, though there was still a large-scale bias arising from the search for foreign finance, the type of finance obtained for these projects happened not to be closely tied to any particular source of technology, and because this permitted the technological choice aspects of the projects to assume a more central role, other factors, not allowed for in the bureaucratic-man formulation, came to be important. These other factors worked, as we shall see, through the same tendency towards interrelatedness of the various aspects of developed-country technology with which it was necessary in the Kenyan cases to supplement the original formulation of the bureaucratic mechanism. But the tendency was not merely appended to the mechanism as a derivative. Rather, it was set in motion by an active set of preferences. That is, the basic components of the explanation of these cases remain the same, but the manner of their combination into an integrated approach differs from what has so far been the case.

Let us, however, first deal briefly with the case studies in Tanzania that closely followed the Kenyan model (James, 1983). These were drawn mostly from the textiles and sugar industries, which were particularly emphasized in the Third Five Year Plan (Table 7.2). Interviews with the managers of the parastatal holding companies responsible for these industries, revealed that the emphasis of the Plan on rapid import substitution had been incorporated into, and seemed to dominate, the objective functions of these institutions. For example, one manager in Texco (the holding company for the textiles industry) described his primary concern as being "to clothe the nation as fast as possible." He stressed that if his concern was simply to maximise profits, he would prefer second-hand machinery to the turnkey projects that were thought best to promote the rapid expansion of output. Similarly, what emerged from interviews with managers at the Sugar Development Corporation could be described as an objective function embodying the primary goals of meeting national excess demand as rapidly as possible subject to the constraint of avoiding losses. From this overriding objective there followed the implication that particular types of products and techniques were ruled out of consideration *ab initio*. The managers stressed that the rapid expansion of the sugar industry based on jaggery and OPS sugar (the small-scale alternative to the large-scale production of refined sugar) would not have been feasible. In the case of the OPS alternative, they pointed out that some 200 small plants would have been required to replace the output of five large ones. The managerial and supervisory problems associated with this alternative, not to mention the training of operatives in the OPS method and the difficulties of raising finance for small-scale techniques, meant to the managers that this method could at best supplement a strategy based on large-scale factories.

In many of the large-scale projects in these industries, to which the objective described in the previous paragraph gave rise during the Third Five Year Plan period, the technology fall-out was closely tied (as in the Kenyan cases) to the sources of finance (and other inputs) that were secured for the (highly packaged) projects. In the Musoma textile mill, for example, with a capacity of 25 million square metres of cloth, a general French contracting company was responsible for financing and constructing the plant on a semi-turnkey basis. This company identified not only the consortium of financing institutions in Europe (whose loans were effectively tied to procurement in each particular country) but also the machinery suppliers. Similarly, in the expansion of the capacity of the sugar mills at Kilombero, Kagera, and Mtibwa, turnkey tenders were floated in the countries to which the external finance was tied.

There were, however, other large-scale projects initiated during the Third Five Year Plan period in which the technological fall-out did not conform at all to this derivative pattern. In these cases, in contrast, technological choice came to comprise a more central element of the decision that had to be made for the projects. Three examples, all financed directly or indirectly (through the Tanzanian Investment Bank) by the World Bank, illustrate this point and demonstrate how other factors impart an independent upward bias to the capital intensity.

The most important of these factors is product choice, the bias from which, as the recently established Morogoro Shoe Company shows, can be imparted through the alleged need to produce exports conforming to international standards. The choice of product for this project was dictated almost entirely by its orientation to exports, as is made quite clear in the Bank's Appraisal Report. Thus, "One fairly modern shoe factory presently produces leather and canvas shoes for the internal market. The output is of acceptable quality within Tanzania, but does not meet international standards. The new shoe factory . . . would produce about 4 million pairs of shoes to international standards, primarily for export, but it is expected that a small part of the production will be sold internally" (IBRD 1977b, p. ii). The same report also makes explicit the link between production for export and the nature of the technology that is required. To quote again from this document, "During the detailed engineering design phase, efforts will be made to substitute labour for capital without compromising product style, quality, and cost competitiveness but the extent to which this can be done is limited in export-oriented industries" (IBRD 1977b, p.29).

Sabuni Industries Limited—the only parastatal in Tanzania which produces powdered laundry detergent—is a clear example of a second main influence on product choice, that which originates in historically determined tastes. The Sabuni project was conceived in the 1960s, when, following the break-up of the East African Community, supplies of the detergent Omo from Kenya were discontinued. It seemed clear to the National Development Corporation (the holding company responsible for the detergent industry at the time), that local production of a substitute was required. In the decision to replicate, or even improve, the brand that had been imported, what appears to have been crucial was the consideration that "since most of the people in the country had used the Kenyan brand of detergent (Omo), which is of very high quality, it was envisaged to produce a detergent of the same standard or even better, in order to capture the market previously supplied by the Unilever Company in Kenya. The intention was also to produce a product which could be exported to neighbouring countries by competing effectively with other high quality brands" (National Chemicals Industries, document). That the choice of this particular type of product had a decisive influence on the choice of technology for Sabuni, can be inferred from the impact it had on the tender process. The tenderers were apparently asked to supply, with their quotations, a sample of their brands. These samples were then analyzed by the research staff of the National Development Corporation. It is surely not without significance that the Italian firm which was awarded the tender, also happens to be the plant supplier to Unilever in Kenya, the manufacturers of Omo.

The final example, the multi-purpose oil mill at Morogoro, illustrates how engineering-man type factors, in addition to those arising from product choice, operated at different stages of the decision process to exacerbate the capital-intensive bias of the technology that was chosen. First, the tender document specified that all the equipment should be new (Industrial Studies and Development Center 1975a, p.14). This prohibition against second-hand equipment is not unique to the acquisition of oil-milling equipment; on the contrary, it is a practice which is endorsed in the bidding rules of the World Bank and by the governments of both Tanzania and Kenya.

In a second respect as well—which concerns once more the link between products and techniques—the specification of the tender document appears to have imparted a bias against the use of more appropriate techniques. Specifically, the document embodies requirements for buildings that require relatively sophisticated products and techniques. Thus, to quote from the document, "Building and construction work must meet local building and hygenic requirements and standards, which to a great extent are of British origin" (ISDC 1975a, p.13). Or, to take another example, the use of locally produced roofing tiles is precluded by "the minimum requirements for roofing materials—corrugated aluminum sheets or corrugated asbestos sheets" (ISDC 1975a, p.13).

If there were therefore biases in the manner in which the tender document was specified, it was also true that in the next stage—the evaluation of the tenders received—engineering-man type factors further reduced the pressures for cost minimisation in the choice of technology. At the very outset of the evaluation procedure, for example, we find that most of the numerous quotations were rejected on the grounds that they had not come "from potentially competent and internationally-known companies" (ISDC 1975b, p.2). And in the selection from among the five contractors that did conform to this description, considerable emphasis was laid on the following factors (in addition, of course, to costs): goodwill of the bidder in his country and abroad, competence and capability of the bidder to successfully complete the project, quality of the end products, experience in export, and establishment of plants in foreign countries (ISDC 1975b, p.3).

One of the major technological issues that confronted the sub-committee formed by Moproco to evaluate the bids, was the choice between a batch and a continuous refining process. Despite the relatively high cost of the latter, this was nevertheless the method selected. With respect to the bleaching component of the refining process, the sub-committee explained its choice with what amounts to a statement of the engineering-man hypothesis. Thus, "Continuous bleaching plants have gained wide acceptance as they are now feasible, but they are relatively costly owing to their expensive control instruments. . . . Continuous bleaching units are favoured by processors because of their independence of human operation, because they permit savings in bleaching earth and oil loss in it, finally because they render a finished product of uniform colour" (ISDC 1975b, p.14). In the opinion of the general manager of Moproco, a member of the sub-committee for evaluating the tenders, the last reason—the uniformity of product quality associated with continuous refining—was perhaps most influential in the process.

The conclusion from these three cases is that active biases in selection led, through the close link between product choice and technology, to the same tendency towards reproducing developed-country technologies that was shown in the derivative process with which the other case studies were associated. An essential difference, however, lies in the implications for policy that seek to alter this outcome. In the one case it is the active biases that need to be tackled directly and in the other it is the prior forces that give rise to the derivation of developed-country technological characteristics. More on this important policy issue will be contained in the concluding section.

The Discretion of Parastatal Managers in Kenya and Tanzania

So far the applied section of the chapter has described the common origins of the bureaucratic mechanism in Kenya and Tanzania and the nature of the technological fall-out from this mechanism in case studies from the manufacturing sectors of the two countries. The analysis has been concerned with how the chosen technologies in the case studies acquired characteristics that rendered them inconsistent with many important development goals (as stated in the respective five year plans). Following the conceptual framework, it remains to consider briefly the relationship between the parastatal holding companies and government agencies that allowed these outcomes to occur.

Table 7.6 summarizes these relationships, which, when juxtaposed, reveal (as with much else in the chapter) a remarkable similarity between the two countries. In both countries it appears that the failure of the elaborate control system has invested parastatal managers with almost complete autonomy and that the weaknesses of the system come from the same fundamental source.

On the one hand, neither government has been able and willing to specify the trade-offs between the multiple and conflicting goals of development that are required for forming a national objective function and without which the agents of government cannot effectively be controlled. One manifestation of this inability is in the lack of clear criteria for project appraisal by the holding companies in both countries (and perhaps also in the orientation to private, rather than social, profitability that is generally exhibited in the appraisals). On the other hand, even if there was no such problem of formulating a clear national objective function, the efficacy of the control system in Kenya and Tanzania would still be severely constrained by managerial and administrative resources that were inadequate to the burgeoning tasks imposed on them during the 1970s (James 1985). Following Killick, it is plausible to argue that such a constraint is necessarily entailed in a strategy that makes major demands on limited skilled manpower (Killick 1978).

V. CONCLUSIONS

Although there are many important respects in which the divergent development strategies adopted by Kenya and Tanzania have produced correspondingly different outcomes, with regard to the factors that are thought to have determined the technological behaviour of public enterprises in the manufacturing sectors of these countries, this chapter has stressed instead the striking similarities between them. It was suggested not only that the two groups of enterprises adopted the same predominant policy goal, but also that the relevant aspects of the policy environment (both domestic and foreign) in which this goal was pursued were similar. Moreover, the achievement of this common goal of rapid and sizeable output increases in key sectors—given the macro-environment that prevailed in the two countries, the similar nature of the constraints to achieving the objective on the basis of small-scale production, the tendency for developed-country offers of finance to be dominant in both, and for these offers to be associated with the reproduction of technologies from these same countries (either merely derivatively when the tie to finance was direct or through an active set of biases when the tie was much less close), and given a similar weak government capacity for control—meant that the resulting technologies were in most respects inconsistent with major goals of development. The rapid and substantial increases in manufacturing output that were achieved during most of the 1970s in Kenya and Tanzania through large-scale, capital-intensive and highly packaged techniques appear to have had adverse consequences for employment, economic efficiency, income distribution, regional policy, products suitable for meeting basic needs, learning effects, and the balance of payments since the exports that were intended often failed to materialize from these projects while their import requirements were extremely heavy (IBRD 1983).

It could be argued that this outcome reflects the fact that national goals other than output maximisation were not in fact accorded much weight by either government. While this interpretation may explain part of what occurred, it assumes that an explicit (or implicit) trade-off between goals was actually made by policy-makers. It may be more realistic, however, to posit an alternative decision-making process in terms of which policy-makers were essentially unaware of the conflicts (and especially the extent of the conflicts) with other goals that output maximisation would entail. In relation to Tanzania, Hyden, for example, suggested that "policy makers often decide on matters without first having obtained full and detailed knowledge of the possible consequences of their decisions. They start 'running' and take the consequences as they occur" (Hyden 1979, p.97).

There are two broad implications for policy that follow from this interpretation of what occurred. One is that a less rapid and more moderate target increase in output would tend to make more feasible a strategy of relying more heavily on small-scale, labour-intensive techniques, since the managerial and organizational constraints on such a strategy would then become binding less quickly (and to this extent dependence on foreign sources of finance would also be reduced). The second broad policy option arises from the fact that even if this goal cannot be altered (for instance because of political factors), one can still seek to alter aspects of the environment in which the goal is pursued, so as to render its achievement more consistent with a different and more appropriate set of techniques than those with which it has been associated in the past.

The components of such an alteration, in turn, can be grouped into two broad categories, comprising policies to enhance the role of small-scale, labour-intensive projects on the one hand, and those seeking to alter the choices that are made by given large-scale projects on the other. Since the goal of rapid and large increases in output is assumed to remain essentially intact, and consequently there is no diminution in the existing constraints on an enlarged role for the small-scale sector, these constraints will need to be surmounted. For this purpose, it is not sufficient merely to advocate intensive training schemes that will produce additional entrepreneurs. In addition, policies will be required to strengthen the regional, district, and village organizations in which the expanded numbers of small-scale projects will have to operate.

The need for simultaneous efforts to improve the technological component of large-scale projects derives from the fact that one cannot realistically expect any rapid and substantial progress from even effective policies indicated in the previous paragraph. A parallel set of policies for the large-scale sector first ought to comprise efforts to restore the link between efficiency and profitability at the enterprise level. In Tanzania, this would require reform of the price-control system. In Kenya it would mean, among other things, ending privileges to public enterprises in financial difficulties. Particularly if they are combined with more emphasis on profitability in the incentive (and accountability) systems, and a move towards a more competitive environment (as is now occurring in Kenya), these policies ought to reduce the slackness in the decision-making procedures of the holding companies, in relation to their search behaviour and appraisal methods. In this way, the behaviour of managers will be subject to a discipline that will make it more difficult for them to ignore the technological choice aspects of projects.

Secondly, a set of policies will be required to address the problems of the finance bias that tend to be especially pronounced when there is a close fall-out from developed-country sources of finance. One way to overcome this bias is to promote a much more active search for developing-country (for example, Indian and Chinese) sources on the one hand (with which more appropriate techniques are likely to be associated), and for more multilateral sources, offering more technological options, on the other. But in the latter case, unless the active biases that were found in the selection mechanism can be overcome, little will be gained from the wider choice that this type of finance potentially affords. Policies to correct these selection biases will have to pay particular attention to the various influences that govern product choice. For one thing, any rationale of the choice of sophisticated products that is based on the need for exports (especially to developed countries) ought to be very carefully evaluated. In many of the sample projects in Kenya and Tanzania this argument was advanced in feasibility studies (partly to rationalize particular product and process choices) but in most cases the intended exports failed to materialize and the output ended up being sold to local consumers, for most of whom it was highly inappropriate. Where the source of the product choice bias originates, instead, in historically conditioned tastes for advanced country imports, countervailing pressures, exercised, for example, through promotional campaigns for local goods, are required. While product policies of this kind may help combat engineering-man type biases, other parts of this problem, such as the prohibition of used equipment, need to be tackled directly. Finally, because there are limits to the extent to which the sources of finance can be altered along the lines suggested above, dependence on developed-country technologies that are closely tied to sources of finance in these countries will remain an important problem for Kenya and Tanzania. In these cases, independent technological advice that is taken early in appraising the project (from say the United Nations Industrial Development Organisation), using some social, rather than private mode of project appraisal, can help reveal grossly inappropriate choices and increase the bargaining strength of the government vis-à-vis foreign collaborators.

Finally, the political economy aspects of these policy proposals need to be considered. In particular, our concern is to indicate that each of the different sets of prescribed policies will be associated with a different—though to some degree overlapping—profile of gaining and losing interests. And insofar as the political significance of these interests varies within and between the two countries, so too will the feasibility of the different policies.

Table 7.7 represents a crude matrix of likely gainers and losers for the three policy areas identified earlier: reform of the macro-environment; enlargement of the role of small-scale, labour-intensive projects; and improved choices for large-scale projects.

Reform of the macro-environment would generally shift the distribution of gains from inefficient enterprises towards more efficient ones and towards consumers and firms previously reliant on the expensive output of the inefficient firms. Some evidence for Kenya indicates these potential gains could be substantial if protectionist policies are eliminated or reduced, since, "It is possible to document high local prices and/or low or deteriorating quality for virtually the complete range of products for which there are import restrictions" (IBRD 1983, p.415). The ban on competing imports of lead pencils, for example, amounts to an implicit tariff of 208 percent, while domestically produced ballpoint pens sell for KSh 1.75 as against a comparable import price of half a shilling (IBRD 1983).

Whereas reform of the macro-economic environment indirectly promotes small-scale projects to the extent that these are relatively efficient, the second policy area shown in the table seeks directly to alter the composition of output in favour of these units. And, particularly if it is pursued in a context of rural industrialization, it poses a challenge principally to urban and allied foreign interests on behalf of rural groups. In this case, as with macro-reform, gains accrue to consumers, but because the gains derive here from the altered characteristics of the products produced on a small-scale, rather than from a fall in the price of existing goods, they tend to be concentrated on those consumers with low incomes.

Unlike the policy prescription considered in the previous paragraph, which challenges the interests associated with large-scale, the final policy alternative impinges only on the form that these interests currently take, namely, those based on the predominance of developed-country finance and techniques. As such, policies to alter the techniques that are chosen by large scale public enterprises threaten a narrower set of interests than those that seek to undermine the enterprises themselves.

Assessing the relative political strengths of the gaining and losing interests shown in the table—and hence the feasibility of different policies within each country—is far from easy, not least because of the substantial disagreement among students of political economy issues in Kenya and Tanzania (Fransman 1982; Swainson 1980; Coulson 1982). Nor, despite the socialistic orientation of Tanzania's leaders, can one cogently argue that the challenges to existing interests that are required will necessarily be easier to effect in that country than in Kenya. For, "What is clear in Tanzania is that the conversion to socialism occurred essentially at the top, indeed at the very top, and has not yet permeated the whole society. As a result there remain many anti-socialist forces in the society. . . . The importance of the urban elite in derailing attempts at radical change has been emphasized by many writers" (Clark 1978, pp.204–5). But one should not infer from this that all the areas of policy intervention will be no more feasible politically in Tanzania than in Kenya. It may be that because of its greater political independence, Tanzania is better placed to implement the switch from predominantly developed-country to alternative (notably developing-country) sources of finance and technology.

NOTES

I am indebted to Frances Stewart for comments on an earlier draft of this chapter and to Leo Mureithi for his kind assistance in Nairobi.

REFERENCES

Aharoni, Y. 1981. Managerial discretion. In *State-Owned Enterprise in the Western Economies*, eds. R. Vernon & Y. Aharoni. New York: St. Martin's Press.

Barclay, A.H. 1977. The Mumias sugar project: A study of rural development in Western Kenya, Ph.D. diss., Columbia University, New York.

Clark, W.E. 1978. *Socialist Development & Public Investment in Tanzania*. Canada: University of Toronto Press.

Coulson, A. 1982. *Tanzania: A Political Economy*. England: Oxford University Press.

Fransman, M., ed. 1982. *Industry and Accumulation in Africa*. Heinemann.

Gillis, M. 1980. *The role of state enterprises in economic development*, Harvard Institute for International Development, Discussion Paper No. 83 (February).

Hopcraft, P. 1979. Industrialization, balance of payments & trade policy in Kenya: Effects of protectionism & government intervention on prices, exports & income distribution. Institute for Development Studies, University of Nairobi. Mimeo.

Hopcraft, P., and J. Oguttu. 1982. *Parastatal development agencies & their relationship with the private sector*. Institute for Development Studies, University of Nairobi, Occasional Paper no. 39.

Hyden, G. 1979. Administration & public policy. In *Politics & Public Policy in Kenya & Tanzania*, eds. J. Barkan and J. Okumu. Praeger.

IBRD. 1977(a). *Tanzania: Basic Industry Report*.

IBRD. 1977(b). *Tanzania: Appraisal of the Morogoro Industrial Complex*.

IBRD. 1978. *Tanzania Second Cashewnut Development Project, Staff Appraisal Report*.

IBRD. 1983. *Kenya: Growth & Structural Change*.

Industrial Studies & Development Centre, Dar-es-Salaam. 1975(a). *Tender Document for a Turnkey Project for a Multi-Purpose Oil Mill Company*.

Industrial Studies & Development Center, Dar-es-Salaam. 1975(b). *Evaluation of Tender Bids for a Multipurpose Oilseed Processing Plant for Morogoro*.

James, J. 1983. *Bureaucratic, engineering & economic men: decision-making for technology in Tanzania's state-owned enterprises*, ILO, World Employment Programme Research, Technology & Employment Programme, Working Paper no. 125.

James, J. 1985. Bureaucratic, engineering & economic men: decision-making for technology in Tanzania's state-owned enterprises. In *Theory & Reality in Development: Essays in Honour of Paul Streeten*, eds. S. Lall and F. Stewart. London: Macmillan.

Killick, T. 1978. *Development Economics in Action: A Study of Economic Policies in Ghana*. Heinemann.

Loxley, J., and J. Saul. 1975. "Multinationals, Workers & the Parastatals in Tanzania," *Review of African Political Economy*, no. 2.

Mihyo, P. Bargaining for technology in Tanzania's public enterprises: some policy issues. Universtiy of Dar-es-Salaam. Mimeo.

Mihyo, P. The legal environment & the performance of public enterprises in Tanzania. University of Dar-es-Salaam. Mimeo.

Ministry of Planning & Economic Affairs, Dar-es-Salaam. 1982. *Structural Adjustment Programme for Tanzania*.

Ndegwa, P. 1979. *Review of Statutory Boards*. Report and Recommendations of the Committee appointed by His Excellency the President. Nairobi.

Ndegwa, P. 1982. *Working Party on Government Expenditures*. Report and Recommendations of the Committee appointed by His Excellency the President. Nairobi.

O'Brien, P. 1982. Relations between transnational corporations and public enterprises in developing countries, with particular reference to technological development: A preliminary analysis. Vienna. Mimeo.

Okumu, J. 1979. Foreign relations: Dilemmas of independence & development. In *Politics and Public Policy in Kenya and Tanzania*, eds. J. Barkan & J. Okumu. Praeger.

Oyugi, W. 1982. *Government and public enterprises: Some observations on Kenya*, Institute for Development Studies, University of Nairobi, Occasional Paper no. 39.

Perkins, F. 1980. Technological choice, industrialisation and development: The case of Tanzania, Ph.D. Thesis, University of Sussex, England.

Perkins, F. 1983. "Technology choice, industrialisation and development: The case of Tanzania," *Journal of Development Studies*, 19 (January).

Raiffa, H. 1980. Decision making in the state owned enterprise. In *State-Owned Enterprise in the Western Economies*, eds. R. Vernon & Y. Aharoni. New York: St. Martin's Press.

Roemer, M., G. Tidrick, and D. Williams. 1976. "The range of strategic choice in Tanzanian industry," *Journal of Development Economics*, 3.

Schluter, M. 1984. *An institutional framework for developing Kenya's food and beverage exports*, Institute for Development Studies, University of Nairobi, Working Paper no. 407.

Stewart, F. 1977. *Technology and Underdevelopment*. London: Macmillan.

Swainson, N. 1980. *The Development of Corporate Capitalism in Kenya 1918–77*. California: University of California Press.

Vernon, R. 1981. Introduction. In *State-Owned Enterprise in the Western Economies*, eds. R. Vernon and Y. Aharoni. New York: St. Martin's Press.

Wells, L. 1975. Economic man and engineering man: Choice of technology in a low-wage country. In *The Choice of Technology in Developing Countries*, C.P. Timmer, et al. Harvard Institute in International Affairs, no. 32.

Williams, D. 1975. *National planning and the choice of technology: The case of textiles in Tanzania*, Economic Research Bureau Paper No. 75.12, Dar-es-Salaam.

Table 7.1

A Comparative Summary of the Technological Characteristics of Public Enterprises in Manufacturing

	Tanzania	Kenya
Degree of Conformity to National Development Goals	"The failure of the post-Arusha companies to distinguish themselves significantly and favourably from the pre-Arusha companies points to one of the most important conclusions which can be made about the performance of the manufacturing parastatals, indeed about all parastatals. There has been as yet no developmental innovation on the part of parastatals to make themselves more consistent with the Tanzanian ideology. They have tended to want the most modern plants. Turn-key projects ... have not been uncommon." (Clark, 1978, p.140) "In general the observed pattern of technological choice ... only reflects to a limited degree Tanzania's articulated development goals." (Perkins, 1980, p. 408)	"This study suggests that the parastatal investment companies have done little or nothing to push the manufacturing sector in the directions specified by the policy statements of government. Rather, they appear to have aided and abetted some of the least appropriate features of the Kenyan industrial structure." (Hopcraft and Oguttu, 1982, p. 193) "While too large a proportion of the development budget has been diverted to investments, the balance of that budget has not been effectively utilized either. The pattern of development outlined in Development Plans has often been ignored in practice in favour of unplanned projects." (Ndegwa, 1982, p. 14)
Relation to the Planning System	"The present system of investment decision-making in the parastatal sector is essentially one of unplanned socialism. ... The results bear only an incidental relation to any formal development plan or to the proclaimed goals of industrial development." (IBRD, 1977a, p. 125)	"Parastatals have played a large and increasingly important role in Kenya's life in recent years. Growth of this sector has been, in many respects, unplanned and uncoordinated."(IBRD, 1983, p. 105)
Technological Characteristics of Public Enterprises	"Despite the rhetoric, Tanzania's industrialization programme has, in general, promoted the establishment of enterprises using large-scale capital-intensive, often technically, and almost invariably economically inefficient techniques." (Perkins, 1983, p. 231) "Almost one-third of parastatals have chosen to manufacture products ... for which a simpler, less technologically specified substitute exists." (Perkins, 1983, p. 226) "There is a strong tendency for parastatals to adopt the most advanced techniques, and build the most modern buildings. In manufacturing this tendency is exhibited as an inclination towards large-scale, capital-intensive, "transformation" projects ... There has been very little change in the orientation of the parastatal sector since the Arusha Declaration. ... There has been no significant development of small-scale rural industries." (Clark, 1978, p. 125)	"The parastatal client firms tend to be large, capital intensive, import intensive and almost exclusively oriented toward a protected, over priced local market." (Hopcraft and Oguttu, 1982, p. 193) "Despite the emphasis in policy statements on assistance to small, African owned and export-oriented firms, firms with government participation tend to be large (half of all Kenya's industrial firms employing more than 200 people have government financial participation)." (IBRD, 1983, p. 85) "Examples of unsound and poorly controlled investments can readily be found in such areas of activity as fertilizer, sugar, textiles and power alcohol. ... this has resulted in uncontrolled cost escalations, inefficient technologies and unprofitable enterprises." (Ndegwa, 1982, p. 42)
Relation to Foreign Finance	"Public investment today remains about as heavily dependent on foreign funds as it did ten years ago. About one-half of public investment has been foreign financed." (Clark, 1978, p. 173)	"A major characteristic of most of the parastatals in Kenya is that they depend heavily on foreign financing and management advice." (Oyugi, 1982, p.64)

Table 7.2
The industrial objectives of government in the 1970s

	Tanzania	Kenya
National goals	"The major objective ... is to achieve a greater degree of economic self-sufficiency." (Third Five Year Plan, p. 43) "The present plan has placed a high priority on the satisfaction of domestic basic needs. Thus the production of food, textiles, shoes and construction materials will have particular emphasis." (Third Five Year Plan, p. 43) "The strategy puts a premium on the earliest feasible development of a basic industry." (Roemer et al., 1976, p. 269) "New projects will have to be consistent with the basic industrial strategy." (Third Five Year Plan, p. 47)	"The overriding industrial strategy of the Government - ... is to accelerate industrial growth." (Second Five Year Plan, p. 326) "The target [for 1974] is an increase in output of over 70 per cent compared with 1967." (Second Five Year Plan, p.12) "The attainment of the income and employment targets in this Plan depends to a significant degree on the country obtaining physical resources from abroad to supplement its own effort. Without making use of these physical resources ... the country cannot develop as rapidly as planned. The Government will therefore endeavour to obtain from abroad the resources necessary to achieve the national goals." (Second Five Year Plan, p. 329-330) "The crucial point in the drive for accelerated industrial development is that highest priority be accorded to projects which make the greatest contribution to improving Kenya's balance of payments position." (Annual Reports and Accounts of the Industrial Development Bank, 1974, p.9)
The Sugar Industry	"The national goal is to achieve self-sufficiency in sugar production at the earliest opportunity, sustaining self-sufficiency at all times and resources and economics permitting produce surplus sugar for export." (Sugar Development Corporation, Annual Report and Accounts, 1976-77, p.33) "Rapid progress in this area is required to satisfy domestic demand." (Third Five Year Plan, p. 46)	"Bearing in mind the sugar production deficit and the need for foreign exchange to purchase additional sugar for the country's consumption requirements, the Government requested funds ... for a study to be made of the industry and the development of a programme for the country to become self-sufficient if economically possible within a period of 10 years." (Government of Kenya, Kenya Sugar Industry, Expansion Study, Vol. V, Nyanza Sugar Belt Improvement Project, Tate and Lyle, May 1976, p. 8) "Kenya's commitment to meeting the consumer demand for sugar by attaining self-sufficiency in its production. The latter theme has been consistently stated as central to agricultural and industrial policy during recent years. Satisfaction of consumer demand has remained a high political priority for the Government." (Barclay, 1977, p. 61-2)
The Textile Industry	"In order to satisfy projected local and export demand in 1985, it will be necessary to produce 220 million square metres of cloth. To achieve this four mills must be established between 1977/78 and 1980/81." (Third Five Year Plan, p. 47)	"The Government attaches great importance to the rapid development of the textile industry." (from the correspondence files of the Rift Valley Textile Project) "Our keen determination to move with utmost speed [to complete the project] as desired by the Kenyan authorities." (from the correspondence files of the Rift Valley Textile Project)

Table 7.2 (cont.)
The industrial objectives of government in the 1970s

	Tanzania	Kenya
The Parastatal Holding Companies and New Projects	"NDC's [the National Development Corporation's] interest is not to run companies for the purpose of profit maximisation, but rather to implement projects in certain sectors. In fact, NDC seems to be evaluated by the number of projects it implements ... The unofficial goal of NDC as expressed by some of its employees, to push through as many projects as possible." (Quoted in O'Brien, 1982, p. 22)	"One of IDB's [the Industrial Development Bank's] important aims has been to attract investment funds from abroad." (Annual Report and Accounts, 1977, Industrial Development Bank, p. 13)
	"The management [of NDC] is anxious to show success. Lever Brothers will come and erect a detergent factory in a year. ... Despite the poor economics of such a project from a developmental point of view, NDC appears more successful than if it had spent the year trying to organize Ujamaa village work shops." (Clark, 1978, p. 189)	"Since December 1974 total investments approved ... have grown by an average of nearly 25% a year ... The total number of projects investigated and considered for investment has increased even more rapidly because of IDB's search for new business." (Annual Report and Accounts, 1977, Industrial Development Bank, p. 12)

Table 7.3
The macro-environment and pressures for cost-consciousness in the choice of technology

Tanzania	Kenya
"Both product and factor markets in Tanzania are nominally under the control of planners. In both areas several aspects of the competitive model have been replaced with devices which operate in quite different directions from market forces. The price-control system, for example, is in many cases based on a cost-plus formulation which both shelters the inefficient and gives only a weak incentive to become more efficient. ... The incentive structure to which the parastatal manager responds offers little in the way of personal financial rewards and, in any case, may focus on surpluses which are more related to windfall gains from the pricing system than to productive efficiency." (Williams, 1975, p.7)	"Financial participation by Government is the best guarantee obtainable that a firm will make high and secure financial profits regardless of its economic efficiency or of its international competitiveness." (Hopcraft, 1979, p. 18) "Firms with Government participation use it to make Government behave in the firm's interest. The complete range of special concessions, licenses, guarantees, and the whole edifice of protective measures, are far more accessible to the firm that has Government financial participation than to one that does not." (IBRD, 1983, p. 419) "The monopsonist position of most parastatals means that there is no competitive pressure to keep operations efficient, whereas their political connections make them immune to the ultimate commercial sanction of bankruptcy and dissolution." (Schluter, 1984, p. 93)

Table 7.4

Managing Agents/Minority Partners and the Source of Technology in Kenyan Parastatals

Firm	Managing agents/minority partners	Main source of technology
Rift Valley Textiles	Seditex (Germany)	Germany
Yuken Textiles	Jugotekstil (Yugoslavia)	?
Salt Manufacturers	Saltec International (Italy)	Saltec
Nyeri Bottling Plant	Coca-Cola Africa	?
Nzoia Sugar	Technisucre (France)	France
South Nyanza Sugar	Buckau Wolf (Germany)[1]	Germany/India
Kenya Furfural	Escher Wyss (Switzerland)	Escher Wyss
Kenya Cashewnuts	Oltremare (Italy)	Oltremare
Ceramic Industries	Ceramic Industries (private owners)	UK/Italy

Notes: 1. One of the turnkey contractors.

Source: Correspondence files of the Industrial Development Bank and the Industrial and Commercial Development Corporation.

Table 7.5
Scale, Products and Technology - Kenya

	Scale	Technology	Products
Rift Valley Textiles	Annual capacity of 11,500,000 linear meters -- "a complete modern integrated textile mill."	"All machinery and equipment selected are brand new, the most modern and of very high quality and reputation."	"Very high quality ... an annual production of approximately 23 million square metres, of which about 7 million metres shall be exported."
Yuken Textiles	"The largeness of premises and their division is a result of the conception of the whole factory and up-to-date technology as well as its flexibility. ... The biggest manufacturer of this line in Yugoslavia."	"Highly developed productive technology ... to compete with the European standards."	"The technological part of the project provides a very high quality of the output (European level)." ... "Activities of the newly established enterprise would be concentrated during its first phase above all on the Kenyan market and on the markets of East African countries, later-on also on other markets."
Molasses Plant	"The plant will be capable of producing 7,300 tons per annum of 99.5% Power Alcohol."	"The Installation shall conform to the latest and most modern technology and development currently available as of the date of this contract as to the Installation and the volume and quality of products produced. ... The opportunities to sell the surplus factory's products ... are fully appreciated and exploited."	
Nyeri Bottling Plant	"The plant will be equipped with a new sophisticated bottling line with ancillary equipment with a capacity for bottling 500 cases per working hour. ... The bottling equipment to be installed is very sophisticated."		"a standard quality product."
Kenya Furfural		"The high capital intensity of the project -- due mainly to the high cost of the proposed plant."	"Most of the end products would be mainly for export."
Cashew Processing	"Mechanical processing in large-scale units with relatively high capital investment costs."	"Equipment considered the best in this field. ... Though mechanised, the project is still labor-intensive. ... All the machinery will be new."	"producing high quality products. ... The project would generate significant additional foreign exchange earnings for the country."

Source: Correspondence files of the Industrial Development Bank and the Industrial and Commercial Development Corporation.

Table 7.6
Managerial Discretion and the Failings of the Parastatal Control System

	Tanzania	Kenya
Overall characterizations of the System	"The elaborate internal and external control system over parastatal activities, which exist on paper are in reality very weak." (Ministry of Planning, 1982, p. 42)	"The President identified ineffective Government supervision as one of the factors contributing to the unsatisfactory performance of parastatals." (Ndegwa, 1979, p. 10)
Managerial Discretion	"It [the party] has remained an institution capable of directing the system only on the most general plane." (Loxley and Saul, 1975, p. 62)	"The weakness of the party system means that the bureaucratic elites are left on their own to determine the major developmental policies." (Oyugi, 1982, p. 70)
	"There was no clear policy especially as regards science and technology. At enterprise level, each corporation remained free to choose its own techniques." (Mihyo, undated (a), p.3)	"Functionally, parastatals do enjoy a very large degree of autonomy with respect to investment decisions." (Oyugi, 1982, p. 71)
	"Parastatals are quite autonomous institutions. Control by their parent ministries is often slight." (Clark, 1978, p. 185)	"The parent ministries tend to leave the organizations pretty much on their own." (Oyugi, 1982, p. 67)
	"There is still a large question mark over the ability of boards effectively to control foreign management." (Loxley and Saul, 1975, p. 69/70)	"In many parastatals, the boards of management have failed to discharge the duties expected of them." (Oyugi, 1982, p. 72)
	"In most of the subsidiaries of the National Development Corporation, the management has taken over the policy decision-making function." (Mihyo, undated (b), p. 16)	"Most of the parastatals have management contracts with foreign based firms or locally based foreign owned management consultancy firms. They have a lot of influence on the operational policies of the organizations." (Oyugi, 1982, p. 69)
Investment Criteria and Accountability	"in the absence of a clearly defined strategy for the socialist transformation of Tanzania there have been no rational criteria by which public sector investment and other spending decisions could be assessed." (Loxley and Saul, 1975, p. 65-6)	"At the moment it is difficult, in the case of many parastatals, to say who is ultimately accountable to the Board, the Government and the public for the proper management of their affairs." (Ndegwa, 1979, p. 9) "Because of the confusion which exists, it is becoming increasingly difficult to say where responsibility for inefficiency or waste lies." (Ndegwa, 1979, p. 3)
	"both the proposing parastatals and the central planning authorities appear to lack clear criteria on which to assess the alternative projects which they develop and evaluate." (Perkins, 1983, p. 236)	"The criteria for accepting or rejecting projects are vague and have not included rigorous economic analysis." (IBRD, 1983, p. 104)
The Limited Capacity for Control	"The central planning ministry does not have the manpower to effectively scrutinize parastatal operations." (Clark, 1978, p. 186)	"While government financial involvement has been expanding, the machinery to control and examine proposed investments in parastatals is inadequate." (IBRD, 1983, p. 42)
	"The country's already weak planning capacity." (IBRD, 1978, p. 10)	
Orientation to Social vs. Private Profitability	"Most parastatals have used commercial profitability -- discounted cash flow -- as their investment yardstick. ... It is however, apparent that ... the use of DCF will almost inevitably give results which have little meaning in social terms." (Loxley and Saul, 1975, p. 67)	"Firms with Government or parastatal involvement find that such agencies behave like any other investor, concerned with the protection and profitability of their portfolio." (IBRD, 1983, p. 416)

Table 7.7
A Matrix of Gaining & Losing Interests

Interest Groups Policy	Major interest groups that stand to lose	Major interest groups that stand to gain
Reform of the macro-environment	For Tanzania, those dependent on inefficient firms (public and private) that are sheltered by the price-control system.	Efficient firms, firms purchasing inputs from currently inefficient enterprises, consumers in general.
	For Kenya, those currently gaining most from government concessions to inefficient public enterprises.	Competing (mostly private) firms, firms purchasing inputs from currently inefficient public enterprises, consumers in general.
Altered composition of output in favor of small-scale enterprises (particularly those in rural areas)	Urban elites (managers, highly-paid workers, bureaucrats, consumers), foreign interests that are allied to urban elites (investors, machinery sellers, managers, skilled workers, etc.).	Rural interests (small-scale firms, the unemployed/underemployed), consumers of products made by small-scale firms (i.e. mostly the poor).
Altered technological choices made by large-scale public enterprises	Developed country interests (aid donors, managers, machinery sellers, workers), consumers of products of developed country technologies, and local interests that most benefit from the presence of developed country interests (e.g. local politicians serving on the boards of joint ventures between foreign and state capital).	Developing country interests (aid donors, financiers, sellers of machinery), sellers of used equipment, the unemployed, consumers of products produced by the alternative technologies.

Eight

Technical Change and Appropriate Technology: A Review of Some Latin American Case Studies

Philip Maxwell

I. INTRODUCTION

The historical record of learning and technical change in industrial firms in LDCs is pertinent to the theory and practice of appropriate technology for at least two reasons.

First, any comparison of alternative techniques should consider the improvements realisable through technical change. To make this comparison operational, empirical evidence is needed about how well the possibilities of technical change with alternative techniques have been exploited (and how constrained these possibilities were) in real situations.

Second is the desire to extend the concepts of appropriate technology beyond advising on the initial choice of technique, and to provide some signposts for the best kinds of technical change for firms to pursue once a particular technique has been chosen and installed. One may hope that a firm that made a good (appropriate) initial choice of technique will subsequently go on to generate an appropriate pattern of technical change with that technique—but this is not a logical necessity. Equally, if a firm has made a poor initial choice of technique, it may be able subsequently to take remedial actions through introducing technical changes to bring it back to a more appropriate technical direction. Thus appropriate (or inappropriate) patterns of technical change may follow from initial choices of technique. Investigation of the empirical record of such patterns in LDCs should, hopefully, generate signposts that could increase the chances that future technical change patterns will be more appropriate.

So the historical record of technical change in LDC industrial firms is worthwhile to explore from an appropriate technology viewpoint. Only fairly recently, however, have studies actually explored this record to any marked extent. Until the early 1970s most research on LDC industrial technology focussed on the issues of choice of technique and transfer of technology rather than on processes of technical change in LDC firms or on indigenous technical effort and creativity. The implicit assumption was that LDC firms were passive technology takers selecting their innovations off the shelf of advanced country technology.

However, the past twelve years or so have seen rapid growth in the amount and sophistication of research into technical change, learning, and innovation in LDC industrial firms—especially in firms from relatively industrially sophisticated or fast growing Newly Industrialized Countries "NICs"—and have shown that a surprisingly large volume of indigenous technical activity and creativity has occurred in some countries, sectors and firms.[1] (For a good overview of the scope of this research see Fransman and King, 1984.)

One of the widely recognized contributions to the study of LDC technical change came from a research programme based on nearly 40 empirical case studies in Latin America during 1975–82, known as the IDB-ECLA programme. The objective of the IDB-ECLA studies was to find out about the characteristics of technical change in several Latin American countries—through detailed empirical case studies of technical change in firms operating either process plants or metalworking and capital-goods plants. A description of the coverage of these studies and a complete list of the resulting publications is given in the appendix to this chapter.

Because of the importance and frequent citation of the IDB-ECLA studies of technical change, it is worthwhile to review these studies to help explore the relationship between technical change and appropriate technology.[2] This indeed is the purpose of this paper.

One should, however, be forewarned of some limitations in extracting conclusions about appropriate technology from the IDB-ECLA studies. First, the studies were never explicitly focussed on issues of appropriate technology such as the use of labour-intensive processes or the design and production of simplified products meeting the basic needs of less well-off consumers. The studies were chiefly concerned with identifying the *locally generated* contributions to technical change in a restricted sample of firms, mainly in the modern sector of the economy (large-scale process plants, and metalworking and capital-goods firms). The insights the IDB-ECLA studies provide on appropriate technology, therefore, are only a spin-off rather than a direct output of the studies[3] and refer mainly to better ways of developing these modern sectors of the industrial manufacturing economy.

The second limitation of this review is that its discussion of technical change is mainly about *process* innovation (and consequent productivity advance). It does not go into the question of *product* innovation and appropriate products. Some light was thrown on product innovation by the IDB-ECLA studies of technical change. However, to review this in detail requires a paper in itself.

Thirdly, our discussion does not attempt to draw on the whole set of IDB-ECLA empirical case studies. It is mainly based on the case studies of steel plants (especially Dahlman, 1978 and Maxwell, 1982), as well as on the reviews of the IDB-ECLA capital-goods and metalworking case studies (Katz, 1982a; 1982b; 1984), and overall programme review (Katz, 1980).

For these reasons the reader will understand that this is a limited exploration into what the IDB-ECLA studies have to offer when viewed from an appropriate technology angle.

II. LOCALIZED TECHNICAL CHANGE

A major contribution of the IDB-ECLA studies relevant to appropriate technology was the demonstration of the *strongly localized and idiosyncratic character of the technical changes* introduced into the studied plants. It was already well known from the literature on transfer-of-technology (for example, Strassmann, 1968) and on appropriate technology (for example, Eckhaus, 1979) that plants installed in LDCs usually required significant adaptations to function properly in the unique local circumstances of a particular LDC, industrial sector and firm. Hence, it was expected that LDC plants would initially be idiosyncratic in their technology compared both to developed-country plants and to other LDC plants producing similar products. The IDB-ECLA studies strongly confirmed this. The great detail about idiosyncracy obtained in the case studies led to a rigorous and comprehensive theoretical and empirical critique of the idea that technologies can be acquired off the shelf without adaptations to local circumstances (see Katz, 1982b).

The IDB-ECLA studies also showed that each plant's pattern of technical change was strongly idiosyncractic due to (a) the successive, cumulative incorporation into plants of hundreds of minor technical changes with a strong tailor-made component; and (b) the less frequent incorporation of major technical changes which also had significant tailor-made elements. The tailor-made component of technical changes arose not only from the specificity of each plant's initial technology and organisation but also from the adaptations to each plant required by the unique succession of external, competitive and policy challenges and constraints arising in its environment.

This evolving *specificity* (uniqueness) found both in a plant's set-up and in its context showed that much of the technological knowledge and know-how for modifying plants through technical changes would have to be generated in-house by a plant's own technical/managerial staff, based on their unique, in situ knowledge of their plant's functioning, problems and possibilities. Thus, endogenous, in-house and localized know-how was found to be crucial in technical change to modify plants.

It was shown that LDC firms have no option but to develop their in-house technical capabilities to generate and apply localized know-how to operating plants and, even more so, to specifying and implementing technical changes in them. Once there are no longer, even in theory, any fully standardised solutions, then technical creativity is needed either to adapt standard solutions with localized know-how or to generate original localized solutions to technical problems.[4] Firms and plants with insufficient in-house technical talent for generating and applying localised know-how are likely, therefore, to have severe problems in implementing technical change and consequently in generating an adequate growth path of productivity in their plants. Appropriate technical change, in the sense of sufficiently localized technical change, is absolutely necessary if productivity is to be maintained and enhanced over time—and this message comes across strongly in all the case studies.

III. LONG-RUN FIRM TRAJECTORIES OF TECHNICAL CHANGE

The IDB-ECLA studies also contributed to a convincing micro-economic description of the complex processes of learning and technical change in LDC manufacturing firms over *long* periods of time. They throw light on the long-run technical change trajectories which constitute actual infant industry maturation paths followed at the firm level.[5]

Several specific features of the long-run technical change trajectories that were found in the case studies are described below:

a. Technical change trajectories imply that firms do much more than just learn how to carry out pre-specified packages of routines efficiently; they have to learn how to introduce scores (or even hundreds) of minor technical changes both (a) to get plants working fully during their start-up periods[6] and (b) to adapt and upgrade already fully operational plants in between periods of major investment to cope with problems and raise productivity.[7]
b. Besides "start-up technical change" and "upgrading technical change", the typical trajectory also involves the less frequent incorporation of major technical changes: that is, participation in the equipment selection, construction and start-up of the major investments represented by the initial plant itself and then by any future major expansions or replacements of it.
c. Firms vary greatly at how good they are at carrying over technically relevant experience from upgrading phases to subsequent major investment phases, and from the investment phases into the succeeding upgrading phases.
d. Much of the technical change which firms introduce is unexpected, and occurs as a defensive reaction when firms are faced by adverse circumstances inside the plants (breakdowns or bottlenecks) or outside them (government interventions or controls, threatening competitors' moves, material supply cutoffs, etc.). In other words, firms do not have perfect information and are often surprised by unfavourable developments to which they must try to muster an effective technical response.[8]
e. Firms are influenced in the rate and type of technical changes which they seek to introduce by the quality and extent of the competition

(by changing market structure), by macro-economic parameters such as interest rates and growth rates, and by developments in the frontier of technology internationally.

f. Because of the differing external contexts they face, and the manifold technological differences between different industries and techniques, it is clear that all long-run plant technical change trajectories differ considerably. Each plant trajectory is differentiated and historically unique, responding to the unique set of technology-specific, firm-specific, industry-specific, context-specific and policy factors which impinge on the plant throughout its evolution.
g. Both the duration and the efficiency of plant learning and technical change trajectories can differ enormously from country to country and from plant to plant. For example, start-up learning periods varied from one to 11 years for different steel plants in the IDB-ECLA case studies (Maxwell, 1982). Also, the time taken by different capital-goods firms to pass through the sequence of four stages of technological maturity noted by Katz (1982a) varied between two and four decades for those firms which successfully made the transition through all four stages.
h. The growth of technological capability inside firms is a critical determinant of the quality and efficiency of the technical change trajectory that will be followed. For neither learning nor technical change are automatic; they depend on internal factors—especially on the firm's skilled technical staff, the sophistication of their organisation, and on management's willingness to invest in technical change.
i. The IDB-ECLA studies have revealed immense inter-firm differences in sophistication of, and resource allocation to, technical change activities, ranging from inexperienced firms with "ad hoc", unsystematic or defensive strategies, to firms with more conscious, systematic, or offensive strategies.
j. The IDB-ECLA studies also provided clear evidence of a technological maturation process occurring within firms, expressed by a gradual transition to more conscious and systematic learning and technical change strategies.[9] Such a maturation process also involved progressive growth in a firm's internal technical capability. It seems to happen in an evolutionary way but only through a deliberate management effort (in response to experience) at building up a firm's technical organisation, skills and know-how. It also is often spurred by marked discontinuities in a plant's trajectory, such as those associated with major expansions, crises or management changes.

It is apparent from the above list that satisfactory long-run technical change trajectories in industrial maturation are not guaranteed, and neither is their efficiency. For example, technical changes might not be introduced when needed, they might not be localized enough, or the firm's learning and engineering efforts might be inadequate. Hence, productivity advance can break down at certain points on the trajectory. Unsuccessful or inefficient technical change sequences and trajectories can occur. *If a trajectory is grossly inefficient, it cannot be appropriate.* This point is taken up in Section 4 on policy reflections.

IV. WAS THE OBSERVED TECHNICAL CHANGE IN AN APPROPRIATE DIRECTION?

A good deal of technical change took place in the plants studied by the IDB-ECLA programme. But the relevant issue from the viewpoint of appropriate technology is: how far did this technical change go in an appropriate direction, not only as regards its localization but also in terms of the several other main characteristics associated with appropriate technology?

It is necessary to have a suitable definition of appropriateness to answer this. The straightforward one is the specific characteristics definition of appropriate technology (Stewart, 1983):

> Among economic characteristics, a more appropriate technology is normally defined as more labor-using than a less appropriate technology (higher L/O); less capital-using (lower K/L); less skill-using; making more use of local materials and resources; smaller-scale; and producing a more appropriate product.

With this in mind, we now take one of the IDB-ECLA case studies, and ask to what extent the technical change introduced there may be regarded as having been appropriate technical change.

The study we look at is frequently cited. It is the USIMINAS state steel firm in Brazil (Dahlman, 1978). As a large-scale, modern industrial process plant, this plant is far removed from small-scale rural technology. (It might therefore be useful as a test-case to see whether the terms "appropriate technology" and "appropriate technical change," in the specific characteristics definition, can be given useful policy meaning for this type of modern industry.) In looking at the record of technical change in the plant we shall focus on three points in particular: how the K/L ratio changed, how scale changed, and the use of local materials.

It will be helpful first to refer to Figure 8.1. This shows various phases/types of productivity-raising technical change in a firm that starts off using Vintage I capital/technology, and operates with it, improves its productivity and then goes on to introduce Vintage II, and (later on) Vintage III.

The kinds of technical change distinguished by Bell in this diagram are labelled Type A, corresponding to start-up improvement (with each vintage); Type B, corresponding to post-start-up incremental improvements which raise plant efficiency above its original design level or rated efficiency (again on each vintage); Type C, which is an inter-vintage technical change of a moderate kind in that Vintages I and II are still recognisably related and the productivity gap between the two vintages is not enormous; and Type

D, which is a radical inter-vintage technical change, involving a large productivity gap between vintages II and III.

The pattern shown in Figure 8.1 was followed by USIMINAS to the extent that its initial plant (that is, Vintage I) was (a) brought on stream in 1963, (b) reached rated capacity of 500,000 tons in 1966 and (c) was then incrementally improved at low investment cost which raised output from this plant to 1,200,000 tons by 1972. Then, from the period 1972–77, a highly capital intensive expansion (Vintage II) was implemented through building large-scale new units along side the Vintage I plant units. This raised the combined output of the expanded plant above 2,400,000 tons per annum by 1977.

From 1966–72, labour productivity and capital productivity at the plant increased dramatically. Both increased at an average rate of about 20–25 percent per year with labour productivity increasing slightly faster—thus altering the K/L ratio in the direction of slightly greater capital intensity.

During the period from 1972–77, labour productivity dipped considerably from 1973–1974 while the new units were being brought on stream, but recovered in 1975 and then in 1976 rose beyond the 1972 peak and continued rising (by about 10 percent) in 1977.[10] In this same 1972–77 period, the capital output ratio (that is, inverse of capital productivity) continued to fall but much more slowly than in the previous 1966–72 period.

From 1966–67 to 1972 labour productivity increased by 14 percent per annum and capital productivity increased by about 13 percent per annum. Thus, the K/L ratio did not alter much. The slight alteration it did demonstrate was in a slightly more capital intensive direction—that is, inappropriate technical change.

The sustained high rates of increase of labour productivity and capital productivity are also noteworthy. With these increased rates of productivity, USIMINAS easily heads the list compiled by Bell of productivity growth rates in developing country firms (Bell, 1982, p. 31).[11] Moreover, from reading the case study one sees that it was USIMINAS's staff's great success in handling Type A, Type B and Type C technical changes that was responsible for its impressive productivity record. We will return to some implications of this later. However, technical change in USIMINAS was not appropriate in terms of the K/L ratio.

Was it appropriate in terms of changes in plant scale? Over the 11 year timespan from achievement of rated capacity in 1966 to 1977, the output level of USIMINAS became a multiple of more than five times its initial output level—a fast rate of growth in only 11 years. But still, the notion of output levels increasing to multiples of some three to ten times their initial levels over periods ranging from 10 to 35 years was a common feature found in most of the IDB-ECLA steel plant studies. Similar multiples of initially rated output were also found in several of the capital-goods and metalworking case studies over 20–40 year periods. However, there was almost certainly a bias in the IDB-ECLA studies towards technologically capable and "successful" firms whose growth rates were probably often above average for their branches of industry.

In USIMINAS (as in other steel plants) most of the increased plant capacity for providing for growing output levels was not met by stretching the rated capacity of existing units (although this was important) but by investing in bigger new plant units built along side the existing ones. The incremental capacity added in USIMINAS's 1972–77 expansion was more than double the initially installed capacity of the original plant, and essentially all the individual main process units in the expansion were larger (for example, the new coke batteries had twice the capacity of the original ones, the steel shop's converters were nearly three times as large as those in the original plant, and the new blast furnace was much bigger than the original ones).

Clearly, then, the technical changes implied by this major expansion were not in an appropriate direction in terms of representing a change to a smaller scale or even a duplication of the pre-existing scale.

However, it must be recognized that in the past 40 years international trends in the technology of integrated coke-based steel plants have been towards larger plant scales—shifting from, for example, 1 million towards 10 million tons per annum plants and also progressively larger individual process units. USIMINAS's decisions were in line with these trends. Increasing plant scale and size of units in the classical integrated coke-based industry have been closely associated with more complex and advanced technology. So major rounds of capital intensive investments in integrated steel plants in recent years have usually involved major increases in both scale and technology.

What about USIMINAS's record of technical changes in the use of local materials? This is an area in which technical changes were clearly in an appropriate direction (especially in those parts of the plant—in the coke ovens, sinter plant and blast furnaces—where the processes are inherently materials-dominated, that is, where most costs relate to materials costs).

From the start of production, adaptative technical changes were needed by USIMINAS due to great differences between the composition of locally available iron ore in terms of its physical and chemical characteristics and the type of iron ore for which the plant had been designed. (Locally available ore was mainly in the form of fines—that is, with small grains—which was more haematitic, had greater amounts of SiO_2 impurities, and had greater variability in its chemical and physical characteristics.)

These special characteristics of the local ore meant that the entire sintering process needed to be studied *ab initio*—both in practical operation and by special tests in a pilot sinter plant—to understand the effect of varying physical and chemical characteristics of the local raw materials on the process of producing sinter. For example, such properties as the physical resistance of the sinter, its basicity,[12] homogeneity, composition, ignition characteristics, the yield of correctly sized sinter emerging from the input—and the performance of the resultant sinter feed in influencing blast furnace output and productivity—all needed to be studied and assessed carefully, based on different combinations of raw material input mixes and different process conditions (Dahlman, 1978).

Thanks to some initial guidance from their Japanese advisers, and through making use of their pilot sinter plant, as well as by actually starting up and carefully studying sinter and blast furnace production,[13] over several years USIMINAS engineers were able systematically to build up their understanding of the physical and chemical processes and use this to specify practical solutions and improvements.

As a consequence they raised the capacity of this sinter plant over seven years (1966–73) by an impressive 101 percent above the rated level through (a) introduction and testing of progressively more sophisticated and efficient raw material input mix combinations—for example, 13 different raw materials were used in the charge to sinter plant in 1973 compared to only 3 raw materials in 1966, and (b) improvement of raw material preparation procedures, sintering procedures and blast furnace procedures to increase yields and productivity (but still requiring only relatively minor investments in embodied technical change).

In consequence not only was sinter plant capacity itself increased, but the crucial coke rate in the blast furnaces (the number of kilograms of coke required per ton of pig iron produced—the main determining factor in steel production costs) was reduced in a similar period from around 600 kilograms per ton to around 420 kilograms per ton.

These types of technical change were clearly appropriate in the sense of modifying processes to match the available local raw materials; improving the quality of the local raw materials through more accurate selection and control; and introducing additional local raw materials to further increase the efficiency of the process.

Adaptations were also made to increase the efficiency of use by USIMINAS of national coal. Although the coal had an undesirably high ash and sulfur content, the government had insisted that it be used in substantial proportions by local steel plants. After the 1973 energy crisis, prices of imported coke more than doubled and a round of energy-saving technical changes was introduced with help from the company's R&D department. This was intended to help cut down the fraction of imported coke and other fuels required by the plant (Dahlman, 1978). Such changes meant to utilize national coal more effectively and save on imported coal were also obviously appropriate.[14]

In USIMINAS, then, we can see technical change was not appropriate in terms of the K/L ratio nor in terms of scale, but was appropriate (or at least went in an appropriate direction) in the use of local raw materials.

In three of the other IDB-ECLA studies which also contained productivity measurements, the K/L ratio did not shift downward in these firms either—in fact, just the opposite took place. In an Argentine lathe producing firm, between 1960 and 1976 labour productivity increased by an average of 5.8 percent per annum while total factor productivity increased by an average of 2.77 percent (Castaño, Katz and Navajas, 1981), suggesting a significant increase in the K/L ratio over the period concerned.[15] In the Argentine rayon plant studied by Katz and others (1978) drastic modernization was introduced 15 years after the plant started so as to meet the threat from new competition, and one-third of the labour force was released. Also, referring implicitly to capital-goods and metalworking firms, Katz (1980) notes that:

> At their starting point almost all of the firms we have examined began with a rather high ratio of labour to capital. In due course, however, most of them, as well as newly arriving competition in the same industries, opted for more capital intensive technologies.

Labour-intensive in-plant transportation procedures and quality control and maintenance procedures were mentioned (also by Katz) as having become more automated in many metalworking plants, in response to both rising wages and increasing output.

The strong impression, then, is that technical change in the IDB-ECLA plants has usually been in the direction of a rising capital-labour ratio (even though the rate may be slow, as in the case of USIMINAS) and towards larger scales of plant output (both in process and capital-goods plants). Both of these trends take the producers in an inappropriate direction.

Nevertheless, if we generalise from the broad findings of the case studies (Katz, 1980), we can also see that technical change was often appropriate in the sense of involving considerable adaptation to local inputs and materials, local market needs (product qualities and models), local competitive pressures (new entrants or demand changes) and the uncertainty of macro-economic policies in the local policy environment.[16] Therefore, much of the observed pattern of technical changes can be considered appropriate in the sense of being minimally or adequately localized.

V. SOME POLICY REFLECTIONS

While the K/L ratio is usually and rightly at the centre of preoccupation for appropriate technology policy, it is obvious that both K/Q and L/Q ratios—that is, productivity—are also important. Persistently high cost output, slow learning, and slow technical change rates—regardless of the technique originally selected—are hardly going to be helpful. Or, to put the matter more bluntly, gross inefficiency is inappropriate, whether it occurs in a small, medium or large-scale plant.

The USIMINAS example already examined was an inspiring, almost textbook example of rapid learning and technical change—suitably localized—and leading to continuous improvement in K/Q and L/Q ratios. At the heart of these favorable changes was the efficient implementation by the firms of Bell's Types A, B and C technical change throughout a long and successful technical change trajectory. Several of the other IDB-ECLA case studies reported quite successful long runs of technical change carried out by fairly efficient Argentine, Brazilian and Mexican firms.

It would, however, be misleading to claim that these success stories were the norm even in those large three Latin American countries, for modern sector firms. Instead, as the IDB-ECLA studies as a whole imply, and as the review of infant industry productivity change by Bell (1982) shows more systematically, the average picture of Latin American (and LDC) industrial infant industry maturation is disappointing. This is especially true when tracking how the K/Q and K/L ratios are faring when compared to steadily improving international standards. In particular, it appears that average rates of productivity advance in many industries are pretty slow, and the cost and duration of industrial infancy are correspondingly high. Instead of infant industry learning periods (catch-up periods) for steel plants and capital-goods industries lasting about 10 years, it emerges very clearly both in the IDB-ECLA studies and in Bell's review that the time involved has been at least twenty years, often thirty years or more. (USIMINAS is an exception.)

While traditionally one measures the duration of infant learning in terms of how long it took a particular plant or national industry as a whole to progress from initiating production to a lowering of its production costs to an internationally competitive level, the IDB-ECLA studies have illustrated that industrial infancy can also usefully be measured along the dimension of increasing internal technological capability as demonstrated by mastery by firms of certain levels or degrees of technological capacity and organisational sophistication—which are a precondition for achieving cost reductions.

For example, in his review of the IDB-ECLA capital-goods studies Katz (1982a) identifies four different stages of technological capability along a trajectory being travelled sequentially by a representative Latin American capital-goods firm using a basically discontinuous technology.

These phases were 1) original implantation of small-scale, unsophisticated workshop/plant; 2) transition through rapid expansion via embodied investment into a more modern factory; 3) digestion and rationalisation of this expanded factory through employment of more technical staff, a more conscious technical strategy, and the progressive replacement of rules of thumb by properly organized plans, standards, manuals and procedures; and finally 4) applying organization and methods techniques systematically to the entire plant and all of its complementary functions.

To complete this sequence of four stages required at least twenty years by those firms which had successfully done it. Most of the firms in the IDB-ECLA sample, however, had not completed this four stage sequence but could still be located at some point in between stages two and three.

It was also emphacized by Katz that there was nothing automatic about firms being able to pass through this sequence or to do so efficiently. Many firms simply do not get through all the interim stages, and get stuck at lower levels of sophistication or actually disappear en route due to competitive pressure.

LDC capital-goods plants are typically different from DC plants as regards their smaller scale, higher degree of vertical integration, lower use of subcontracting and idiosyncratic technical organization.[17] Given these differences, and a goal of aiming for the optimum choice of technique, the need is for flexible yet efficient layouts, machinery choices and organizational arrangements to be implemented for scaled-down plants at the *start* of the selection/installation process, rather than being reached only after costly trial and error and remedial technical change.

In this regard, all developments which have promoted economies of scale in small and medium sized plants in LDCs need to be scrutinized. In this sense, techniques such as group technology are important (Katz, 1982a). So too are policies for the standardization and normalization of parts, which can be conducted first at the intra firm level and then, to have a greater influence, coordinated by government industrial policy at the sector level (Katz, 1982a).

Turning to policy ideas from the steel plant studies, the data from the case material shows that it has often required several years of remedial technical change efforts to get initial plants or subsequent plant expansions working properly. This was true in some of the major investment projects of the Peruvian, Colombian, Argentinian and Mexican state steel plants (Maxwell, 1982). The need was usually to overcome serious plant design errors, as well as subsequent construction phase errors and general inexperience among plant staff in operating procedures. In other words there was considerable scope for many of the firms studied to have made better choices of techniques. Because this did not happen, expensive remedial technical change paths often had to be followed.

Moreover, not only were there problems with the initial plants built by some of the steel firms studied, but some major design, conceptual, construction, and operational errors were made in the expansion projects for the Colombian, Mexican and Argentine state steel plants (Maxwell, 1982). These errors helped to cause long start-up periods and the need for prolonged and costly remedial learning and investment before these expansions could be made fully operational. Evidently, then, the learning and experience acquired in the first plant cycle was insufficient to equip these firms to cope with the major new complexities imposed by their expansions in the second cycle. In terms of Bell's diagram (Figure 8.1) type C technical change was badly mishandled.

So, it is not only the absolute scale of a steel plant or the identity of its physical technology which can sometimes be inappropriate. It is also possible that *the rate of change of scale and/or the extent of the jump in technology that a firm undertakes when expanding can be inappropriate* too. This will be so when the technological capability of the firm concerned falls short of the level needed to assist in specifying its new scale of plant or technology properly and subsequently to learn to implement and master it in a reasonable time frame.

For major process plants, such as steel plants, the IDB-ECLA findings suggest the need to revise the methodology of the feasibility reports carried out by governments and international and national development banks. Such reports strongly influence—or rubber-stamp—the choice of technique decisions for major investments in such plants. (Choice of technique is not merely the actual set of process choices constituting a plant's technology. It is also the set of plant scaling and sizing decisions taken, the selection of the international and local technology suppliers contributing to the project, the financing package, and also, in some ways most crucial of all, the set of decisions regarding precisely how the firm itself will (or will not!) gear-up for and participate in the specification, construction, and start-up of its plant or expansion.)

The revision needed is to bring learning and technical change considerations explicitly and fully into the feasibility analysis—that is, explicitly to estimate learning times and learning cost of major scale changes and major technical changes as part of the *standard* cost-benefit analysis procedure for such investments.

As suggested earlier, an important issue for appropriate technology when applied to modern sector infant industries in LDCs relates to industrial efficiency—that is, to K/Q and L/Q measures. Many researchers and policy analysts take a hard line on the question of industrial efficiency, by defining industrial infancy as a condition of "being uncompetitive on the world market"; and they define industrial maturity as, "a condition . . . of being competitive and of being able to remain competitive." Maturation, in this definition, is "the process of getting competitive and staying competitive" (Bell, Ross-Larson and Westphal, 1983).

This viewpoint is shared by other authors. Katz (1984) criticises the outcomes of technical change trajectories in certain Latin American capital-goods plants using continuous technology on the grounds that the empirical evidence from the case studies showed that these plants "operate in the Latin American region behind international standards."

We think, however, that putting the issue in this tough way is not very helpful. The important question to ask about long-run trajectories in most LDCs is, so far as their end results are concerned, "how far are these plants behind international standards?" This is a quantitative problem. However, value and policy judgements will be required regarding the extent of the productivity gap that can be regarded as tolerable. In this context, both scale of plant and choice of technique are important issues whenever the fundamental scale and/or technology of an LDC plant are inherently smaller or less efficient than competing large-scale plants or technologies in advanced countries. For then a situation can arise in which there will still be a significant productivity gap between these two kinds of plants even when the LDC plant has managed to traverse a complete sequence of technological maturation with its plant. The size of this gap is determined by the inherent design limits of the small-scale technology versus the large-scale technology in advanced countries.

However, at the level of industrial protection and tariff policies, the issue seems to be wrongly put if one states that because small and medium-scale plants can never produce as cheaply as larger scale plants in advanced countries, therefore such small and medium-scale plants should have no place in international production. This would make complete nonsense of industrialization policy throughout most of the developing world.

Rather, one has to accept that if societies are going to industrialize, then, with a few exceptions such as the largest LDCs like Brazil or India, the incidence of small and medium-scale plants is going to be the general order of the day.

The challenge, therefore, is to design an industrial protection policy and consistent technology policies (including appropriate technology policies) which will encourage *rapid learning* and *systematic strategies towards technical change* by the managements of these small and medium-scale plants, so that a high degree of efficiency and productivity can be achieved.

NOTES

1. The NIC countries include Brazil, Mexico, Argentina, India, South Korea, and Hong Kong.

2. One of the foremost practitioners in this research field has stated that (see Lall, 1984): ". . . the seminal work, sponsored by the Inter-American Development Bank (IDB) and the United Nations Economic Commission for Latin America (ECLA) on technological development in Latin American enterprises . . . (has) . . . provided a substantial part of the analytical underpinning of most recent research on third world technology and technology exports."

3. An important further limitation to deriving appropriate technology policies—even for these modern sectors—from the IDB-ECLA studies (and this would also apply to trying to derive protection or infant industry policies from them) is that they focussed almost entirely on the "internal economies" of the technical changes introduced by manufacturing firms, and touched only incidentally on the generation of the external economies of technical change which could benefit other firms (for example, competitors or customers). This is an important limitation when evaluating policies for setting up or strengthening LDC capital goods industries, given that these have been posited as important transmitters of external economies to other segments of LDC industry. Also the IDB-ECLA studies did not significantly explore the technical performance of local engineering or consulting engineering firms. Yet these kinds of firms, perhaps even more than local capital goods firms, have been posited as major generators of external economies both for their customers (such as local project owners) and for the local capital goods and metalworking industry.

4. Nelson (1979) points out that much of plant technology and know-how is not 100% replicable or transferable even in theory. When two plants are engaged in essentially similar activities, they will always be operating a somewhat differentiated and specific "package" of operational routines, some of which they will have had to develop for themselves.

5. Lall (1978), Katz (1982), and Bell (1982) have all talked of the infant industry learning process as one involving "technological maturation" by firms.

6. A significant fraction of these minor technical changes were introduced in the start-up periods of new facilities to get them working properly at design capacity in local conditions. Dahlman (1978) offers a particularly good and detailed account

of technical change in the start-up period of the blast furnaces in a Brazilian steel plant. Sercovich (1978) also provides an excellent detailed empirical and theoretical account of technical change in start-up periods.

7. In many cases, the stimulus to these upgrading types of minor technical change was the emergence of production bottlenecks. In other cases, it was to cope with adverse external changes: for example, supply shortages, price rises, or competitive changes. Achieving cost reductions through increased productivity was also an important stimulus, as was the desire of managements to seize new market demand opportunities either through raising plant output, raising product quality, or launching new products.

8. In the Latin American countries studied in the IDB-ECLA programme, a significant part of the observed pattern of technical change in firms was an adaptive, induced response to emerging bottlenecks, imperfections, distortions, and uncertainties in the surrounding supply context and policy context. This is well described in Teitel (1979), Canitrot (1978), and Teubal (1979).

9. This phrase is used (and its meaning developed in detail) by Lall (1979), Katz (1982a), and Bell (1982).

10. These figures follow the account given by Bell, based on his reading of the case study data (see Bell, 1982, p.31).

11. In this listing, labour, capital, and total factor productivity growth rates drawn from 32 different firm case studies are collated.

12. Basicity is a chemical property, the opposite of acidity. Bases and acids react with and neutralise each other.

13. During start-up, rated sinter plant capacity was achieved in a series of carefully controlled stages in which first one, then another of the basic raw materials were tried out, the idea being to introduce and study relatively few parameters at any one time in order to build up experience and understanding of the sintering process (see Dahlman, 1978).

14. We should nevertheless note that the classical integrated coke-based plants like USIMINAS continue to be considerably dependent on imported metallurgical grade coke, with its foreign exchange implication. In contrast, in Brasil are also located the world's leading firms in the adaptation and development of much smaller scale charcoal-based blast furnaces which can be fed by local plantation-reared eucalyptus trees.

15. These productivity figures are taken from Bell's table already cited (Bell, 1982, p.31).

16. Two of the IDB-ECLA studies, namely Canitrot (1978) and Fidel and Lucangeli (1978), explore the behaviour of firms in introducing technical changes when faced by macro-economic instability and the likelihood of wide variations in factor prices over the planning horizons of their investments. Among other things, these studies show that the decision on whether to upgrade (modernize) equipment rather than replace it with new equipment is strongly dependent on the availability and salary levels of skilled technical labour, the exchange rate, and the length of the planning horizon. Decisions to upgrade (modernize) a plant usually substituted *skilled* engineering labour for new capital-intensive imported equipment and constituted a significant kind of appropriate technical change.

17. The idiosyncracies of capital goods plants may be even greater than in process plants because of product heterogeneity, component complexity, and the vast range of technical alternatives for arriving at similar end results, matched by organizational alternatives for implementing the process.

REFERENCES

Bell, M., B. Ross-Larson, and L. Westphal. 1983. The cost and benefit of infant industries: A summary of firm-level research. Washington, D.C.: the World Bank. Mimeo (March).

Bell, M. 1982. Technological Change in Infant Industries: A review of empirical evidence. Science Policy Research Unit. Mimeo (April). (A more recent version of this paper "Technological change in infant industries: a review of the evidence" is available from the World Bank.)

Canitrot, A. 1978. *Method for evaluating the significance of macro-economic variables in the analysis of technology incorporation decisions*, Working Paper No. 12. Buenos Aires: available from CEPAL.

Dahlman, C. 1978. *From technological dependence to technological development: The case of the USIMINAS steel plant in Brasil*, IDB-ECLA Working Paper No. 21. Text (Vol. 1) by C. Dahlman and Appendices by F. Fonseca and C. Dahlman. Buenos Aires: available from CEPAL.

Echkaus, R., ed. 1979. *Appropriate Technology for Developing Countries*. Washington D.C.: National Academy of Sciences

Fidel, J., and J. Lucangeli. 1978. *Cost-benefit of different technological options in the context of a differentiated oligopoly: the case of the Argentine cigarette industry*, Working Paper No. 18. Buenos Aires: available from CEPAL.

Fransman, M., and K. King, eds. 1984. *Technological Capability in the Third World*. London: Macmillan.

Katz, J.M., M. Gutkowski, M. Rodrigues, and G. Goity. 1978. *Productivity, technology and domestic efforts in research and development*, IDB-ECLA Working Paper No. 13. Buenos Aires: available from CEPAL.

Katz, J.M. 1980. *Domestic Technology Generation in LDCs: A Review of Research Findings*, IDB/ECLA Working Paper No. 35, Buenos Aires: available from CEPAL.

Katz, J.M. 1982(a). *Cambio tecnológico en la industria metal mecánica latinoamericana: Resultado de un Programa de Estudios de Casos*, IDB-ECLA Working Paper No. 51. Buenos Aires: available from CEPAL. (Available in Spanish only. The English translation of the title of this paper is: Technological change in the Latin American metal-working industry: Results from a programme of case-studies.)

Katz, J.M. 1982(b). Technology and Economic Development: An Overview of Research Findings. In *Trade, Stability, Technology and Equity in Latin America*, eds. M. Syrquin and S. Teitel. Academic Press.

Katz, J.M. 1984. Technological innovation, industrial organisation and comparative advantages of Latin American metal-working industries. In eds. Fransman, M., and King, K., op. cit.

Lall, S. 1979. Developing countries as exporters of technology and capital goods: the Indian experience. Oxford, June.

Lall, S., ed. 1984. "Exports of technology by newly industrializing countries," special issue of *World Development*, Vol. 12, Nos. 5 and 6. See the overview by S. Lall.

Maxwell, P. 1982. *Steel plant technological development in Latin America: A comparative study of the selection and upgrading of technology in plants in Argentina, Brasil, Colombia, Mexico and Peru*, IDB-ECLA Working Paper No. 55. Buenos Aires: available from CEPAL.

Nelson, R. 1979. *Innovation and economic development: theoretical retrospect and prospect*, IDB-ECLA Working Paper No. 55. Buenos Aires: available from CEPAL.

Sercovich, F.C. 1978. *Design engineering and endogenous technical change: A microeconomic approach based on the experience of the Argentine chemical and petrochemical industries*, IDB-ECLA Working Paper No. 19. Buenos Aires: available from CEPAL.

Stewart, F. 1983. *Macro-policies for appropriate technology: An introductory classification*, A.T. International Working Paper. Washington D.C.: A.T. International.

Strassmann, W. 1968. *Technological Change and Economic Development: The Manufacturing Experience of Mexico and Puerto Rico*. Ithaca, New York: Cornell University Press.

Teitel, S. 1979. *Notes on technical change induced under conditions of protection, distortion and rationing*, IDB/ECLA Working Paper No. 34. Buenos Aires: available from CEPAL.

Teubal, M. 1979. *Innovation and Development*, IDB/ECLA Working Paper No. 33. Buenos Aires: available from CEPAL.

APPENDIX: SCOPE OF THE IDB-ECLA STUDIES AND COMPLETE REFERENCE LIST

In the first phase of the IDB-ECLA programme (1975–78) the main focus was on empirical case studies of the technological behaviour of individual Latin American firms (and sometimes of complete branches of industry) in the field of large-scale process plants, including chemical, petrochemical, rayon, steel, cement and cigarette production plants. There were some 16 studies of this kind (see refs. 4, 7–9, 11, 13, 15, 16, 18–21, 24, 26, 27). There were also two studies on technology-linked exports from Argentina (2, 14), three country studies of the contribution of technical change to productivity growth in manufacturing industry in Colombia, Argentina and Peru, respectively (1, 22, 25), and a valuable study of technical change in the Argentine construction industry (3, 17). As can be seen from the references, many of the above studies are available in English.

In the second phase of the programme (1979–82), the focus shifted to metal working and capital goods producing firms—where some 22 different case studies were conducted on individual firms (or in a few cases on specific branches) in the metal working and capital goods industries of Argentina, Brasil, Colombia, Mexico and Venezuela. The different kinds of production covered by the case studies included the manufacture of lathes and other machine tools, production of automobile parts and components, production of electric motors, some consumer durables, agricultural implements and machinery, and the output of foundries and forgings plants. For the 22 studies, see refs. 37–50, 52–54 and 57–61 inclusive.

According to the reference list, only two of these 22 capital-goods firm case-studies, both related to numerically controlled machine tools (37, 44), appear to have been published in English, and the others published in Spanish. The review paper which supplies an overview and conclusions from all these studies is by Katz, see item 51 in references, and is in Spanish. However two much shorter, distilled versions of this review have been published in English (Katz 1982b; 1984).

The main characteristic of the case studies of IDB-ECLA was their focus on the micro-level and microeconomic conduct of the plants concerned with developing and changing their technology—explored through very detailed fieldwork and interviews at the firm and plant level.

The case studies looked at technical change over long periods (five to 40 years) in the chronology of plants and firms, and thus avoided a one-sided focus on only the periods of major investments. Consequently, the studies could offer a proper long-run perspective on technical change in firms, which did not leave out the greater part of the life-cycle of the firms and plants concerned.

Most of the studies achieved a detailed qualitative description of the technological history of each firm or plant, and usually useful descriptions of the firm's sectoral and macro-contexts. Although many of the studies did not go much beyond this, nearly all came up with some clear qualitative and/or quantitative evidence of significant productivity improvements due to the introduction of technical changes. Only a few, however, undertook systematic quantitative investigations of the productivity advances achieved (in this regard see, for instance, Katz, and others 1978 [see ref. 13] and Dahlman, 1978 [see ref. 21], and Castaño, Katz and Navajas, 1981 [see ref. 38].

Although the unit of analysis was usually the individual firm (or group of firms) being studied, information was also produced in most of the case studies about how specific historical features of the different sectoral, macro, and policy contexts in each country had influenced the technical change undertaken at the firm level.

It is not easy for researchers to use the IDB-ECLA findings since the empirical case studies usually contain heavy technological detail without, in some of the studies, much in the way of organising hypotheses to lighten the story. However the technological detail was one of the great strengths of the programme. Moreover there are a number of review papers of various aspects of the studies which lighten the task of utilizing the findings.

In particular, to help evaluate and utilise the valuable "trawl" of empirical data from the individual case studies, a serious effort was made within the IDB-ECLA programme to produce some review, theoretical, comparative, and summary papers which would distill the important results from the case studies and point towards policy conclusions. The main published outputs of this kind were (i) Katz, 1980 (ref. 35) which summarises some overall results from the programme; (ii) Katz, 1982a (ref. 51) which reviews and compares the capital goods and metal working case studies; (iii) Maxwell, 1982 (ref. 55) which compares and discusses the programme's five steel plant case studies; (iv) Teitel, 1979 (ref. 34) who examines how distorted macro contexts affect the types of technical change undertaken; (v) Canitrot, 1978 (ref. 12) on how technical change is affected by changes in the values of macroeconomic parameters; (vi) Teubal, 1979 (ref. 33) which models learning in response to bottleneck situations; and (vii) Nelson, 1979 (ref. 31) who explores the tacitness and non-imitability dimensions of industrial technology.

REFERENCE LIST OF IDB-ECLA STUDIES

1. *The creation of technology in the Argentine manufacturing sector*, Katz, J. July 1978. (Spanish original noviembre 1976).
2. *Technology and industrial exports. A micro-economic analysis of Argentina's recent experience*, Katz, J.; Ablin, E.; August 1978. (Spanish original diciembre 1967).
3. *Competition, oligopoly and technological change in the construction industry. The Argentine case*, Vitelli, G.; August 1978. (Spanish original diciembre 1967).
4. *Learning and technical change in the steelplant of Acindar S.A. in Rosario*, Argentina, Maxwell, Philip; August 1977.
5. *Estudio sobre tecnología en la siderúrgica latinoamericana*, Instituto Chileno del Acero para el Programa Regional de Investigacion en Ciencia y Tecnología BID/CEPAL; diciembre 1976.
6. *El marco jurídico de la innovación tecnológica en América Latina.* Vol. I & II Convenio INTAL/Programa BID/CEPAL de Investigaciones en Temas de Ciencia y Tecnología en America Latina; diciembre 1976.
7. *The Argentine cigarette industry: technological profile and behaviour*, Fidel, J.; Lucangeli, J.; Shepherd, P.; September 1978. (Spanish original diciembre 1976).
8. *Cambio tecnológico en la industria de generación de energía eléctrica de Colombia*, Ramirez Gomez, M.; diciembre 1976.
9. *Technology, innovation and transfer of technology in the cement industry*, Pearson, R.; diciembre 1976.
10. *Desarrollo de la capacidad de ingeniería en el sector quimico-petroquimico. Delimitación metodológica de un campo de estudio*, Sercovich, F.C.; junio 1977.
11. *The Mexican cement industry. Technology, market structure and growth*, Pearson, Ruth; September 1977.
12. Method *for evaluating the significance of macro-economic variables in the analysis of technology incorporation decisions*, Canitrot, A.; July 1978. (Spanish original septiembre 1977).
13. *Productivity, technology and domestic efforts in research and development*, Katz, J.; Gutkowski, M.; Rodrigues, M.; Goity, G.; July 1978. (Spanish original marzo 1978).
14. *From infant industry to technology exports: The Argentine experience in the international sale of industrial plants and engineering works*, Katz, J.; Ablin, E.; October 1978. (Spanish original abril 1978).
15. *The Argentine cement industry. Technology, market structure and growth*, Pearson, R.; April 1978.

Source: IDB-ECLA Programme Document.

16. *First-best technological strategy in an "Nth-best" economic context. A case study of the evolution of the Acindar steelplant in Rosario, Argentina*, Maxwell, P.; April 1978.
17. *Technological change, market structure and employment in the Argentine construction sector*, Vitelli, G.; May 1981. (Spanish original agosto 1978).
18. *Cost-benefit of different technological options in the context of a differentiated oligopoly: the case of the Argentine cigarette industry*, Fidel, J.; Lucangeli, J.; October 1978. (Spanish original mayo 1978).
19. *Design engineering and endogenous technical change. A micro-economic approach based on the experience of the Argentine chemical and petrochemical industries*, Sercovich, F.C.; October 1978. (Spanish original agosto 1978).
20. *Análisis microeconómico de las características del cambio tecnológico y del proceso de innovaciones. El caso de Furfural y Derivados*, S.A. Mexico, Perez Aceves, L.; Perez y Peniche, J. de J.; junio 1978.
21. *From technological dependence to technological development; the case of the Usiminas steel plant in Brazil*, Text: Dahlman, C. (Vol. I). Appendices: Valadares Fonseca, F.; Dahlman, C. (Vol. II); October 1978.
22. *Tecnológia en el sector manufacturero colombiano*, Ramirez Gomez, M.; Sandoval Peralta, D.; octubre 1978.
23. *Implicit R&D strategy and investment-linked R&D. A study of the R&D programme of the Argentine steel firm*, Acindar S.A., Maxwell, P.; March 1979.
24. *Decisiones tecnológicas a nivel de empresa. El caso de Altos Hornos de México, S.A. (AHMSA)*, Perez Aceves, L.; Perez y Peniche, J. de J.; septiembre 1980.
25. *Crecimiento, industrialización y cambio técnico: el caso del sector manufacturero peruano*, Vega Centeno, M.; octubre 1978.
26. *El desarrollo tecnológico en la industria siderúrgica en Colombia*, Puerta R., German; abril 1979.
27. *Selecao, absorcao e geracao de tecnologica na petroquimica brasileira. Um estudo de caso*, Jorge, M.J.; marzo 1979.

(There is no document no. 28.)

29. *El fenómeno tecnológico interno*, Cibotti, R.; Lucangeli, Jorge; agosto 1980.
30. *Technological change, economic development and intra and extra regional relations in Latin America*, Katz, J.; October 1978. (Spanish original agosto 1978).
31. *Innovation and economic development; theoretical retrospect and prospect*, Nelson, R.; April 1979.
32. *On the micro-economics of technical progress*, Stiglitz, J.E.; April 1979.
33. *Innovation and development*, Teubal, M.; April 1979.
34. *Notes on technical change induced under conditions of protection, distortions and rationing*, Teitel, S.; April 1979.

35. *Domestic technology generation in LDCs: a review of research findings*, Katz, J.; November 1980.
36. *Capacity-stretching technical change: some empirical and theoretical aspects*, Maxwell, P.; Teubal, M.; December 1980.
37. *The use and production of numerically controlled machine-tools in Argentina*, Jacobsson, S.; December 1980.
38. *Etapas históricas y conductas tecnológicas en una planta argentina de máquinas herramientas*, Castaño, A.; Katz, J.; Navajas, F; enero 1981.
39. *Evolucao tecnológica no setor de maquinas de processar cereais. Um estodo de caso* Nogueira da Cruz, Helio; julio 1981.
40. *Productividad, escala y aprendizaje en una planta argentina de motores*, Berlinski, J.; agosto 1981.
41. *Cambio tecnológico en la firma Distral S.A. fabricante de calderas y equipos de presión*, Ramirez Gomez, M.; Leibovich G.; Jose; agosto 1981.
42. *Análisis de la trayectoria de una planta automotriz en Colombia; el caso de Sofasa*, Sandoval P., Diego; M., Mauricio; Guterman, L.; noviembre 1981.
43. *Innovaciones en productos y aprendizaje (el caso de una planta argentina de implementos agrícolas)*, Berlinski, J.; enero 1982.
44. *Technical change and technology policy. The case of numerically controlled lathes in Argentina*, Jacobsson, Staffan; March 1982.
45. *Innovaciones en el proceso y aprendizaje en una planta argentina de fundición*, Berlinski, J.; abril 1982.
46. *Inovacao tecnológica no setor de maquinas ferramentas brasileiro—Um estudo de caso*, da Silva, M.E.; mayo 1982.
47. *Observacoes sobre a mudanca tecnologica no setor de maquinas ferramentas do Brasil*, Nogueira da Cruz, H.; da Silva, M.E.; Hugerth, L.; mayo 1982.
48. *Cambios en la información técnica y aprendizaje en una planta argentina de motores*, Berlinksi, J.; junio 1982.
49. *La industria de máquinas herramientas en colombia. Estudio de una firma productora de tornos y otras máquinas para trabajar metales*, Sandoval, D.; Jaramillo, L.; junio 1982.
50. *Análisis de desarrollo industrial de forjas de Colombia. 1961–1981*. Sandoval, D.; Mick, M.; Guterman, L.; Jaramillo, L.; junio 1982.
51. *Cambio tecnológico en la industria metalmécanica latinoamericana. Resultados de un programa de estudios de Casos*. Katz, J.; julio 1982.
52. *El cambio tecnológico en la industria venezolana de maquinaria agrícola. Estudios de caso*, Turkieh, M.; Pirela, A.; Martinez, J.; Levin, P.; julio 1982.
53. *La industria de astilleros en Colombia: un estudio de caso de la empresa Conastil*, Sandoval P.; Diego; Jaramillo, L.; agosto 1982.
54. *Un estudio sobre el cambio tecnológico de una empresa mexicana productora de maquinaria para molinos*, Mercado, A.; Lombo, L.; agosto 1982.

55. *Steelplant technological development in Latin America. A comparative study of the selection and upgrading of technology in plants in Argentina, Brasil, Colombia, Mexico and Peru.* Maxwell, P.; August 1982.
56. *Basic issues emerging from recent research on technological behaviour of selected Latin American metalworking plants* (Argentina) Berlinski, J.; (Brazil) Nogueira da Cruz, H.; (Colombia) Sandoval, D.; (Venezuela) Turkieh, M.; August 1982. (4 brief review papers, some in Spanish).
57. *El cambio tecnológico en una empresa mexicana productora de máquinas para el vidrio y el plástico,* Mercado, A.; Toledo, P.; septiembre 1982.
58. *Evolucao tecnologica em una firma de processo produtivo continuo no setor metal-mecanico brasileiro,* Nogueira da Cruz, H.; da Silva, M.; septiembre 1982.
59. *Innovaciones en el proceso y aprendizaje. (El caso de una planta argentina de motores),* Berlinski, J; septiembre 1982.
60. *Innovaciones en productos y aprendizaje. (El caso de una planta argentina de implementos agrícolas)* Berlinski, J.; septiembre 1982.

Figure 8.1 Phases/types of productivity-raising technical change. From Bell, 1982, p. 21.

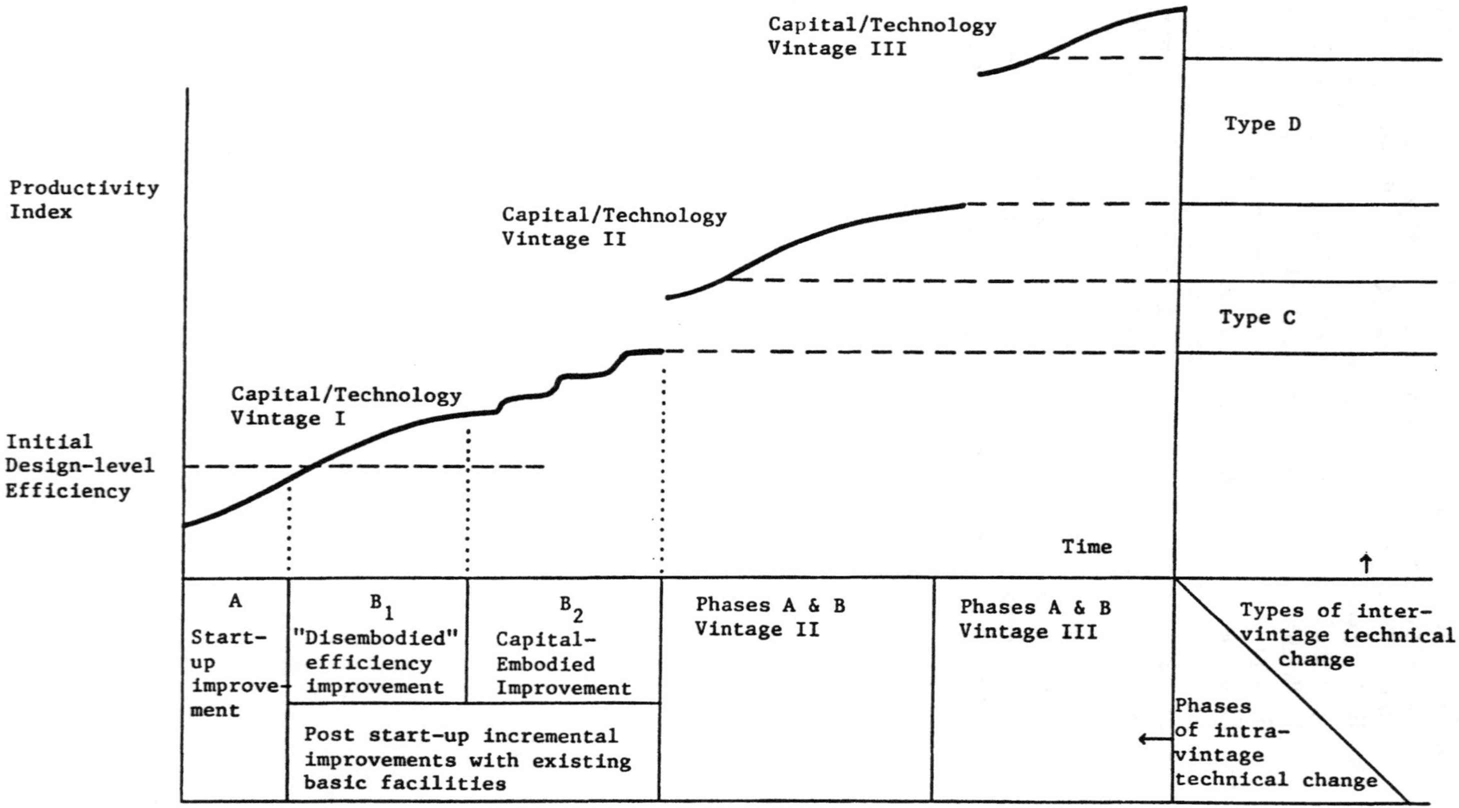

Nine

Overview and Conclusions

Frances Stewart

I. INTRODUCTION

Over the past two decades the concept of appropriate technology (AT) has gained increasing acceptance as an essential part of any development strategy which aims to combine economic growth with equity. The spread of productive employment throughout the adult population is necessary for full participation in economic development, and for generating sufficient incomes among the poor to enable them to meet their basic needs. The adoption of efficient appropriate technologies is intrinsic to spreading productive employment and eliminating unemployment and underemployment.

Although the need for appropriate technology is widely agreed upon, as evidenced by the enormous literature (see Carr, 1985, for many examples), and the many institutions which promote AT (see Jequier and McRobie), the achievements in terms of actual use of appropriate technologies have been relatively small. There are, of course, numerous examples of successful ATs. But there are more examples, even in countries where the need for AT is explicitly accepted by the government, of inappropriate technologies being introduced often displacing appropriate alternatives. In many countries the problems of unemployment and underemployment remain acute, while the continued growth of population, with increasing numbers falling below the poverty line, has further accentuated the need for AT.

The hypothesis underlying this book is that a major reason for the relative failure of AT—in terms of actual on-the-ground investment—has been a near exclusive focus by those promoting AT primarily (and often exclusively) on micro-interventions—that is, the development and introduction of specific ATs in specific contexts.

Unavoidably such interventions can only affect a very small proportion of the total investment decisions even when (as is increasingly the case) they begin to work on issues of dissemination and replication after a successful pilot project has been initiated. Moreover, by looking exclusively at particular projects (including dissemination and replication), no attention is paid to developments at the other end of the investment/technology spectrum—that is, to the inappropriate technologies being introduced in the modern industrial sector which pre-empt resources, create inequalities and regional imbalances, and may undermine appropriate technologies.

While micro-interventions have a role to play, the widespread adoption of AT requires that all decision-makers—public and private, foreign and domestic—adopt more appropriate technologies. To achieve this requires changing the *general context* or *macro-policies* within which individual decision-makers operate. The aim of this book has been to explore the nature of the macro-policies which would push all decisions in an appropriate direction. While chapter one presented a preliminary classification of the relevant policies, the empirical studies (chapters two through eight) examined these policies from the perspective of particular technologies in actual situations in different parts of the world.

Identification of correct policies is one essential step. However, if these policies are to be introduced in concrete situations, they must have sufficient political support. One of the hypotheses in the introductory essay was that forces of political economy often provided the decisive obstacle to the introduction of appropriate macro-policies because the policies would change the distribution of benefits from economic activity in a way that might conflict with dominant interest groups. The empirical studies were intended to elucidate how the policies identified as promoting AT would affect the nexus of interests in the society being studied.

This chapter presents an overview of the empirical studies and analyses the main conclusions. Section two will briefly review the findings of each of the studies. Section three highlights the main conclusions and analyses how the hypotheses put forward in the introductory classification require modification in the light of the empirical work. Before coming to the empirical studies, the rest of this introductory section briefly sketches the classification presented initially in chapter one so that the findings of the empirical studies may be viewed against this framework of analysis.

* * *

The introductory classification suggested four areas relevant to the identification of macro-policies for the promotion of AT: those related to *objectives* of decision-makers, access to *resources*, the nature of *markets* and the availability of *technology*.

Objectives

It was argued that each type of decision-maker (for example, family, parastatal, small local private company, or large private, multinational company) had its own objectives, but these could be influenced by the environment in which the decision-making unit operated. Consequently, objectives might be changed by changing the balance of different types of decision-makers within the economy. This was described as the *composition of units*.

Resources

It was suggested that the resources available to each decision-maker, in price, quality and quantity, determined the quantity of investment each could make, and also influenced the nature of each investment decision. Policies towards resources include policies influencing the prices of different resources (for example, subsidies and taxes, investment allowances, and minimum wage laws); policies towards imports (tariffs, quotas, exchange rates) which determine the price and availability of imported resources; and policies towards credit which determine access to finance for investment by different decision-makers.

Markets

The type and extent of the market served by each micro-unit was argued to be an important determinant of technological choice, influencing both the nature of the product, and thereby the method of production, and the scale of production. In general, different types of decision-making units serve different markets, ranging from the world market to informal sector consumers. Government policies could influence both external and domestic markets. External markets depend on developments in the world economy but are much more influenced—in terms of domestic decision-makers—by policies towards international trade (for example, import-substitution versus export-orientation). Domestic markets are influenced by internal income distribution and by the consumption regime, both of which could be changed by government policies.

Technology

The fourth determinant of choice of technology suggested was knowledge about and price of technological alternatives. Decision-makers normally have access to only a subset of the world technological shelf, and this subset varies with the type of unit. For example, multi-national corporation subsidiaries have easy and cheap access to the latest technology in use by the parent company, while sources of technology for the small-scale sector are largely confined to the technology in use by other firms in the region and the occasional machinery salesman. Over time the world technological shelf shifts and the subsets known to various units also shift. The direction of this shift depends on R & D and more informal innovations both abroad and in the country concerned. Policies to affect the change over time include policies towards local R & D, dissemination channels, and informal sources of technical change.

Analysis of the four categories separately suggested that there was likely to be a systematic difference in choice of product and choice of technique according to the type of decision-making unit. Government policies might therefore affect choices towards more appropriate technology, both by changing the environment so that each type of decision-maker would make more appropriate choices and by shifting control over investable resources towards those types of decision-makers that tend to make more appropriate choices, that is, changing the *composition of units.*

II. FINDINGS OF THE EMPIRICAL STUDIES

The studies divide broadly into two groups. The first five (chapters two through six) are concerned with rural and agriculture-related technologies. The last two (chapters seven and eight) relate mainly to industrial urban processes.

Technology Choice in Indian Agriculture

In chapter two Ashok Rudra reviews technology choice in Indian agriculture over the past three decades. He argues that after an initial period in which more-or-less appropriate technology was promoted, since around 1959 the Indian government, aided and abetted by its foreign (primarily U.S. government and Ford Foundation) advisers, systematically supported inappropriate technological decisions. The policy switch occurred with the emphasis on a Green Revolution package, involving the application of fertiliser, irrigation, and mechanisation in combination with the new seeds; the package of technology and inputs was promoted in relatively large amounts and concentrated on relatively few areas of high potential.

An agricultural strategy that started in the immediate post-independence period with the philosophy of all-round and self-reliant development of the rural community was transformed into one narrowly focussing on production concentrated in regions, crops, and on rich farmers and depending exclusively on purchased inputs from distant and sophisticated large-scale industries.

Rudra shows that this tendency towards concentrating resources on the larger farmers and richer regions, which led to growing rural inequality and regional imbalance, occurred for each of the main elements in agricultural technology: mechanisation, where, despite strong evidence of zero or negative social returns, employment displacing mechanisation was promoted; fertiliser policy, where there are large subsidies on chemical fertiliser production and no promotion of organic alternatives; pesticides, where a similar situation prevails; and irrigation, where mechanised tubewells were promoted, while canals and other forms of traditional irrigation were neglected. In each case the interests of large farmers, and foreign and domestic machinery and fertiliser producers, combined to bring about policies favouring inappropriate technologies at the expense of small farmers, landless labourers, and rural artisans, and of large regions in the country where the "package" was inapplicable.

The policies which led to inappropriate technology in Indian agriculture—and which would need to be reversed to promote appropriate technology—

include price and credit policies, which subsidised the production, sale, and finance of chemical fertilisers, tractors, and mechanised tubewells. In addition, R & D (mainly carried out by public institutions, domestic or international) largely neglected the development and improvement of appropriate alternatives. Where appropriate R & D did occur, dissemination and promotion of the results was almost totally neglected, in contrast to the efficient network which developed for the promotion of the inappropriate technology package.

Rudra's analysis puts major emphasis on policies in the area of *resources* and *technology*. He presents a clear view of the forces of political economy which led to the policies favouring appropriate technology—namely the dominant interests of large farmers, and domestic and foreign machinery producers, supported by bilateral and multilateral aid-donors.

Irrigation in Bangladesh

In chapter three, Stephen Biggs and Jon Griffith examine an example of an appropriate irrigation technology in Bangladesh which, in microcosm, illustrates many of Rudra's findings for Indian agriculture as a whole. The example is the manually operated shallow tubewell (MOSTI). This consists of converting an established technology for providing domestic water supplies to a technology for irrigating crops. MOSTIs are shown to be more appropriate than the mechanised shallow tubewells (ST) by several criteria: MOSTIs are much smaller in terms of the area covered, which is on average one-twentieth of the STs; they are much cheaper at about one-eighteenth the cost; they use only manual labour compared with diesel fuel required by the STs; and they create far more employment—twenty times as much per acre, while investment cost per acre is 1/320 of the ST.

The two techniques achieve similar rates of irrigation for every Tk. spent on capital costs, measured at market prices. But the market prices include a heavy tax on the materials used to make the MOSTI, and subsidies on the STs. The STs are more profitable at these prices, if labour is costed at the ruling market rates and the capacity of the tubewells is fully used. But with less than full use of the tubewells or if the labour is family labour with very low opportunity cost, then the MOSTIs become profitable. The MOSTIs are especially suitable for very small family farms with limited access to credit, where the low capital costs, low scale, and high use of labour are particularly advantageous. Surprisingly, research into the results of projects supporting MOSTIs has shown that they are bought by relatively large farms. Biggs and Griffith speculate that this might be because of the subsidies involved in these programmes, and that some who buy them might do so to resell to small farmers.

The study reveals the following policy obstacles to the promotion of AT:

1. Very limited R & D on appropriate technologies. In fact, the MOSTIs are not a new technology but a new use for an old technology. Biggs

and Griffith argue that there would be very large potential gains from devoting more resources to R & D for more appropriate technologies in improving the efficiency of existing techniques and developing new ones.

2. Price policies in Bangladesh generally favoured the more inappropriate technologies. In this case there was a heavy tax on the steel pipes used in the MOSTIs and subsidies on mechanised methods.
3. The system of credit was such that small farmers had virtually no access to institutionalised credit, and had to pay high rates for informal sources of credit.
4. The financial and administrative procedures of the aid agencies were better suited to mechanised techniques with a large import content. Recently, a MOSTI-type pump has been developed using bamboo instead of steel. The pump may be produced entirely within the village. But this type of development cannot be handled by most aid agencies which need to deal with recognised, formal sector organizations. There were also problems within the Bangladesh administration which exhibited biases towards mechanised techniques. A USAID project to support MOSTIs in 1976 had difficulty in securing cooperation from the Bangladesh Agricultural Development Corporation.

The policies identified thus fit into those of *resources* (prices and credit), *technology* (research and development) and *objectives* (the objectives and organisation of aid organisations and the Bangladesh parastatal administration), in terms of the introductory classification.

Analysis of the interest groups involved in the decision about irrigation technology showed that the major gainers from the appropriate technology were small and landless peasants and rural artisans while the groups gaining from mechanised techniques included large peasants, bureaucrats, and equipment producers and installers (see table 3.7).

Paddy Threshing Technology: Thailand and the Philippines

In chapter four, Bart Duff tells the story of the small thresher designed by the International Rice Research Institute (IRRI) and its impact in the Philippines and Thailand.

Two versions of a thresher suitable for small rice farms were developed by IRRI, the outcome of research and development starting in 1967. Local manufacture of the threshers was initiated in the mid-1970s and by 1985 there were 70 firms producing the threshers in the Philippines and 20 in Thailand. In each country, there was a very high adoption rate among small farmers in irrigated areas.

Analysis of the effects of the thresher shows that it was significantly labour-displacing, saving between one-quarter and one-third of labour used in post-production processes. A general equilibrium analysis in the Philippines showed that total labour use following an increase in rice production was 7 percent less with the thresher than without it. The reduced labour-use in the Philippines affected hired labour more than proportionately. Landless labourers are among the poorest groups in the Philippines. Labour's share of output declined with the introduction of mechanised threshing.

In the Philippines, this labour displacement occurred at a time when the labour supply in aggregate was growing faster than demand and real wages were falling. In contrast, in Thailand where there was an expanding land frontier and only a small landless labourer class, real wages were rising.

In both countries, the technology was highly profitable from a private point of view (hence its high rate of adoption). But whereas in the circumstances of Thailand it was also socially beneficial, in the Philippines it seems to have had negative effects, contributing to the surplus labour and depressed real wages. Whether on balance, the social effects are deemed positive or negative in the Philippines must depend on how the incomes of different groups are weighted.

The high private profitability in the Philippines—despite the uncertain social effects—was partly due to government policies towards credit and tariffs. The research and promotion provided free by IRRI also contributed to private profitability. The technology's profitability was also due to the yield increasing effects (of from 0.7 to 6.0 percent of the grain) because greater losses tended to be associated with manual methods, unless there was a high degree of labour supervision.

The study suggests a number of important conclusions. First, it underlines the fact (argued in chapter one) that appropriateness is relative. What is appropriate in one context (Thailand) may be inappropriate in another (the Philippines). Second, it shows the potential for R & D, but also suggests that very great care is needed to ensure the appropriateness of new technologies, especially in a labour surplus economy. In the Philippines what appeared to be appropriate—being small-scale, locally produced, simple—in fact turned out to have important labour-displacing effects. Examination of the likely effects of the technology should have been carried out by IRRI before launching the technology on a large scale. Third, the case provides an example of a classic conflict between output and employment. The thresher appears to maximise output in the Philippines, but at the expense of employment and a deterioration in income distribution.

Rural Linkages in the Philippines and Taiwan

The study by Gustav Ranis and Frances Stewart (chapter five) uses material from the Philippines and Taiwan to analyse rural linkages as a way of promoting appropriate technology. It is shown that in general, rural industrialisation uses more appropriate technologies. A dominant factor leading to the growth of non-agricultural activities in the rural areas are linkages arising from agricultural development. Agricultural growth generates non-agricultural activity through consumption linkages (i.e., extra demand for consumption goods and services from those whose agricultural incomes have risen), forward linkages (processing agricultural crops), and backward linkages (supplies of inputs to agriculture). Examples from the Philippines show the very extensive nature of these linkages, with a one percent increase in agricultural output leading to a more than one percent increase in non-agricultural employment in the rural areas. Consumption linkages were generally quantitatively the most significant. In Taiwan the rate of growth of non-agricultural employment in the rural areas was more than twice the rate of growth in the Philippines at a time when agricultural growth rates were similar. Comparison between the two countries revealed a number of reasons for such a difference. First, more capital-intensive technology choices in agriculture in the Philippines generated less additional consumption from employment, and smaller rural backward linkages, since mechanised techniques had a markedly higher urban and import content while the less mechanized techniques were more often manufactured and serviced in the rural areas. The high rate of large-scale mechanisation in the Philippines was due to a set of price interventions, including subsidised credit, which favoured tractors, and to unequal land distribution. In Taiwan the rapid growth of very labour-intensive crops—mushrooms and especially asparagus—also enhanced consumption linkages and generated employment in local canning factories.

In Taiwan, processing agricultural crops was generally more decentralized. A major reason for this situation in the examples of bananas and pineapples was the presence of small-scale local companies that carried out the processing in Taiwan, whereas in the Philippines processing was done by multinational companies in large-scale plants. In rice processing in the Philippines, aid-donors and the government together promoted large-scale capital-intensive integrated rice-processing plants, at the expense of small-scale village mills. The availability of infrastructure—roads and rural electrification—was generally much more deficient in the Philippines, discouraging rural linkages.

The study concludes that strong rural linkages are a powerful mechanism for promoting AT and identifies a number of policies which would strengthen these linkages. A general policy conclusion is that policies which effectively promote agricultural development also have a substantial positive effect on the promotion of AT. For any given rate of growth in agriculture, policies which favour labour-absorption in agriculture increase rural linkages. These policies include egalitarian land reform, reforms in price interventions to avoid favouring mechanisation, reform in credit institutions, and policies to promote the growth of high value labour-intensive cropping patterns. Generating more decentralised and appropriate choices in agro-processing requires changes in organisational structures (that is, a shift from MNCs to local companies) as well as improved provision of rural infrastructure. Local small-scale entrepreneurs tended to adopt more appropriate techniques than either MNCs (as shown in the case of bananas and pineapples) or parastatals supported by aid agencies (as in the case of rice).

Policies suggested by the study fall into four categories. The emphasis on policies to promote agricultural growth, however, falls outside the initial classification.

Analysis of the political economy of the policies identified as promoting AT reveals similar interests to the findings of Rudra and Biggs and Griffith. The major gainers from the policies favouring AT would be small farmers and the landless and small rural entrepreneurs, while the main losers would be foreign machinery suppliers, local bureaucrats and cronies, and large farmers. The latter present a powerful constellation of interests, but the study identifies some policies—notably general promotion of agriculture, especially support for labour-intensive crops and provision of rural infrastructure—which would impose fewer losses on powerful groups, and might be less vigorously opposed by dominant interest groups.

Sugar Processing in India and Kenya

Chapter six by Raphael Kaplinsky contains a case study of one example of forward linkage—sugar processing—drawing on material from Kenya and India. In sugar manufacture there are two distinct types of technology: (1) the vacuum pan sulphitation technique (VP), which is intrinsically large-scale and capital-intensive, with a tendency for technical change to lead to increasing scale and capital-intensity over time; and (2) the open-pan sulphitation technique (OP), which is much smaller in scale. The VP technology ranges in capacity from 1,000 to 7,000 tons of cane crushing capacity per day, with optimal plant size in the 1970s of around 5,000 t.c.d., the OP techniques are designed for 100 or 200 t.c.d. The OP technique is far more labour-using than the VP—the capital/labour ratio of the VP plants range from four to 20 times the K/L ratio of the OP plants. In Kenya the VP technology involved greater dependence on foreign supplies (the machinery was all imported) and foreign management. In contrast, the OP plants were owned and managed by small local firms and the machinery was manufactured locally. This difference did not apply in India where both types of machinery were manufactured in the country and managed by local companies. But the OP machinery was produced in dispersed workshops in India, while production of VP machinery was concentrated in a few sites.

Because of the small-scale and decentralised location of OP technology, it is far better suited to processing the small quantities of sugar cane produced by small farmers. The large farmers find the large processing capacity of the VP technology more convenient.

In the past there has been considerable debate about the relative efficiency of OP and VP techniques because of the lower recovery rate of the OP technology of crystal sugar from a given quantity of sugar cane. In addition, the product produced by the OP technology is often regarded as inferior, being less even and of a variable colour. In India, this has led to a price discount; in Kenya there is no such discount as the product of the VP technology is also of rather uncertain quality. As a result of innovations conducted in India, the OP's efficiency was significantly increased and is now competitive with the VP technology in many circumstances.

It is evident that the OP technology represents the appropriate technology in most conditions of capital-scarcity and underemployment. However, in Kenya only 1.7 percent of output is processed by OP techniques. In India, 30 percent of output is OP-processed.

Kaplinsky identifies a number of policies that have led to this situation. The price of sugar is an important influence since the higher the price, the greater the cost of a lower recovery rate. In India, there is no single price but a complex pricing system whose effect on choice of technology varies according to the precise situation, while the overall effect—because of the complexity of the regulations—is unclear. This raises an important issue which has wider implications than the example being considered here. Government regulations over prices—or other types of intervention—can have unintended but important effects on choice of technique. This is especially likely to be true where the interventions are complex. Governments committed to AT need to incorporate AT considerations into the decision-making process not only where choice of technique is evidently directly affected but also in cases, such as this one, where the effects are indirect.

The aid community has been a major influence on choice of technique in Kenya since most of the plants have been aid-financed. Bilateral donors have favoured VP technology because they permit tied-aid to finance the machinery while their own nationals provide the management contracts and expertise required. Multilateral aid donors have also broadly favoured the VP technology. Here the motivation is more complex. One reason is that the VP technology involves large-scale formal sector projects which are generally preferred by the aid donors since they permit rapid flow of funds and may be subject to the normal control procedures. (A similar story was told for irrigation projects in Bangladesh.)

Government price and subsidy policies have been a major factor in Kenya. The VP mills are not required to write off their heavy depreciation costs so that capital is effectively subsidised; the OP mills (which have much less heavy capital costs) are required to write them off.

The study identified significant policy influences over choice of technology in each of the categories of the classification. Objectives of aid-donors supported the inappropriate technology in Kenya. Large farmers' objectives were best met by the VP, while those of small farmers were better served by the OP. As noted, cheap and abundant capital supplies, resulting from policies of aid-donors and government, helped the VP technology in Kenya (the *resource* classification). The variable quality of sugar from the OP made markets an important influence; low income consumers bought cheaper and lower-quality sugar produced by OP techniques in India. Higher-income consumers were prepared to pay more for the VP produced sugar. The availability and efficiency of different *technologies* turned out to be critical, with the recent innovations in OP techniques greatly improving their relative efficiency.

Analysis of the political economy behind the relevant policies reveals a situation which is familiar from the previous studies. In Kenya, the gainers from the VP technology were foreign machinery suppliers and foreign firms supplying management services, large farmers (many of whom were absentee landlords with positions in the government), and the aid community. The gainers from the OP technology were small farmers, the unemployed and underemployed in the rural areas, and small local firms producing the OP techniques. In Kenya, the latter group are politically weak while aid finance has been dominant—hence the small use of the OP technology. In India, the distribution of interests was a little different since the VP technology was produced and managed by local firms and the aid community played only a marginal role. In addition, small farmers and small machinery producers form a larger and more powerful group. This difference in the way various interests are affected and in their political power may explain why the OP technology is much more prevalent in India.

Parastatals in Kenya and Tanzania

Some of the earlier chapters touched on the role of parastatals and aid agencies in relation to the choice of technique. The parastatals are a central topic of James' analysis in chapter seven, but his chapter also contains material on the role of aid agencies. Parastatals account for a large proportion of investment in many developing countries, often half or more. In theory, it might be expected that this large amount of public sector investment would permit governments to realise their objectives more efficiently. And, since in most cases the objectives include increasing employment, promoting equity and regional balance and supporting small-scale activities, it would seem that parastatals should be a powerful instrument for the promotion of appropriate technology. Yet the few references to choice of technology and the role of the parastatals made in the earlier chapters suggest that this is not the case. James—looking at the apparently different environments in capitalist Kenya and socialist Tanzania—provides strong and systematic evidence that parastatals in these countries have tended to select *inappropriate* technologies. Many examples from both countries show parastatals selecting large-scale capital-intensive technologies and producing high quality Western-style products even where there is an obvious alternative:

> "Despite the rhetoric, Tanzania's industrialisation programme has, in general, promoted the establishment of enterprises using large-scale capital-intensive, often technically and almost invariably economically inefficient techniques." (Perkins on parastatals in Tanzania)

> "The parastatal client firms tend to be large, capital-intensive, import-intensive and almost entirely directed towards a protected overpriced local market." (Hopcraft and Oguttu on Kenya)

Ignorance of technological alternatives cannot be more than a minor cause of the inappropriate choices since James quotes several examples where the choice was explicitly questioned and alternatives suggested but the initial inappropriate choice nonetheless prevailed.

In searching for causes James pointed to the overriding objective of bureaucrats within parastatals and government departments to maximise output in a short period as being a central factor. Maximisation of the rate of increase of output required maximising the number of new projects initiated. With the foreign exchange and financial stringencies prevalent in both countries, bureaucrats found that seeking foreign finance was the most effective way of maximising new projects. Heavy dependence on foreign finance in turn led to dependence on Western sources of technology and machinery, with the consequence that methods of production dominant in the source country were introduced unquestioningly into the very different conditions of Kenya and Tanzania. The connection between foreign finance and inappropriate technology is clear-cut in the case of bilateral aid. However, James establishes that the same situation prevailed for multilateral finance, in the examples he examines. One reason for this was that it was accepted by multilateral agencies that the technology must produce products which would meet international product standards, either because exports were intended, or because consumers were believed to demand these standards. A second reason was that small-scale activities would require far more administrative and supervisory resources and would therefore delay securing the desired increase in output. This was the reason given for rejecting an OP sugar mill in Tanzania in favour of a VP mill; the OP technology would have involved 200 plants compared with five for the VP.

James' analysis leads to a number of policy conclusions. First, he suggests changing the balance of investment away from the large-scale parastatal organisations to small-scale plants—that is, changing the composition of units. Second, he identifies ways of improving the decisions made by the parastatals. These include reduced emphasis at all levels on maximising output increases, reducing the autonomy of the parastatals, and restoring the links between efficiency and profitability. In the Tanzanian case this would require a reform in the system of price controls which, by operating on a cost plus basis, left little incentive for efficient choices. In both countries reduced financial privileges to parastatals—which often permitted open-ended subsidies—would be necessary, as well as a move towards a more competitive environment. James argues that the strong bias in technological choice imparted by the requirement of securing the latest product standards needs to be tackled directly by a products policy. The technological bias which is the outcome of financial dependence on developed country sources might be reduced by active search for developing country sources of finance and technology.

The study of the parastatals gives greatest emphasis to *objectives* and to *product standards* in analysis of the policies which led to inappropriate choices. *Resource* access was critical because of the link between financial source and technology source, while price and subsidy policies of the governments permitted parastatals to make inefficient choices without affecting their viability. Unlike the previous studies, James' analysis did not conclude that R & D on appropriate techniques was an important policy requirement. This is because James found that parastatals made inefficient choices from within the existing technological alternatives, rejecting more efficient appropriate techniques. Consequently, the problem was one of the choice mechanism, not the efficiency of appropriate techniques. R & D would not therefore be likely to affect the outcome.

The political economy of the required policy changes was found to be similar to that in previous studies. The gainers from more appropriate decisions would be the unemployed, underemployed, and small entrepreneurs; the losers include bureaucrats, bilateral aid donors and foreign machinery producers.

Technical Change in Industrial Firms in Latin America

Chapter eight reviews the lessons learned from the numerous studies of industrial technical change undertaken in a major IDB/ECLA project. Philip Maxwell surveys the studies from the perspective of AT. As Maxwell points out, the IDB/ECLA studies were not undertaken with the intention of examining the appropriateness of the technical change. Consequently the lessons learned are somewhat incidental to the main findings of the project.

One of the major findings of the studies was the importance of in-house technical capability. The studies established that firm capacity to initiate technical change was far more widespread than previously believed; moreover, they also showed that some such effort was vital to fit imported technologies into the local environment. They found that in many cases local technical change contributed to a sizeable expansion in output and substantial productivity improvement. The precise pattern of learning and technical change varied widely according to the capability of the firm and the circumstances it faced.

Investigation into how appropriate this sizeable (and previously underestimated) effort was gave a conflicting picture. On the one hand, in the examples examined the changes tended to raise rather than lower the K/L ratio (chiefly as a result of being more effective in raising labour productivity than capital productivity, not through developing new capital-using and labour-saving techniques); secondly, many of the innovations increased the scale of the enterprise, further away from the small-scale AT ideal. On the other hand, the efforts resulted in a greater use of local materials and locally available fuels and, from this perspective, they contributed to more appropriate technologies. Maxwell does not investigate product specification and product changes, but here there also have been conflicting examples in the literature. On the one hand, in some cases adaptions have been undertaken which make the products suit the local environment better (for example, more rugged cars and buses)—that is, appropriate changes. On the other, some of the quality upgrading has been inappropriate, upgrading products to what may be excessive standards.

The direction of technical change achieved by these efforts depends on the general economic environment as well as the specific opportunities and constraints of the particular firm. The IDB/ECLA studies covered Latin American economies in the 1970s when the macro-economic environment—in terms of factor prices, credit availability, income distribution, and trading strategy—tended to support a rather capital-intensive choice of technique and the production of rather sophisticated products for elite markets. It is therefore of interest to contrast these findings with an earlier study of Taiwan and South Korea (see Ranis, 1973).

Ranis found, in contrast to the findings of the IDB/ECLA studies, a number of appropriate adaptions of imported techniques by local firms, which reduced the capital/labour ratio, in response to the pressures of the environment. The macro-economic environment in Taiwan and South Korea in the 1960s was very different from that of Latin American economies of the 1970s. Factor markets were more unified and factor prices facing the modern sector more closely reflected factor availability; income distribution was much more equal and the elite market was therefore less important while the mass market was more important; and the trading environment was much more open, with greater emphasis on exporting manufactured products. The contrast between the two cases suggests that there is no inexorable tendency for technical change to be unavoidably in an inappropriate direction, but local firms may respond in an appropriate way where the macro-economic environment is pressing in that direction.

III. LESSONS FROM THE STUDIES

The policy findings of the empirical studies generally support the classification of policies suggested in chapter one and summarised above. They indicate the relative importance of different policies in different contexts, and identify some additional policies for AT, not included in the initial classification. The analysis of the political economy of AT policies in the studies—especially as similar conclusions emerged from several studies—throws considerable empirical light on this difficult area. This section starts by reviewing the initial classification in the light of the findings. The section concludes with a review of the findings on the political economy of AT.

Classification

Objectives

Of the many actors involved in investment and technology decisions the studies provided most careful analysis of and evidence on the objectives of decision-makers in parastatals. Also some evidence was gathered on decision-making within governments and by aid-donors. For each of these categories, the nature of the objectives identified has important implications for technology decisions and for the development of policies to promote AT.

Parastatals. The bureaucratic objectives of decision-makers within parastatals have been shown to be an important element which, combined with heavy dependence on foreign finance, has led, systematically, to inappropriate technology choices. This emerged not only from James, who produced much supporting evidence for the conclusion, but also from more indirect evidence in other studies (Biggs, Ranis and Stewart). Since parastatals account for a large proportion of investment, choice of technique within parastatals is of major significance, in many countries, for technology choice in the country as a whole. An important area of policy for AT is to change the operations of parastatals to secure more appropriate technology decisions. Policies would include:

1. Changing the economic environment in which parastatals operate so that they have to be more efficient in order to generate surpluses. Such a change might include increasing competition within the industries in which parastatals operate by increasing domestic competition and/or international competition; reducing price controls and/or changing their form; and reducing the role of quotas and licenses in allocating resources. These moves would all strengthen the relationship between efficient (which means more appropriate) decisions and profitability. Such a change in the environment would also be needed to improve the technology decisions of the private sector.
2. Reducing the special financial privileges of parastatals (and others) so that their viability in the medium term depends on their ability to generate surpluses. (This should not rule out loss-making activities which have explicit social purpose, but prevent the many other loss-making areas which have no such justification.) Open ended subsidies and capital write-offs are examples of policies which have permitted parastatals to take inefficient and inappropriate technology decisions.
3. Improving procedures for investment appraisal and investment decisions within parastatals. James' study reveals haphazard procedures with more-or-less any project getting the go-ahead so long as external finance was available, and with *no* systematic technology search and no appropriate technology considerations incorporated into the decision-making apparatus. The net result was a costly and arbitrarily selected set of projects, using inappropriate technologies and operating with low capacity utilisation. A systematic appraisal procedure should include a technology search with an explicit AT element, AT considerations in the appraisal, and a search for and appraisal of financial sources. Availability of foreign finance would be one consideration, but only when it is properly costed (the idea that foreign finance is costless is nonsense). Proper technology search and investment appraisal procedures would significantly reduce the influence of foreign finance on technology decisions.
4. Reducing the influence of Western financial sources on technology decisions. This would be achieved in part by the procedures just discussed. In addition, governments should seek more sectoral and

programme finance and less project-finance; they should search for alternative sources of finance which might involve more appropriate technologies—that is, more developing country sources.

5. Generating new forms of public enterprise whose structures are likely to favour AT. This implies that they should be much smaller in scale than most parastatals and the role of bureaucrats should be smaller. Small cooperatives provide one possibility (see Stewart (ed.), 1983 for others).

Foreign aid donors. Foreign aid donors were not included as major decision-makers in the initial classification. But the studies make it clear that in many countries they are critical in many technology decisions. For example, Rudra traces the whole development of policy making towards technology in Indian agriculture to the interaction of advice and assistance from the aid community and policy makers in India, with the aid community playing the leading role for the most part. Aid was also of major importance in irrigation in Bangladesh, in many choices made in Kenyan and Tanzanian parastatals, and in rice processing and agricultural mechanisation in the Philippines.

On balance the influence of the aid-community—according to these studies—is overwhelmingly in favour of inappropriate technology. Bilateral aid donors systematically supported technologies exported from their own economy, which almost invariably meant large-scale and capital intensive technologies. There were a few exceptions to this—USAID, for example, supported one of the MOSTI projects. But the net effects of bilateral project aid, according to these studies, was to support inappropriate technology. There was a little more ambiguity about multilateral aid, but the net effect seems to have been similar to bilateral aid: in most cases the multilateral aid donors supported inappropriate choices. UNICEF's support for the MOSTI in Bangladesh was an exception. In addition, James notes examples where the World Bank questioned choices of technology on the grounds that they were inappropriate, but the choices went through nonetheless. The studies cite a number of cases where there was initiation of and support for inappropriate technologies. For example, in the Philippines, tractorisation—which displaced labour and had little positive effect on output—was financed by joint programmes between the Philippine government and the World Bank, providing subsidised credit. The Asian Development Bank was largely responsible—again in collaboration with the government—for the large-scale integrated rice complexes which reduced opportunities for village rice mills. In Tanzania, the World Bank supported a VP sugar project, generating a fraction of the employment of the OP alternatives.

Part of the reason for the aid-donors support of inappropriate technology lies in the same kind of bureaucratic objectives that James identified within parastatals. An overwhelming objective of aid administrators in many cases is to meet their target flow of finance, while ensuring that the projects financed meet the procedures that have been laid down. Questions of project efficiency and social desirability often come second. It is always easier to meet financial flow targets with a few big projects than with a multitude of small ones. Moreover, many small project managers may not be able to fulfill the mandatory auditing requirements. When, as with much bilateral aid, these objectives are combined with the objective of tying the aid, the forces favouring inappropriate technology become overwhelming. Multilateral aid donors normally finance only the foreign exchange component of the capital cost of a project which automatically imparts a bias in favour of projects with heavy capital costs and a high foreign exchange component of the capital costs.

One important area for AT policy is to change motivations and procedures of bilateral and multilateral aid agencies towards promotion of AT. This would involve:

1. switching from project aid to general or sectoral aid;
2. giving priority to aid for small-scale projects;
3. to avoid heavy administrative costs associated with small-scale projects, major aid agencies could use intermediary national institutions which could help finance and supervise small-scale projects. Consequently, an effort is needed to build up suitable national institutional capacities;
4. incorporating AT into project aid explicitly, so that the search for efficient AT methods becomes an explicit element in project aid;
5. using LDC consultancy firms;
6. eliminating aid-tying;
7. eliminating the capital cost only, foreign exchange element only, aspects of aid financing; and
8. changing auditing and paperwork requirements to ease the problems of very small firms.

It is evident that for both categories just discussed—parastatals and aid-donors—decisions were taken in interaction with the government concerned. In the case of the parastatals, the government determined the output-maximisation objective which was ultimately responsible for many of the inappropriate decisions. In the case of the aid community, all the big inappropriate decisions were taken in collaboration, or after discussion, with the government. Governments have undoubtedly favoured inappropriate technology not only in the cases just cited but also in the determination of many of the macro-policies discussed throughout this book. The reason for this lies largely in political economy, to be discussed later. But in addition, the government itself is subject to similar bureaucratic influences that apply to the parastatals and the aid institutions. These bureaucratic influences naturally support decisions favouring projects that can be executed quickly, and lead to maximum plan fulfillment. Governments also have administrative procedures, like the aid institutions, and these procedures are most readily followed by managers of large projects, especially those involving foreign management, who are more accustomed to dealing efficiently and speedily with many of the administrative requirements. Thus extending the analysis of the biases imparted by "bureaucratic man" to government helps to explain the systematic support many governments have given to inappropriate technology.

Resources

The studies strongly endorse the view that price and availability of resources to different micro-units affected the choice of technique within each unit and also the distribution of investment as between different types of units. Many instances were identified of government policies towards prices—especially tax and subsidy policies—which favoured inappropriate decisions. One example was the depreciation write-off permitted to VP technologies in Kenya; another was the subsidisation of mechanisation in Philippine agriculture; and a third was the tax on materials in the MOSTIs in Bangladesh. Credit institutions were found to favour larger borrowers.

Evaluation of the USAID MOSTI project in Bangladesh found that "credit sales had been very disappointing, explaining this was due to red tape and the reluctance of the banks to handle small credit applications." Although the MOSTI projects were designed to help very small farmers, the average land holding of those affected was quite large. Informal sector activities were by definition excluded from securing loans from formal sector credit institutions. Any credit they received came from informal sources at high interest rates.

There was clear evidence that family labour was regarded as having a lower cost than the wage for hiring labour. This was the case, for example, in irrigation in Bangladesh and in harvesting and rice threshing in the Philippines. This difference meant that family farms found more labour-intensive techniques to be efficient, as compared with commercial farms which adopted more mechanised methods.

Policies towards tariffs and exchange rates also affected choice of technique. For example, in the Philippines the protection and overvalued exchange rates led to relatively low prices for imported tractors, encouraging mechanisation. In Taiwan, the successful export expansion of highly labour-intensive crops—which in turn led to high rural linkages—was in part due to the exchange rate regime which favoured exports.

One finding of the studies was that government interventions on prices may affect choice of technique even where this is not the obvious or intended effect of the interventions. One example was the price control system in Tanzania; another was the sugar price regulations in Kenya and India. In all the cases of this sort which were discussed, the effects tended to be towards support of inappropriate choices.

Markets and Products

A near universal finding of the studies was the dominating influence of *product* quality on choice of technique. This was true of parastatal's choices in Kenya and Tanzania; in rice-processing in the Philippines; in sugar processing in Tanzania and India. In each case more capital-intensive techniques produced "higher" quality products, where quality is defined by uniformity of quality and acceptability in international markets. The fact that a technology produced higher quality was universally regarded as a decisive argument in its favour, irrespective of the cost or whether there was sufficient need to produce the higher quality. Since so many sins are committed against appropriate technology in the name of product quality, it is important to analyse clearly the considerations involved.

It is helpful to do so by taking three different situations:

1. where the product is intended for the domestic market (an import substitution (IS) product);
2. where the product is ultimately intended for export, but where there are no or few actual exports and the product is wholly (or largely) consumed domestically;
3. where the product is largely exported.

In the case of an IS product, considerations of product quality are a matter of the domestic costs and benefits of different qualities of product. Other things being equal, a "higher" quality product would be preferable where there is an unambiguous ranking of what it means for a product to be "better" or "worse." (This is by no means always the case; some products may have more nutrients but be less uniform or less well packaged, for example.) However, other things are not equal since the higher quality has the undoubted cost, normally, of involving a less appropriate technology. For example, in the Philippines the big rice processing plant produced a high quality rice in terms of uniform size of grain and few broken grains (although nutritional content was the same), but at the cost of tremendous loss of employment and income-earning opportunities throughout the rural areas. In many of the cases examined the "higher" quality meant that some richer urban consumers had "better" products, but poorer people had lower incomes and lower consumption.

Adopting high quality products of the same standard as those designed for advanced country consumers generally involves inappropriate standards for much lower income consumers. This means that a small proportion of consumers may enjoy the standards prevalent in the West, while the majority are deprived. For this reason, an important aspect of appropriate technology is *appropriate products*, which are products with characteristics suitable for low-income consumers. The need to produce and consume appropriate products represents the consumption side of appropriate technology.

For products intended for domestic consumption there are therefore two reasons for rejecting the argument of "product quality" as an automatic and decisive factor leading to choice of capital-intensive techniques. First, the products may be considered superior in advanced countries but may be inappropriate in poorer countries. Secondly, even if they are considered superior in the developing country context, the *costs* of employment and output foregone must also be weighed.

An interesting example of the wrong products policies for IS products is cited in James' study. In Tanzania a project was planned to replace the detergent OMO, previously imported from Kenya, with a locally produced product. It was decided to replace it by an identical powder, produced with the inappropriate technology (supplied by the same firm as had previously provided the Kenyan technology), because consumers were accustomed to the product. No search was made for more appropriate products using more appropriate technology. More appropriate substitutes do exist in both product and technology (see Langdon). These were not even considered because of the automatic and unjustified assumption that product quality must be "maintained." One interesting aspect of this example is that it comes from a country which is, relatively speaking, rather egalitarian, does not have great respect for multinational companies or Western consumer values, and is heavily interventionist in many areas.

AT policies therefore also involve products policies. Domestic income distribution is one important determinant of the market for different types of products. Poorer consumers buy different types of products and also, within each category, tend to consume more appropriate products, normally produced with more appropriate technology (for example, less packaged items, less regular quality, as in the case of OP sugar in India where the price discount on this type of sugar makes it accessible to lower income consumers). A successful AT strategy would spread income earning opportunities more widely, which would automatically lead to the consumption of more appropriate products, in turn providing further support for the AT strategy. Governments may also intervene more directly to influence consumption patterns.

One possibility is limitation of advertising. Advertising is confined to advanced country products so tastes are artificially tilted away from more appropriate local products. For the most part, there are few restrictions on advertising in developing countries; advertisements for products with strongly (and well known) negative effects (for example, cigarettes, baby milk) are often permitted without restriction. Secondly, governments can provide information services to identify, assess, and inform about alternative products. Thirdly, governments may develop and adapt regulations about product quality. (See James and Stewart for more discussion of products policies.)

It is sometimes suggested that for governments to have active products policies—as advocated here as an intrinsic part of AT policies—involves a severe limitation of personal liberty. This argument is completely misplaced. Consumers' freedom is severely limited in developing countries by the lack of income. So, while consumers may be said to have the freedom to buy what they want, they have insufficient incomes to buy enough even to ensure adequate nutrition. A policy which gives them enough income to ensure their health but reduces the ability of some to advertise would not constitute a severe infringement of liberty. Secondly, consumers' freedom in developing countries is limited by their ignorance about alternative products, while their tastes are manipulated by the partial information from advertising. Thirdly, consumers' freedom is already limited by myriad government regulations; if these regulations were reformed to promote appropriate rather than inappropriate standards this would not involve a loss in consumer freedom.

The second type of situation is where the possibility of exporting the product is used to justify more capital-intensive methods to produce products of an international standard. In the studies this occurred, for example, in rice-processing in the Philippines and in a shoe factory in Tanzania. In neither of these cases did any substantial quantity of exports result, but the export possibility was still taken as a decisive argument in favour of inappropriate technology. This is clearly not justified. The extent and benefits from exporting must be clearly assessed and weighed against the cost of adopting inappropriate technology.

The third situation where product quality is used to justify inappropriate technology choices is where the product actually is exported, and consequently international standards of product quality are required. Even here the argument is not cut and dried for two reasons. First, as in the previous cases, there must be some assessment of the benefits and costs. Secondly, there is no unique phenomenon "international standards." The world market represents a vast array of different markets with different consumption patterns and product requirements. Products may be suitable for some parts of the international market but not for others. Developing countries need not pursue the "highest" standard markets but can sell to the low-income end of the market, either in developed countries in other developing countries. A clear example of the possibilities is provided by the case of pineapple canning in the Philippines and Taiwan. Both countries exported a large quantity of canned pineapples. In the Philippines, the multinational companies used large-scale capital-intensive technology and produced a high quality product which they exported to high-income markets. In Taiwan, local companies adopted more labour-intensive methods, producing lower quality (more broken and uneven) canned pineapples. These were exported successfully to lower income consumers in advanced countries. The case illustrates that there is no unique "international standard" which justifies particular product standards and technology choices.

The studies have shown that the question of product quality is often critical in technological choice, usually supporting inappropriate choices. This is normally not justified. An essential aspect of macro-policies for AT is to adopt appropriate products policies not only for domestic consumption but also exports. As far as exports are concerned, countries which have chosen "high" standards to facilitate exports of particular goods have also often adopted exchange rate regimes which inhibit labour-intensive exports. The example of Taiwan showed that changing the trade/exchange rate regime to support such labour-intensive exports leads to further growth of exports and more labour-intensive techniques than adopting trade regimes which tend to constrain manufactured exports, and compensating for this by promoting product "quality" through the adoption of capital-intensive techniques. South-South markets offer considerable potential for trade in appropriate products. Policies to promote such trade—e.g. by mutual preferences, mutual trade liberalisation, monetary arrangements, or countertrade—form part of the array of AT policies.

The studies strongly support the view that *appropriate products* are an essential aspect of appropriate technology both because the production of inappropriate products generally requires inappropriate technology, and because meeting the basic needs of poor people requires the production of appropriate goods to meet their consumption needs and to provide appropriate productive equipment. The appropriate products aspect of appropriate technology has generally been given inadequate attention by supporters of appropriate technology.

Technology

While several of the studies identified particular techniques with appropriate characteristics, it was clear there was considerable potential for improving their efficiency—and therefore their ability to compete effectively with inappropriate techniques—and that in some areas few appropriate techniques existed, owing to the neglect in research and development programmes.

The thrust of advanced country technological change is towards improved efficiency of technologies which have increasingly inappropriate characteristics. A typical example is the VP sugar technology whose efficient minimum scale has risen from a crushing capacity of 1,000 tons a day to about 7,000 tons, while the capital/labour ratio has also increased. Since world research and development is concentrated in the advanced countries, the major direction of technical change is in an inappropriate direction. And, since the resulting technical change usually increases the efficiency of the technology, as well as changing its characteristics, it makes it increasingly difficult for appropriate technologies to remain competitive. Moreover, a good deal of R & D in developing countries is of a similar kind to developed country R & D, focussing on large-scale and capital-intensive technologies. Rudra argues that much of Indian R & D in agriculture has focussed on inappropriate technological change. As Maxwell's study shows, much technical change emerges from rather informal in-house firm activity; in the context of Latin America this change has also been, on balance, in an inappropriate direction, generally increasing scale and capital/labour ratios, though making greater use of local materials.

There are examples of innovations improving the efficiency of or developing new appropriate technologies. The work in improving the efficiency of OP sugar technology has made this technology competitive with the VP technology in many circumstances, whereas previously it had been regarded as an inferior technology (see Forsyth). The use of the MOSTI wells—and more recently the bamboo version of the wells—are other examples of appropriate innovations. Biggs and Griffith argue that there is considerable potential for further improvements in efficiency, since so far little serious work has been done in this area. New developments in small rice mills (combining a rubber roller with a steel huller) have permitted these inexpensive and small-scale mills to produce a much higher quality of rice, and consequently to become competitive with the more expensive cono-type mills. This innovation was the result of work by IRRI. As chapter four shows, the small-scale thresher developed by IRRI reduced employment and labour's share of output in the Philippines, even though it increased grain output. However, this was in comparison with manual methods. It was much more appropriate than large-scale mechanized threshers. In Thailand, where labour surplus was much less, the small-scale thresher was appropriate.

These examples point to the potential for improving the productivity of ATs so that the dynamic efficiency of appropriate technology may be secured. Without such changes, inappropriate techniques will inevitably displace those with appropriate characteristics because of the inexorable progress in their efficiency that emanates from the systematic application of R & D in advanced countries to these technologies. While there have been some cases of improvements in ATs following R & D, these represent only a minority of cases, even within the innovations of the R & D institutions in developing countries. According to Rudra, there is tremendous potential for improving the productivity of traditional methods in Indian agriculture; this potential has not been realised partly because of deficient R & D, but more importantly in this case because of inadequate dissemination and promotion of the results. The study of technical change in Latin America indicated that *no efforts* had been made to channel innovations towards appropriate technology.

Deficiency in quantity and quality of R & D and in the dissemination of resources devoted to appropriate technology is a major problem for the continued viability of AT, and should be a priority area for policy.

Appropriate technologies are by their nature normally small-scale, and often adopted in the informal sector. Consequently, it is extremely unlikely—in contrast to activities in large firms—that the firms (or families) using the ATs will have either resources or incentives enough to generate new or improved technologies in any systematic way. Outside intervention is therefore essential—either to finance institutions which generate technical change in AT, or to finance individual users of technologies to initiate appropriate technical change.

There is a need to promote a network of institutions—nationally and internationally—for the development and dissemination of appropriate technology (see Bhalla (ed.)). Foreign aid agencies could play a role in selecting a priority area (for example, food processing) for developing and disseminating technology. However, the IRRI case study shows that care is needed to ensure that the technologies that emerge are appropriate in all dimensions.

* * *

In two areas, there is a need to extend the range of policies beyond those in the initial classification. These were in the use of *standards* and in *rural linkages*.

• *Standards*: This has emerged as a powerful instrument for achieving improvements in technology, as shown in a study by Kiyokawa and Ishikawa. But it is necessary to incorporate appropriateness into the development of standards before this can be an effective tool of AT. This is an area in which detailed work at an industry level is required.

• *Rural linkages*: Chapter five showed these to be an extremely powerful way of promoting AT. This means that agricultural growth as such tends to generate AT, especially if accompanied by policies (described in that chapter) to strengthen these linkages.

Composition of Units

The discussion above has summarised ways in which the studies have illuminated the categorisation of policies contained in the initial classification. In addition, the studies strongly support the view that choice of technology varies systematically according to type of decision-maker so that changing the composition of units is a very important aspect of policies to promote AT. Table 9.1 summarises the findings with respect to each type of decision-making unit. It represents a somewhat over-simplified view, especially as it does not incorporate differences in particular contexts, due to differences in the policy environment. In general, the more the whole policy package supports AT, the less the difference in choices between types of units. Nonetheless, as can be seen from the table, the various units are subject to rather systematic pressures, from each aspect of the classification—objectives, resources, markets and technology—which make for consistent differences in choice of product and choice of technique between types of micro-units. At one extreme, parastatals and multinational companies both most effectively fulfill their objectives, given markets and resource constraints, by producing high-quality, sophisticated products using capital-intensive and large-scale techniques. At the other extreme, family farms and informal sector firms produce simple products for local consumption and use labour intensive and small-scale techniques.

The studies gave numerous examples of these differences; for example, OP sugar technology was adopted by small firms while parastatals and multinationals adopted the VP technology. Small farms used the IRRI small tools, while large farms bought tractors and used large mechanised threshers. Local companies in Taiwan used more labour-intensive and small-scale processing than the multinationals in the Philippines. There were many other examples of such differences, as would be expected by the differences summarised in table 9.1. It follows that changing the composition of units would have a major effect on choice of technology in the economy as a whole. If more investments were undertaken by small local companies, the informal sector, and small and family farmers, then both product choice and choice of technique would be markedly more appropriate than if investment decisions were dominated by multinational companies, parastatals, large local companies and large farmers.

Policies which would change the composition of units include:

1. more unified credit markets with higher interest rates for large borrowers and lower ones for the small-scale sector;
2. reformed credit market procedures so that they discriminate less (for example, in collateral requirements) against the small-scale;
3. land reform to increase the proportion of land owned by small farmers;
4. income redistribution reducing the size of the elite market and increasing the size of low-income markets. An effective AT strategy would automatically achieve this by spreading employment and income earning opportunities and therefore purchasing power and markets;
5. a variety of administrative interventions favouring small-scale and limiting large-scale investments. In many countries, a substantial change would be effected by stopping the special discrimination in favour of large firms;
6. provision of infrastructure, technical assistance, etc. for the small-scale sector.

These policies, which change the composition of units towards more appropriate decisions, need to be accompanied by policies designed to improve the productivity of the small-scale sector.

Political Economy

This book has identified a large number of policy changes which would promote appropriate technology. The studies also established that in many countries which explicitly support the objectives of an appropriate technology strategy, such as the spread of productive employment and the elimination of poverty, the policies pursued by government have been broadly inappropriate for these objectives, supporting inappropriate technological choice. This was shown, for example, in the studies of technology choice in Indian agriculture and parastatals in Tanzania respectively. To some extent this apparent contradiction between objectives and policies may be due to ignorance about effective policies to secure the desired goals. A major purpose of this book has been to elucidate these policies. But many of the policies identified are familiar to those who have studied the connections between policies and technology choice. It appears, therefore, that to a considerable extent, the adoption of an inappropriate set of policies is the consequence of the political economy of the required policy changes. Many of the policies necessary to promote AT would strongly conflict with the interests of dominant groups. This situation was elucidated by an analysis of the political economy of policy change in a number of the studies.

All the analyses of the political economy of policy changes in the book came to remarkably similar conclusions, despite the differences in countries and sectors covered by the various authors. The gainers from AT policies were invariably the unemployed and underemployed and small local firms; the potential losers were bureaucrats, large-scale domestic producers, large farmers and foreign technology, management and machinery suppliers from the advanced countries. Aid institutions, which might have been expected to be neutral (or pro-AT), were in fact, for the most part, vehicles for inappropriate technology transfer, and presumably, therefore, would be losers by pro-AT policies. The balance of political power in the countries studied strongly favours those who would lose by AT policies. Hence the decision-makers in government generally adopted inappropriate policies. Bureaucratic support for inappropriate policies partly stems from recognition of this political reality, and partly from the fact that bureaucrats' own objectives are usually best met by inappropriate choices.

This analysis of the political economy of policy formation derives from countries of very different types, in terms of the usual classification of political economy. For example, it includes the planned economy of India and the more laissez-faire Philippines; socialist Tanzania and capitalist-oriented Kenya; countries which have relied heavily on aid, such as Tanzania and Bangladesh and countries where aid is of lesser importance proportionately, such as India; countries where multinational companies are welcomed (Philippines and Kenya) and countries where they are kept at arms length (Tanzania and India). Nonetheless, Taiwan managed to escape the inexorable pressures and to adopt a set of policies broadly supportive of appropriate technology. Relevant factors explaining this are briefly discussed in chapter five. They include the displacement of local elites in decision-making by people from the mainland in 1949 and an early effective land reform which, together with the development of a dynamic small scale industry, established a powerful combination of interests favouring many AT policies. In addition, geography and colonial heritage provided favourable conditions for the development of rural industry.

One major conclusion from the analysis of political economy of AT policies is that in most of the countries examined, the complete set of AT policies are unlikely to be introduced without major changes in political power—in particular a switch in power from the existing dominant interests who gain by inappropriate technologies to the groups who would gain by AT. But this does not mean that no policy change can occur without such a major change in political power. Some potential for change does exist in those countries which at present promote inappropriate technologies.

First, aid agencies have some potential—especially in some countries—for changing the direction of their own influence and pushing government policies to favour AT. This would require a big change in the attitudes of aid agencies which themselves tend to reflect dominant interests in the donor nations. For bilateral aid such a change seems unlikely to be more than marginal. The same might be said—in view of past experience—of multilateral agencies. But this is an area where change might be possible either within the agencies or by a switch in financial flows towards agencies which are sympathetic to AT.

Second, some of the policies identified as promoting AT are much more likely to meet overriding political opposition than others. The earlier analysis suggests that policies to promote appropriate R & D and dissemination, to support agriculture, to improve rural infrastructure and to develop appropriate standards would be of the type to give positive support for AT without being directly and overtly negative to inappropriate technology. From the perspective of identifying policies likely to be adopted, the aim should be to find non-confrontational policies.

Third, the political process is a cumulative one; as small farms and the small-scale industrial sector develop in economic strength, they also acquire political strength. A cumulative process may then be set in motion which, from small beginnings, results in a political economy favouring AT.

IV. CONCLUSION

The studies in this volume have strongly supported the view that government policies are critical to the success or failure of appropriate technology. They are of far greater importance for AT than the specific micro-interventions which have been the main vehicle of those who support appropriate technology. The studies have identified a large range of policies which would promote AT. They have also shown that in many cases government policies have promoted inappropriate technologies. Analysis of the politics of the required policy changes has shown that the major problem in securing the desired policy changes lies in political economy; this is the overriding obstacle to the promotion of appropriate technology in many countries.

NOTES

I am grateful to Ted Owens and participants at the Washington, DC, seminar, January 1986, for comments on a previous draft.

REFERENCES

Bhalla, A., ed. 1979. *Towards Global Action for Appropriate Technology*. Oxford: Pergamon Press.

Carr, M., ed. 1985. *The A. T. Reader, Theory and Practice in Appropriate Technology*. London: Intermediate Technology Publications.

Forsyth, D. 1977. "Appropriate technology in sugar manufacturing," *World Development*, 9.

Hopcroft, P., and J. Oguttu. 1982. *Parastatal Development Agencies and Their Relationship with the Private Sector*, Institute for Development Studies and University of Nairobi, Occasional Paper no. 39.

James, J., and F. Stewart. 1981. *New Products: A Discussion of the Welfare Effects of New Products in Developing Countries*, Oxford Economic Papers, 33, 1.

Jequier, N., ed. 1976. *Appropriate Technology, Problems and Promises*. Paris: O.E.C.D.

Kiyokawa, Y., and S. Ishikawa. 1985. The Significance of Standardization in the Development of the Machine-Tool Industry: the Cases of Japan and China. Institute of Economic Research, Hitotsubashi University, Japan. Photocopy.
Langdon, S. 1981. *Multinationals in the Political Economy of Kenya.* London: Macmillan.
McRobie, G. 1981. *Small is Possible.* New York: Harper and Row.
Perkins, F. 1980. Technology Choice, Industrialisation and Development: the Case of Tanzania, Ph.D. thesis, University of Sussex.
Ranis, G. 1973. "Industrial sector labour absorption," *Economic Development and Cultural Change,* 21.
Stewart, F., ed. 1983. *Work, Income and Inequality, Payments Systems in the Third World.* London: Macmillan.

TABLE 9.1

COMPOSITION OF UNITS AND CHOICE OF TECHNOLOGY

TYPE OF DECISION-MAKER	OBJECTIVES	RESOURCES	MARKETS	TECHNOLOGY	CHOICE OF PRODUCT	CHOICE OF TECHNIQUE
INDUSTRY						
AID DONORS	Maximise flow of funds: use of foreign technology	Cheap capital		Advanced countries		
GOVT/PARASTATALS	Bureaucratic - output/project maximising	Cheap capital if foreign financed	Local elite	Advanced countries - source of finance	Sophisticated/ inappropriate	K-intensive large scale
MULTINATIONAL CO.	Maximise international profits satisficers	Cheap capital	International & local elite	Parent Co. Normally advanced	"	"
LARGE SCALE CO.	Profit maximisers	Cheapish capital	Mainly local elite	Foreign in-house	Mainly inappropriate	"
SMALL LOCAL CO. (FORMAL)	Profit maximisers	Limited access to cheap capital; Labour cheap	Local elite & middle income	Variety of sources	More appropriate	More labour intensive
INFORMAL CO. & FAMILIES	Maximise family income and employment	Expensive capital & limited; very cheap labour	Local low income	Primitive; AT support institutions	Appropriate	Very labour intensive & small
AGRICULTURE						
LARGE FARMERS	Maximise profits	Cheap credit: subsidised tractors	Urban & international	Government & foreign companies and aid institutions	Cash Crops	Mechanized large tractors
MEDIUM/SMALL	Maximise profits	More expensive credit - limited	Urban & rural	Same but more limited	Mainly cash crops	Small scale machines
FAMILY	Maximise family income	Little credit, expensive. Very cheap labour	Mainly rural	Primitive	Mainly locally consumed foods	Mainly local and primitive tools

About the Contributors

Stephen Biggs is a lecturer of agricultural economics at the School of Development Studies, University of East Anglia, Norwich, U.K., whose current work focuses on problems in the generation and diffusion of rural and agricultural technology.

Bart Duff is an agricultural economist with the International Rice Research Institute in Los Banos, Philippines.

Jon Griffith is an irrigation engineer who worked with water development projects in India and Bangladesh for many years. He currently works with UNICEF in Laos.

Jeffrey James is assistant professor of economics at Boston University.

Raphael Kaplinsky is a Fellow at the Institute of Development Studies in Brighton, England, whose research has been mainly on the topics of industrialisation, technology and MNCs. He now works in the areas of technical change (with particular reference to microelectronics) and appropriate technology.

Philip Maxwell was a full-time member of the IDB/ECLA Technology Research Program in Buenos Aires from 1975–1980. From 1981 onwards, he has held senior positions at Pergamon Press in Oxford.

Gustav Ranis is a Frank Altschul Professor of International Economics at Yale University.

Ashok Rudra is a professor of economics at Visva-Bharati Santiniketan and Indian Statistical Institute, Calcutta.

Frances Stewart is senior research officer at Queen Elizabeth House and a Fellow of Somerville College, Oxford.

Index

www.ingramcontent.com/pod-product-compliance
Lightning Source LLC
LaVergne TN
LVHW011114300926
849160LV00008B/376
9780367161538